A Critical
Spirit

A Critical
Spirit

The Thought of
William Dawson LeSueur

Edited and with
Critical Commentary

by A.B. McKillop

The Carleton Library No. 104
Published by McClelland and Stewart
in association with the Institute of Canadian Studies,
Carleton University.

© *1977. McClelland and Stewart Limited*

ALL RIGHTS RESERVED

0-7710-9802-2

The Canadian Publishers
McClelland and Stewart Limited
25 Hollinger Road, Toronto

Printed and bound in Canada

For
P.G.R.

who shares
the critical spirit

Contents

Preface

William Dawson LeSueur was the most wide-ranging Canadian-born intellectual of his generation. A controversial essayist and historian who dedicated himself to the spirit of critical enquiry, he probed relentlessly into the dominating concerns of the age of Macdonald and Laurier. This volume contains the major writings of this neglected figure in the intellectual history of Canada: his defense of the intellectual life; his advocacy of a scientific, evolutionary ethics; his indictment of the political morality and popular government of his day; and his application of the critical spirit to the writing of Canadian history. LeSueur's work constituted a major response to the transatlantic currents of late nineteenth-century thought.

W.D. LeSueur's thought deserves to be considered in its own right. Yet there is another reason for the publication of this volume. On the day before the publisher's deadline, a special issue of the journal *American Quarterly* (Vol. XXVII, December, 1975) reached my desk. The issue was devoted to "Victorian Culture in America", and it contained many insights and perspectives which this editor could well have used. Most of them were as significant for Canada in the age of Victoria as they were for America. William Dawson LeSueur was pre-eminently a Victorian, and his thought was largely a synthesis of various values and concerns central to many Victorian minds on both sides of the Atlantic. This volume, *A Critical Spirit*, could easily have been given the title, "Victorian Culture in Canada: the Thought of W.D. LeSueur", without doing a great injustice to its subject. Similarly, the concluding plea of the Special Editor of the *American Quarterly* issue, Daniel Walker Howe, is also an accurate reflection of my second general aim in putting together this volume of LeSueur's essays: "Now it would seem, the time is ripe for a kind of understanding that can go beyond an immediate need to celebrate or derogate, that can take a fresh look at the characteristics and dynamics of American Victorian culture. Only then, when we have imaginatively recreated the world the Victorians experienced, and at the same time put that world into a perspective of our own, will we be in a position to comprehend the true nature of their achievement." (p.532)

In providing a commentary for this volume, I have attempted to show how the thought of W.D. LeSueur involves a consideration of certain tendencies of thought and clusters of assumption which gave shape to Victorian culture in Canada. No scholarly synthesis of Canadian cultural life in the nineteenth century yet exists. I have taken the risk that the reader might occasionally lose sight of LeSueur himself as he examines the contextual background provided in the editor's essays, but it has been a calculated risk taken in order to point toward certain areas of research which need to be explored before such a synthesis can emerge.

Of editorial criteria in a more narrow sense little needs to be said. The items in this volume have been selected from about seventy of LeSueur's essays. Unless otherwise noted they appear in their entirety, including LeSueur's original footnotes which appear at the bottom of the page. I have regularized these footnotes somewhat, and have shorn the essays of many marks of punctuation (mainly commas) which, even by Victorian standards, appeared to be needless. I have also attempted to provide the background necessary to understand many of the literary, historical and biographical allusions and references made by LeSueur. These appear in the form of the ''Notes on the Text'' at the back of the book.

A Critical Spirit would not have been published without a great deal of aid from various quarters. Professors Donald Swainson and George Rawlyk, of the History Department at Queen's University, and Professor Carman Bickerton, History Editor of the Carleton Library series, offered important encouragement and advice when the idea for the volume was in its initial stages. At the University of Manitoba, Professors Mark Gabbert, John Finlay and R.A. Swanson read parts of the manuscript and Lovell C. Clark gave a close reading of it all. Errors of fact, judgement, and style were eliminated as a result of their discerning eyes. Professors L.A. Desmond and J.J. Gahan, of the University of Manitoba's History and Classics departments, respectively, translated the Latin and Greek phrases found in the text.

Mr. Jim Holmes and Miss J.M. Buller were more than capable research assistants at different stages in the preparation of the manuscript. Canada Council research grants administered through the University of Manitoba Faculty of Graduate Studies and a travel grant from the J.S. Ewart Memorial Fund provided the finances necessary for archival work in Ottawa and Toronto and for the typing of the volume. Mrs. Carol Adam carried out this latter chore with both exemplary patience and skilful efficiency. Mrs. Jean Birch did likewise when tackling the frustrating task of typing a revised version of parts of the manuscript. And last, a great debt is owed to Graham Reynolds, who kindled my initial enthusiasm for the project on a cold winter's morning in Kingston, several years ago now, when *A Critical Spirit* was just a phrase.

A.B. McKillop,
February, 1976,
University College,
University of Manitoba.

Introduction

> *In every society . . . there are some persons with an unusual*
> *sensitivity to the sacred, an uncommon reflectiveness about the*
> *nature of their universe and the rules which govern their society.*
> *There is in every society a minority of persons who, more than the*
> *ordinary run of their fellow men, are inquiring, and desirous of*
> *being in frequent communion with symbols which are more general*
> *than the immediate concrete situations of everyday life and remote in*
> *their reference in both time and space. In this minority, there is a*
> *need to externalize this quest in oral and written discourse, in poetic*
> *or plastic expression, in historical reminiscence or writing, in ritual*
> *performance and acts of worship. This interior need to penetrate*
> *beyond the screen of immediate concrete experience marks the*
> *existence of the intellectuals in every society.*

> Edward Shils, "The Intellectual
> and the Powers: Some Perspectives
> for Comparative Analysis" (1958).

In April, 1871, an article on the French poet and critic, Sainte-Beuve, appeared in the *Westminster Review*. It was for the most part highly appreciative of Ste.-Beuve's life-long commitment to "the critical spirit." In 1830, Ste.-Beuve had written: "It is the nature of the critical spirit to be quick, suggestive, versatile, and comprehensive. The critical spirit is like a large, clear stream, which winds and spreads out around the works and monuments of poetry . . ." Quoting this passage in the original French, the author of the *Westminster Review* article added that "No words could more happily or accurately describe what criticism was, in his hands, throughout the whole of his long career."[1] Moreover, the writer claimed, Ste.-Beuve was important not simply because he was critical but also because he was systematic about it. "The first thing that strikes us when we look into [Ste.-Beuve's] works is, that criticism with him is not a mere thing of rules and precedents, but, so to speak, a living science." Ste.-Beuve had been averse to all rigid systems of thought, and therefore was suspicious when criticism was subordinated to any preconceived idea or pre-established authority. Nevertheless, his criticism was not without its own controlling idea: it should consist of systematic intellectual enquiry. "One consequence of the effort which Ste.-Beuve made to pursue criticism in a scientific spirit, is that of all critics he is the least dogmatic." Indeed, concluded the anonymous reviewer, he is "less a judge than an enquirer who tells us of his discoveries, and invites us to verify them for ourselves."[2]

The author of that essay had also been an enquirer more than a judge. Exactly a year earlier he had appeared before the Literary and Scientific Society of Ottawa to deliver a shorter version of the *Westminster Review* piece. Then entitled "The Greatest Critic of the Age," this critical appreciation of the French poet-critic (who had died only a few months earlier) was by a young Canadian civil servant named William Dawson LeSueur.[3] By the year 1871, LeSueur, born in 1840, had worked for the Post Office Department of the Canadian civil service for fifteen years. He had by then completed his formal education, which had taken him from the Montreal High School to the Ontario Law School and the University of Toronto. There he graduated as Silver Medallist in Classics in 1863. In his career as a civil servant he remained with the Post Office until his retirement in 1902 (from 1888 to 1902 he was chief of the Post Office money order system). After his retirement he became the Secretary of the Dominion Board of Civil Service Examiners.[4]

W.D. LeSueur's connection with the Literary and Scientific Society of Ottawa was also a long one. Almost every year from 1871 until the turn of the twentieth century, LeSueur held an executive position with the group, either as Librarian, Vice-President, or (most frequently) President.[5] This long association with an organization dedicated to the joint study of Literature and Science indicates that while LeSueur's occupation was that of a civil servant, his preoccupations far transcended the normal concerns of the administrator. Much of his biography must therefore be seen as an inner one, for his significant life was primarily that of the mind.

Ste.-Beuve had been twenty-five years of age when he put forward his conception of the nature of the critical spirit; LeSueur was thirty-one when he revealed to his Ottawa audience an acceptance of the necessity for—and dictates of—such a spirit. A long and distinguished career in Canadian letters had begun. For the next forty years and more, LeSueur put before Canadian and international audiences alike a constructive criticism of various aspects of the life and thought of his day. This career was to see him engaged constantly in debate with various orthodoxies which in his view hampered the activity of the critical intellect. Whether attacking an orthodoxy that was religious or scientific, political or historical, LeSueur insisted throughout his life that the essence of civilization lay in an individual's ability to exercise, in a responsible fashion, a critical enquiry that asked nothing more than honesty and sincerity and sought nothing less than truth. His was a moral as well as an intellectual vision. The thought of William Dawson LeSueur, as set forth in scores of essays published over the last quarter of the nineteenth century, provides abundant evidence of a mind that knew few intellectual boundaries. The range of its interests and the sources of its concern were those of its age. LeSueur deserves, then, the attention of anyone interested in the intellectual and cultural history of Canada. The modern student will not only re-discover the most diverse and pre-eminent Canadian intellect of the age of Macdonald and Laurier, but also enter into the trans-Atlantic nature of the controversies in which those of LeSueur's generation engaged.

II

Modern observers of the cultural life of late nineteenth-century English-Canada have not been unaware of LeSueur's place in it. His earnestness, his devotion to the positivist ideal, have been noted briefly by Claude Bissell, R.L. McDougall, F.W. Watt, and Carl Berger. In his collection of essays, *Culture and Nationality*, A.G. Bailey makes the claim that LeSueur "was typical of the best minds" of his generation: "Well acquainted with the ancient literatures, he wrote extensively on the major scientific, philosophical, and literary questions of the time, and always in an interesting and persuasive manner. So wide and varied were his interests that they almost epitomize the influences, British, European, and American, then current in Canada."[6]

Such assessments portray LeSueur as typical, yet unique: typical in his earnest Victorian concern, unique in his particular set of convictions. As scholars pass toward their major areas of interest—whether literary taste, Canadian periodical literature, literary radicalism, Canadian imperialism or Canadian nationality—they afford LeSueur the passing reference which from their particular perspectives he deserves. Yet that an individual such as the one described by Bailey has received so little treatment is a significant commentary upon the current nature and state of Canadian cultural and intellectual history. Bissell, McDougall, and Watt were interested primarily in literary aspects of the Canadian cultural experience, and insofar as LeSueur, an essayist, is also a man of letters he receives mention. The preoccupation of Berger and Bailey was with what might be termed "political culture" (Berger more narrowly so than Bailey). Yet in the case of neither approach, literary or political, does the actual substance of any of LeSueur's several interests receive attention.[7]

A major problem in assessing figures such as W.D. LeSueur at the present time is that there is little historiographical context into which to place them.[8] Studies have been made of English and American cultural life in the late nineteenth century, but there is no equivalent for Canada of Stow Persons' book, *The Decline of American Gentility* (1971), John Tomsich's *A Genteel Endeavor*; *American Culture and Politics in the Gilded Age* (1971), or Frank Miller Turner's *Between Science and Religion*; *the Reaction to Scientific Naturalism in Late Victorian England* (1974). The purpose of this volume is, therefore, two-fold: first, to introduce William Dawson LeSueur to the modern Canadian student; and, second, to suggest something of both the intellectual and social context against which his ideas may be viewed. For this reason the introductory essays which preface each of the sections of this book, the chapters of LeSueur's inner biography, are longer than may normally be found in edited collections of essays.

Fortunately, W.D. LeSueur's writings indicate several fairly distinct, although overlapping, areas of dominant concern which help to make a contextual background reasonably easy to establish. These areas of interest, which roughly follow the chronology of LeSueur's writings, indicate fairly clear shifts in the direction of his thought. This volume is structured to outline these chapters in the inner biography of the author.

The primary theme which pervades all LeSueur's writings is the nature of the intellectual life and the necessity for critical intellectual enquiry. His publishing career began on this note, and among his last published words were those which insisted that "the essential nature of history . . . is not affirmation but enquiry." (p.285) Having established in a series of essays the various premises from which he worked, LeSueur turned in the 1870s and 1880s to a more specific subject, involving one of the major intellectual preoccupations of his day: the relationship between science and religion. Here LeSueur was clearly on the side of what he called "the scientific spirit," yet his prior commitment to the critical intellect required that he tread a difficult intellectual path bordered on one side by the dogmatism of what he believed to be a decaying Christian orthodoxy and on the other by a Science that had the tendency, in the hands of some exponents, to become equally dogmatic. One of the most distinctive features of LeSueur's thought was the fact that he was largely successful in remaining on the critical path he had chosen. A follower of Comte's positivism, he could nevertheless warn that the positivistic science of his day "too easily falls into the snare of dogmatism" (p.107); and although he was a defender of the evolutionary naturalism of Herbert Spencer, his thought showed little trace of the rigid Social Darwinism of William Graham Sumner.

The combination in LeSueur of a commitment to the critical path with an equally strong moral sensibility made the third major area of his concern both logical and all but inevitable. From the 1870s until his death, LeSueur was a constant critic of the political culture of his day—whether in Canada, the United States, or Great Britain. LeSueur's criticisms of "popular government" were wide-ranging, and they were not of the sort which stood to make him popular with the general public. His insistence was that politics and political action must be informed by clearly-articulated moral conviction if it is to be anything other than the politics of self-interest. Lacking such conviction, no political party could claim to be truly working for the "highest good of the community," especially in an age when politicians increasingly looked to "public opinion" for their election platforms. Such assumptions led LeSueur to question critically certain characteristics of the political culture of his day by examining the implications of such commonplaces of popular political discourse as "Democracy," "Popular Government," "Party Politics," and above all "Responsible Government."

It was therefore also inevitable that LeSueur should have turned toward the study of history, as well as politics, in order to understand the true origins, meanings, and significance of the various political and cultural shibboleths of his age. Towards the end of the nineteenth century, and continuing until his death, he spent much of his time engaged in archival research on Canadian history. His published studies in Canadian history were a biography of Count Frontenac, written for the "Makers of Canada" series, and translations of certain writings of Champlain and LaVerendrye.[9] Yet the area of his main historical concern was primarily that of the history of Canada from the 1760s to the 1840s.[10] The fruition of this research was LeSueur's study of *William Lyon Mackenzie*—less a biography of the Upper Canadian reform leader than an attempt to place Mackenzie fully into the social context of his age. Because of opposition from the heirs of Mackenzie, the book was never published. Neither libellous to Mackenzie nor lacking in scholarly balance, the typescript has gathered dust for the past sixty years, testimony to the negation of the very principles of sustained critical enquiry upon which W.D. LeSueur had based his life's work.[11]

The "LeSueur-Lindsey controversy," as the long litigation over LeSueur's study of Mackenzie came to be called, lies somewhat beyond the scope of this volume. Although some attention will be given to it, detailed consideration of the matter must be left until such time as the book itself, still somewhat revisionist, can be published. Of primary concern here are the critical essays written by LeSueur between the 1870s and the end of the nineteenth century. During those years he, more than any other native-born Canadian, addressed himself to the major intellectual and social questions of his day; and it was upon his many contributions to British, American, and Canadian periodicals during the last three decades of the nineteenth century that his reputation rested.[12]

That reputation was a substantial one. Within five years of LeSueur's first appearance in print, Goldwin Smith suggested to George W. Curtis, editor of *Harper's Weekly*, that he solicit articles from the young essayist. "He is *far* away the best writer in our nation's periodicals on all serious subjects, including religious and philosophical topics," Smith wrote. "He is highly cultivated; a liberal all-round, yet perfectly temperate and catholic; and I think an eminently high minded and high toned man in whom you would find a worthy associate."[13] A few years later, the American social reformer, Henry George, noted in a letter that Canada's LeSueur had come to look very favourably upon George's *Progress and Poverty* (1879). "Here is a man," he wrote, "who in my opinion is worth half the college professors in the United States." George added that E.L. Youmans, editor of the prestigious magazine, *Popular Science Monthly*, held a "very great opinion" of LeSueur.[14] This was very likely the case, for soon LeSueur was invited to join the staff of the magazine as a contributing editor. He continued to publish articles in it for two decades. His first contribution to the *Popular Science Monthly*, in 1880, was an exposition and defence of Herbert Spencer's book, *The Data of Ethics* (1879). Spencer had been impressed with LeSueur's critical assessment (first published in the *Canadian Monthly and National Review* and sent to him by the author), and forwarded the essay to Youmans. Shortly thereafter, the article appeared in the American journal. In 1882, when Spencer was given a now famous testimonial at Delmonico's Restaurant in New York City, LeSueur was asked by Spencer's American hosts to represent Canada.[15]

By the twentieth century, LeSueur was well-established as Canada's leading native-born social critic. In 1901 Queen's University honoured him with a Doctor of Laws degree. In 1912 his long service to the Royal Society of Canada was rewarded with his election to its Presidency. The same year, Adam Shortt, political economist and archivist, was quoted in Henry J. Morgan's *Canadian Men and Women of the Time* describing LeSueur as "a recognized leader among those who are striving to maintain an interest in the things of the mind." And at the time of LeSueur's death in 1917, John Reade, a Montreal poet, noted in an obituary of his friend that "so diverse and comprehensive were his endowments that one may well hesitate to say where he most excelled." The same brief survey of LeSueur's life provides an additional reason why his writings, his internal biography, merit examination by the student of nineteenth-century Canadian thought and culture. LeSueur, Reade said, "was among the rare students of Canada who recognized at once the significance of the new science and its destined ultimate effects on religious and philosophic thought."[16]

Reade's claim for LeSueur's significance is not that he was alone in Canada in being caught up in the nineteenth-century debate between exponents of science and those of religion, but that he recognized the future implications of the various issues raised. It also raises, by implication, certain problems of context. Were literate Canadians of the last quarter of the nineteenth century so caught up in the material life of their day, so preoccupied with the expansion of their new nation westward, so enraptured or enraged by Macdonald's National Policy, that they were exempt from the intellectual agonies, the "spiritual crisis" of many of their peers in England and America? "Scientific investigation as an enemy of religion was a common theme in the Gilded Age," one American historian has concluded of the United States after 1870.[17] Another, examining certain aspects of the relationship between science and religion in Late Victorian England, considers the major individuals in his study to be "part of the English contingent in the widespread late nineteenth-century protest against the pretensions of science to dominate thought and culture."[18] Were Canadians so unconcerned with affairs of the mind that the only contingent of which they found themselves a part was the one that saw service in South Africa at the turn of the century?

A glance at a list of W.D. LeSueur's nineteenth-century writings will indicate at the very least that such questions need to be asked. S.F. Wise has written that the major task of the Canadian intellectual historian must be "to analyze the manner in which externally-derived ideas have been adapted to a variety of local and regional environments, in such a way that a body of assumptions uniquely Canadian has been built up; and to trace the changing content of such assumptions."[19] For anyone who wishes to study the configuration of "externally-derived" assumptions within the framework of one mind, W.D. LeSueur is indeed a discovery. Consider some of the sources of his ideas and the subjects of his criticism: John Stuart Mill, Fitzjames Stephen, Herbert Spencer, Auguste Comte, Henry George, Arthur Balfour, F.W. Newman, J.B. Stallo, T.H. Huxley, Thomas Carlyle, Matthew Arnold, Ste. Beuve, Bernardin de St. Pierre, John Tyndall, E.L. Youmans, Charles Lyell, Charles Darwin, George J. Romanes, Goldwin Smith, Frederic Harrison, Noah Porter, Lyman Abbott, John Fiske, Dwight Moody and Ira Sankey. This list excludes a number of LeSueur's Canadian critics, who themselves drew from what they conceived to be the best and most significant which the Western intellectual experience had to offer.

III

As difficult and perhaps undesirable as it may be to make generalizations in something of an historiographical vacuum, perhaps some are warranted here. The thought of W.D. LeSueur may be said to represent one manifestation of what might be called the Anglo-Canadian moral imagination, a mental stance which for much of the country's history has consisted of the largely self-imposed obligation to extend and to articulate various conceptions of religious, political, institutional, and cultural traditions inherited from Europe and in particular from the British Isles. There has been a distinct continuity in this fundamental moral concern exercised by literate Anglo-Canadians—a concern rooted in the assertion of duty and obligation.

"A moralist," said a philosopher at a prominent Canadian university over CBC Radio in 1965, "is someone who seeks to draw a moral lesson either from an edifying story, from some event that has taken place, or from his observations on human behaviour."[20] One may trace the continuity of the moral imagination, so conceived, in a variety of forms throughout the course of Canadian history from the Conquest. It is to be seen in John Graves Simcoe's concern for the creation in British North America of a society which was to be the "image and transcript" of the England he had left, in Thomas McCulloch's emphasis in *The Stepsure Letters* (to use Northrop Frye's phrase), "not on raising the standard of living [of Nova Scotians], but on making sure that it is a standard," in Judge Haliburton's ambivalent mind, and in the defensive gentility of Susanna Moodie. It is evidenced in the structure and aims of Anglo-Canadian higher education throughout the nineteenth century and well into the twentieth, in the articulation of a mythology of loyalism to a once-united British Empire and later in the development of an imperial ideal which was similarly meant to serve as the basis of a form of desired cultural identification. One sees it in a less political form as part of the debate in the 1870s and 1880s over the cultural implications of modern scientific modes of thought, and here too it took a variety of forms—from the "positivism" of W.D. LeSueur to the British Hegelianism of G.M. Grant and John Watson to the orthodox Christianity of John William Dawson and Bishop John Travers Lewis.[21]

The continuity of this tradition into the twentieth century is reflected in much of Stephen Leacock's serious social criticism and in a number of the articles that may be found in the pages of Andrew Macphail's

University Magazine between 1907 and 1920. The publication by Canadian men of letters of similar articles by no means disappeared after 1920, as a careful reading of the *Canadian Forum* and a simple glance at an index of *Queen's Quarterly* or the *Dalhousie Review* will indicate. A deeply-ingrained sense of moral concern also lies near the heart of the thought of several of the figures who have dominated the modern intellectual landscape of Canada. This will be borne out if one turns to the writings of Harold Innis on the nature and implications of communications, the novels of Hugh MacLennan, the historical writings of Donald Creighton, the philosophy and criticism of George P. Grant, or the literary criticism and critical theory of Northrop Frye.[22]

It must be stated, however, that the moral imagination of Anglo-Canadians has not always manifested itself in ways with which the student or scholar of the late twentieth century is enamoured. The force of obligation can be an oppressive one, and a suspicious attitude toward enquiry and criticism is generally repugnant to those who take such processes as part of their birthright. Yet birthrights are won, and in Canada it has been won in an environment where the pressures for cultural uniformity helped to create an intellectual atmosphere that was at times both stifling and oppressive. Within the past thirty years the spirit of cultural self-criticism in Canada has advanced markedly, largely due to the writings and inspiration of Northrop Frye. Frye's counterpart for the nineteenth century—in aim if not in influence—was W.D. LeSueur, who articulated his own moral vision, one based, like that of Frye, upon the notion of criticism as both an individual and collective way of life. Moreover, LeSueur attempted to do so in a social environment which was by no means propitious to the ideas he put forward, and in a period when in Canada the intellect was looked upon with suspicion and critical enquiry accepted for the most part only in safely-moderate Canadian measures. The place of W.D. LeSueur within the history of the Anglo-Canadian moral imagination, and Canadian history in general, is an important one, for it was he who first introduced the spirit of modern criticism into Canadian life.

NOTES

1. "Ste.-Beuve," *Westminster Review* (April, 1871), p.216.

2. *Ibid.*, p.213. The best short treatment of Sainte-Beuve's place in French letters is probably in Roger L. Williams, *The World of Napoleon III* (New York: Macmillan, 1957), pp.113-131. See also Irving Babbitt, *The Masters of Modern French Criticism* (New York: Houghton Mifflin Company, 1912), pp. 97-188, and C.K. Trueblood, "Sainte-Beuve and the Psychology of Personality," *Character and Personality*, Vol VIII (1939-40), pp.120-143.

3. *Transactions of the Ottawa Literary and Scientific Society* (1897-98), p.12.

4. Biographical materials on the life of W.D. LeSueur are scarce. Those provided here are mainly from standard sources: John Reade, "William Dawson LeSueur," *Proceedings of the Royal Society of Canada* (1918), pp. iv-vi; P.G. Roy, *Fils de Quebec*, Vol.4 (Quebec, 1933), pp.173-74; Henry James Morgan (ed.), *The Canadian Men and Women of the Time*, 2nd ed. (Toronto: Wm. Briggs, 1912), p. 654; *University of Toronto Calendar, 1891-92* (Toronto: 1892), Appendix 1. p.34; Norah Story, *The Oxford Companion to Canadian History and Literature* (Toronto: Oxford University Press, 1967), p. 453.

5. *Transactions, op. cit.*, pp.17-20, contains a list of the Ottawa Literary and Scientific Society's officers from its beginnings in 1869 (as an outgrowth of the Ottawa Natural History Society) to 1898.

6. A.G. Bailey, *Culture and Nationality* (Toronto: McClelland and Stewart, The Carleton Library, No. 58, 1972), p.66.

7. C.T. Bissell, "Literary Taste in Central Canada During the Late Nineteenth Century," *Canadian Historical Review*, Vol. xxxi (Sept. 1950), p.244; A.G. Bailey, *op.cit.*, pp.58-74; R.L. McDougall, "A Study of Canadian Periodical Literature of the Nineteenth Century" (unpublished PH.D dissertation, University of Toronto, 1950), chapt.v, pp.252-365, 402n; F.W. Watt, "Radicalism in English-Canadian Literature since Confederation" (unpublished PH.D. dissertation, University of Toronto, 1957), chapt. II, pp.37-79; and F.W. Watt, "Literature of Protest," in Carl F. Klinck (ed.), *Literary History of Canada* (Toronto: University of Toronto Press, 1973), pp. 460-61; C. Berger, "The Vision of Grandeur" (unpublished PH.D dissertation, University of Toronto, 1966), pp.433-435.

8. This is indicated in the bibliography of the most comprehensive modern survey of late nineteenth-century Canada, Peter B. Waite's, *Canada, 1874-1896: Arduous Destiny* (Toronto: McClelland and Steward, 1971). The book's contents reflect this absence of historical writing on the cultural and intellectual history of Canada.

9. *Count Frontenac* (Toronto: Morang and Co. Ltd., 1906), pp.382; *The Works of Samuel de Champlain* . . . ; reprinted, translated and annotated by Six Canadian Scholars under the general editorship of H.P. Biggar, Vols. v (1620-1629) and vi (1629-1732) (Toronto: The Champlain Society, 1922-36); *Journals and Letters of Pierre Gaultier de Varennes de la Vérendrye* . . . , edited with introduction and notes by Lawrence J. Burpee (Toronto: The Champlain Society, 1927).

10. LeSueur's research notes are still extant: see W.D. LeSueur Papers, Public Archives of Canada [PAC].

11. One typescript copy, accessible to researchers, is in Vol.vi of the Mackenzie-Lindsey Papers, in the Public Archves of Ontario [PAO]; another, on microfilm, may be read in the Rare Books and Special Collections section of the University of Toronto Robarts Library. The copy of the biography in the W.D. LeSueur Papers, in the PAC, is now available to researchers. The prohibition of publication of LeSueur's book was made on the basis of LeSueur's "breach of contract and good faith" in obtaining access to the Mackenzie Papers, not on the grounds of libellous statements contained within the book itself. See "Copy of Judgment of Britton, J., delivered 9th January, 1913" [in the Appellate Divi-

sion of the Ontario Court of Appeal], in Mackenzie-Lindsey Papers, Vol.v, PAO.

12. It should be mentioned that from the 1870s until his death LeSueur was also a regular contributor of editorials to the *Montreal Star*, *Montreal Gazette*, and *Ottawa Citizen* (see Reade, *op.cit.*, p.v). These editorials were unsigned, however, and it is not possible to establish which editorials LeSueur wrote. (C.M. Lapointe, Chief Librarian, *Montreal Star*, to the editor, November 4, 1972; Miss Agnes McFarlane, Librarian, *The Gazette*, to the editor, November 8, 1972).

13. Goldwin Smith Papers, Smith to George W. Curtis, October 24, 1876, pp. 2-3.

14. Henry George, Jr., *The Life of Henry George* (New York: Doubleday, 1904), pp. 340-341. See also Crauford D.W. Goodwin, *Canadian Economic Thought* (Durham, N.C.: Duke University Press, 1961), pp. 31-32, for LeSueur's defence of George's *Progress and Poverty*.

15. Herbert Spencer to W.D. LeSueur, April 27, 1880, W.D. LeSueur Papers, Vol. I file 4. PAC; Reade *op. cit.*, p.v; Richard Hofstadter, *Social Darwinism in American Thought*, rev. ed. (Boston: Beacon Press, 1955), p. 48.

16. Queen's University Domsday Book, 1901, Queen's University Archives; *Acts and Proceedings of the Royal Society of Canada, 1914*, N.S., Vol. 8, p. xiv; Morgan, *op. cit.*, p. 654; Reade, *op. cit.*, pp. iv-v.

17. Paul A. Carter, *The Spiritual Crisis of the Gilded Age* (DeKalb: Northern Illinois University Press, 1971), p. 14.

18. Frank Miller Turner, *Between Science and Religion*; *the Reaction to Scientific Naturalism in Late Victorian England* (London: Yale University Press, 1974), p.5.

19. S.F. Wise, "Sermon Literature and Canadian Intellectual History," in J.M. Bumstead (ed.), *Canadian History Before Confederation* (Georgetown, Ontario: Irwin-Dorsey, 1972), p. 255.

20. A.R.C. Duncan, *Moral Philosophy* (Toronto: CBC Publications, 1965), pp.5-6.

21. There is an "historiographical vacuum" mainly in the sense of an absence of monographic studies. For an indication of some of the sources which will help to document these generalizations, see the following: W.R. Riddell, *The Life of John Graves Simcoe* (Toronto: McClelland and Stewart, 1926), pp. 17, 31, 32, 86; John Graves Simcoe, [Speech] "At the Opening of the Second Session of the First Parliament of Upper Canada," 31 May, 1793, in Henry Scadding (ed.), *Letter to Sir Joseph Banks, and other Documents* (Toronto: Copp Clark, 1890), p. 12; Keith Walden, "Isaac Brock: Man and Myth" (unpublished M.A. thesis, Queen's University, 1972); Terry Cook, "John Beverley Robinson and the Conservative Blueprint for the Upper Canadian Community," *Ontario History*, Vol. LXIV (June, 1972); S.F. Wise, "God's Peculiar Peoples," in W.L. Morton (ed.), *The Shield of Achilles* (Toronto: McClelland and Stewart, 1968); Susanna Moodie, "Education the True Wealth of the World," *The Victoria Magazine*, Vol. I, no. 4 (December 1847), p. 89, in *The Victoria Magazine 1847-1848*, ed. by Susanna & J.W.D. Moodie, with an introduction by William H. New (Vancouver: The University of British Columbia Press, 1973); Thomas McCulloch, *The Stepsure Letters*, Introduc-

tion by H. Northrop Frye (Toronto: McClelland and Stewart, 1960), pp. vii and *passim*; Fred Cogswell, "Haliburton," in Carl Klinck (ed.), *Literary History of Canada* (Toronto: University of Toronto Press, 1973), pp. 92-101; Carl Berger, *The Sense of Power* (Toronto: University of Toronto Press, 1970).

22. See Stephen Leacock, *The Social Criticism of Stephen Leacock*, edited and introduced by Alan Bowker (Toronto: University of Toronto Press, 1973), esp. pp. 41-50; Andrew Macphail, "Certain Varieties of the Apples of Sodom," *University Magazine*, Vol. x (February 1911); Pelham Edgar, "A Confession of Faith and a Protest," *ibid.*, Vol. viii (April 1909); A.B. McKillop, "Science, Values, and *The Canadian Forum*, 1920-1927," unpublished ms in the possession of the editor; J.W. Carey, "Harold Adams Innis and Marshall McLuhan," *Antioch Review*, Vol. xxvii (1967) and H.A. Innis, *Empire and Communications*, rev. ed. (Toronto: University of Toronto Press, 1972); George Woodcock, "A Nation's Odyssey: the Novels of Hugh MacLennan," in A.J.M. Smith (ed.), *Masks of Fiction* (Toronto: McClelland and Stewart, 1961); P.A. Morley, *The Immoral Moralists* (Toronto: Clarke, Irwin, 1972); Donald Creighton, *Towards the Discovery of Canada* (Toronto: Macmillan, 1972); G.P. Grant, *Philosophy in the Mass Age* (Toronto: Copp Clark, 1966), *Lament for a Nation* (Toronto: McClelland and Stewart, The Carleton Library, No. 50, 1970), and *Technology and Empire* (Toronto: Anansi, 1969); Northrop Frye, "Culture and the National Will" (Convocation address at Carleton University, 1957), *The Modern Century* (Toronto: Oxford University Press, 1967), and *The Critical Path: an Essay on the Social Context of Literary Criticism* (Bloomington: Indiana University Press, 1973).

PART ONE
The Critical Intellect

. . . An open mythology has no canon.

—Northrop Frye,
The Modern Century (1967)

*The main element of the modern spirit's life
is neither the sense and understanding nor
the heart and imagination; it is the imaginative
reason.*

—Matthew Arnold,
*Essays in Criticism,
1st Series* (1865)

Introduction

The publication of W.D. LeSueur's first essay, on Ste.-Beuve, was a declaration of his personal commitment to criticism as a way of life. All his subsequent writings—whether on criticism itself, science and "modern thought," morality and politics, or the function of the historian—were extensions of this central concern into different but related areas. The years between 1855 and 1872, the period in which LeSueur gradually arrived at his commitment to critical intellectual enquiry, were important ones for the history of critical expression. The year 1855 marked the abolition of the newspaper tax in England and the intervening years saw the publication of a number of critical works, including Charles Darwin's *The Origin of Species* and John Stuart Mill's *On Liberty* (both in 1859), *Essays and Reviews* (1860), Bishop Colenso's *The Pentateuch . . . Critically Examined* (1862), Matthew Arnold's *Essays in Criticism* (1865) and *Culture and Anarchy* (1867-68), T.H. Huxley's *Lay Sermons* (1870), and Darwin's *The Descent of Man* (1871). Any young man or woman with a reflective or speculative bent of mind with access to any of the major Anglo-American periodicals or even the library of a well-stocked Mechanic's Institute would have had little difficulty finding a variety of "heterodox" views which challenged preconceived notions and intoxicated the intellect.[1]

The enquiring and critical frame of mind which produced the various forms of heterodoxy prevalent in the third quarter of the nineteenth century was in direct conflict with accepted notions as to the proper function of the mind in British North America. In order to show the extent to which this was the case, and to indicate why William Dawson LeSueur's essays on criticism and the intellectual life were unique in Canada and were seen to contain dangerous notions, it is necessary to establish in some detail the intellectual context of his ideas and arguments. LeSueur will not appear on several of the pages that follow, for it was not he who reflected the attitudes and values dominant in Canada during the 1870s. More accurate barometers of accepted intellectual views are those clerics and academicians who were responsible for nurturing the thought of young Canadians who attended various denominational colleges and universities. Their ideas must be ex-

3

amined before the significance of LeSueur's thought can be fully
determined.

I

Any discussion of the life of the mind in the English-speaking
sections of nineteenth-century Canada must take two major and inter-
related cultural forces into account. The first is the conservative nature
of much of that thought, derived from the anti-revolutionary reaction to
the American and French revolutions, and which at times reached the
point of obsession with the necessity of upholding and extending
inherited European cultural legacies. The second is evangelical Christianity, which was relied upon heavily in Canada to provide the moral
cement with which to maintain the social bond. It is difficult to
over-estimate the pervasiveness or strength of either of these formative
influences. The political affinities of the various Protestant denomina-
tions may have differed, but virtually all were united by the fundamental conviction that all threats to the established social order as inherited
from England or to the foundations of Christianity were to be thwarted.
Hence, in British North America, responsiveness to European
ideologies was far more closely related to religious than to political
institutions: "it was the clergy, not the politicians, who bore the chief
responsibility for interpreting the meaning of Europe's convulsions to
society at large," writes one prominent Upper Canadian historian,
"and because of this they made a lasting contribution to the nature of
Canadian conservatism."[2]

Not the least of these "convulsions" were those of the mind. From
the point of view of those who wished to instil conservative social
values it was no less dangerous to have a populace given over to the
elevation of the "intellectual" side of human thought than it was to
have a public sympathetic to liberal or republican ideals. Indeed, it was
the role of the intellect within the life of the mind that concerned many
Anglo-Canadian educators. In the decades when Canadian students
such as W.D. LeSueur were reading Darwin and Mill, most Canadian
educators—virtually all of them clergymen—were concerned lest, as
Nathaniel Burwash (later to become a prominent Canadian Methodist)
expressed it, "the confidence secured by an intellectual process . . .
was substituted for the deep and regenerative convictions and revealing
liht of the Holy Spirit."[3]

In such a context the function of the university was conceived to be
not the gradual acquisition of knowledge and insight through the
promotion of the process of critical enquiry but the cultivation of a
pious disposition of mind. The student was above all to be made aware
of the extent to which his life and his thought must be governed by a

proper relationship between himself and his God. Under this conception of the working of the educated mind the "intellect" was a threatening presence, for by its very nature it was no respecter of orthodoxies. And to Anglo-Canadian educators, to speak of "orthodoxy" was to speak of nothing less than a conscious effort to preserve the framework of spiritual, cultural, and political tradition inherited from the European experience. Uncontrolled, it was thought, the intellect could seriously hamper the successful instillation (to use the words of Acadia College's President, John Mockett Cramp) of "that moral conservatism, without which, the advantages of knowledge itself may prove comparatively valueless."[4] It would not be inaccurate to say that Principal William Leitch of Queen's College echoed the convictions of virtually all the leaders of British North America's universities in 1868 when he told his students at convocation to "Forget not that, though you never enter the sacred profession of the Ministry, you are bound to be priests of God, and to serve Him in the various secular callings to which you may devote yourselves in life. Your education here is designed to dignify those callings so that they may be subservient to God's glory."[5] The intellectual callings of the various academic "disciplines" must also, in Leitch's view, be "subservient" to the more important task of recognizing the magnificence of that glory, as may be seen in Leitch's book, *God's Glory in the Heavens* (1862), an extension of William Paley's natural theology into the realm of mid-nineteenth century astronomy.[6]

The frame of mind deemed acceptable and desirable by those in positions of power at institutions where Canadian minds were to be cultivated and expanded was one in which "enquiry" of any sort was severely restricted by the conscious and willing subordination of purely "intellectual" effort to the dictates of the religious conscience. Had W.D. LeSueur been an undergraduate at Queen's College in 1855, the 15 year old student would have heard the Reverend James George, Vice-Principal and Professor of Moral Philosophy, give this set of priorities its most overt expression. In an address before the university community, George spoke on the subject of "The Relation Between Piety and Intellectual Labor." Scientists such as Humphrey Davy had accomplished what they had, George said, only because their intellects were guided by the pious disposition. "[T]he enthusiasm which enabled them to accomplish so much in unfolding the laws of nature," he noted, "was but the form that their piety took in doing homage to the God of nature . . . [T]heir piety furnished them with a kind of compass, telescope, and microscope, which enabled their intellect to go farther and see farther and deeper into nature than it otherwise could have done." Intellect divorced from piety, like Reason divorced from the gift of divine revelation, was at best only a half-blind wanderer in search of truth. At its worst it could be a positive evil,

> [for] . . . if the intellect be severed from God, and the heart in opposition to Him, the mind can give forth nothing but mere corruscations of light, which rather bewilder than guide, and are sure to land us in some disastrous folly. Unsanctified genius lives on the edge of madness, and may drive the world mad. For what, in truth, is the highest intellectual power without piety, but a Satanic light, leading in the end to the darkness of the pit. Real piety, we repeat, is the believing knowledge of the true God.[7]

It was with such a conception of the place of intellect within the structure of the mind that Canadian students were trained in the middle decades of the nineteenth century. And this was the case irrespective of discipline or denominational affiliation. Students in Divinity and at the Medical Faculty of Trinity College, as well as those in arts at the University of Toronto, were asked to accept without question the Paleyite evidences for design in nature found in the textbooks of two of their professors, James Beaven's *Elements of Natural Theology* (1850) and James Bovell's *A Manual of Natural Theology, for the Use of the Canadian Student* (1859).[8] Bovell explicitly warned his students of the dangers of an unwarranted extension of the scientific imagination through the exercise of sheer intellect. "While false systems of philosophy may tantalize and fret the mind," he wrote, "the calm and reflecting reasoner on revealed truth is content to curb his imagination, and to accept the creator as He has thought fit to shew himself."[9] The work of Daniel Wilson and John William Dawson, two of Canada's most eminent scientists and educators in the nineteenth century, was, in a sense, testimony to the operation of Bovell's dictum within their own minds. Their reviews of Darwin's *Origins* for Canadian journals in 1860, Wilson's peculiar combination of literary criticism, ethnology, and sheer fancy, *Caliban: the Missing Link* (1873)—written to rebut Darwin's *The Descent of Man*—, and Dawson's various popular defences of Biblical cosmogony, such as *The Story of the Earth and Man* (1873) and *Nature and the Bible*(1875), show the extent to which the critical enquiry which they claimed of their own fields was in fact seriously circumscribed by limitations upon the intellect which they themselves imposed.[10]

The works of Beaven and Bovell, the scientific writings of Dawson and Wilson, and the calendars of virtually every college in English-speaking Canada, indicate that Natural Theology, the proof of God's existence through the evidence of design and contrivance in Nature, was meant to instil into Canadian students—the future leaders of the nation—a moral and social conservatism that would check the disruptive influence of critical thought and democratic social ideals. It was conceived to be a major source of social orthodoxy.

This was also the case with the study of philosophy. One example may suffice. Students at the Free Church College in Halifax (and later at Dalhousie University) were informed by the Reverend William Lyall, Professor of Mental and Moral Philosophy, that "The right state of the affections . . . is a circumstance of more importance than the mere operation of mind, than any exercise of the intellectual faculties merely. . . . Thought is the staple of mind; emotion or feeling is the state, however, for which thought exists."[11] Two years later, in 1855, Professor Lyall published his *Intellect, the Emotions, and Man's Moral Nature*, which showed in a ponderous 627 pages the clear inferiority in the scale of mental faculties of the intellect to both the emotions and the Moral Nature of man.[12]

Professor Lyall's book was a major example of the influence of a second system of ideas used in mid-nineteenth century Canada to establish social and religious orthodoxy. Along with Paley's "Natural Theology," the tenets and teachings of the Scottish "Common Sense" school of philosophy were almost universally in use at Anglo-Canadian universities between 1840 and the 1870s. This philosophical "school" had grown out of the Enlightenment in Scotland, and was developed by several moral philosophers at Scottish universities, especially Thomas Reid, Dugald Stewart, and Sir William Hamilton. The essential nature of the school was that it sought to make the British empirical tradition introspective. All truths were within any man's reach through the common understanding: he had only to observe the nature of his own consciousness. Such psychological observation would allow one to determine principles—and to arrive at moral judgements—from the very constitution of the mind. But this assumption was based upon a certain conception of the morphology of the mind: that it was divided into many "senses" or "faculties" which corresponded to the actual physiology of the mental constitution. Names for these faculties varied from philosopher to philosopher, but always among them were man's "moral sense" or "moral nature," the innate capacity to arrive at moral truth. Also essential to the "Common Sense" school was its epistemological dualism. It set the external world against the world of consciousness, thereby helping to keep the traditional distinction between material and spiritual intact.[13]

Together, these various assumptions came to be used in the United States and Canada to meet several socially and intellectually desirable ends. The American religious historian, Sidney Ahlstrom, has clearly and forcefully set forward the use made of "Common Sense" in

America. Ahlstrom's description applies equally to the Canadian experience:

> On the mind-matter problem dualism facilitated an all-out attack on both materialism and idealism, as well as the pantheism that either type of monistic analysis could lead to. Furthermore, by a firm separation of the Creator and His creation, the Scottish thinkers preserved the orthodox notion of God's transcendence [sic], and made Revelation necessary. Dualism also made possible a synchronous affirmation of science on one hand, and an identification of the human intellect and the Divine Mind on the other. Scottish philosophers could thus be monotonously consistent in their invocations of Bacon or Newton and at the same time certify those rational processes of man which lead toward natural theology and contemplative piety and away from relativism and romantic excesses.
>
> The Scottish Philosophy, in short, was a winning combination. . . .[14]

In Canada the Natural Theology taught by James Beaven and James Bovell and the natural science investigated by John William Dawson and Daniel Wilson shared the dualism of Mind and Matter, Reason and Revelation. The epistemological foundations for that dualism were provided by their study in England and in Scotland of the philosophers whose theories have been outlined above. Meanwhile, the subject-object dualism, faculty psychology, and the appeal to introspection were made a basic part of the Canadian student's elementary assumptions by the teachings of various philosophers who were usually newly-arrived in the British North American colonies. In the middle decades of the nineteenth century, "Common Sense" seemed to be a "winning combination" in Canada as well as in the United States. It served the intellectual needs of Anglo-Canadian educators for several decades by helping to keep the intellect (and hence potentially dangerous intellectual enquiry) in a position in the scale of faculties clearly subordinate to the "moral nature." And its central assumptions maintained a grip on the educated Canadian mind long after it ceased to be taught.

Yet at precisely this time the Anglo-American world abounded with the evidence of material progress brought about by the triumphs of that "inferior" faculty, the intellect. "I find myself falling behind the age and cannot keep pace with the 'March of Intellect'," a Canadian railroad entrepreneur confided to a friend in 1851.[15] The age was one, said the speaker at a public lecture in Kingston in 1860, in which everywhere was "recorded the triumphs of the human intellect, the achievements of the human mind."[16] Yet A.J. O'Loughlin, a local cabinetmaker and secretary of the school board, was concerned. Those very triumphs created the possibility that men might forget that the essential nature of man was that he was moral and spiritual as well as intellectual. The speaker could scarcely deny the importance of intellect in bringing about the world of The Great Exhibition of 1851, but he could remind his audience just where it should be placed in the scale of things. He therefore took pains to stress that "the intellectual mind answers the purposes, and subserves the convenience of the rational and reasonable immortal soul." Intellect, that is to say, is one *function* of mind, not its constitution. "So by intellectual mind," he added, "we would simply imply a mind *which* when brought into connexion with, would suit the purposes and harmonize with the reasonable faculties of a soul or spirit essentially intellectual."[17]

A key to the popular nineteenth century conception of a well-balanced mind was, as the above quotation indicates, its insistence on the harmonious relationship of the various faculties. Since the cognitive, affective, and moral faculties each were seen to have specific and separate functions, such a harmony was deemed to be a hallmark of education and citizenry. And on the contrary, disproportionate emphasis upon any one faculty—especially the "intellectual"—was often considered to be an unhealthy form of mental life. The mind was a unity of all faculties: none should reign supreme.

Recognition of this fact helps explain, for example, the popular appeal—and indeed the nature—of the kind of poetry found in E.H. Dewart's *Selections from Canadian Poets*, published in 1864. Dewart notes, in the introduction to the volume, that "A national literature . . . is not merely the record of a country's mental progress: it is the expression of its intellectual life, the bond of national unity, and the guide of national energy."[18] Hence, the volume is often cited by historians to illustrate the growth—on the very eve of Confederation—of a national (as opposed to a colonial) consciousness. Yet the volume's introduction also provides a lengthy articulation of the desired nature of that intellectual life. It does so in its description of the nature and function of poetry.

Those who regard poetry as a "tissue of misleading fancies," wrote the editor, have ignored a fundamental truth: "the essential unity of mind." Such critics, Dewart insisted, have forgotten just what poetry is:

Poetry is not the product of any one faculty of the mind: it is the offspring of the whole mind, in the full exercise of all its faculties, and in its highest moods of sympathy, with the truths of mind and matter. It is not some artificial distortion of thought and language by a capricious fancy: it has its foundation in the mental constitution which our Creator has given us. . . . It ministers to a want of our intellectual nature. This is the secret of its power, and the pledge of its perpetuity . . . Poetry is the medium by which the emotions of beauty, joy, admiration, reverence, harmony, or tenderness kindled in the poet-soul, in communion with Nature and God, is conveyed to the souls of others.[19]

As with the philosophy of mind taught by William Lyall and James George, or with the science of Daniel Wilson and J.W. Dawson, the poetic experience described by E.H. Dewart presupposed the subordination of intellect to emotion. Cognition was made to be a process clearly inferior to, and dependent upon, man's aesthetic capacity. The function of intellect was not to conceive, to create, or to organize for its own sake; it was, instead, to give expression "to the emotions which throb for utterance at the heart. The influence of beauty or grandeur, moral and physical. . . . To this feeling, which exists in a stronger or weaker degree in all minds," Dewart concluded, "Poetry appeals."[20]

Such a conception of the structure and function of mind may have had certain emotional benefits, but it also assumed that, intellectually, man must primarily be a passive creature: intellect should operate when prodded by sense impressions or emotional (including spiritual) needs, and must then kindle equally passive traits such as admiration, devotion, and the desire for harmony. This conception of the passive role of intellectual power was meant to hold true whether men reflected upon their relationship to their families, their race, the national entity of which they were a part, or their God. It was meant to establish and maintain proper social relationships and values, and to curb social theorizing which would upset them. It was, in short, an elaborate means by which the pious disposition of mind could be preserved.

This was the cultural milieu in which W.D. LeSueur first began to publish articles which urged the necessity of criticism and declared his belief in the values of the intellectual life. Only when set against the backdrop of this context can the significance of LeSueur's various writings on the critical spirit be assessed. Between 1875 and 1882 four such articles were put before the Anglo-Canadian reading public. By the time "The Intellectual Life" (1875), the first of these articles, was published, LeSueur had already established something of a reputation as a Canadian critic of significance. By that time, he had published not only his *Westminster Review* article on Ste.-Beuve but also studies of Matthew Arnold and Bernardin de St. Pierre in the *Canadian Monthly and National Review*. He had also turned to political and social criticism in a severe indictment of "Party Politics," published under the pseudonym, "A Radical," in 1872, and had reviewed the general state of political culture and intellectual life in Canada in a perceptive essay, "Old and New in Canada," which opened the January, 1875, issue of the *Canadian Monthly* (see pp. 181-92). Yet LeSueur's articles on the critical intellect remain more important than these for any consideration of the premises from which he worked. Together they provide his philosophical *credo*, a declaration of faith in the critical path which he was to follow for the rest of his life. They therefore constitute the first and most fundamental chapter of his internal biography.

II

The essays which together comprise this philosophical testament were, by necessity, a defence of intellect and its role in human thought. Yet it is significant that LeSueur's argument was not a defensive one. He was concerned with dispelling certain criticisms levelled against the intellectual life: that the intellectual life is dominated by a narrow rationalism; that the training of the intellect (given such a conception of reason) may subvert one's primary duty to consider moral and ethical questions; and that such a life leads inevitably toward skepticism, materialism, and other forms of heterodoxy. Yet LeSueur attempted to rebut these charges not by searching for chinks in the enemy's armour but by asserting what he hoped was a consistent and superior philosophy of life.

One of the fundamental tenets of this philosophy was the insistence that the intellectual life consists of a unity of "mental act" and "moral colouring." The intellectual life is above all a moral life; hence intellectual concern is also moral concern. It therefore followed for LeSueur that such a life was not, as many of his contemporaries in Canada believed, something to be feared. He denied that it undermined the cultivation of love, disinterestedness, admiration, or enthusiasm for the true and the beautiful. Indeed, it enhances one's esteem for such values—for the person who follows the intellectual life is also one whose life must be guided by moral purpose. This claim nears the heart of LeSueur's *credo* and deserves to be emphasized:

> The life that such live is pre-eminently a life of thought, animated and kindled by strong moral feeling. If we call it "The intellectual life," we shall not, perhaps, use the words very inappropriately, or assign to them more meaning than they are adapted to bear. For is there not in the word "intellect" itself, something noble and imposing, and should we care to dignify with the name *intellectual activity* thought devoted to idle or selfish purposes? In such a life as I refer to, there is a pervading unity of tone and purpose. The man who thinks a

noble thought does not distinguish between the mental act and its
moral colouring; to him it is simply one moment of his life in which
high thoughts and high aims are thus harmoniously and indissolubly
blended, I know of none more suitable than the word "intellectual."
(p. 29)

The implications of this basic insistence upon uniting intellectual
enquiry and moral purpose may be examined through a consideration of
the concepts which pervade LeSueur's *credo*. The keys to his
philosophy of life lie in the meanings he ascribed to the words
"reason," "truth," "liberty," "culture," and "criticism."

"The Intellectual Life" and "Idealism in Life" both open with the
assertion that man is distinguished from brute creation by the fact that
he is self-conscious. "To man alone," he states, "is it given to regulate
his own inward life, and so govern his thought that, instead of being
dependent on momentary sense-impressions, they shall follow a path,
and proceed in an order, of his own determining." (p. 27) Man, like
other animals, is subject to the operation of the laws of the natural
world; yet his ability to reflect upon their operation and upon his own
relationship with physical nature affords him a form of liberation from
physical laws. "The moment . . . that self-consciousness enters upon
the scene, everything is altered. Law is not abolished, and yet in a very
real sense liberty is established,—liberty within the bounds of law. . . .
The self-conscious being knows what he wants, and within certain
limits can gratify his own desires. He does not escape from the control
of mechanical or chemical laws; but he can, to a large extent, modify
the incidence of those laws." (pp. 42-43) And it is the intellect, along
with the powers for rationality that go with it, which is the main agent
by which man asserts this capacity, the basis of his humanity.

If LeSueur saw the intellect as man's vehicle for expressing his
self-consciousness, he also saw reason as its workhorse. What is
reason? LeSueur denied vigorously that it can be conceived in any
narrow sense. It is not, he insisted, "a narrow kind of calculating
faculty" (p. 30); nor is it "wholly independent of the moral nature," as
some had claimed. (p. 63) It is, instead, the only means by which man
can arrive at truth, and is vitally connected with moral concern because
it is in fact "the moral or emotional nature that gives a direction to the
operations of reason. . . . Reason only occupies itself with what the
perceptive faculties furnish to it; and the perceptive faculties only see
what they are told to see, in other words, what the mind has an interest
in." (p. 63) One must have faith in reason as a means of pursuing truth;
yet to commit one's self to the *supremacy* of reason is to divorce it from
the moral imperative that must provide its direction. Man must, therefore, not "make an idol of his own individual reason," for to do so

would be to negate the search for unity that is the basis of the intellectual life.

Hence, just as the pious Christian, aware of his alienation from the mind of God, searches for a means of re-establishing that unity, so the man with faith in reason also seeks to re-establish functionally a similar unity.[21] Just as piety demands a submission to authority, so does reason. "No one knows better than he who believes in reason," LeSueur wrote, "how to submit to authority, for no one is more impressed than he with the advantage that knowledge has over ignorance, or with the inexorable character of all natural laws. . . . In the intellectual life there is no spirit of revolt, but rather a desire to be brought into harmony with whatever may be recognized as the decrees of Providence or the laws of Nature, in a word, with whatever is permanent and essential in the general constitution of things." (p. 32)

Yet it was precisely LeSueur's conception of what was "permanent and essential" in life that forced him to differ philosophically from those whose moral concerns did not vary greatly from his own. This difference was an immensely important one, for it derived from conceptions of what constituted "truth" that were fundamentally at variance. The most dogmatic of anti-Darwinian religionists would have agreed with LeSueur's assertion that every man should "devote himself with singleness of purpose to the discovery and diffusion of truth." (p. 40) Yet they certainly would have disagreed with his conception of what constituted "truth" itself. These differing conceptions of truth can best be understood by noting briefly the nature of modern social mythology as put forward by the Canadian literary critic and theorist, Northrop Frye.

Darwin, as Frye has noted, "finally shattered the old teleological conception of nature as reflecting an intelligent purpose," and that "From then on design in nature has been increasingly interpreted by science as a product of a self-developing nature."[22] Frye puts this observation into the context of the larger transition in social mythologies in which the "Darwinian revolution" was but a stage: a transition from the "closed mythology" that had characterized the Judaeo-Christian tradition to the "open mythology" of the modern century. Those in the second half of the nineteenth century who began to articulate this latter mythology were seldom revolutionaries; seldom did they reject the entire substance and thrust of the closed Christian mythology. They, too, possessed (to continue with Frye's terminology) a "myth of concern":

The myth of concern exists to hold society together, so far as words can help to do this. For it, truth and reality are not directly connected with reasoning or evidence, but are socially established.

What is true, for concern, is what society does and believes in response to authority, and a belief, so far as a belief is verbalized, is a statement of willingness to participate in a myth of concern. The typical language of concern therefore tends to become the language of belief. In origin a myth of concern is largely undifferentiated: it has its roots in religion, but religion has also at that stage the function of *religio*, the binding together of the community in common acts and assumptions.[23]

Frye's conception of the nature of modern social mythology does not, however, end there, for central to the modern myth of concern is another informed by a specific configuration of beliefs which have arisen over the past several hundred years. This configuration he calls the "myth of freedom," the verbal expression of certain dominant mental attitudes such as "objectivity, suspension of judgment, tolerance, and respect for the individual." The various attributes which constitute the myth of freedom are part of the modern myth of concern; yet the myth of freedom

. . . is a part that stresses the importance of the non-mythical elements in culture, of the truths and realities that are studied rather than created, provided by nature rather than by a social vision. It thus extends to the safeguarding of certain social values not directly connected with the myth of concern, such as the tolerance of opinion which dissents from it. . . . The myth of freedom . . . constitutes the "liberal" element in society, as the myth of concern constitutes the conservative one, and those who hold it are unlikely to form a much larger group than a critical, and usually an educated, minority. To form the community as a whole is not the function of the myth of freedom: it has to find its place in, and come to terms with, the society of which it forms part.[24]

This "open mythology" of the century after Darwin, characterized by the preoccupation both with "concern" and "freedom," is the broadest intellectual and social context into which W.D. LeSueur's writings can be placed. Like many of the greater intellectual figures of the nineteenth century—Hegel, Comte, Mill, Arnold, and Huxley—LeSueur sought to reconcile the basic forces of freedom and authority, progress and order, liberty and culture, and attempted to do so on the basis of an open mythology founded upon a progressive view of man and society. For all their differences, John Stuart Mill and Matthew Arnold were each "progressivists." That is, they agreed fundamentally, in Maurice Mandelbaum's words, on "the possibility of regarding man as a progressive being, capable of transforming himself through the cultivation of his capacities for higher forms of sensibil-ity."[25] This observation applies equally to LeSueur, as do the words which open a study of Arnold and Mill: "In their attempts to reconcile the ancient and the modern, literature and science, above all culture and democracy, Arnold and Mill were also trying to synthesize the partial and diverse elements of their age into a unified whole which would survive into the next."[26]

We may now consider LeSueur's conception of "truth." As a progressivist, he saw the course of thought as "a progressive reduction of facts to a rational or thinkable order." (p. 62) Yet he also insisted that "facts . . . are not in themselves truths; they are only the material out of which truth can be distilled." (p. 39) "Truth" does not consist of external data whether from the natural world or revelation. Nor, in one sense, can any conclusion be true for all time. The most that can be said is that our considered conclusions harmonize with existing knowledge: "Whether it will harmonize with the knowledge of some future age," he admitted, "it would be rash in us to attempt to predict." (p. 61) LeSueur rejected the notion of an eternal "truth" conceived as an external body of "facts." In that sense he was a relativist. Yet in another way he did conceive "truth" to be eternal. The man who is imbued with the spirit of intellectual liberty, he said, "is prepared to welcome truth from any quarter, and the universe seems to him full of truth. . . ." Such a man knows that, "though he were proved wrong on every point, there is a *right* elsewhere." (p. 30) What was important to LeSueur was the cultivation of a disposition of mind—a critical spirit—in which men could freely pursue certain ends while remaining open to the possibility—indeed, the inevitability—of error. This is what he meant by the phrase "there is a *right* elsewhere," for he continued the sentence by adding ". . . that in fact, only in the light of higher truth could he be rationally convinced of his own errors." LeSueur's was an open mythology: he advocated not a rigid creed but a set of mental co-ordinates.[27]

At the level of epistemology, LeSueur's progressive view of mind allowed him, without being a Hegelian, to follow Hegel's conception of truth, as put forward in *The Phenomenology of Mind*. (p. 27) "The truth is the whole," Hegel had said. "The whole, however, is merely the essential nature reaching its completeness through the process of its own development."[28] At the social level, LeSueur's progressivism caused him to see a close alliance between man's faith in reason and his faith in progress. He was more concerned, however, with the means by which progress comes about than with its manifestations. "For in what does progress consist," he asked, "if not in the gradual assimilation, so to speak, by the social organism, of successive discoveries of truth?" The progress of society will be checked only if "the conquests of the human mind'' cease. (p. 34) Material progress is dependent totally upon mental progress.

But in what direction should the critical mind turn for these conquests? What are the ideals to which it should aspire? What should be the basis of its moral concern? Again one turns to LeSueur's conception of the progressive course of thought and to the universalistic nature of the ''truth'' which will inevitably result from enquiry—for from them is derived his conceptions of liberty and culture, and his commitment to the criticism which is an outgrowth of both.

The great problem of thought, LeSueur claimed, is to achieve a ''harmony with what is already known or assumed to be known.'' (p. 61) But how can any lasting contribution to social progress be made if one's conclusions can at any moment be discarded as erroneous? The answer, he concluded, lies in the fact that the best thought is never pursued for individual ends: ''it springs, instead, almost wholly from the social nature of man.'' (p. 62) Successful thought will fundamentally be that which is pursued for social ends:

What a man thinks—if he thinks sincerely—holds good, or should hold good, not for himself alone, but for all men. . . . But as we all err more or less in the conceptions we form, it is manifest that the most satisfactory progress will be made in thought where there is the freest possible social comparison of views, and where men most frequently remind themselves that thought is not destined to serve merely individual purposes. Thought will make its best advance when men consciously or unconsciously try to think together. . . . The man who has a strong impulse to think, desires to think with others, or at least desires others to think with him; for he knows that whatever is true is true for all, and whatever is important is important for all. He does not therefore seek to fence himself off from the rest of mankind, but takes up his work as a continuation of what others have done before him. . . . Better [by] far, in a social point of view, the most dogmatic and absolute spirit than the mere worship of *la petite culture* in matters intellectual. It has not been by standing apart from one another, each man with his private thought and purpose, that the greatest triumphs of humanity have been won, but by the effort of all to universalize truth and to mere individual differences in a common intellectual and spiritual life. (pp. 62-63)

This passage from ''Free Thought and Responsible Thought'' is especially important because it provides a crucial link between two seemingly disparate ''isms'' with which LeSueur was later to be linked: positivism and conservatism. When identified with the former in the 1870s and 1880s, he was seen as a dangerously heterodox social radical; yet in Mackenzie King's Canada he was portrayed as a tory reactionary. In one sense, LeSueur *was* dangerously radical, for he openly advocated the use of positivistic assumptions in shaping social ethics. He had little use for the closed-minded dogmatism of traditional Christianity. Moreover, his writings in defense of modern thought were consistent with the generally-accepted tenets of positivism:

> that science is the only valid knowledge and facts the only objects of knowledge; that philosophy does not possess a method different from science; and that the task of philosophy is to find the general principles common to all the sciences and to use these principles as guides to human conduct and as the basis of social organization.[29]

Because of his basic acceptance of these general principles, his pronouncements—no matter how gracefully put—were seen to be challenges to Christian metaphysics (indeed, to the very idea of "metaphysics") and to the knowledge gained through faith as opposed to the scientific method.

In fact, as will become apparent, LeSueur was a radical only insofar as he challenged an authority based upon Christian dogma. His "positivism" owed far more to the spirit of Christianity than his opponents cared to admit. Furthermore, his understanding of social reality was profoundly not a radical one, for it was based upon the notion of society as an historically-evolved social organism. Here was the point of union between the Comtean positivism of his youth and the Burkean conservatism of his later years: the organic nature of society, and the necessity of subordinating individual for social ends, when necessary, whether in the political process or the process of thought.

LeSueur's essay on "Free Thought and Responsible Thought" also illustrates the complexity of his social thought. In it can be seen an articulation of aspects of the myths of freedom and concern which together constituted his particular brand of the nineteenth century progressivist creed. Indeed, it is as a progressivist (positivism must be seen as one variant of "progressivism") that LeSueur must primarily be viewed, for only in so doing can one adequately understand his acceptance of some tenets of the liberal and positivist doctrines and his rejection of others. In an earlier article he had defended Mill's insistence upon intellectual tolerance and the free expression of opinion, and had severely criticized Fitzjames Stephen for putting forward the claim that in certain circumstances such tolerance should end.[30] Yet while, like Mill, LeSueur was committed to free enquiry, he took issue with the conception of "liberty" put forward by Mill in 1859. "Let men but be allowed to think freely, and give free play to their several individualities," went LeSueur's version of Mill's creed, "and a new and better order of things would speedily arise." (p. 60) The weakness of such a view was not that freedom of thought was not a good thing, but that it could be abused. It could be abused because it does not follow that free thought is necessarily responsible thought. Again LeSueur turned to the positivist variant of progressivism.

If the course of thought consists of "a progressively wider interpretation of the universe in which man's lot is cast," it becomes apparent, said LeSueur, "that individual thought cannot properly, or with any advantage, separate itself from the thought of the race. . . . When, therefore, a demand is made for freedom, it becomes a question of much importance," he went on, "whether the freedom claimed is freedom to pursue truth in a social spirit for social ends, or mere freedom to think what one chooses without regard to ends and without any sense of responsibility." (p. 65) LeSueur insisted that both views be permitted; it was sufficient to point out the fallacies contained in the latter:

> The great lesson which "free-thinkers" have to learn is that all true thought is universal in character, not individual; and that nobody can be said to be thinking in the right sense of the word unless he is thinking for all, and endeavouring to promote the general harmony of human thought. It is unfortunately too common to find "free-thinkers" look upon the privilege of free thought as a mere private possession, something for the use of which they owe no account to any one, not even to themselves. They only realize their intellectual freedom in differing from others not agreeing with them. This is, no doubt, a not unnatural reaction from the intellectual tyranny of the past; but none the less does it lead to a hurtful dissipation of mental energy as well as to a dangerous weakening of social bonds. (p. 66)

We see put forward here one of the most critical relationships of the nineteenth century: "intellectual freedom" and the "social bonds", liberty and authority, freedom and concern. Positivism embodied both elements: it sought to be a force for liberation from entangling superstitions and institutions in its advocacy of the scientific method; yet its social theory lent itself to the establishment of a new orthodoxy which could subjugate individual freedoms for the social aggregate and replace one set of priests and prophets with another.

LeSueur's particular attempt to reconcile the demands of liberty and authority (in their various forms) was not simply a combination of the spirits of Mill and Comte, the fusion of an insistence upon the necessity for sustained individual enquiry into all matters with a refusal to elevate the individual above the social whole.[31] It was also one which sought to wed Comte's concern for humanity with a conception of culture not unlike that of Matthew Arnold. LeSueur, like Arnold, read widely in the literatures of classical antiquity and his appreciation of the classics remained with him to the end of his life. [32] Arnold, like LeSueur, viewed Sainte-Beuve as the literary critic who most helped to shape, as he admitted to a friend in 1872, his "habits, methods, and ruling ideas." [33] In that year LeSueur published his second article; its subject was the poetry of Matthew Arnold.

It was the combination of universalism with a "warmth of moral emotion" which LeSueur admired in Arnold's poetry. In commenting upon the last two stanzas of Arnold's "Lines Written in Kensington Gardens," he contrasted the moral stance of Marcus Aurelius (who was no less an influence upon LeSueur than upon Arnold), whose stoicism called for man to find peace of mind by "bringing his own nature into subjection," with that of Arnold, which "finds a support for his good resolutions in the very constitution of the universe." [34] Arnold's stance, like the stoic's, offered justice and dignity, yet it did so with a humility that the latter sometimes lacked. Moreover, it offered modern man "the power of sympathy, the power of feeling not merely *for* others but *with* them," a power which could potentially "become a distinct object of desire with even the best of men." [35]

This potential was in perfect harmony with LeSueur's positivistic commitment to "humanity"—itself an extension of his own belief in the existence of a cosmic moral order. This belief found parallel expression in the petition of prayer expressed by Arnold in "A Wish," a poem which LeSueur viewed as "one of the best Mr. Arnold ever wrote." The poem, LeSueur stated, was "full of that noble faith which looks upon the universe as a divine work, and the destinies of man in the future as wholly beyond the power of any human agencies or artifices to control." [36] LeSueur' universalism found perfect poetic utterance in Arnold's desire to

> . . . let me gaze, till I become
> In soul with what I gaze on wed!
> To feel the universe my home;

and his positivism offered him the belief that he was free to control his destiny in a way that Arnold felt impossible. In "A Wish," Arnold asked only "that my death may find/ The freedom to my life denied."

Lionel Trilling once wrote that Empedocles' misery in Arnold's poem, "Empedocles on Etna," was that "he cannot endure the social world; not only has he lost community with Nature, he has lost community with his fellow-men." [37] Trilling added that Arnold chose Empedocles "to embody his own social feelings," emotions which saw "the very social organism . . . [to be] fatal to the best of human values."[38] Arnold's Empedocles, faced with the death of imagination and the loss of self through the force of his own rationalistic and materialistic knowledge, commited suicide. LeSueur's would have found a life fulfilled: *his* Empedocles would have been a nineteenth century Frazier presiding confidently and optimistically over the positivist's Walden. "From one point of view," he said of "Empedocles on Etna," "it may be regarded as a poetical rendering of the Positive Philosophy: there are verses in it which breathe the Positivist spirit in its purest and most essential form."[39]

LeSueur also shared many of the imperatives of Arnold's moral imagination, and this was not inconsistent with his own commitment to the positivist spirit. Indeed, it says something about the nature of that positivism. His essay on Arnold's poetry concluded with the declaration that while one may find faults and deficiencies in Arnold's work, "it is beyond dispute that his influence as a writer, whether in prose or verse, tends constantly to the refining of our taste, and the ennobling of our moral sense."[40] LeSueur, like Arnold, found philosophical and religious moral creeds negative and incapable of affirming life.[41] Like Arnold, he was less concerned with formulas for morality than with the force of moral vision. He warned against such a restrictive view of morality in his essay on criticism. "In some cases," he wrote, "an undue preoccupation with moral interests destroys, or at least impairs, the sense for art." (p. 55)

The thrust of moral vision, unlike the concern for enforcing one's own moral lessons, leaves this essential connection between morality and art intact. It is essential because it is the quintessence of Culture. Arnold's declaration in *Culture and Anarchy* that Culture is "the best that is known and thought in the world" is well known; less-so is his declaration of the aims of Culture. To express these aims Arnold used the words of Bishop Wilson, "to make reason and the will of God prevail," and by "the will of God" Arnold meant "the universal order which seems to be intended and aimed at in the world, and which it is man's happiness to go along with or his misery to go counter to."[42] Arnold's Culture was a quest for inward perfection. It was life as art, and this was no less true for LeSueur. If LeSueur's commitment to the scientific spirit meant that there were natural laws in the physical world which were inviolable, his commitment to the cause of Culture equally meant the operation of moral laws for the spiritual world. Life in the natural world meant that man was bound to the face of the earth by the law of gravity; the ideal life meant that he must be equally governed by "the law that binds him to the true and beautiful." (pp. 44-45) The ideal life, the life of Culture, is a life of humility, disinterestedness, and patience. The man who attempts to live this ideal life recognizes the existence of "a moral order of the universe" and is willing voluntarily to subject himself to 'law'—"not to an outward code of observance, but to that inward voice which bids a man ever to seek and practice the best." (p. 47) It is life conceived as "something whose rules were not to be sought in the customs of the market-place, but deep down in the most secret and intimate convictions of the individual soul, as something whose standard was nothing short of the eternal beauty of holiness." (p. 45) It is life as embodied in Christ and the New Testament.

III

The first and most fundamental chapter in William Dawson LeSueur's internal biography is thus the story of his attempt to construct a workable philosophy of life, one which harmonized with the various laws—natural and spiritual—which many men of his day conceived to be in conflict.[43] While abundantly eclectic in the sources of its inspiration, it nevertheless achieved a high degree of consistency and integration by a basic commitment to a progressive view of man and history, an organic conception of social reality, and a universalistic conception of life in general which was the product of both progressivism and organicism. These themes pervade the pages which follow.

Civilized life rested, for W.D. LeSueur, upon an almost sacred connection between the critical spirit and the spirit of Culture. The invocation of moral sanctions which hindered the critical process— whether by dogmatists of religion, science, politics, or history—had necessarily to be combatted: "perpetual fussiness in morals is not the great preservative of moral order," he wrote; "the world lives, and is likely to live, by such laws as conduce to its well-being, and can do without the leading strings of even the best-intentioned nurses. To know this is culture, and is one foundation at least for a true criticism of life and whatever claims to represent life." (p. 56) LeSueur's search for these laws of social life in an age when science was making great and obvious advances resulted in his articulation of a scientific spirit which owed much to Auguste Comte; yet this "positivistic" commitment to the cause of humanity, it may now be seen, was derived just as much from classical culture and the spirit of the Christian tradition. In a word, LeSueur's "positivism" owed as much to the Pauline dictum which went: "Finally be of one mind, united in feeling." Whether derived from Comte or St. Paul, this message, LeSueur claimed, nevertheless led to a widening of experience, knowledge, and sensibility. It disturbed the pre-critical state of mind; it led to a wider culture; it created a temperament in which a man will "become a critic in spite of himself."

NOTES

1. See John Beattie Crozier's remarkable autobiography, *My Inner Life; being a Chapter in Personal Evolution and Autobiography* (New York: Longmans, Green, and Co., 1908), Vol. I, Ch. VI: "Evolution Not to Be Jumped," pp. 176-184 ff. A contemporary of LeSueur, Crozier, born in Galt, Canada West, in 1849, attended the University of Toronto where he was both University and Starr medallist in Medicine in 1872. Finding the intellectual atmosphere of Canada stifling, he emigrated to England where, while practicing medicine, he spent most of the rest of his life attempting to write a synthetic history of the evolution of the human intellect. Because of the gradual failure of his eyesight only two of three projected volumes were completed. He died in 1921. Publications of Dr. Crozier, who achieved a considerable degree of eminence within British philosophical and literary circles, included *The Religion of the Future* (1880), *Civilization and Progress* (1885), *History of Intellectual Development*, Vol. I (1897), Vol. II (1901), and *Last Words on Great Issues* (1917). For estimates of Crozier's career and philosophy, see: Arnold Haultain, "A Search for an Ideal," *Canadian Magazine*, Vol. XXII, no. 5 (March 1904), pp. 427-430; *Nature*, Vol. 106 (Jan. 27, 1921), p. 700; "Death of Dr. Beattie Crozier; Philosopher and Social Economist; Services to Speculative Thought," *Times* [London], Monday, January 10, 1921, p. 15. It is interesting to speculate what degree of eminence LeSueur might have achieved within British circles had he emigrated to England with Crozier in 1872.

2. These two themes have been given extended consideration by Canadian scholars. The writings of S.F. Wise have done much to reveal the ramifications of the anti-revolutionary nature of the Canadian experience, especially with regard to Canadian attitudes toward the United States. See: "The Origins of Anti-Americanism in Canada," Fourth Seminar on Canadian-American Relations, Assumption University of Windsor (1962), pp.297-306, in which he stresses the connection between anti-Americanism and the Canadian conservative tradition (pp. 298-299); also "Colonial Attitudes from the Era of the War of 1812 to the Rebellions of 1837," in S.F. Wise and R.C. Brown (eds.), *Canada Views the United States* (Toronto: Macmillan of Canada Ltd., 1967), where he stresses the nature of the "disbelief system" created by the British North American rejection of the American and French revolutions: "it was essential for Canadians not to believe in the United States and to assume that the country they lived in was not a kind of subarctic, second-best America, but rather a genuine alternative to this revolution-born democracy, and organized upon principles and for purposes quite different from it." (p.22) The French Revolution served to cement "the bond between psychological need and conservative ideology." (p.22) Another essay by Wise in the same collection, "The Annexation Movement and Its Effect on Canadian Opinion, 1857-67" (pp.44-97), continues the same theme to the period of Confederation. A further essay by Wise, elsewhere, stresses the positive functions and widespread popular acceptance of conservative ideas and leaders in the period prior to the 1837 rebellions: "Upper Canada and the Conservative Tradition," in *Profiles of a Province: Studies in the History of Ontario* (Toronto: Ontario Historical Society, 1967), pp.20-34.

John S. Moir, in "The Upper Canadian Religious Tradition," *ibid.*, pp.189-

195, sees Upper Canada between 1825 and 1850 as "almost exclusively a Christian community," whose religious institutions, while adapting to the needs of the North American environment, nevertheless "were and still are transplants from Europe." (p.189) Moir stresses the great preoccupation of Canadian churchmen with the question of "voluntarism." It was from this issue that most Canadian religious controversies arose. Yet this must not be made to obscure the fact that, beyond questions of polity, even such traditionally bitter rivals as John Strachan and Egerton Ryerson shared certain basic convictions.

In "Sermon Literature and Canadian Intellectual History," *The Bulletin* of The United Church of Canada, No.18 (1965), pp.3-18, S.F. Wise deals largely with two important sermons of John Strachan in order to reveal the nature of the social psychology of the Canadian Tory. Two excellent articles that stress the importance and widespread influence of evangelical Protestantism in English-speaking Canada during the first half of the nineteenth century are those by G. French, "The French Evangelical Creed in Canada," and S.F. Wise, "God's Peculiar Peoples," both in W.L. Morton (ed.), *The Shield of Achilles, op.cit.*, pp.15-35, and 36-61. French argues persuasively for the necessity of viewing Christianity as a "powerful formative factor in the growth of this nation." (p.15) Wise argues that despite the exhortations of clergymen, "providential theory [failed] to furnish a unifying myth for English-Canadians in the early Victorian era." (p.36)

3. N. Burwash, *The History of Victoria College* (Toronto: University of Toronto Press, 1927), pp. 466-467.

4. Quoted in T.A. Higgins, *The Life of John Mockett Cramp* (Montreal: n.p., 1887), p. 417.

5. William Leitch, "Introductory Address at the Opening of Queen's College, November 8, 1860" (Montreal: John Lovell, 1860), p. 7.

6. William Leitch, *God's Glory in the Heavens* (London: Alexander Strahan & Co., 1862).

7. Rev. James George, "The Relation Between Piety and Intellectual Labor. An Address Delivered at the Opening of the Fourteenth Session of Queen's College" (Kingston: The Daily News Office, 1855), p. 9.

8. James Beaven, *Elements of Natural Theology* (London: Francis and John Rivington, 1850); James Bovell, *A Manual of Natural Theology, for the Use of the Canadian Student* (Toronto: Rowsell & Ellis, 1860). Along with the Scottish Common Sense philosophy, William Paley's natural theology was one of the intellectual touchstones in Anglo-Canadian education during the middle decades of the nineteenth century.

9. *Ibid.*, p. iii.

10. Daniel Wilson, "The President's Address," *Canadian Journal*, Ser. II, Vol. 5 (1960), pp. 109-127; J.W. Dawson, "Review of Darwin on the Origin of Species By Natural Selection," *Canadian Naturalist and Geologist*, Vol. v (1860), pp. 101-120; C.F. O'Brien, *Sir William Dawson: a Life in Science and Religion* (Philadelphia: American Philosophical Society, 1971).

11. Rev. William Lyall, "The Philosophy of Thought; a lecture delivered at the opening of the Free Church College, Halifax, Nova Scotia, Session 1852-3" (Halifax: James Barnes, 1853), p. 3.

12. Rev. William Lyall, *Intellect, the Emotions, and Man's Moral*

Nature (Edinburgh: Thomas Constable, 1855), Section One: "The Philosophy of Intellect," pp. 13-279 ff.

13. See S.A. Grave, "Common Sense," in Paul Edwards (ed.), *The Encyclopedia of Philosophy*, Vol.2 (New York: Macmillan, 1967), pp.156-157; Sidney Ahlstrom, "The Scottish Philosophy and American Theology," *Church History*, Vol.24 (1955), pp.260-261; Gladys Bryson, *Man and Society: the Scottish Enquiry of the Eighteenth Century* (New York: Augustus M. Kelley, 1966), *passim;* George Elder Davie, *The Democratic Intellect; Scotland and Her Universities in the Nineteenth Century* (Edinburgh: University Press).

14. Ahlstrom, *op.cit.*, pp.267-268; John Irving, "The Development of Philosophy in Central Canada to 1900," *Canadian Historical Review*, Vol. XXXI (September, 1950), pp.252-287. See also Wilson Smith, *Professors and Public Ethics; Studies of Northern Moral Philosophers before the Civil War* (Ithaca: Cornell University Press, 1956).

15. Isaac Fraser to John Macaulay, September 9, 1851, Macaulay Papers, PAO. The editor is grateful to Dr. Peter Baskerville for this reference.

16. A.J. O'Loughlin, "Man, a Material, Mental, and Spiritual Being: A Lecture delivered in the City Hall, Kingston, C.W., January 6th, 1860" (Kingston: James M. Creighton, 1860), p. 6.

17. *Ibid.*, p. 37.

18. E.H. Dewart, "Introductory Essay" to *Selections from Canadian Poets . . . ,* "Literature of Canada . . . Poetry and Prose in Reprint" series, Introduction by Douglas Lochhead (Toronto: University of Toronto Press, 1973), p. ix.

19. *Ibid.*, pp. xi, ff.

20. *Ibid.*

21. For various discussions of what might be termed the morphology of piety, see: Emile Durkheim, *The Elementary Forms of the Religious Life* (London: George Allen and Unwin, 1964), pp. 36-42, *passim*; Robert A. Nisbet, *The Sociological Tradition* (New York: Basic Books, 1966), pp. 261-163; George Santayana, *The Life of Reason*, One Vol. Ed. (New York: Charles Scribner's Sons, 1955), pp. 258, *passim*.

22. Northrop Frye, *The Modern Century* (Toronto: Oxford University Press, 1967), pp. 110, ff.

23. Northrop Frye, *The Critical Path* (Bloomington: Indiana University Press, 1973), p. 36.

24. *Ibid.*, p. 45.

25. Maurice Mandelbaum, *History, Man, and Reason; a Study in Nineteenth-Century Thought* (Baltimore: Johns Hopkins Press, 1974), p. 199.

26. Edward Alexander, *Matthew Arnold and John Stuart Mill* (New York: Columbia University Press, 1965), p. 1. See also pp. 12, 243.

27. On the notion of an "open mythology," Frye writes: "Beliefs and convictions and courses of action come out of an open mythology, but when such courses are decided on, the area of discussion is not closed off. No idea is anything more than a half-truth unless it contains its own opposite, and is expounded by its own denial or qualification." *The Modern Century, op. cit.*, p. 116. See also "The Noisy Conflict of Half-Truths," in Alexander, *op. cit.*, pp. 34-73.

28. Hegel quoted in Mandelbaum, *op. cit.*, p. 175.

29. Nicola Abbagnano, "Positivism," in Paul Edwards (ed.), *The Encyclopedia of Philosophy* (New York: Macmillan, 1967), Vol.6, p. 414. Another authority, Abraham Kaplan, has also provided a brief summary of the essential nature of positivism: ". . . a continuation of the eighteenth-century philosophy of the Enlightenment. Metaphysics and theology are again brought before the bar of reason, with the insistence that the institutions appealing to them for justification be reformed or replaced. Science is claimed to provide the standards applied in this critique. The name 'positivism' derives from the emphasis on the positive sciences—that is, on tested and systematized experience rather than on undisciplined speculation." "Positivism," *International Encyclopedia of the Social Sciences* (New York: Macmillan, 1968), Vol.12, p.389. See also Stanislav Andreski (ed.), *The Essential Comte* (New York: Barnes and Noble, 1974), pp. 7-18.

30. W.D. LeSueur, "Liberty of Thought and Discussion," *Canadian Monthly and National Review*, Vol. x, no. 3 (September 1876), pp. 202-212. LeSueur's article was largely a critical review of Stephens' book, *Liberty, Equality, and Fraternity* (1872). The title of LeSueur's essay is essentially the same as those of the second chapter of both Mill's *On Liberty* and Stephen's *Liberty, Equality, Fraternity*. Fitzjames Stephen's argument for limiting the toleration of free discussion was based on the assumption (to use his own words), that "people should not talk about what they do not understand," and that "most people have no right to any opinions whatever . . . except in so far as they are necessary for the regulation of their own affairs." It should be added that LeSueur doubtless took umbrage at Stephen's book because much of it (Chs. IV-VI) was a devastating attack on the political manifestations of the positivist religion of humanity. For an excellent treatment of the premises from which Stephen worked in formulating his views see R.J. White's "Introduction" to *Liberty, Equality, Fraternity*, R.J. White, ed. (Cambridge: Cambridge University Press, 1967), pp. 1-18.

31. See Auguste Comte, "Plan of the Scientific Operations Necessary for Reorganizing Society," in Philip Rieff (ed.), *On Intellectuals* (New York: Doubleday, 1969), p. 277 ff.; Mandelbaum, *op. cit.*, pp. 164-174; W M. Simon, *European Positivism in the Nineteenth Century* (Ithaca: Cornell University Press, 1963), p. 4.

32. His last literary endeavour, undertaken at the end of the "LeSueur Lindsey controversy," was a Latin metrical translation of John Mason Neale's hymn, "Art Thou Weary, Art Thou Languid," *University Magazine*, Vol. XIV (December 1915), p. 563.

33. Cited in Alexander, *op. cit.*, p. 6.

34. W.D. LeSueur, "The Poetry of Matthew Arnold," *Canadian Monthly and National Review*, Vol. 1 no. 3 (March 1872), p. 222. See also Lionel Trilling, *Matthew Arnold* (New York: The World Publishing Co., 1965), p. 175.

35. *Ibid*.

36. *Ibid*.

37. Trilling, *op. cit.*, p. 103; also pp. 80-83.

38. *Ibid*.

39. "The Poetry of Matthew Arnold," *op. cit.*, p. 229.

40. *Ibid.*

41. Trilling, *op. cit.*, p. 202.

42. *Ibid.*, pp. 241-242.

43. Paul A Carter, *The Spiritual Crisis of the Gilded Age* (DeKalb: Northern Illinois Press, 1971), *passim*; Frank Miller Turner, *Between Science and Religion* (London: Yale University Press, 1974), pp. 1-37, 247-256; John Dillenberger, *Protestant Thought and Natural Science* (New York: Doubleday, 1960), pp. 217-238 ff; Richard D. Altick, *Victorian People and Ideas* (New York: W.W. Norton, 1973), pp. 226-237.

1. The Intellectual Life (1875)

To man alone of all sentient beings, is it given to regulate his own inward life, and so govern his thoughts that, instead of being dependent on momentary sense impressions, they shall follow a path, and proceed in an order, of his own determining. The lower animals have thoughts, but their thoughts are chained, as it were, to the objects that suggest them, and their lives may thus be conceived as broken into an indefinite number of separate movements, each dominated by its own special impression. When a horse stops at a gate at which he has been accustomed to stop, I cannot believe that he retains what we would call a remembrance of any of the previous occasions on which he has done so, or that he distinguishes in any way between his last act of the kind and former ones. He stops, as we say, mechanically, by virtue of an association established between the visual impression of the gate, and the order to stop so often given at the same point. How this may be we know from our own experience, for we continually find ourselves doing things in the same way, sometimes much to our own inconvenience. Very many acts of forgetfulness are the result simply of the force of established habits: we have some special thing to do at a certain time, something out of the usual course, but, trusting ourselves to our daily routine of duty, we are insensibly carried past the point at which the special action was to be performed, and are only reminded of it when perhaps it is too late. The very attempt, however, to keep a thing in mind is a mark of the higher intellectual development at which human beings have arrived; we cannot imagine such an attempt being made by any of the lower animals. It is our prerogative to contemplate our own thoughts as phenomena: in other words, man has risen to self-consciousness, and with self-consciousness comes the impulse, and not the impulse only, but the power to control the successive manifestations of his life. In the self-consciousness of man, Spirit, to use the language of the Hegelian philosophy, realises its own essential freedom. The forms in which it clothes itself perish, but it remains, and it

SOURCE: *Canadian Monthly and National Review*, Vol. VII (April, 1875), pp. 320-330.

thus recognizes itself as superior to change, the true type of the incorruptible and eternal.

The freedom of spirit, however, is realised in different degrees in different races, and individuals. Throughout a large portion of the human family, the life of sense predominates altogether over the life of thought, and man is seen as the slave of passion, and of custom, rather than as master of his own faculties and destinies. There is, no doubt, a radical distinction between the thought even of savages, and that of the lower animals; but if the glory of mankind is to be found in the power of self-control and self-education, and in the possession of interests wholly unconnected with the physical appetites, there are numerous races of men to whose humanity little glory can be said to attach. Among savage tribes there seems an absolute lack of capacity for the exercise of abstract thought, or any disengagement of the mind from material objects and interests; but I am not sure that in civilised communities, we do not sometimes witness what, strictly judged, is a more painful subject of contemplation, namely, a kind of voluntary ignorance of all the nobler springs of human action, a voluntary clinging to a mode of life, such as, in all its moral elements, might be lived by beings very far down in the scale of civilisation.

In cases of this kind how much should be attributed to sheer inferiority of organization in the individual, and how much to the lack of favourable formative influences? The balance is often difficult to strike, but probably no case comes under our notice in which we are not disposed to believe that, *had circumstances only been different*, a better result might have been brought about. Strange characters no doubt are born into the world, but what these might become under a thoroughly natural and healthy system of education no one, perhaps, is in a position to say. Certain it is that, by unwise and vicious methods of education, many a naturally good disposition has been spoilt, and gifts of intellect that might have proved of the highest value to society have either been condemned to uselessness, or directed into positively mischievous courses. The great dramatist has told us of a "Divinity that shapes our ends, rough-hew them how we will." This may perchance hold true of human destinies; but in the development of human character it would seem as if nature did the rough-hewing and left education and circumstances to do the shaping. And the shaping is a great deal. The turn that it gives to our thoughts, our interests, our tastes, our manners, may make all the difference between happiness and unhappiness, between success and the want of it; may make our lives noble or make them mean, make them a blessing to the world or a burden even to ourselves. Very few human beings have even moderate justice done to them in the way of education. Carlyle has said: "A wise, well-calculating breeding of a young genial soul in this world, or alas of any young soul in it, lies fatally over the horizon in these days.'' The statement is an extreme one, but to those who know how to read Carlyle, it contains a truth. ''Wise and well-calculating breeding'' does not lie completely ''over the horizon'' even in these days; but, like all excellent things, it is rare. To make it more common is the one great problem in education; a problem, however, the full importance of which few appreciate. By education is too commonly understood the mere acquisition of ''useful knowledge,'' in other words, of an equipment for the great life-struggle for wealth. The moulding of the character, the awakening and strengthening of the intellectual powers, the cultivation of the tastes and the emotions, scarcely enter into the popular idea of education at all. Yet surely an education that makes no provision for these things is unworthy of being offered to a being like man, susceptible of reverence, of love, of disinterestedness, of admiration, of enthusiasm for the true and the beautiful; a being formed for rational enquiry and discourse, and capable of governing his life by devotion to high ideals. That there is in average humanity a capacity for something better than we ordinarily see is proved by the success that attends the efforts of all really eminent teachers. One man like Dr. Arnold gives a tone to the thoughts and sentiments of hundreds of youths, so that those whom he has trained are distinguishable by their intellectual and moral qualities for the rest of their lives. A recent writer in *Blackwood's Magazine* held that Dr. Arnold made his boys too conscientious; but if there was an error on that side, which I am slow to believe, it was an error that very few teachers could commit if they tried, and one of which very few have ever been accused.

Whether as the result of fortunate, or in spite of unfortunate, influences and agencies, some souls in every generation are seen to rise above the commonplace of human existence, so as to derive from the habitual exercise of their higher and nobler faculties an interest at once keen and satisfying. The life that such live is pre-eminently a life of thought, animated and kindled by strong moral feeling. If we call it ''the intellectual life,'' we shall not, perhaps, use the words very inappropriately, or assign to them more meaning than they are adapted to bear. For is there not in the word ''intellect'' itself, something noble and imposing, and should we care to dignify with the name *intellectual activity* thought devoted to idle or selfish purposes? In such a life as I refer to, there is a pervading unity of tone and purpose. The man who thinks a noble thought does not distinguish between the mental act and its moral colouring; to him it is simply one moment of his existence. If, therefore, one word is to be chosen to express a life in which high thoughts and high aims are thus harmoniously and indissolubly blended, I know of none more suitable than the word ''intellectual.''

The first step in this life is to have faith in reason; to believe sincerely, thoroughly, and once for all, that man has faculties adapted for the discovery of truth, and that a faithful use of these must be attended by good results. Such a faith is so natural to the human mind that it can hardly fail to be developed in any one who in youth sees examples, or perhaps even a single example, of its active exercise. In default of living companionship of the right kind, a book casually met with will sometimes awaken the mind to a sense of its powers and privileges; but, in whatever way the effect is wrought, it is always one of the very greatest moment. A too common idea of human reason is that it is a narrow kind of calculating faculty, useful in business operations and in the ordinary affairs of life; but, in wider or deeper questions, more likely to lead to error than to truth. The true view of reason is that it is the *only* faculty man has for arriving at truth on any subject great or small, so that any truth which reason cannot grasp is entirely out of human reach. If we are to guard against being led astray by reason, what faculty are we to employ for the purpose? Shall we better ourselves by giving the reins to imagination, or jumping at conclusions with our eyes shut? This is what in certain quarters we are counselled to do, on the understanding, of course, that the conclusions we jump at shall be those of our counsellors; otherwise our faith is vain. Madame de Stael understood pretty well a certain class of philosophers when she wrote:

> The defenders of prejudices, that is to say, of unjust claims, of superstitious doctrines, of oppressive privileges, try to call into existence an apparent opposition between reason and philosophy, in order to be able to maintain that reason may lay an interdict upon reason, that there are truths which we should believe without understanding them, principles which we must admit, but forbear from analysing; in a word, a sort of exercise of thought which serves the single purpose of persuading us how useless all thought is.*

There must have been "Grammars of Assent," and treatises on "The Limits of Religious Thought"[1] in those days as well as in these, for here they are described as regards their spirit and purpose to the very letter.

He who once fully realizes that truth is made for man and man for truth, enjoys a sense of freedom that nothing else can give. He breathes a larger and more invigorating air, and feels himself a citizen, not of the world only, but of the universe. He is delivered from bondage to his own opinions, for he knows now that, though he were proved wrong on every point, there is a *right* elsewhere—that in fact, only in the light of higher truth could he be rationally convinced of his own errors. The

*De la Littérature, p. 514.

poet Clough, whose life was almost a type-example of what we would here describe, has nobly said—

It fortifies my soul to know
That, though I perish, Truth is so;
That, howsoe'er I stray and range,
Whate'er I do, Thou dost not change.
I steadier step when I recall
That, if I slip, Thou dost not fall.

Most men, on the contrary, speak and act as though the fortunes of the universe were bound up with their own infallibility, and as if, therefore, any demonstration of radical error in their opinions would imperil all the happiness and hopes of humanity. Hence follows, by a natural process of development, a kind of fetish-worship of opinions that leaves out of sight almost entirely the question of their truth or falsehood, and looks only at their supposed utility. The more assured a man is of possessing the truth, the more confident should be his out-look upon the world, the more prepared he should be to examine the opinions of those who are so unfortunate as to disagree with him, and ascertain the grounds on which they are held. We find, however, that just the contrary is the case; that people whose opinions rest, as they say, on an immovable basis, are, as a general thing, particularly reluctant to acquaint themselves directly with other forms of belief. They will, perhaps, look into some travesty of hostile opinions prepared for them by hands they can trust, but as for a personal survey of the hostile territory, they would rather be excused. In such cases the thing dreaded is not the loss of truth, but the loss of a persuasion; that truth *may* be on the other side they cannot help at times suspecting, but they are determined never to be brought face to face with the proofs. If they thought that a thorough and candid examination of their opponents' position would confirm them in their present opinions and set their minds for ever at rest, they would gladly and eagerly resort to it; but they think nothing of the kind. Instead of setting truth above opinion, they set opinion above truth. Truth is a far-off Mikado, a dignified kind of entity always to be spoken of with respect, but opinion is the *praesens divus*, the Tycoon, or, to come back to Europe, the mayor of the palace—the actual ruler of men's lives. Is there no word to express this disposition of mind? Certainly there is: the word is *scepticism*. The sceptic, in any sense of the word, that can live in this century is not he who, after candid examination, decides that he cannot accept this or that system of belief, but he whose mind is full of dark places that he does not care to have illumined, who fears that his structure of belief is tottering, yet dreads to examine its foundations, or even so much as to put out his hand to steady it, who piteously begs everybody near to keep quiet, lest a breath or a vibration should lay the whole fabric in ruins.

Directly opposed to the spirit of scepticism is the spirit of intellectual liberty. He whose thought has been emancipated may find himself compelled to deny, or at least to question, many things commonly accepted, but the general tone of his mind is not negative, but positive. In a certain sense he feels as though he could believe all things, for he is prepared to welcome truth from any quarter, and the universe seems to him full of truth, while error dwindles away to the most insignificant dimensions. Even errors, when understood in their genesis and development, yield up their quota of truth, and may thus serve, like any other objects of study, to help forward the education of the mind.

It by no means follows that he who has arrived at a conviction of the supremacy of reason must make an idol of his own individual reason, or set up any form whatever of self-worship. Of course he will be accused of this, and probably of numerous other absurdities, but he must learn, as a reasonable man, to bear the charge with patience, knowing how plausible it must appear to those who urge it. Reason itself teaches that, in certain matters, the reason of others is to be preferred to our own; and, in such cases we shall use our reason simply to guide us to those whom it may be prudent for us to trust or follow. If these, instead of doing us good, inflict injury on us, or lead us astray, we pay the penalty of our ignorance, as men have been doing, more or less, from the beginning of the world. Our duty was discharged if we made the best selection that the state of our knowledge, or the information within our reach, enabled us to make. No one knows better than he who believes in reason how to submit to authority; for no one is more impressed than he with the advantage that knowledge has over ignorance, or with the inexorable character of all natural laws. "A pious soul," says Carlyle, writing of his friend Sterling, "we may justly call him; devoutly submissive to the will of the Supreme in all things; the highest and sole essential form which Religion can assume in man, and without which all forms of religion are a mockery and a delusion in man." In the intellectual life there is no spirit of revolt, but rather a desire to be brought into harmony with whatever may be recognized as the decrees of Providence or the laws of Nature, in a word, with whatever is permanent and essential in the general constitution of things.

The great truths of the universe are not of any private interpretation——their application is to all mankind, their benefits are for all. He, therefore, who has seen reason in its beauty and its infinitude will feel that *his* life, at least, must afford some feeble reflection of that which has dawned upon his spirit. He has become a debtor to humanity, and woe to him if he preaches not some kind of gospel. Was the revelation made to him that he might thereafter shut his lips and live a life of selfishness among his fellow-men? Or can he avail himself of the wider and deeper views of things to which he has been admitted simply to increase his own personal prestige and power? That men cannot be thus unfaithful to the highest gifts it would be rash to assert, but surely it must be hard for them to be; for does not all illumination, like the first rays of sunlight on the lips of the fabled statue, seem to smite into music the very ''chords of self,'' attuning them to a vaster harmony than they had ever before known? There is nothing in the world so catholic as reason. Interests and traditions divide men and arm them against one another, but reason would unite them, if they would but listen to its voice. Edgar Quinet[2] has well pointed out that what the mightiest church the world ever saw failed to accomplish—the unification of humanity—science, which is nothing but embodied reason, is every day hastening to a consummation. Let me try and translate here a few of his eloquent sentences:—

> This reign of unity, which the church is still pursuing, science, in its ceaseless progress, has all but grasped, if indeed, she has not fully grasped it. You heap upon her your lofty scorn, but all the while she is accomplishing that which you content yourself with promising. What is she doing? Why, she is the same for all peoples, she speaks, and makes her authority respected in all languages: she brings together different climates and does away with space. Always in agreement with the vast book of Nature, wide open from East to West, she knows nothing of sects or heresies. She works; she imitates the Creator, and brings nature to its perfection. While you are discoursing, she is advancing; and the modern world, which you refuse to follow, is resting itself more and more upon her laws, as upon eternal reason, the one truly catholic reason brought to light by the very men you have condemned.*

The intellectual life, therefore, is a life of sympathy with humanity and of harmony with nature. It finds its natural aliment in general truths, and the satisfaction of its active impulses in the enunciation of these truths, and, so far as may be, in their practical application to human affairs. All sustained intellectual life must have its root in human interests of one kind or another, and we find, as a matter of fact, that the keenest students, those who grasp at the most encyclopaedic knowledge, are those whose labours bear most directly on the progress of society. And here it may be remarked that faith in reason and faith in

*L'Ultramontanisme, Leçon v.

progress are sentiments so closely allied that they are seldom seen apart. For in what does progress consist, if not in the gradual assimilation, so to speak, by the social organism, of successive discoveries of truth? If, therefore, there are no assignable limits to the conquests of the human mind, there can be none to the progress of society. It has been truly remarked that the idea of progress is a wholly modern one. The thoughts of the ancients seem scarcely to have wandered beyond their own time, and after the introduction of Christianity, the whole stress of human hopes (and fears) was transferred to a future life, this mundane state of existence being regarded as a provisional dispensation which might at any moment be abruptly terminated. Of course men continued to follow their instincts; they married and gave in marriage (though the thought of the approaching end of the world was often an incitement to celibacy), they fought and traded and built; but the idea that here on this earth the human race had a glorious destiny to fulfil was one for which the system in which they believed allowed no room. It was with the much-abused French philosophers of the 18th century, that the idea of progress may be said to have originated. In the face of a hierarchy still powerful and dangerous, they ventured to dispute the doctrine of the total corruption of human nature, and to contend that the free exercise of thought, instead of leading inevitably to error, was the only means by which men could hope to escape from their errors, and to advance in the knowledge of the truth. They held, too, that the free play of human instincts and feelings, instead of involving the ruin of society, would lead to the evolution of a far better social order than the one then existing. That they were over-sanguine in some of their anticipations, that they expected too much from the mere removal of restrictions on human action, may readily be admitted; but it is their glory to have believed in liberty in a larger sense than it had ever been believed in before; and to have seen in prophetic vision that golden age of the future to which all the noblest minds of the present generation instinctively look forward, and the hope of which grows stronger in the breast of humanity with each succeeding year. The ideas which these men cast abroad worked like leaven in French society, and no doubt hastened the downfall of the corrupt and fast-decaying French monarchy; but to-day, no longer revolutionary in their tendency, they are a faith to thousands and furnish the inspiration of much noble and unobtrusive effort for the general good.

To lead a truly intellectual life, prizing the perception of truth above the rewards of the world, requires an elevation of character that not every man of superior intellect possesses. The world is ever at the elbow of the man of talent, urging, tempting him to devote to its service—but not in the highest sense—the gifts at his command. A thousand voices cry:

Amuse us, enliven us, startle us, flatter us, or, if you like, satirize us; but in some way or other excite and please us, and you shall not have to wait for your recompense. We will pay you cash down, and leave no debt for posterity to settle. Your name and fame shall be in all the newspapers, and if criticism ventures to attack you we will laugh it out of countenance; for are we not the great public, and can we not protect our favourites?

Yielding to such solicitations, many a man has abandoned art and truth, and devoted himself to the ignoble task of gratifying tastes which he recognized as frivolous or vicious. He has given the world what it ordered, allowed it to dictate what he should write or speak or create, and he has had his reward in popularity and pay. Perhaps if he has been very successful he has been proclaimed a true classic, and promised an immortality of renown. True classics, however, are not often those who take their own generation by storm,* and are never those who write simply with a view to immediate popularity. The fame of Shakespeare, Spenser, and Milton is vastly greater in this age than it was in their own, not only because this age is able to understand them in a wider and deeper sense than the one in which they wrote, but because these great names have received the cumulative admiration of every generation through which they have passed. It is not too much to say that a man who has the stuff in him of a true classic will not be thoroughly comprehended or enjoyed by the mass of his contemporaries, for the simple reason that, in point of thought, he is in advance of them. It rests with posterity to do him full justice, and if he be a writer of the first eminence, a Dante, a Shakespeare, a Goethe, a dozen generations are not too much for the purpose.

There are many enemies to intellectual life, but they may be all classed under the one head as *the world*. One man is tempted to write rubbish for popular consumption, another to compose trashy music, another to fall in with vulgar tastes in architecture or in the decorative arts. Others again are summoned to bear a part in the political struggles of their day; and nothing will satisfy the multitude but that they should visibly ally themselves with some existing party organization, and aim at the ordinary rewards of political partisanship or leadership. According to the popular view, ability is, like wealth, a personal possession to be used for the benefit of the possessor; and why a man who has ability should not employ it to procure his worldly advancement is a mystery that passes all vulgar understanding. Not only so, but many men

*Il n'est pas bon de paraitre trop vite et d'emblée classique à ses contemporains; on a grande chance alors de ne pas rester tel pour la postérité." Ste. Beuve, *Causeries du Lundi*. Vol. 3, p. 40.

become irritated and vexed whenever they hear of any one whose apparent aim in life is simply to investigate the truth of things, and bring that truth to bear as much as possible on the minds of others.

Urit enim fulgore suo qui praegravat artes
Infra se positas.[3]

They have an uncomfortable feeling that the business of the world, and perhaps their own particularly, could not go on if it were a matter of general obligation to pursue only right ends, and to pursue those only by right means. The man of ideas thus appears to many in the light of a dangerous innovator, simply because, having forsaken the rule of thumb for the rule of logic, and the morality of expediency for that of principle, there is no knowing what doctrines he may some day bring forward for the confusion of society. He may not have announced anything revolutionary as yet, but his method seems to contain in it "the promise and potency" of every form of revolution.

Let a man but renounce his devotion to truth and principle, and the more brain-power he can bring to the aid of a party or cause the more welcome his alliance will be. He will become a champion athlete in parliamentary or journalistic struggles; weaker men will rally round him; and in due time he may scale the highest seat of power. There will be plenty of work for him to do; plenty of glory to gain. Instead of hiding in obscurity, he will be ever in the eye of the world. Instead of inspiring aversion and distrust by his very talents, he will secure admiration and, in a certain measure, sympathy. Instead of straining, more or less painfully, after a high ideal, he will have SUCCESS, the great ideal of nearly all the world, brought within easy grasp. The one condition is that he shall do as others do, fight the world with its own weapons, and forget as much as possible that he was ever summoned to any nobler task.

"Do you mean then," someone here may ask, "that men of high character and ability should stand aloof from public affairs and leave them to be managed by men of inferior qualifications, intellectual and moral?" I should be sorry to mean anything of the kind; but this I do mean: that if, to any man in particular, participation in public life involves a sensible lowering of his standards of duty, or the sacrifice of more important principles than any he can hope to vindicate or establish, then *for that man* participation in public life is an error, if not a crime. And to how many men such as I refer to has a public career of any length involved less than this? Where is the name among men who have been long in politics in this, or I might almost say, in any country that is capable of exciting the enthusiasm of rational men? There are party leaders of ability who receive daily flattery from those whose interest it is to flatter them; but where is the man who has shown in the struggle of parties a spirit superior to stratagem, to evasion, to unworthy compromise, the man who has neither alienated his judgment nor sacrificed his conscience, the man upon whom good men may fix their hopes and whose public virtues the youth of our country may be urged to imitate? We have seen men go into politics who might have been all this, some perhaps who we trusted would be, but—some change has passed over them: to those whose hopes were brightest they are "lost leaders."

If the only choice to a man of intellect were between absolute passivity and nullity, in respect to the political interests of the country, and an active political career with all its moral risks, there would be much to say in favour of the latter course; but such fortunately is far from being the case. A man does not need to be a practical politician in order to influence public opinion. As a private citizen he may uphold true principles and help to guide those around him to right conclusions. The important question, if we would estimate any man's work aright, is not, How widely his name has been repeated? but, what have those who repeat his name learnt or received from him? What kind of moral impulse has he communicated to those who have come into contact with him? Surely to have done good to a few is infinitely better than merely to have provided talk for many. When Alcibiades wanted to set the Athenians chattering he cut off his dog's tail, and no doubt the experiment was perfectly successful. The press in these days furnishes a means of influence second to none in importance, and fortunately it cannot be entirely usurped for purposes of party warfare. There are channels here and there through which disinterested thought can find expression; and the influence which one able and thoroughly impartial writer can exert on public sentiment outweighs that of a score of special pleaders in Parliament or out of it. The practical politicians of the day in England look to the press for direction far more than the press looks to them; the thinkers lay down the law for the doers; themselves unseen, and for the most part unknown, they guide in no small degree the destinies of a great empire.

If the atmosphere of politics is unfavourable to high intellectuality, not less so is the atmosphere of what in a special sense is called "society." The intellectual man, as conceived in these pages, is serious, earnest, sincere; he must put on a mask if he is to appear otherwise; society will have nothing to do with seriousness or earnestness, and though it does not as openly banish sincerity (nobody likes to profess himself, in so many words, "a fraud"), it succeeds in reducing that virtue within such narrow limits that those who fail altogether to see it may well be excused. The intellectual man's converse is with ideas and truths: society interests itself only in the most frivolous and insipid of facts. The intellectual man pursues culture: society pursues common-place. The intellectual man is above all things a *man* and, in all his most intimate thoughts, he takes his stand on common ground with the mass of his fellow-creatures; he is raised above them in point of advantages, but he feels the strength of the bond that unites human heart with human heart. His "society" is the world, not that handful of people who usurp the name and who, with a fatuity almost inconceivable, seem to think that for them the whole economy of nature was planned, and that, if other classes exist, it is that they may minister to *their* wants, and supply an effective contrast to their brilliance and gaiety.

But, alas! as a poet I have already quoted, has said,

The heart is prone to fall away,
Her high and cherished visions to forget.

There is a weak side to even the best characters, a side to which the fascinations of society can appeal with dangerous force; and much of high purpose has e'er this been lost in the whirl of dissipation, or extinguished in the unworthy and ungenerous rivalries that make up so large a portion of fashionable life. But as

E'en in a palace life may be lived well,

so it is possible to be in "society" and yet not of it, to observe its forms while rejecting its spirit; what is *not* possible is to accept its spirit, to adopt its tone, and yet to cultivate the life of the intellect and of the soul. As well try to unite political philosophy with slavish partisanship, or devotion to art with constant consultation of popular tastes.

To very few is it given to devote themselves wholly to intellectual pursuits; but it is by no means necessary to do so to live in the truest sense an intellectual life. As has often been remarked, much of the best thinking and of the highest order of literary work has been done by men actively engaged in the business of the world. The names of Bacon, Milton, Clarendon, and Burke would be as seriously missed from the political, as from the literary, history of their country. It is indeed an inestimable advantage for the thinker who would deal with political or social questions to have had his own share of action in society, provided always the relations into which he has entered with men or with parties have not been such as to cripple or pervert his judgment. In the same way, and with the same proviso, the best narrator of events will be he who can say "*quorum magna pars fui.*"[4] The importance of the proviso has been illustrated in many cases, and quite lately in a very signal instance: Lord Russell has had a very large place in the history of

England for forty years past; but his lately published "Recollections" are pronounced by competent judges to be a very faulty and partial record of the period over which they extend.

Be a man's occupations what they may, he must furnish himself with facts before he can theorise with advantage. If any one imagines that the intellectual region is one in which facts become of little importance, he is very greatly mistaken. The only difference between the thinker and other men is that he, having gathered his facts, sifts, arranges, questions them, and thus forces them to yield up whatever of truth they contain. For facts, be it remembered, are not in themselves truths; they are only the material out of which truth can be distilled. By dint of practice, the man of thought acquires a wonderful facility in referring special facts to the class or order to which they belong, and thus obtaining a ready insight into their significance. For persons unacquainted with his method and resources, he might appear to be dealing with matters in a most arbitrary way; whereas, in reality, he is but availing himself of previously-acquired knowledge, or previously-established conclusions. It need not be denied that even great philosophers do sometimes base their theories on insufficient foundations; such mistakes (which men of the world, little as they think it, are making every day of their lives) are incidental to the imperfection of human faculties, and do not arise from any failure to recognize that the whole value and virtue of every theory must depend upon its exact agreement with all the facts it purports to explain. Not the philosopher only, but the poet as well, must have facts in his possession before he can produce any work that shall deserve to live. We think of the poet as dealing in fancies, but who has so wonderful a gift as he in opening our eyes to the facts of the world in which we live? He has seen with his own eyes, and noted a thousand things that have passed before our eyes too, but to which we never gave heed. His verse is more expressive to us than the face of nature itself. Why? Because his eye is keener than ours, and because he speaks to us in human accents that nature cannot command. We have lived in the world; we have had intercourse with men; we think we understand pretty well the springs of human action; but here is a man who will tell us all we ever knew and a great deal more. Whence hath he this knowledge? That sometimes is a mystery, but he has it; and we, who thought ourselves knowing, stand abashed.

The intellectual life should be a life of patience—patience in gathering knowledge, patience in drawing conclusions, and patience in waiting for results. It may be hard sometimes to reconcile enthusiasm with patience but they may be reconciled, and they must be, if the best results are to be achieved. The patience of the believers in a cause is no less a presage of victory than their enthusiasm; indeed, of the two it is the fuller of promise. Let cynics or fatalists say what they will, the hope of a rational ordering of human society, the hope of some future harmony of human beliefs, does spring eternal in the human breast. And the life is one that maketh not ashamed; those who possess it must avow it, and must work towards its realization. Not only in the prophet-minds of every age has it asserted itself, but in the minds of the people at large there has ever been a dim foreboding of some great good in store for humanity. We see not as yet the outlines even of the future edifice of civilization; but we see errors and falsehoods which it is a manifest and immediate duty to combat, and the destruction of which we cannot but believe will hasten the advent of the better time. What the world lacks is faith; it has long been taught that it is very evil, and the lesson has been learnt so thoroughly that it is hard now to make people believe that in themselves there are infinite capacities for good, and that nearly all the good they do is done independently of laws or enactments of any kind. The persuasion of an evil often has as serious effects as the evil itself; a "malade imaginaire" may be the most hopeless of invalids. The world is at this moment, to some extent, a "malade imaginaire," but unfortunately the great multitude of its physicians are exerting themselves only to prolong its delusion.

A great mark of the true intellectual life is simplicity. How can a man who is devoting himself with singleness of purpose to the discovery and diffusion of truth, or whose mind has in any way received the stamp of intellectual elevation, burden himself with refinements of luxury, affectations of pedantry, or any of the multiplied forms of vain glorious pretence? The more closely a man's attention is concentrated on abstract or general questions, the more his own personality sinks out of sight. It cannot, indeed, be maintained that literary men and *savants* are always exempt from vanity; but it is undoubtedly true that this failing has very seldom been exhibited by the greatest among them. It is also true that just in proportion to a man's intellectual eminence, to his capacity for high thinking, are we struck by the incongruity of any exhibition on his part of vanity or affectation. It is satisfactory to note in this matter a marked advance in public sentiment. The literary men of to-day would be ashamed to indulge in personal quarrels such as their predecessors of a century or more ago paraded before the world. They studiously avoid (of course I speak generally) all personal issues, rightly conceiving that their proper business is to throw light on the questions they undertake to treat; not to demand attention for themselves.

No one needs companionship and sympathy more than he who is leading, or trying to lead, an intellectual life: unfortunately none are more often deprived of these advantages. It is easy to have a "chum," or any number of them, if a pipe of tobacco and talk on the local news of the day make up your ideal of social enjoyment, but not if your thoughts run very much on higher themes. In the centres of population the earnest student can probably find a few like-minded; but elsewhere he must, generally speaking, pursue his career solitary and unaided except by books and journals. A useful thought for such is that others here and there are treading the same path under the same difficulties; for it is cheering to know that we have fellow-labourers, even though we may never see them nor even learn their names. Here are a couple of sentences from Edgar Quinet's "Histoire de mes Idées," which many perhaps may read with encouragement:

I had a presentiment that what was wanted was an almost complete revolution in intellectual matters; and, as I saw no one working towards the accomplishment of the change, I fancied myself alone. This feeling of solitude was weighing me down at the very moment when so many immortal works, yet unknown to the world, were being prepared in silence, germinating, as it were, under ground.

Every one imagined himself alone as I did, and thought and meditated as though upon a desert isle. And yet all were being wrought upon at the same time by the newborn spirit of the century, and all were feeling in their very bones the pangs of moral growth. How many complaints were there exhaled! How many sincere tears were shed! Nature herself groans when she is about to bring to the birth.

The intellectual life is a serious life, but it knows nothing of ennui; and its pleasures, to those who have tasted them in their purity, must ever seem the noblest that the constitution of man has placed within his reach. Let me close with a word from one who could speak with authority: "Pure ideas, visible only to the inward eye, are of all things that men can know the most beautiful. To live in them is true enjoyment —happiness with no admixture of cloud."*

*William Von Humboldt: quoted in an article in the *London Quarterly Review* for April, 1868.

2. Idealism in Life
   (1878)

The great problem of philosophy is to render an account of consciousness. The conscious mind arranges, and in a certain sense explains, the facts of which it is conscious; but how it stands related to those facts is a question which has hitherto evaded solution. The metaphysician has applied to it his subtlest formulas; but the true equation has never been reached, and perhaps never will be reached. The highest form of consciousness is self-consciousness. We can imagine a certain sensibility to impressions without any reference of these impressions to a permanent personality to whom they constitute moments of experience. But when an organism not only feels, but says "I feel," then the highest mode of being known to us, or indeed conceivable by us has sprung into existence. Mr. Spencer tells us that there may be some mode of existence as far transcending conscious intelligence and will as the latter transcends mere mechanical action. Possibly. It would indeed be arrogant in man to claim to have exhausted the highest possibilities of being, and to say that what his faculties cannot grasp can have no existence anywhere; but certain it is that our highest thought at present stops at personality,—at the mode of existence which our own self-consciousness reveals to us.

A being possessing mere sensibility without self-consciousness must necessarily be under the law of external circumstances. It is acted upon and re-acts but it is powerless to shape its own destiny or even to step for one moment aside from the narrow path in which it has been bidden to move. The moment, however, that self-consciousness enters upon the scene, everything is altered. Law is not abolished, and yet in a very real sense liberty is established,—liberty within the bounds of law. The self-conscious being says: "I feel, I desire, I know." The whole mystery of the universe is wrapped up in these words, and it were vain to ask ourselves now how their utterance becomes possible, how a mode of being that has absolutely no analogy with the laws of physical

SOURCE: *Canadian Monthly and National Review*, Vol. XIII (April, 1878), pp. 414-420. An address to the Progressive Society of Ottawa, Sunday, 10 March, 1878.

nature is superinduced, so to speak, upon a physical organism. What we are concerned with now is the enormous change which the development or apparition of self-consciousness works. The self-conscious being knows what he wants, and within certain limits can gratify his own desires. He does not escape from the control of mechanical or chemical laws; but he can, to a large extent, modify the incidence of those laws. He cannot make the wind blow less keenly, but he can provide himself with clothing; he cannot bring down more rain from heaven, but he can dig wells; he cannot avert a storm, but he can shelter himself from it. He can court this natural influence and shun the other, and thus he can make nature do his work, and subserve his highest interests. Only as his knowledge widens, however, will he thus free himself from the thrall in which all unconscious beings abide. The pestilence and the lightning will smite him till he has learnt the conditions which call the one into malign activity and those which render the other innocuous. Thus he suffers *till he knows*. St. Paul has spoken of all creation "groaning and travailing together being burdened," and true it is that the human race, just in proportion to its ignorance of the laws of nature, does groan and travail, being burdened. There have been cases in which even prolonged and multiplied experiences of the most painful kind have failed to set the essential facts in such a light as to suggest a remedy. The obstruction in some cases is a false theory, in others it is the absence of the habit of analysis; in other again the complexity of the phenomena defies all analysis. Yet for all that, self-consciousness means freedom, for it involves the power of choice, gives promise of the future solution of many questions hopeless enough now.

The highest realization of liberty lies in that force of self-consciousness to which I propose at present to give the name of "Idealism." If self-consciousness involves the perception of an end, idealism, I should say, involves and is based upon the perception of a perfect end. To the mind exercising its faculty of choice, many objects, many possible courses present themselves. Of these, which shall it choose? Shall it be the easiest or the most difficult? the one which promises immediate gratification, or the one which necessitates a long waiting for the desired results? Shall appetite or reason be listened to? the suggestions of selfishness or the dictates of justice? Shall the standards of society, of the world, be accepted as adequate and final, or shall a higher law prompt to higher deeds? I call that man an idealist who aims at bringing his life under the government of a perfect law,—who asks, regarding an action, not whether it is profitable, or safe, or calculated to win applause, but whether it is *the* action which, under the circumstances, ought to be performed. Why do I call him an idealist? Because he pursues ideals; because he believes in something as the best, and tries to realize that best in action. Everybody acknowledges that the artist should be an idealist,—he must be either that or a mere copyist; and the least reflection will enable any one to perceive that if art had confined itself to copying, its highest glories would never have been won. The questions, therefore, which the artist has to ask himself continually,—be he poet, painter, sculptor, or musician,—are, how would this or that sentiment or passion express itself in its purity? What forms would it take? What accessories would be best adapted to bring it into most effective relief? And with these questions he grapples and struggles with an intensity of effort which even the lust of gold has never drawn from its votaries. The world understands, or at least in a general way consents to this. Let the artist, if he will, consume himself in the task of finding perfect forms and bringing to light hitherto unimagined combinations. That is his business; and as his works sometimes bring a high price, the business is perhaps as legitimate as another. So judges the world, not, however without a secret contempt for a class of men who, though they may occasionally make money, do not as a rule seem to *think* money, and who would much rather miss making money than be unfaithful to their art. In most pursuits, money, broadly speaking, is the great criterion and measure of success. In the region of art it is a standard no longer; for the artist worthy of the name does not ask what people are willing to pay for, but what, in the highest sense, it is best he should produce. If he cannot work for this generation he will work for the next, and let who will minister to the taste of the hour.

But the great truth to which the eyes of the world are sealed is this, that the law which the artist is indulgently allowed to govern himself by—the law that binds him to the true and beautiful—is the law which ought to govern all mankind. If we are not all artists it is our own fault; for there is an art ready to our hand which we all might practice, in which we could all do faithful and lasting work, in which some of us might perchance rise to great pre-eminence,—in which we all at least might have the satisfaction of feeling that we were working in the artist spirit, patiently, humbly, loyally, trustfully, looking within and not without for our rule of action and our reward. Do you ask what this art is for which we all have capacity? I answer, it is the *art of life*. Truth and beauty are not confined to the realm of art in its narrow or professional sense; they may shine forth in the actions of the humblest son of toil, or they may add lustre to a throne. "E'en in a palace," said Marcus Aurelius, "life may be lived well"; and, if in a palace, then anywhere. But how many are they who conceive of life as an art, having its own rules quite apart from the maxims which teach how to win what, in the world, is called success. How many are they who ask what is best and highest in their own natures, and who seek above all things, to do justice to *that*, to bring it to its highest development? How many are they who have an equal respect for what is of most worth in others, and who would therefore refuse to have any part in what might tend to lower the tone of another's thought, to debase his taste, or make him less sensitive to the appeals of his higher nature? I should be sorry to underrate the good that is in the world: the human race has lived too long upon the earth not to have learned many lessons of mutual helpfulness; but, at the same time, if I say that the conception of life as an art— not as a trade—is as yet present to but few minds, I shall hardly encounter contradiction. Yet eighteen hundred years ago there was one who dealt with life in his addresses to the multitude, and who never presented it in any other light than as something more solemn, more sacred, than any special art that ever engaged human genius in its service, as something whose rules were not to be sought in the customs of the market place, but deep down in the most secret and intimate convictions of the individual soul, as something whose standard was nothing short of the eternal beauty of holiness. Say, if you like, that he was an enthusiast, that some of his maxims were impracticable, and that the great mass of the Christian Chruch, in its worship of wealth, and the general poverty of its aims, has turned its back on nearly all that he taught. All this may be admitted, but the great fact remains that he dealt with life in the light of eternal principles, that he raised the hearts and roused the consciences of men, that he made truth and duty supreme over all lower motives, and pronounced a condemnation that has rung, and shall ring, through the ages against every unworthy form of compromise, against every bartering of gold for dross, against every act that could dim the light of truth in the human soul. He was the highest type of an "idealist," as I am now using the word; and the maxims he uttered, he uttered as binding on all mankind. And why not? A gospel like this may in point of fact be embraced by but few; its beauty may be seen by but a few; but no one can be shut out from it, inasmuch as there is no valid reason why one man, as much as another, should not embrace the highest rule of life, and reap the reward of perfect peace.

Now the practical question for us to consider is, whether we shall strive to maintain our conception of life at the level established by the founder of Christianity; or whether we shall discard that conception for a lower one. Whatever we do let us do it with our eyes open. The great world—the world of business and of fashion—says, in effect, that it will not have this man to rule over it; and accordingly it makes maxims of its own which it does not require any great exercise of virtue to observe. Self-interest is supposed to be a sufficient guide for every one, and by the balancing of opposing interests social equilibrium is maintained. If any man is better than his fellows, better than he need be in fact, he is a fool for his pains. The first great commandment of society is to make money: the second is like unto it—make more money. If you do not make money it is not said that you shall go to hell; but it is tacitly assumed that you are in hell already—the one palpable, material hell about which the modern world has no shadow of doubt. But let us seriously ask ourselves if there is any moral safety in the renunciation of a high ideal, of high conceptions of duty, for a rule of life more consonant with what we are pleased to regard as our interests. Where are we to stop? We adopt a compromise; we are not going to be "righteous overmuch"; we will just give ourselves fair play in a world where a good deal of sharp practice prevails. Supposing then our "interests" seem to require just a little more scope yet—and a little more. Why should they not have it? We have abandoned the ideal; we have come down to the practical; why should we cramp ourselves? And so the world abounds with dishonesty that just stops short of the penitentiary, while now and then an over close calculator finds that he has crossed the line.

But some one will say: "How can *one* adopt an ideal rule of life when all around him recognize nothing higher than custom or expediency." To this question I am not bold enough to reply as Christ would have replied: "He that saveth his life," i.e., carefully and narrowly guards his interests by the ordinary means used in the world, "shall lose it; and he that loseth his life," i.e. risks everything for duty, for the ideal, "shall save it." Yet though I do not feel like using these words, something tells me they are true—something tells me that the world owes much to those who have thought enough of their principles, of their ideals, to suffer and even die for them. What or where would we be now if no patriot had ever faced death, if no martyr had ever triumphed over agony, rather than betray the cause in which he believed? We can only say that our moral inheritance from the past would have been a much poorer and meaner one than it actually is, and that human history would have been robbed of all its dignity, pathos, and grandeur.

Without, however, attempting to solve any radical question—such as whether absolute subjection to the ideal is possible in a world so full of imperfection as ours—I would endeavour to throw out a suggestion or two in aid of idealism in life. The first thing, it seems to me, that a man has to do who has any desire for imitation in the higher life, is to reduce himself to moderate and reasonable dimensions in the great map of humanity. The natural man has a projection of his own for making maps of the world, according to which self stands out considerably larger than all the rest of mankind put together; and this same exaggerated self he carries about with him as no small burden, though perhaps he may not see the burden nor realize its existence. There can be no ideal life, however, while this distortion exists in a man's thoughts. He must realize that he is *not* of so much consequence as he has hitherto imagined; and that upon a map of the world, drawn upon any true scale, he is a very small speck indeed. This is the beginning of wisdom, and the beginning of peace—of wisdom, for now he can see other things in their true proportions; of peace, because he feels that he has got rid of a pestilent delusion, that he will no longer tax the indulgence of others by an inordinate self-love, and, lastly, that what is left of him is the true man, and is all there. The ways in which this wholesome reduction would work are very numerous. "Who am I that I should assume this tone, that I should hold others in subjection and sacrifice their comfort, their wishes, their tastes to mine?" are questions which never occur to many men, but which to the "regenerate" man seem to be at hand as often as he is tempted to transgress the bonds which moderation, and a just regard for the rights of others impose upon his conduct. To observe how some men comport themselves, in their households particularly, one would imagine that they were absolutely irresponsible beings, raised high above all law, and free to indulge every passing humour, without a moment's consideration for the inferior beings by whom they are surrounded. They may refrain from actual blows, but their words are blows which bruise the heart and crush self-respect. Or perhaps it is mere contempt and indifference which the lordly being's actions express. He was made to be amused, and when his household cannot amuse him, he feels entirely free to seek his amusement elsewhere. He never dreamt of entering into any engagement which would bind him to do his full share towards making others happy: he is a master; do not ask him to descend from his high eminence and help others to bear the burdens of life. Oh man, have *you* then no master? one is tempted to exclaim. If you have lost all sense of an eye that watches your every action, is there still nothing that tells you that your whole line of life is false, that there is nothing in it that is either true or sweet or wholesome, but that it is a fraud, a tyranny, and a nuisance—a thing that the world were well rid of—a thing for Oblivion to hide with her darkest mantle? If there be no master for such, there is at least a moral order of the universe, the violation of which brings its own punishments. Are such men, with their tempestuous passions and selfish ways, happy? Far from it. Happiness is not won upon these terms. "Great peace have they," said the Psalmist, "who love the law;" and happiness ever comes, not of a constrained, but of a voluntary subjection to *law*—not to an outward code of observances, but to that inward voice which bids a man ever to seek and practice the best.

There are all grades in human character; and the cases are perhaps rare in which we see a systematic ignoring of the higher law; yet how often men of whom better things might be expected give way to despotic or inconsiderate courses of conduct, acting as though their advantages of position, whether as husband, as father, as master, as capitalist, or be it what it may, carried no responsibility whatever. I think that the idea presented in the New Testament, that we are all servants of a higher Master, is a very wholesome one; and, at any rate, whether we can entertain the idea or no, it is well, it seems to me, to put the case from time to time to ourselves thus: "If I had a master, one who judged of things by a perfect standard, what would he think of my dealings with my fellow-servant?" To judge thus, to apply such a check to ourselves in our daily business, is what I call idealism in life; it is the pursuit of the perfect and the true.

It would be a very great mistake to suppose that a man, by reducing himself to his proper place and dimensions in the world, must lose either force of character or influence. A French writer, I forget who, has said that this is an age when modest people are very quickly taken at their word; but it is a small loss to the modest man to lose the advantages he might gain by brag or bluster. There are abundant means of influence open to him in his intercourse with his fellow-men; and when people see that he does not make too much of himself, that he has no wish to engross an undue measure of attention, or to encroach on anybody else's rights, they give him ready access to their minds and hearts. The humility enjoined in the New Testament has nothing mean or grovelling about it. Neither Jesus Christ nor Paul will ever teach any man to be a flunkey. "Let no man think of himself more highly than he ought to think, but let him think soberly." *Soberly*—that is the word.

There is another form which idealism will take which I should be sorry not to commend to your attention, viz., the idealism that craves for intellectual truth, which abhors compromise where truth is concerned, which refuses as far as posssible to allow convenience, or interest, or prejudice, to arrest enquiry, to suppress its results, or to have any voice whatever in the shaping of opinions. Madame de Stael, in her brilliant and instructive book on Literature, says that "multitudes of men will never admit any general principle without first comparing its results with their own actions and interests,"—of course to see whether they can admit it without inconvenience to themselves. It is needless to say that this habit is far from having died out of the world; and it is equally needless to say that it is the very negation of idealism. Truth is a word that has been sadly bandied about in all ages; it has had abuse enough to crush all meaning out of it, had that been possible; but it was not possible, and so the word and its meaning survive. To arrive at truth, however, is not the prerogative of everyone. Some men in all their reasonings and observations simply dig pitfalls for themselves. They collate facts, they go through forms of reasoning, and they are not wiser, but less wise, than they were at the beginning. They fare precisely as those do who go to the Bible to prove a doctrine true; the proofs come to hand with delightful ease, and the ingenious individual wonders that all the world is not of his opinion. The first requisite for the discovery of truth is disinterestedness, and the second, I should say, is patience. How is a man to know, some one may ask, whether another man is disinterested? Every student of physics knows that the generation of heat in certain cases is the result of undue friction. Now, where I see undue heat or bitterness developed in connection with the discussion of a question, there I suspect the friction of interest or prejudice. The intense heat that an Orangeman, for example, will display in talking of Popery is hardly to be set down to a disinterested sympathy for those of his fellow-men who are bound in Romish superstition, or to a purely patriotic zeal for civil rights. The bitterness, again, that characterizes the language of some Radicals when speaking of the doctrines of Christianity, *may be* pure zeal for truth, but I confess I am apt to suspect an admixture in it of something else. As to the language which we sometimes hear from the pulpit in regard to free-thought and free-thinkers it bears too obviously the stamp of self-interest and fear to be accepted for a pure apostolic fervour. Let a man, then, judge himself as he would judge another, note the points where he breaks into language more violent or less charitable than he is wont to use, and try to overcome the friction *there*.

I have spoken of patience as the second great condition for the discovery of the truth. Some excellent people insist on treating certain questions as vastly more simple than they really are. They like short deductive cuts—"cross lots," as our neighbours say—to their favourite conclusions. To such I could respectfully tender this advice: When the process of reasoning by which you reach your conclusions is *very* obvious, *very* simple, rather suspect that it is unsuited to the matter in hand than that men as honest and able as yourselves have failed to see it. It has an odd effect to find a person holding up his hands in astonishment that so and so—a man of great eminence and high character, perhaps—had failed to perceive something which, if it had any bearing on the case, would be as conspicuous as the sun at noonday. Far better, I think, to conclude that there are other elements in the question which we do not allow for, than that men who enjoy in a high degree the respect of their contemporaries, are either stark fools or shameless knaves. Suppose that we hve to sacrifice in some measure the definiteness and absoluteness of our own opinions in order to do full justice to those of others—what of that? Any sacrifice for *justice* is worth making; and it is enough for a man to surround himself with an atmosphere of truthfulness, to know himself, and to be known by others, as open to the truth at all times, and above all as true in deed. A man who can do this may keep a great many speculative questions open without much injury to his character.

And now a few words in conclusion as regards the main sources of idealist inspiration. I have already stated that I find in the New Testament idealism in its most perfect form. In saying this I do not for one moment shut my eyes to all that modern criticism has established in regard to that book; but I see there the teaching of one who presented life in its highest conceivable aspect, as a struggle towards perfection. Next to the New Testament for intensity of ethical emotion, I would place the immortal work of Thomas à Kempis—the "Imitation of Christ". I need not tell the members of this Society that the book in question is pervaded by the monastic spirit; its origin and the date of its production would answer sufficiently for that. Its monasticism, however, does not rob it of its power as an instrument of moral culture, does not destroy its hold upon the hearts of many who have left, not monasticism only, but much else, far behind them. When I read such sentences as the following: "What does it profit thee to engage in deep discussion on the Trinity, if thou art lacking in humility, and so render theyself displeasing to the Trinity?" "Many words do not satisfy the soul; but a good life does refresh the mind, and a pure conscience gives great confidence towards God." "O divine truth, make me one with thee in perpetual charity!" "What is a greater impediment and trouble to thee than thine own immoderate self-love?" "A humble knowledge of thyself is a surer way to God than a profound search after knowledge; yet is not knowledge to be blamed, which is a good thing considered in itself, and ordained of God; but a good conscience and life are to be preferred to it." When, I say, I read such sentences as these and scores of others, I feel that the author was toiling in the upward path, and his strong yet simple words are as a helpful voice from the darkness of the past. There is idealism of the highest order in Shakespere and in Milton. Shakespere, it is true, gives us everything; but the pure mind chooses and dwells on what is best, and the best is incomparable. As a literary artist alone Milton carries the mind to a very high elevation; but in addition he makes life what every poet should make it,—a theatre of noble effort and pure aspiration. Coming down to more modern times, we find in the poet Shelley a passionate idealist. His "Alastor," his "Hymn to Intellectual Beauty," and his "Hellas," are each sufficient to make an epoch in the intellectual history of any one who can read them with adequate preparation of mind. In our own day, Tennyson and Browning, not to mention many other lesser poets, are full of the finest enthusiasm for the perfect life. To read these poets sympathetically is indeed to see the world with purified eyes, to see evil in all its hatefulness, and virtue in all its beauty. And yet there is, perhaps, a greater name still to be uttered,—Thomas Carlyle, with all his faults one of the noblest of human souls, and a mighty preacher to this generation. Such a man, overflowing with prophetic fervour, can afford to make a thousand mistakes, and the world will be his debtor still. He takes his stand upon no creed, but he makes the human conscience itself thunder against all baseness and falsehood. In the case of a lesser man his errors might have been more potent than his truths; but the impulse to righteousness that Carlyle has given will, I believe, be more than sufficient to carry his readers safely over the dangerous portions of his philosophy. Nor can I forbear, in this enumeration, to mention the name of Emerson,—a pure soul if ever there was one, a man of infinite delicacy, tact, and insight, inflexible in principle, radiant with hope, and unconquerable in faith. It is his especial gift to refine everything he touches, to breathe upon everything the best and richest influences of human culture. Let us make these men our company, without making them our oracles, and we shall grow into the likeness of what we behold, we shall imbibe their spirit, and receive a portion of their power. The great question for each of us is not, Shall we be free from this or that false opinion? but, Shall the world be beautiful for us, shall our minds be filled with pure thoughts and generous purposes? Shall we form a noble or a mean estimate of men and things? Shall we walk in a narrow, treadmill path of barren reasoning or shall we have some sense of the richness and fulness and glory of the universe, and of the infinite resources of the spirit of man? Shall our lives be harmonized and dignified by a moral aim of which reason shall approve; or shall we shuffle through life, infirm of purpose, and trying to content ourselves with a partial rationalization of our conduct? In a word, shall we idealize life, or shall we vulgarize it? That, I say, is the question which concerns us all. Of the two courses open to us, if we choose the second our path may be an easy one, but it will lead away from the proper goal of human effort, and clouds may settle heavily upon it before the close; if we choose the former we choose struggle, but the struggle will be ever upward, and our last days shall be our best.

3. A Few Words on Criticism
   (1879)

A critic, says Ste.-Beuve somewhere, is a man who knows how to read and who teaches others. The remark is a profound one, and serves to set criticism at once in its true light—a light altogether different from that in which it is ordinarily viewed. To the vulgar mind the critic is the fault-finder, a being of artificial tastes, who loves to pour scorn on the common judgments of mankind—who finds admirable what no one else can understand, and commonplace what the rest of the world crowns with applause. A certain amount of misunderstanding of this kind is indeed inevitable. The majority of men, carried away by what is admirable in their idols, resent being told that some clay is mixed with the gold. Tell an ardent admirer of Byron that the poet, wide and powerful as is the sweep of his passionate rhetoric, is, when all is said and done, a trifle commonplace in thought, and he will likely denounce you as an unimaginative prig, upon whom the splendid flights of the bard are thrown away. Tell one who has made Macaulay his Bible that the style of that great writer, forcible and lucid as it is, is often overladen with epithet, and antithetical at the cost both of sense and of truth, and he will set you down as some envious Dryasdust, who would fain make the approaches to knowledge as dreary and uninviting as possible. Or gently insinuate to a Dickens-worshipper that there is a lack of art in the construction of the great novelist's plots, that his colours are too strong and his work here and there too coarse, that neither his mirth nor his pathos stir very deep thoughts, and that he is, in general, too contented with cheap effects, and you will be looked upon at once as a most outlandish and inhuman creature.

Yet these are things that criticism must say, or else forever hold its peace. They may be beyond the grasp or comprehension of many, but some are from time to time rising to the point at which such observations become instructive and stimulating. There is no law of nature which binds every healthily-constituted being to go on indefinitely in a

SOURCE: *Rose-Belford's Canadian Monthly and National Review*, Vol. III (September, 1879), pp. 323-328.

bland, indiscriminating admiration even of such undeniably great writers as Byron, Macaulay, and Dickens. On the contrary, nothing can be more certain than that, with wider culture, comes a disturbance of the state of mind which renders such indiscriminating judgments impossible. If the devotee, say, of Dickens has not been utterly spoilt by over indulgence in his favourite author, he will find in Thackeray something which was wanting in the writings of the more popular novelist, a subtler analysis of character, a higher tone of thought, a general flavour of intellectual refinement. Or let him, if he can, turn to French literature, and see how Balzac, for example, will build up a character, by what a succession of delicate touches, and by what strokes of penetrative insight. Let him extend his reading, and he will, if he but uses his opportunities aright, become a critic in spite of himself. He will find when he returns to his Dickens, that his point of view is no longer the same, that he sees now what he never saw before; makes distinctions where he would not have dreamed there was room for any, and, in a word, is a wiser, though not necessarily a sadder, man.

And herein we catch sight of the true answer which should be made to those who, speaking from a lower level, challenge the conclusions at which all higher criticism has unanimously arrived. In these days, where so many profane voices are raised against the study of the classics, it is not uncommon to hear men who confessedly know not a word of Greek or Latin disputing the value of the Greek and Latin literatures. Of course it may be said, "Why dispute with such people?" but it is not always as easy as it would seem to avoid disputing with them. We may, however, safely challenge them to make an experiment for themselves, or to examine the results of the experiments already made. Who that ever, by adequate preparation, obtained an introduction for himself into the realm of classical literature failed to find it incomparable in form, that is incomparable *as literature*? What thorough classical scholar ever turned round and pronounced classical literature poor and unprofitable? So with the art of the ancients, their sculpture, and architecture. If you want any one *not* to admire that, and place it in the front rank of what man has achieved in the world, you must take care to keep him away from the best examples of modern art. All culture leads up to this in the most inevitable manner, just as all musical culture leads up to admiration of Beethoven and Bach. Those whose taste in literature and art is poorest have still some rudimentary perceptions of what is excellent; and we may, therefore, confidently say to them when they are foolish enough to sit in judgment upon the dicta of a culture to which they have not attained:

Extend your knowledge, multiply your experiences, allow yourself a wider range in the enjoyment of such things as you can enjoy, and see if you do not work towards an admiration of those things which the highest criticism pronounces to be supreme.

We might despair of art if, as men became more familiar with beautiful forms, they did not verge towards agreement in their critical judgments, if in the higher regions of artistic creation *the true* did not visibly shake itself free from the false, and stand forth for the homage of all. Happily this is the case, making all allowance for momentary disputes over contemporary art; the world acquires definitive possession, one by one of the masterpieces of genius, and counts up its treasures with a feeling of security. And who shall separate it from the love of what is truly great and noble? Surely neither life nor death nor any other creature!

We thus see that culture leads directly to criticism, and that, if you would suppress criticism, you must suppress culture. We begin also to see more clearly the meaning of Ste.-Beuve's declaration that the critic is a man who knows how to read and who teaches others. He knows how to read in the sense of knowing the meaning of what he reads, and not merely its signification but its significance, its relative position in the world of literature, the degree in which it is original or imitated, and a hundred other things about it which it would take too long to mention. The unsuspecting reader who takes up a book thinks that, provided he can exercise average intelligence, he is master of the situation. So he is perhaps if the author is Dickens, whose demands upon his readers are perhaps the lightest ever made by any author of equal fame. But so he is not in a thousand other cases. The very phraseology used will at times stagger him, for, though the words may not be unusual, the sense in which they are here and there employed is such as he is not accustomed to. I remember a case in point. M. Guizot,[5] in his 'Memoires,' makes the observation that men who cannot make allowances for the imperfections of humanity, and the very unsatisfactory conditions (from a moral point of view) under which government has to be carried on, should hold aloof from politics, and confine themselves to "pure speculation," meaning, of course, philosophical speculation. Showing the passage to a friend who was well acquainted with the French language, I found that by "pure speculation" he understood *commerce*. In fact, he so translated it, and thus robbed the sentence of all its point; for why on earth should men who are over-scrupulous in politics betake their tender consciences to the "pure speculation" of business? Nothing could be more inconsequent.

This may, perhaps, be an extreme case, but it is as good an illustration as any of the way in which the uncultured reader will hack and hew any author whose level of thought is much higher than his own. And, two to one, such a reader, when he comes across anything that does not yield up its meaning at once, will assail his author for using unmeaning language, it being settled in his mind that what is unmeaning to him must be equally so to all the world. Many of the phrases which the science of to-day has made the common property of the reading world are wholly void of meaning, unless understood in the precise sense in which they may happen to be employed, though the words of which they are composed are as common as words can be. What words, for example, are better understood than "protective" and "resemblance"? but ask some one who is wholly unacquainted with the literature of Darwinism, what a "protective resemblance" is, and he will be utterly at a loss for an answer. You might give him a day to think over it, but nothing would, or could, come of his cogitations. The same remark applies to the much more familiar term "natural selection"; you must either know the special sense in which the words are used or else find them a meaningless formula. Many phrases of a scientific or semi-scientific character have been caught up by the multitude and are used with very slight reference to their true signification. How many of those whom we hear repeating the phrase, "fly off at a tangent," have the slightest conception of what "flying off at a tangent" means? But to know the meaning of such phrases, so as to feel their force, is *a part* of knowing how to read.

Some persons are unable to read (in our present sense), not because they have read so little, but because of the narrowness of their emotional range, and a certain want of what may be called moral flexibility. I have heard Clough's beautiful "Easter Day Ode," cited by a devout enemy of all theology as a stirring denial of the Resurrection. All the pathos and regret of the poem were lost sight of in the simple iteration of the words occuring several times as a refrain:

> He is not risen, no—
> He lies and moulders low;
>   Christ is not risen!

The whole moral drift of the poem was mistaken; and instead of sympathy with a faith which had raised men to a lofty level, and might yet have great possibilities of action on humanity, nothing was seen but a categorical denial of the central doctrine of that faith. One is inclined to trust that the poet was never himself confronted with such an interpretation of his Ode.

In some cases an undue preoccupation with moral interests destroys, or at least impairs, the sense for art. There are those who for want of a wide familiarity with ideas, look with suspicion upon everything which does not directly enforce their own favourite moral lessons. We could not have a better example of the contrary of this than the poet Milton.

Here was a rigid moralist, a man whose own conduct was above reproach, and who understood as well as any one else, to say the least, the importance to society of established moral rules, but whose extraordinary breadth of culture and range of feeling made him as much at home amid images drawn from classic mythology, the encounters of irresponsible gods and nymphs, the idyllic loves of shepherds and shepherdesses, as amid the serious political and theological controversies of his time. Art symbolises the free powers of nature, and where it is true to its mission can no more teach individual license than the lilies of the field, or than sunshine, wind and rain. Lucretius, in the splendid exordium to his immortal work, and Clough, in such a poem as "Natura Naturans," fill the mind with a sense of the glory of the universe, and do more to destroy the deadly sin of prurience than a thousand moral discourses. But to feel this, and to yield oneself to the poet so as to be carried with him far above the level of all gross conceptions, one must needs have taken a wide survey of things, and learnt the salutary lesson that perpetual fussiness in morals is not the great preservative of moral order—that the world lives, and is likely to live, by such laws as conduce to its well-being, and can do without the leading strings of even the best-intentioned nurses. To know this is culture, and is one foundation at least for a true criticism of life and whatever claims to represent life.

Prejudice, it is needless to say, blinds many a one to the true sense of what they read, and to this extent they must of course, be classed among the incapables. I have known narrow religionists try to read such authors as Spencer and Tyndall, but all in vain. The hatred they felt for the author choked all understanding of him, or else the line of thought was so totally different from what they were accustomed to, that they felt as though they had embarked on an open sea in a rudderless boat. On the other hand, I have known sceptics take in hand such a work as Newman's "Grammar of Assent," and lay it down without having clearly understood the drift of one page or recognised the force of a single sentence in the book. They read clad in a triple panoply of wilful opposition to the author, and of course they might better have left it alone. In such cases it is not ignorance that has to be overcome so much as passion, and when, in grown-up people, passions have run to this length there is little to be done to moderate them. With the young, however, there is more hope, and we need not hesitate to mention, as the great solvent of not yet irremediably hardened prejudice—culture.

From the definition we have given of criticism, and from our representation of it as an out-growth of culture, it is evident in the first place that it cannot be a limited thing. There is no end to it in fact. The perfect critic would have to be omniscient, and then, it may be feared, he would find criticism or anything else dull work. In a certain sense it may be said that every one is a critic up to a certain point, criticism being essentially based on comparison, and comparison of some kind, if only with one's own experiences, being inseparable from the reading of any book. But the critic, in an adequate sense, is he who is fitted by education, by culture, by sympathy, by insight, by acquired tact, to *appreciate* a literary work; who knows its *real* merits, and who, therefore, if he praises it, praises the right things, and not, as is so often done, the wrong; who knows its defects and can speak of them in duly-measured language; who sees into the composition and make-up of the book, and knows both what aids the writer had, and what difficulties he overcame; divines the prevailing mood under which it was written, and its essential character; sees it as the development and embodiment of a central thought and purpose, or, contrariwise, as a haphazard combination of more or less incongruous materials; finally, makes the distinction between what belongs to the author—what bears the special imprint of his own mind, his mark in the corner, as the French say—and what reflects simply the current literary ideas of the time. Such a man, it seems hardly necessary to say, is not by nature a fault-finder, nor is he so by profession. I forget what writer it is— Rivarol, I think—who says that the critic before he inflicts one wound has received twenty; but it is very true, and worth bearing in mind. Far from seeking matter of blame the happiness of the critic consists in finding something to praise; his true goal is, to quote Ste.-Beuve again, "une admiration nette, distincte et sentie." The world at large is content to admire vaguely and confusedly, and, in so doing, it includes in its admiration things noway excellent. Thus it is that popularity has spoilt so many authors; the indiscriminating applause of the multitude leads them to think their very faults admirable, or at least effectually prevents them from recognising their faults as faults. They see that they have only to exert their special talent in order to win success, and they exert it with little thought of bringing it under discipline, or putting it to the worthiest use. They do not act, as old Phocion did, who, when the multitude applauded anything he had said, turned sharply round and asked what absurdity he had uttered. The question rather is, "How did I make that hit? I must try it again." And the thing is tried again, perhaps through a series of attempts, each feebler than the one before.

A true criticism discerns where the real strength of an author lies; and there have been critics whose insight and power of analysis have been such as to reveal the author to himself in a manner that has filled him with surprise. To be praised in a general way is but little satisfaction to a superior mind, but to have one's true points of superiority or originality clearly discerned and adequately expressed, to feel that a moment of recognition has been given to one's real self, is a satisfaction almost unique. Beranger said that a certain criticism of his poems by Ste.-

Beuve drew tears from his eyes, such was the intellectual sympathy that the criticism displayed. And this is indeed what constitutes the critic's highest pleasure, the disengaging of the real from the conventional, and coming into immediate contact with the spirit of an author. Every mind has its own essential quality, or, so to speak, its own peculiar flavour, masked of course to the majority by all that is not essential or peculiar, but discernable by the few. The critic is an amateur in such things. An original talent is to him like a fragrant flower the odour of which he inhales till he learns to know it among a thousand. To point out faults and short-comings, therefore, is but a necessity of his trade, not that which lends its attraction in his eyes, or which constitutes the crown and reward of his labours. Robert Browning is not addressing critics in particular when he says:—

Because you spend your lives in praising—
To praise you search the wide world over.

but he might be, as criticism is ever on the search for beauty and truth, and, but for the desire that these create, would have no existence.

Many are the taunts that have been thrown at critics, and no doubt the profession has had, like all others, its unworthy representatives, purblind pedants, fatuous fops, and incompetents of every grade. But after all has been said that can be said about "irresponsible reviewers" and about men who have failed in every other walk in literature betaking themselves to criticism, the fact remains that criticism is a permanent necessity of civilization, and is becoming more and more a necessity as civilization becomes more complex. The task of criticism moreover is one which no broken-down literary adventurer is fit to undertake. The original creators in the world of letters and of art occupy, no doubt, a supreme position, and deserve the homage of mankind; but the well-equipped critic, the man of wide reading, of cultivated taste, of well-balanced mind and complete intellectual disinterestedness is a man whom society may well honour. The balance of faculties which we require in the critic is something in which the greatest geniuses are sometimes sadly lacking. In fact the business of a genius would seem to be simply *to be a genius*, and give the world his one special gift; and, that done, we find him even as other men. On one side there is preponderant development, on another there is possibly deficiency. It is ungracious perhaps to look such noble gift-horses in the mouth; but their surpassing merits should not lead us to disparage men who, if less brilliantly endowed, possess, nevertheless, special faculties of no common order. The accomplished critic, with his calm penetrative glance and infinite tact, is a man whom those who know and love literature best know how to value.

It would be a great mistake to suppose that the critic finds all the materials for his criticism in the work before him. Far from it: he has materials in his own mind, derived from his wide experience of human thought; he knows the ways of men, and has grasped so many relations that nothing can touch his mind that does not waken countless associations and vibrate along a thousand lives. So that in interpreting an author he takes of his own and weaves it in with his presentation of the author's thoughts. To know what critics have done and can do for the illustration of great texts, and the cultivation of the minds of the educated classes, let any one run through a number of volumes of the *Revue des Deux Mondes*, and try to do justice to a few of the numberless essays that will there be found under such names as De Rémusat, Schérer, Janet, St. Réné-Taillandier, Renan, Réville, to mention only a few of the more prominent ones. The work of these men is immense, and executed with a faithfulness that is an honour to them and to French letters. Our own Review literature will show the same thing, but in a less striking form. It is not the work of broken-down literary men that we see in such periodicals, but work, in many cases, vastly better than any that the brilliant phrase-maker to whom the sneer to which we allude is due ever put off his hands.

Criticism should be the voice of impartial and enlightened reason. Too often what passes for criticism is the voice of hireling adulation or hireling enmity. Illustrations of this will occur to everyone, but there is no use in blaming criticism, which, as has been said, is an intellectual necessity of the age. The foregoing remarks have been made in the hope that they may help to clear away some prevalent misconceptions by showing the organic connection, so to speak, that exists between criticism as a function, or as a mode of intellectual activity, and the very simplest intellectual processes. Such a mode of regarding it should do away with the odium that in so many minds attaches to the idea of criticism. Let us all try to be critics according to the measure of our abilities and opportunities. Let us aim at seeing all we can, at gaining as many points of view as possible. Let us compare carefully and judge impartially; and we may depend upon it we shall be the better for the very effort.

4. Free Thought and Responsible Thought (1882)

The publication of Mr. Mill's book on "Liberty" marked probably the culminating point of the modern worship of free enquiry. Up to that time the demand for intellectual freedom had never been fully satisified; and the powerful plea put forth by Mr. Mill was therefore enthusiastically welcomed by all forward looking minds as the precise statement of the case which their intellectual position required. The errors of the past, it was then felt, had been largely due to the restrictions imposed on thought; complete liberty of thought was consequently the chief thing necessary for the successful pursuit of truth and the reconstruction, on a sound basis, of philosophy and of human life. Let men but be allowed to think freely, and give free play to their several individualities, and a new and better order of things would speedily arise. This phase of thought, which, as remarked, had its culmination at the date of Mr. Mill's celebrated treatise, shows to-day signs of diminished and perhaps diminishing force. It is rare to find such enthusiasm for the abstract idea of liberty as was common a generation or half a generation ago. What Mr. Mill in his "Autobiography" represents as having happened to himself, in regard to the high hopes he had entertained of the adoption of "liberal" ideas in legislation has happened to many since in regard to their fond anticipations of the effects of unchecked freedom of thought. Mr. Mill acknowledged with regret that an extended franchise, free trade, and other radical reforms had not made such a wonderful change in the state of the nation as he and others had counted on; and in like manner many to-day are coming to the conclusion that thought may be very free, so far as the absence of civil or social restraints can make it so, and yet very unproductive. Those who incline to this view of the matter do not deny that freedom of thought is in itself a good thing; they only say that like other good things it is liable: 1. to non use, and, 2. to abuse. Give a man a freedom which he does not care to exercise, and what better is he? Give him a freedom that he is not fit to exercise, and what better is he?

SOURCE: *Rose-Belford's Canadian Monthly and National Review,* Vol. VIII (June, 1882), pp. 614-620.

Nothing, but possibly the worse. Let us therefore look a little into this matter of free thought and see what there is in it, and what conclusions it is safe to form respecting it.

Thought may be defined sufficiently well for our present purpose, as the activity of the knowing faculty in man. How man knows, how the blending of subject and object is accomplished in the act of knowledge, or what are the true relations of object and subject, are problems with which the highest minds of every age have successively grappled, but the exact solution of which is probably as distant now as ever. Fortunately I do not need to await a solution before adopting such a practical view of the matter as serves the purposes of every-day thought. We place on one side the observing, reflecting, mind; on the other an objective universe in which that mind seeks its aliment. The mind absorbs the universe and ideally recreates it. Knowledge is the mental reproduction of an external, or assumed external order. When we are confident in our power to think of things *as they exist* we say we know them. If, however, we look a little closely into the matter, we shall see that the mind progressively makes the order which it seems to discover in the universe. Arrest the thinking faculty at any stage, and what shall we find it doing? Trying to discover the explanation of something, in other words trying so to conceive a new fact as to make it harmonize with an already existing scheme of thought. That is to say, the mind has established a harmony amongst its previous observations; the new fact as it first presents itself threatens to disturb that harmony, and the question then is: is there not some other way of viewing it which will bring it into harmony with what is already known or assumed to be known? The apparent backward movement of the planets was a disturbing fact of this nature in regard to the primitive geocentric theory of the heavens; and as that theory was too firmly rooted to be easily shaken, or rather, as the means for a complete revision of it were lacking, the disturbing fact was reduced to order by the very ingenious theory of epicycles. That theory was not destined to hold good for all time; but it held good at the time, and that is really as much as we can say for any theory we adopt—that it harmonizes with the sum of our existing knowledge. Whether it will harmonize with the knowledge of some future age it would be rash in us to attempt to predict; for the system that seems to us unshakable to-day may, through some extension of our knowledge, have to be as thoroughly reconstructed as have been the ancient views of astronomy. At whatever point, as I have said, the progress of thought may be interrupted, we shall find two things—first, that the mind has already created a certain order of thought for itself; and second, that it is trying to build more and more of the universe into the system so established. Every now and again it has to tear down a large portion of its work, in order to build on a better place and a wider foundation; but still the work goes on—the great work of giving laws to phenomena, and creating ideal unity out of actual diversity.

This is not only the *work* of the mind; it is its life; it is the one law of its being. Mind is only mind in so far as it progressively knows, that is, in so far as it progressively enters into things, and so moulds and masters them, as to be able to *think* them. The mind digests facts, and turns them into a vital current of rational thought. A fact—as some apparently supernatural manifestation—which the mind cannot digest, acts as a poison upon the system, and may result in insanity or death.

Such being the course of thought, a progressive reduction of facts to a rational or thinkable order, we are, perhaps, prepared to understand what are likely to be the most favourable conditions for vigorous and successful thought. One condition certainly will be the common pursuit of truth by a multitude of minds. Instead of thought being, as so many seem to imagine, a purely individual thing, it springs almost wholly from the social nature of man. What a man thinks—if he thinks sincerely—holds good, or should hold good, not for himself alone, but for all men; and in our social intercourse we instinctively presume that the impressions made on us by outward facts are shared by others. But as we all err more or less in the conceptions we form, it is manifest that the most satisfactory progress will be made in thought where there is the freest possible social comparison of views, and where men most frequently remind themselves that thought is not destined to serve merely individual purposes. Thought will make its best advance when men consciously or unconsciously try to think together, and not when the tendency is to think as far apart as possible. The ideal of many so-called free-thinkers is an independent life of thought for each individual, the cultivation by each of a little area upon which no other man shall have a right to set a foot. Each, as it were, puts up a notice on his lot: "These are my opinions. Trespassers will be prosecuted with the utmost rigour of the law." Now, most certainly, I do not believe in trespassing upon a man's intellectual premises against his will; but I am strongly of opinion that, just in so far as a man thinks in this separated spirit, will he think to no purpose, or to worse than no purpose. After all, a man cannot think in this spirit; he may think that he thinks, but he doesn't think. To think, as before explained, is to construct, to build in, to harmonize; and nobody goes to this trouble for the mere sake of self-assertion. The man who has a strong impulse to think, desires to think with others, or at least desires others to think with him; for he knows that whatever is true is true for all, and that whatever is important is important for all. He does not therefore seek to fence himself off from the rest of mankind, but takes up his work as a continuation of what others have done before him. The real work of thought is too full of interest, and brings the labours of others too frequently to mind, to be carried on by one whose main desire is to preserve his property rights. Better far, in a social point of view, the most dogmatic and absolute spirit than the mere worship of *la petite culture* in matters intellectual. It has not been by standing apart from one another, each man with his private thought and purpose, that the greatest triumphs of humanity have been won, but by the effort of all to universalize truth and to merge individual differences in a common intellectual and spiritual life. Thus have all societies been founded and extended, and all enterprises of great pith and moment undertaken and accomplished.

Another important condition for the successful pursuit of truth is the cultivation of right moral dispositions. This is a principle which is quite too much overlooked. It is commonly held, particularly by people of our own argumentative temper, that reason is wholly independent of the moral nature, and is always ready to perform its office of discovering truth. They forget that it is the moral or emotional nature that gives a direction to the operations of reason, just as it does to the practical activities. That reason is not an all-seeing eye, discovering all facts and relations with equal facility, is evident from the very partial manner in which the faculty is exercised by different individuals. The man whose taste is for books will, in a week, acquire more knowledge about books and their authors than another man, whose tastes lie wholly in the direction, say, of practical mechanics, will gain in a whole lifetime. The botanist wonders that any one can talk or walk in the country without seeing what he sees; and yet he may be blind as a bat to the most obvious phenomena of language, even as they occur in his own daily speech. The sportsman has a degree of lore as to guns and their makers, as to the varieties of wild fowl and their several habits and habitats, that strikes with amazement any one who is not of the craft. Every one of these specialists may have had abundant opportunities, so far as the mere passing of certain images before the eye is concerned, to pick up a great variety of knowledge outside of his favourite pursuit; but in point of fact he has not picked it up, for he has not seen what he has not been interested in, or has seen it only to forget straightway what manner of thing it was. Reason only occupies itself with what the perceptive faculties furnish to it; and the perceptive faculties only see what they are told to see, in other words, what the mind has an interest in. In many other ways, however, reason is affected in its workings, for good or for evil, by desire. The vain man will desire to see the things that will minister to his vanity; the selfish man the things that will minister to his selfishness; the just and social man the things that make for the general welfare; and each will be more or less successful in seeing the things he wishes to see, and avoiding the sight of things that conflict with his desires and purposes. Now the Universe, like Scripture, is not of any private interpretation; and neither the vain man nor the selfish man will obtain a key to it. The order they create will not be a durable order; it will have flaws precisely corresponding to the admixture of impure motive in their speculations. The history even of physical discovery is full of vicissitudes, due not so much to the weakness of the reasoning or perceptive faculties of men, as to erroneous assumptions dictated by personal bias or passion.

This is a truth which might with advantage receive extensive illustration; but as this would transcend the limits within which this paper is necessarily confined, it may be sufficient to quote the testimony of one of the profoundest scientific minds of this or any other century, the late Michael Faraday. In an address delivered by him before the Royal Institution on "The Education of the Judgment," we find the following observations:—

> Among those points of self-education which take the form of mental discipline, there is one of great importance, and moreover difficult to deal with, because it involves an internal conflict, and equally touches our vanity and our ease. It consists in the tendency to deceive ourselves regarding all we wish for, and the necessity for resistance to these desires. It is impossible for any one who has not been constrained, by the course of his occupation and thoughts, to a habit of continued self-correction, to be aware of the amount of error arising from this tendency. . . . It is my firm persuasion that no man can examine himself in the most common things, having any reference to him personally, or to any person, thought or matter related to him, without being soon made aware of the temptation and the difficulty of opposing it. I could give you many illustrations personal to myself, about atmospheric magnetism, lines of force, attraction, repulsion, unity of power, nature of matter, &c., . . . but it would be unsuitable, and also unnecessary, for each must be conscious of a large field sadly uncultivated in this respect. *I will simply express my strong belief* (the italics are Faraday's own) *that that point of self-education which consists in teaching the mind to resist its desires and inclinations, until they are proved to be right, is the most important of all, not only in things of natural philosophy, but in every department of daily life.*

The first and the last step in the education of the scientific judgment this eminent philosopher declares to be—*humility*. Such testimony as this from a man like Faraday is of infinite value. If in such matters as "atmospheric magnetism, lines of force, attraction, repulsion, &c," he could feel his judgment swayed by influences connected with his own personal desires and preferences, what must have been, and what must be, the case with men destitute of his admirable sobriety of character and conscientious self-restraint?

The truth that Faraday has thus laid down has been expressed with even greater force and in a much more systematic manner by Auguste Comte. "Goodness of heart," says the latter, "helps forward a theoretical career more than force of character." Of the great physiologist, Blainville, one of his own disciples, he observed:

> Impulses of too personal a kind enfeebled the ardour and constancy required for Blainville's intellectual task; and the full strength of his mind was never put forth. . . . He saw rivals where he should have seen colleagues, and sometimes superiors. Always unjust to Broussais, he failed to recognise the transcendent greatness of Bichat. When personal feeling extends so far as this, it hinders the working of general views not less than of generous feelings.*

The bearing of all this upon the question of Free Thought may, perhaps, begin to be seen. It has been shown that thought in its dynamic aspect consists in a progressively wider interpretation of the universe in which man's lot is cast. This being its task, it is apparent that individual thought cannot properly, or with any advantage, separate itself from the thought of the race. The only true and serviceable thought is the thought that, either now or hereafter, all men may think. A thought, or a mode of thought that is essentially peculiar to an individual—that is, so to speak, the mere expression or outcome of the accidents of his individuality—is of about the same value to himself and the world as would be a wart on the hand or a squint in his eye. The branch, except it abide in the vine, dies; and so the individual man, except he abide in the great vine—humanity. When, therefore, a demand is made for freedom of thought, it becomes a question of much importance whether the freedom claimed is freedom to pursue truth in a social spirit for social ends, or mere freedom to think what one chooses without regard to ends and without any sense of responsibility. In either case the demand should be granted, for no good can come of any attempt to interfere by way of control with men's thinkings, or what they choose to regard as such; but, in the one case, the demand is entitled to all the sympathy that can be given to it: in the latter, it is entitled to just as much as we accord to the desire for any other purely individual indulgence.

The more this distinction is dwelt upon, the more important, I believe, it will be seen to be. Not that it affords the means of discriminating between claims for freedom of thought that ought to be

*See Comte's *Positive Polity*—English translation—Vol. I., Appendix, p. 599.

allowed, and claims that ought not to be allowed; for all such claims should be allowed lest the very disallowance should tend to the perversion of thought. The importance of the distinction lies in the use that may be made of it by those who are demanding free thought for themselves. "What am I going to do with it when I get it?" or, "Having got it, what am I doing with it?" are questions, as it seems to me, of extreme pertinency. And if the only answer to such questions is to the effect that I am going to think just as I choose, and without any regard to what others may think, all that can be said is that the conclusion is a very poor one. To talk about thinking as one chooses is nonsense and worse; for one cannot *choose* his way of thinking without doing what is distinctly immoral. To choose in such a matter is deliberately to allow the judgment to be swayed by personal feelings and interests. Put these aside, and there is no choice; there is simply obedience to the laws of thought, or to the truth of things in so far as the mind is fitted to apprehend it. The great lesson which "free-thinkers" have to learn is that all true thought is universal in its character, not individual; and that nobody can be said to be thinking in the right sense of the word unless he is thinking for all, and endeavouring to promote the general harmony of human thought. It is unfortunately too common to find "free-thinkers" look upon the privilege of free thought as a merely private possession, something for the use of which they owe no account to any one, not even to themselves. They hold it as a kind of character to contradict every opinion with which they do not immediately agree, and generally to disport themselves in the world of thought with the most perfect feeling of irresponsibility. They only realize their intellectual freedom in differing from others not in agreeing with them. This is, no doubt, a not unnatural reaction from the intellectual tyranny of the past; but none the less does it lead to a hurtful dissipation of mental energy as well as to a dangerous weakening of social bonds.

The battle of mental freedom, so far as external control is concerned, may be said to have been fought and won. The Church may scold, and the State, through her magistrates, may sometimes frown; but no man to-day is compelled to profess to believe what he does not believe, nor are any restraints worth mentioning imposed upon the expression of opinion. There is, however, another battle to be fought before the spiritual freedom of mankind can be complete; and that is the battle against anarchy in the guise of liberty. So far as men insist upon thinking what they choose, there is from one point of view anarchy, and from another enslavement—anarchy inasmuch as the very idea of law is set at naught, and enslavement because each man, instead of struggling against the personal influences that pervert opinion, as Faraday has so well shown, resigns himself to them entirely.

We are thus brought round by a road which is perhaps not often travelled, and which many "advanced thinkers" particularly dislike to travel, to the old truth that true liberty lies in a reasoned subjection to law. How can human powers be carried to their highest? By a knowledge of, and conformity with, the laws of nature. He who rebels is shorn of power and cast forth from Nature's protection. He who rebels against humanity is disowned by humanity, and his life dwindles to the narrow limits of his infinitely narrow self. Free thought is of no value unless it be also *responsible* thought. To think should be regarded, not as a means of self-pleasing, but as a sacred ministry; and we should value our thoughts just in so far as they enable us to understand and sympathise with the great life of the world, just in so far as they quicken our sense of kindred with all mankind. The triumph of thought is not to enable a man to stand aloof from his fellows, superior to what he regards as their prejudices and indifferent to their hopes and fears. The triumph of thought is to seize what an excellent French writer, the late M. Ernest Bersot, calls "the durable aspect of things."[6] The triumph of thought for each individual is to enlarge in some small degree the thought of humanity, or even to think over again the great thoughts of humanity with sympathetic insight into their meaning. The latter may seem a humble office, but only to those who know not what it is. There are thousands and millions who daily use, in a sort of symbolic or empirical fashion, the thoughts that the ages have wrought out—just as the mariner uses the "Nautical Almanacs"—with very little conception of what has gone to form them, or of their true reach and significance. The mind of humanity is known to none but those who are in a peculiar manner its sons.

The social weakness that comes of excessive individualism in thought is too obvious and notorious to need dwelling on. "Liberals" (in the theological sense) are constantly heard complaining how difficult it is to secure any joint action among persons of their way of thinking. To organize even Unitarians, has been said by one of themselves, to be very much the same as trying to "cord stumps," what it is to organize "Liberals" let those who have tried it say. If we seek for the cause of the trouble, we shall find it in the erroneous impression that liberty is only realized in difference; and that, as organization and system tend to obliterate differences, they must also be dangerous to liberty. But, when once men in general begin to think under a sense of responsibility, they will see that all thinking should tend to unity, and that the crown of thought should be the discovery of a true philosophy of human life. To say that the natural result of free thought is infinite and hopeless divergence, in as many different directions as there are thinkers, is fatally to discredit the thinking faculty. Better far, one would be compelled to say, that thought should not be free, than that there should be no harmony or coherence in men's opinions, but that what is true to one man should be false to every other. It is not so, however. When, by the subjugation of egoism, thought becomes truly free, it will be seen to be not a dispersive but a unifying force; and when men begin to look to it, not for little individual allotments of opinion, but for conclusions of universal validity, the foundations of a true philosophy is to believe it possible. If it be possible, why should we not have it? If it be not possible, then to little purpose have we emancipated ourselves from the philosophies and theologies of the past.

I began this paper by observing that the zeal for free-thought simply for its own sake, seemed to have abated somewhat of late years. If the fact be as I believe, the symptom is not wholly an unfavourable one. A true instinct whispers to mankind that something better than endless wranglings should be the outcome of the exercise of the highest human faculty. The world has had enough of criticism of the past, its institutions and beliefs. Many doctrines and systems have no doubt, been badly shaken; but, for all that, the great majority of men cling to them still for the practical guidance and help they afford in life. What is wanted now is a philosophy which, while doing justice to the past, will do what the old systems cannot do, rightly interpret the present, and give the keynote of the future harmony of society. When such a philosophy is in a forward state, men may not be found clinging so tenaciously to doctrines which they acknowledge are in many respects far from satisfactory. But such a philosophy will not come from any amount of irresponsible thought directed to no definite ends; it will come as the result of the earnest efforts of many minds, and from the growth of the conviction that thought was given not for individual but for social ends.

PART TWO
Science, Ethics, and Modern Thought

I understand by modern science the body of rules, instruments, theorems, observations, and conceptions with the aid of which man manipulates physical nature in order to grasp its workings.

—Jacques Barzun
Science—the Glorious Entertainment (1964)

What is the power that rules the universe, what is the estate, what is the destiny of man? Those who think that such questions as these will be laid aside by a being whose speculative faculties have once been raised to activity, and that man will rest content with a knowledge of physical phenomena and of the material laws which regulate his brief existence here, have not at present the evidence of the bookstores on their side.

—"Bystander,"
The Week (February 7, 1884)

Introduction

I

Everybody, wrote Sara Jeannette Duncan in 1887, talks about "the age." Moreover, they do so almost as if "the age" has an existence independent of the actual lives of men. This, she said, indicates an attitude as curious and interesting as anything men in fact said of their age: "Forgetting, apparently, that we are part and parcel of it, and individually responsible for its having done those things which it ought not to do, and left undone those things which it ought to have done, we elect ourselves a grand jury to indict and try the age."[1] Miss Duncan was writing for a Canadian periodical, *The Week*, her audience a Canadian one; and while her accusation was by no means applicable only to her own readers, by the time she put her comments to paper she could have provided numerous examples of Canadians' judgements about the age in which they lived.

This was the case partly because by the late 1880s Canadians had been able to publish their views continuously in one national forum or another for almost two decades.[2] It was equally the case, however, because the "age" in which Canadian periodical literature came into its own was also that of Charles Darwin, Herbert Spencer, and T.H. Huxley. The age that was observed and characterized in the 1870s and 1880s was thus one in which the various claims of science and religion were set forward and debated by the literate middle classes, including those in Canada. "Whatever sins of omission or commission may be fairly laid to the charge of our age and generation, indifference to the momentous problems of human life and destiny is not one of them," wrote W.J. Rattray in 1878. "Men are far too seriously-minded in their search after truth . . . to treat the solemn questions which persistently obtrude themselves for solution on every age, with levity, scorn or a flippant superficiality."[3] The opening sentences of many articles published in Canadian literary periodicals during these decades clearly illustrate the extent to which Rattray's claim was true. "If any one thing is more characteristic of this age than another," Kingston's Agnes Maule Machar wrote, "it is the restless mental activity which questions all things formerly received; a general 'shaking' and revising of opinions, which, however much temporary pain and disorganization it may produce, must at least end in the result 'that the things which cannot be shaken should remain.' "[4]

Agnes Machar was one of the most articulate and intelligent Canadian lay defenders of Christian orthodoxy during one of the most difficult periods in the history of the Christian religion. Well-read and open-minded, yet deeply committed to her Presbyterian heritage, she never doubted the fundamental truths of her religion. Yet not everyone in Canada at the time was able to enjoy such certitude. Goldwin Smith opened one article in *The Canadian Monthly* with the words: "The intellectual world is at present the scene of a great revolution, one of the most dangerous features of which is that the clergy, an order of men specially set apart as Ministers of Truth, are rendered incapable of performing the intellectual part of their functions properly by the pressure of creeds. . . ." The consequences of this "intellectual revolution" for Smith were both profound and painful, for while the claims of modern science convinced him of the weakness of many traditional articles of the Christian faith, they provided no adequate substitute for the certainty that was lost. "Doubt," he wrote, "is no longer locked in the bosom or only whispered in the ear."[5]

The spectre of Doubt was abroad. "The visible encroaches on the invisible," said the American Anglican divine, James DeKoven, in 1878: "Between us and God appear to come laws and forces, and powers, the duration and extent of which we can grasp and measure. . . . What, then, if these laws begin to take . . . the place of God?"[6] By the 1870s and 1880s the progress of science seemed to be making its mark everywhere, especially when science was extended into the area of technology. Few attacks were made upon it on that account by English-speaking North Americans. It was the extension of science into the realm of cosmogony, ethics, and man's spiritual life which turned many who accepted the desirability of the material progress brought about by science into its strongest accusers, and rendered others unable to believe in either a science seemingly validated by "progress" or a religion that stood only on faith. The claim by one Canadian university student of the 1870s that "There can be little doubt that of late years the argument for the existence of a God from the proofs of design in Nature, has not met with so general an acceptance as formerly" was understandable in a decade when traditional Christian teleology was in the process of dissolution. This particular student's conclusions illustrate clearly the dilemma in which many of his fellow students probably found themselves. First, he accepted the validity of the findings of modern science: it ". . . steps in and dispels such fancies" as the evidences in Nature of "a great and invisible Design and Lawgiver." Indeed, science proclaims physical nature to be solely under the dominion of natural laws. Yet the consequences of that acceptance were immense, for the student found that the tendency of modern science was "to remove God more and more into the background. . . ." Even worse, ". . . some of its professors in their wisdom even think that they can dispense with him altogether." While the student thus accepted the reality of a world governed by physical laws, and while he noted that "Everywhere around us, if we will but open our eyes, are the signs of a great and terribly struggle for existence," such "explanations" nevertheless did not further his own understanding. The Darwinian world provided abundant evidence of the "agency of evil," he said, but no *reason* for it. In the end the student was left to fall back upon the rhetoric rather than the substance of an earlier Natural Theology. Science had invalidated the premises of the argument from Design, but the student had been given nothing to take its place. For this student the traditional Christian teleology had been shattered by the findings of modern science, yet the traditional Christian conception of rationality, the correspondence of human reason with the perception of design and purpose in nature, remained very much with him. For this reason he could not trust the evidence of a Reason guided solely by intellect: "Starting indeed with the knowledge of its great Architect, we can trace his handiwork in pillar and cornice, ceiling and floor: but with our own unguided reason we could never regard it as in all its parts a fitting monument of Omnipotence and Wisdom divine." Nor could he even trust the empirical evidence of his own observations of Nature, for "Nature furnishes us with no solution of the enigmas of life: [it is] Revelation [which alone] reveals the essential truths of existence to every humble enquirer."[7]

The problem of reconciling Christianity, as a Revealed religion, with the findings of modern science was one which preyed upon the minds of many young men and women at Anglo-Canadian universities during the 1870s and 1880s. John Fiske and others, as Carl Berger has claimed, may have affected a reconciliation of evolution and religion during the 1870s, but their efforts were perhaps most satisfactory to their own psychological needs.[8] One sees little evidence of solace derived from such sources in the pages of Victoria College's newspaper, *Acta Victoriana*, Queen's University's *Queen's Journal*, or Dalhousie University's *Dalhousie Gazette* in those years. To be sure, there is a note of optimism in students' opinions that the problems of reconciliation between Revelation and Science will ultimately be worked out once "the book of nature" is "rightly understood" and a "*true* science" developed. But it is a superficial optimism at best. The day was fast approaching, concluded one such student, "when all mysteries shall be unfolded before our rejoicing intellects."[9] Another waited for the day when "the rays shot into the darkness by intellect" would reveal that perhaps the Darwinian theory of Descent and the traditional Christian conception of Design were consistent with one another.[10] In the meantime, however, their student essays, always utterly serious in tone, bespoke far more of the generally optimistic enthusiasm of youth than of any true reconciliation within their own minds of the twin systems of scientific and religious belief. "We have but launched our bark on the Ocean of Life," said one student in a paper with a furrowed brow title, "The Age and Its Tendencies," "and though we see a current in one direction, and a counter-current in another, we have yet scarcely found out in what direction the whole mass is drifting; yet we know the course is ever onward."[11]

While Anglo-Canadian university students wrote articles such as these for their college newspapers, men and women of their parents' generation put into print their own views on the question of science. In a host of articles in the *Canadian Methodist Magazine,* as Berger has pointed out, Canadian clergymen felt compelled to draw upon whatever sources they could in order to plead for the necessary oneness of the Author of Revelation and the Author of Nature. Evolution itself, they argued, was part of the on-going Design of God.[12] Yet, like those of their sons and daughters, theirs was at best a defensive argument. It could offer no certitude, only the possibility of new directions in which to follow "truth"—whatever that now was. A poem entitled "One Faith in Many Forms," reprinted in *Rose-Belford's Canadian Monthly* from the London *Spectator* in 1881, expressed the dilemma well:

>   Him,—
> What is His Name? What name will all express
>   The mighty whole, of whom we are but part—
> So that all differing tongues may join a worship
>   Echoing in every heart?
>
> Then answers one—'God is an endless sequence,
>   Incapable of either break or flaw,
> Which we discern but dimly and in fragments!
>   God is unchanging . . . Law.'
>
> 'Nay,' said another, 'Law is but His method;
>   Look back, behind the sequence to his source!
> Behind all phases and all changes seek Him!
>   God is the primal Force!'

The poet denied in subsequent stanzas that God was either "unchanging Law" or "primal Force." Nor was he solely manifested through a Love for an equally vague Humanity. God incorporates all—"Love, beauty, Wisdom and force": "God includes them, as some great cathedral/Includes each separate shrine.''[13] The effect on the poem's readers was probably to further the desire for such an all-embracing God; yet the basic problem remained unresolved—for the shrines remained separate.

II

It was from separate shrines, each devoted to fundamentally the same end, that W.D. LeSueur and his Canadian critics engaged in polite, yet utterly serious, argumentative battle from the mid 1870s through the 1880s. Thus began the second chapter of his internal biography. The opposing battlements were those of modern scientific thought and Christian orthodoxy; the battlegrounds the newspapers, periodical press and pamphlets. At stake was the nature of the ethical systems by which men govern their lives. As an editorial writer for the Toronto *Mail* wrote, when responding critically to LeSueur's article, ''The Future of Morality'': ''one of the questions which our age is debating somewhat anxiously is the connection between the ethics of a nation and its faith.''[14]

Basically, the various charges made by critics of the ''Science'' of the day fell into a few general areas. First, they claimed that—extended into the realm of ethics—Science led to materialism, agnosticism, and scepticism. Secondly, as such, it was devoid of any real spiritual substance; hence it could put forward no adequate guide for human conduct. Third, it was guilty of the very sin with which it charged Christianity: dogmatism. These were the charges which LeSueur sought to dispel in his various writings on science and ''modern thought'' during the 1870s and 1880s. He did so in a number of articles published over a twenty year period; yet the essentials of his defence of ''modern thought'' can be gleaned in the half dozen pieces which are reprinted in this volume.

The articles ''Science and Materialism'' (1877) and ''The Scientific Spirit'' (1879) extended LeSueur's fundamental commitment to critical enquiry into the scientific endeavour. These articles also attempted to disabuse science of the charge that it was guilty of a negative scepticism and a crass materialism. In ''Morality and Religion'' and ''A Vindication of Scientific Ethics'' (both published in 1880) he sought to elaborate further his conviction that the scientific spirit *could* exert an ethical influence. He did so through an explication and defence of Herbert Spencer's book, *The Data of Ethics*, published a year earlier and at the time under fierce attack.[15] It was as reasonable to believe that systems of morals could be developed from the study of the history of human conduct in the natural world, Spencer had claimed, as it was to assume that the regulation of conduct could only come about through credal dicta derived from supernatural agencies.[16] Finally, in "Materialism and Positivism" (1882) and "A Defence of Modern Thought" (1884), he attempted to divorce positivist social theory from the charge that it was materialistic and denied that "modern thought" in general, which sought to rebuild society around scientific principles, was agnostic in its spirit or its tendencies.

That science fostered a materialistic and sceptical outlook on life was the most frequent charge made against it in the 1870s and 1880s. Indeed, some critics claimed that by its very nature it was materialistic and sceptical.[17] Defenders of Christianity could give substance to the truth of these propositions by pointing out the influence of both Epicureanism and sensationalism upon scientists; they could note the way in which the Scottish philosopher, Alexander Bain, took the empiricist tradition into the realm of psychology by tracing both thoughts and "moral apprehensions" to the bodily system; they could illustrate the agnostic "materialism" in Herbert Spencer's social evolutionism by quoting him without due regard to the corpus of his thought; similarly, they could support their arguments by drawing evidence from T.H. Huxley's article on protoplasm as the physical basis of life. They could also allow such "materialists" to ridicule themselves by quoting, equally without adequate regard for context, such snippets as: "The brain secretes thought as the liver secretes bile;" "The soul is the product of a peculiar combination of matter;" or "Mental activity is a function of the cerebral substance."[18]

Charges that modern science was materialistic reached their peak, however, after the delivery and publication of John Tyndall's "Belfast Address," given to the British Association for the Advancement of Science in 1874. Tyndall, Professor of Natural Philosophy in the Royal Institution, enjoyed a widespread reputation in the 1860s and 1870s, due mainly to the many lectures he gave for laymen. The opinions expressed in his 1874 Presidential Address to the B.A.A.S. were all the more horrifying because they came from one of the most eminent and respected British scientific authorities.

Tyndall infuriated his listeners, and later his readers, because he sought to unite the findings of the science of his day—in biology, physics, chemistry, and psychology—with the philosophical atomism of the ancients, especially Democritus. Tyndall's own religious convictions led him to advocate a vague sort of pantheism and to put forward his belief that religious feelings could not aid man in arriving at an objective understanding of his place in nature. Only science could do this. Science, he concluded, had by 1874 reached an "impregnable position" which he claimed could be described in a few words: "We claim, and we shall wrest, from theology the entire domain of cosmological theory. All schemes and systems which thus infringe upon the domain of science must *in so far as they do this*, submit to its control, and relinquish all thought of controlling it.''[19] Here, it seemed, was excellent evidence of the materialistic nature of an agnostic, dogmatic, and arrogant Science.

Within hours of the delivery of the Belfast Address, its author was under attack in England. The next day, a London merchant suggested to the Home Secretary that Tyndall be brought to trial under a British statute which dealt with the expression of blasphemous opinions. *Punch* satirized him in poems and cartoons. So did the Scottish physicist, James Clerk Maxwell, in the following light verse: ''From nothing comes nothing they told us,/ naught happens by chance but by fate;/ There is nothing but atoms and void, all else/ is mere whims out of date.''[20] The debate between Tyndall, his defenders, and his opponents continued into the late 1870s. The very phrase, ''Belfast Address,'' became synonymous with the words, such as ''materialism'', which were seen to pose dire threats against orthodox religious belief.

This was no less the case in the new Canadian nation than it was in the more serene atmosphere of the English parsonage. In 1876 the Professor of Mathematics and Natural Philosophy at McGill University, Alexander Johnson (who was also Vice-Dean of the Faculty of Arts), was called upon to convince the university's students in engineering and theoretical physics that in entering their new professions they were not enlisting in the ranks of the materialists. ''My subject is one that has been agitating the minds of many during nearly two years past,'' he said:

a wave of disturbance originating in the address of the President of the British Association for the advancement of Science in 1874 has rolled over the mother country, and crossing the Atlantic, diffused itself here far and wide. The disturbance then excited, the agitation of men's minds, and the discussions that followed, are still in full vigour, not only in Great Britain, but here in Canada . . .

The discussions are carried on or noticed, not only in books, reviews and pamphlets, but in newspapers and in the social circle. When the newspapers teem with quotations from Tyndall, Huxley, Darwin and Herbert Spencer (no later than this morning I saw one from the last mentioned), and the mind of the nation in general is agitated, it is not to be supposed that the student's mind will escape that apprehension which lays hold of many when they are told that Science and Religion are irreconcileably at variance. When after this, the student hears, as he must do, in his lectures, of ''molecules,'' ''atoms,'' ''vibrations,'' and other terms which are bandied about so freely in these discussions, he may have some fears that he is entering on dangerous ground, and a feeling of uneasiness may seize hold of him, though he can see no precise cause of it.[21]

Professor Alexander judged that by the questions asked of him in the classroom during the academic year that had just concluded such an uneasiness was indeed present in the minds of his students. The remainder of his address was therefore an attempt to persuade them that, in his own words, "there are no good grounds for the impression that what are called the Atheistic or Materialistic conclusions, so loudly proclaimed by certain scientific men and, among them, by Dr. Tyndall, have any support in Physical Science."[22]

The spectre of Tyndall and his "Belfast Address" was thus part of the intellectual context within which the debate over science and religion was conducted in Canada. Both Graeme Mercer Adam, the energetic editor of the *Canadian Monthly,* and Goldwin Smith, mentor of the Canadian periodical press for the last quarter of the nineteenth century, were well-read in much of the "heterodox" thought of the day; and not a little of it found its way into the pages of their various journalistic enterprises. John Tyndall's "Reply to Critics of the Belfast Address" appeared in the *Canadian Monthly* in February, 1875. A month later appeared a long exposition and review of George J. Romanes' book, *Christian Prayer and General Laws.*[23] From then until the last issue of the *Canadian Monthly* was published in 1878, its pages were filled with articles which attacked or defended the arguments set forward by Tyndall and Romanes. They were of three basic sorts: first, those the subject of which was "materialism" proper; secondly, those which debated the extent to which the physical laws which governed the natural world also exercised a control over the world of the spirit; third, those which debated the possibility of an evolutionary system of morality. The first of these centred around Tyndall, whose "heresies" were kept in the reader's mind by the republication of articles such as his address, "Materialism and Its Opponents." LeSueur's essay, "Science and Materialism" (1877), was written in the midst of this debate.[24] The second area of controversy, that over the domain of physical laws, took Romanes' book as its launching point. "The Prayer question," as Romanes himself called it when opening an article for the *Canadian Monthly*, was among the most fiercely-argued of the religious debates in the Canadian 1870s.[25] Without mentioning this controversy specifically, LeSueur's 1880 article, "Morality and Religion," was a summation of his general attitude toward Christianity as set forward in the 'Prayer question.'

This article, written shortly after the publication of *The Data of Ethics*, also marked his entrance into the third area of debate, for this was in large measure an enlargement of that over natural laws. The Prayer question had begun with the query: 'Given the fact that we live in a world which science shows is governed by natural laws, to what extent can we petition God to have our prayers answered?' (To what extent, that is, can we expect God to "violate" those natural laws?) The debate over evolutionary ethics began essentially with the question: 'Given the fact that we live in a world which Science shows to be governed by natural laws, to what extent can those laws serve as the basis for our systems of belief and conduct?' The debate thus included discussions of the validity of evolutionary theory, the evidences for the truth of the Christian doctrine of the immortality of the Soul (as well as the question of the very existence of such an entity), and the possibility of establishing an evolutionary or natural system of morality. This last debate began with considerations of the scientific work of Darwin and the speculations of Goldwin Smith, continued with attacks upon and defences of *The Data of Ethics*, and came to a conclusion (as an on-going debate, not as a question) with the Canadian reactions to Goldwin Smith's pessimistic essay, "The Prospect of a Moral Interregnum."[26]

It is not necessary to trace here the arguments set forward by the major participants in these controversies. Our purpose may be served by noting that W.D. LeSueur found himself in the midst of each. It is sufficient to say that, with few exceptions,[27] LeSueur's contributions to the debates were the only ones which derived from the framework of scientific assumptions; and with the exception of certain articles by John Watson, the British Hegelian philosopher at Queen's University, Kingston,[28] LeSueur's were the only pieces which sought to move beyond special pleading to a larger synthesis that could reconcile the two warring camps by setting forward a coherent philosophy of life. It cannot be said that his viewpoint was without significant points of weakness, or even that he managed at all times to measure up to the standards of criticism he set for himself.[29] Yet the articles which constitute the core of the second chapter of his internal biography indicate clearly that LeSueur's writings in defense of science were above all an extension of his plea for a critical spirit in all areas of enquiry. The scientific spirit was, in essence, simply the critical spirit in a special form, and whether LeSueur addressed himself to such American eminences as the cosmic evolutionist, John Fiske, the evangelical preacher, Lyman Abbott, and the ex-President of Yale University, Noah Porter, or to their Canadian counterparts such as the Presbyterian divine, G.M. Grant, or the Anglican Archbishop of Ontario, John Travers Lewis, this spirit underlay all his arguments.[30]

III

It was entirely appropriate that W.D. LeSueur's essays on science, ethics, and modern thought began to appear at about the same time as his essays on the critical spirit, for his conception of the nature of science was derived from the same premises as his theory of criticism. In its essence, he claimed, the purpose of science is not to determine inviolable truths. It is a simple matter of enquiry. From the time of Bacon, science had "kept to the true path," because it had been Bacon who first conceived of science as "a progressive interrogation of nature." Its prime function is "to interpret to man the world in which he lives." (p. 96) Since at the level of the mind, it is the intellect which renders the randomness of experience into an intelligible order, thus making such an interpretation possible, the intellect itself—in a very real sense—*is* science. "Science," LeSueur wrote, "is the minister of man's thinking faculty"; it "is simply the intellect of man, exercising itself in a certain direction." (pp. 98, 101) Once again LeSueur's insistence that "truth" is not an objective body of data is to be noted. Just as he conceived the critical spirit to be a continual and open process of affirmation and rejection by which judgements are made, so he saw the scientific spirit as simply the critical process extended into the observation of the natural world. "Science," he wrote in 1889, "is nothing else than knowledge of the facts and laws of the universe." But these "facts and laws" do not constitute an absolute truth any more than do religious creeds. Science does not advance the interests of an Absolute Truth. Those engaged in modern science, LeSueur concluded, have a far more humble task: they "are simply gathering facts and deducing laws, subject to rectification when further facts shall have been gathered."[31]

This commitment to a scientific spirit conceived largely as the process of continual critical enquiry was most evident in LeSueur's response to the charge that the science of his day was as dogmatic as the institutional Christianity which was then under attack. No article published in Canada set this charge forward more clearly, or with more force, than "'The Marvels of Scientific Logic,' " by 'G,' of Toronto. The triumphs of physical science since the time of Bacon, said 'G,' were both magnificent and indisputable. Science had liberated itself from the "fetters" of theological "slavery" and the "tyranny of mind" that such a restriction imposed. Yet it had liberated men from one form of mental slavery only to subject them to another, "a dogmatism which makes man the foolish sport of undesigning chance."[32] With its emphasis on the reality of the 'Seen' as opposed to the 'Unseen' and its commitment to sensory experience as the datum of consciousness and belief, it declares triumphantly that Haeckel and Huxley have a better *a priori* claim on "truth" than St. Paul. It insists on positive "proof" for the verification of all laws, yet though it cannot disprove the existence of an intelligent Creator of the universe or the existence of a universal moral order derived from laws of the world of the Spirit, it nevertheless rejects these as patently false mainly on the basis of their inconsistency with scientific postulates. "If she cannot fully explain the mystery that lies all around her," concluded 'G,' "let her confess that for her at least the *super*natural exists, and let her learn humility."[33]

LeSueur was scarcely one to take the problems of dogmatism lightly. "The great intellectual issue of the present day," he wrote in 1886, "however, some may try to disguise it, is that between dogma on the one hand and the free spirit of scientific enquiry on the other."[34] He made no attempt to conceal the fact, as his article "Morality and Religion" shows, that to his mind specific religious "systems"—theologies—constituted "dogmatism" as he elsewhere defined it: "a traditional opinion held and defended on account of its assumed practical value, rather than on account of its truth."[35] The scientific spirit stood in direct opposition to dogmatism; yet LeSueur admitted that science was not always undogmatic. Its very success in enlargening men's understanding of their world had led it to this dangerous trap. "Dogmatism," he warned when discussing the scientific spirit, "is nothing but the temper of command unreasonably exercised. Science in the present day wields command, and it only too easily falls into the snare of dogmatism." (p. 107) The remedy for this situation was for scientists constantly to remind themselves that all scientific theories are essentially provisional, and any theory framed by them is "a working hypothesis and no more." (p. 109) Hence the scientific spirit, like the critical spirit in general, must also be characterized by humility. Again like the critical spirit it must also have as its ultimate end the pursuit of culture, the quest for individual, social, and moral perfection. If the scientist is to assume the momentous task of aiding man "to interpret [to other men] . . . the world in which he lives," he has assumed a burden which he must not take lightly: "[I]t is, therefore, of vast importance that the leaders in scientific investigation should set clearly before the world where the chief interest and glory of science lies, that they should visibly make it the instructor of humanity to all noble ends, that they should put it forward as the great liberaliser of thought, the enemy of superstition and confusion, the beautifier of life, and that in which man's highest faculties can find unfailing exercise and satisfaction." (p. 111)

This assertion of the cultural aims of science would have been severely undermined, however, if LeSueur had been unable to counter the charge that science was materialistic. LeSueur's conception of social progress was that of an evolutionary and positivistic naturalist. How, then, could he separate himself and his philosophical outlook from this charge? One writer in *Rose-Belford's Canadian Monthly* had asked, rhetorically, what "materialism" was and then defined it: "It is the supposition that all the changes of the universe, all the phenomena of the natural and of what *we* may call the spiritual world, are due to the combination of primordial atoms whose 'essential properties are extension and solidarity.' "[36] Was this not a more or less accurate description of LeSueur's philosophy, and was his talk of science as the "beautifier of life" and the minister of "man's highest faculties" not simply a gratuitous addendum to a materialistic view of life?

The answer to this question lies not in LeSueur's social philosophy but in his psychology. In his thinking about the mind he accepted the "scheme of scientific ideas" which, as Alfred North Whitehead claimed, has dominated thought since the seventeenth century. This thought, Whitehead stated, "involves a fundamental duality, with *material* on one hand, and on the other hand *mind*."[37] This was one of the costs of the scientific revolution of that century, for it resulted, as one historian of psychology has observed, in "the isolation of mind from nature and the study of purposive behaviour from the advance of the scientific method. The fragmentation of the world into primary and secondary qualities, outer and inner, body and mind, and the exclusion of final causes from science have plagued the study of mind and behavior at least since Descartes."[38] LeSueur was a dualist within this tradition, an observer whose belief in the inviolable distinctions between "mind" and "matter" was entrenched by the authority of science. Yet his dualism, perhaps reinforced by his original training in the tenets of "Common Sense," was articulated at a time when scientists such as Karl Vogt and his followers, working in the area of physiology, were uncovering the mysteries of the central nervous system and making the distinction between "mind" and "brain" increasingly murky.[39] The fragmentation of the old mind-body dichotomy introduced immense problems for many individuals, especially those who dealt professionally with the mentally ill. In Canada, for example, both Dr. Daniel Clark, in charge of the Toronto Asylum for the Insane, and Dr. R.M. Bucke, Superintendant of the Provincial Asylum in London, Ontario, went through much intellectual agony to reconcile the findings of the new developments in physiology with their own moral and emotional constitutions.[40]

The extent to which LeSueur knew of the work of such psychologists as Franz Joseph Gall, Johannes Muller, and Sir David Ferrier is not known. What is certain is that he did not relinquish his belief in the dualism of mind and body. For him, as for R.M. Bucke, the mind and the body were essentially distinct: the processes of thought and the processes of biology operated at different yet parallel planes. LeSueur therefore rejected flatly the findings of "the typical physiologist" of his day, "whose passion was to show that the various modes of social action were nothing more or higher than the processes of secretion, digestion, nutrition, &c., with which his peculiar studies had rendered him familiar." (p. 100) Even more reprehensible to LeSueur than this materialistic physiologist, who extended the principles of biology into the study of social action, was the materialist who "loves to dwell on the physical basis of mind, and to ignore the utter impossibility of expressing any of the phenomena of mind in terms of matter." (p. 100) Here LeSueur agreed with Tyndall: matter cannot be transformed into thought. To accept such an unthinkable notion would undermine the basis of moral judgement and render statements of value—words like "wise or foolish, just or unjust, brave or cowardly"—meaningless. Furthermore, it would degrade the idea of thought itself. The "true scientist," whose aim, like the philosopher, is the pursuit of Culture, will not accept such a false view of the scientific spirit: "no one knows better than a true man of science," LeSueur wrote, "that nerve vibrations and molecular movements in the brain are no more the equivalent of thought than the pen with which Tennyson wrote, was the equivalent of 'In Memoriam.' " (p. 101)

Here is a perfect example of the way certain scientific findings can be drawn upon and others ignored to support an individual's moral and intellectual point of view. LeSueur clearly recognized that an acceptance of the findings of certain of the physiologists and psychologists of his day would have called severely into question the whole superstructure upon which Christian metaphysics rested; yet such an acceptance would thereby have also challenged the reality of a spiritual world independent of both matter and Christianity. He was unwilling to give that world up.

An examination of LeSueur's essay, "Materialism and Positivism," shows a fundamental belief in two inviolable orders of phenomena, one of mind or spirit and another of matter. Comtean positivism appealed to LeSueur not only because it was progressivist, organic, and universalistic, but also because it did not essentially challenge the existence of the spiritual world. It did not doubt the existence of a universal moral order. It was a "positive philosophy" because it did not seek to invoke spiritual authorities; it was content to deal with facts—that is, with "whatever produces a complete and definite impression upon the mind." (p. 132) Yet it was *not* materialistic, for it did not necessarily limit "facts," positive knowledge, to the world of material substance. "Now, the difference between the materialist and the positivist lies in just this," he wrote, "that the former is embarrassed at the decided effects which he sees produced by impalpable things, while the latter escapes such embarrassment entirely, simply by not having set up any arbitrary standard of what constitutes reality. The materialist does not want to recognize anything as real that does not more or less resemble his piece of granite, that does not affect the tactual sense; while the positivist is content to recognize all things as real that reveal their existence to the mind by affecting it in a definite manner." (p. 133) Here LeSueur's dualism came in very handy. Just as there is a faculty of mind which operates at a separate plane from the bodily functions, so there is also a distinct emotional and moral nature which functions in relationship to a "reality" different from that involved in man's physical relationship with nature. The hold upon the Victorian mind of the school of Reid and Stewart was a tenacious one indeed.

It is important to recall the extent to which such a view was as fundamental an intellectual assumption in LeSueur's day as the "reality" of the "stimulus-response" construct is to ours. In 1879, LeSueur reviewed R.M. Bucke's book, *Man's Moral Nature* (1879), and confessed that he was "struck" by it. By 1879 Bucke had begun to acquire a reputation on the North American continent as one of the most innovative medics engaged in psychological research. One passage in particular from the book of this authority on human psychology engaged LeSueur's interest:

> The activity and efficiency of the intellectual nature is largely dependent upon the degree of development of the moral nature, which last is undoubtedly the driving-power of our mental mechanism, as the great sympathetic is the driving-power of our bodily organization. What I mean is, and I think everyone will agree with me here, that, with the same intellectual power, the outcome of that power will be vastly greater with a high moral nature behind it than it will be with a low moral nature behind it. In other words, that, with a given brain, a man who has strong and high desires will arrive at more and truer results of reflection than if, with the same brain, his desires are comparatively mean and low.[41]

Bucke, like LeSueur, assumed that the moral nature had a distinct and autonomous existence within the human constitution. Like LeSueur (and like Comte), he also believed that this moral nature existed in different men at different levels.

LeSueur was convinced that Bucke was right: the lessons of everyday experience told him so. Some men, even though intelligent, fail to make a mark on society because they have a poorly-developed moral nature. They have no distinct "moral aims," do not "aspire to moral influence," are not "compelled to any enterprises of moral conquest," and "do not appeal to the emotional side of any one's nature."[42] On the other hand, men of "culture and humanity" do not lead such narrow lives. Theirs is an intellectual power energized and given direction by a highly developed moral nature. They see what others fail to see: *They see into themselves,* and, seeing into themselves, they see into others. They are at home, so to speak, in the region of the soul." The ultimate lesson of Bucke's book was thus also the lesson of Arnold's *Culture and Anarchy*: Bucke showed "in a very striking manner how natural is the connection between 'Sweetness' and 'light'."[43]

The operation of these assumptions within LeSueur's mind made Herbert Spencer a likely authority upon whom to draw for ideas. In the 1870s and 1880s Spencer's reputation as the greatest man of his age reached its peak in the Anglo-American community. His "synthetic philosophy" was both comprehensive and scientific and made the British social philosopher, in the words of Richard Hofstadter, "the metaphysician of the homemade intellectual, and the prophet of the crackerbarrel agnostic."[44] His was a philosophy that—because of its comprehensiveness—was all things to all men, and scarcely an intellectual in the transatlantic community remained unaware of "Spencerism."[45]

The dominant view of Spencer's social philosophy that emerges from Richard Hofstadter's book, *Social Darwinism in American Thought*, (1944) is of a grand "scientific" justification for an economic enterprise unimpeded by government regulation or control, a philosophy which in the hands of Spencerian disciples such as the American social theorist, William Graham Sumner, could give sanction to such claims as that which said: "The millionaires are a product of natural selection, acting on the whole body of men to pick out those who can meet the requirement of certain work to be done."[46] W.D. LeSueur drew no such conclusions from his own reading of either Spencer or Darwin. He objected strenuously in 1885 to John Fiske's claim that "in the desperate struggle for existence no peculiarity has been too insignificant for natural selection to seize and enhance," for such a view seemed to suggest that natural selection was "some vigilant intelligence watching for opportunities to advance its designs."[47] Natural selection, he insisted, carries with it no differentiation into "good" or "bad." "Darwin has discovered no law in nature by which good qualities (as such) are produced; he has simply discovered a law by which all kinds of qualities (differentiations), good, bad, and indifferent, are produced, and by which the bad ones (bad, i.e., in relation to the environment) are knocked off, like so many projection angles, by the destruction of the individuals manifesting them. . . . If, therefore, we believe in natural selection, let us believe in it as it is, and be content to speak of it as it is. *Let us not make a god of what is, in its essence, the very negation of intelligent action.*"[48]

LeSueur's insistence upon a radical separation of ethics from the mechanism by which evolution took place did not presume, however, a divorce of ethics from the evolutionary process itself. It was precisely because Spencer's "synthetic philosophy" was also fundamentally an ethical one (see note 16) that he was attracted to it. Furthermore, while Spencer's comprehensive system treated all things as subject to natural laws it did not deny the possibility of a divinity and the existence of universal moral laws, or obliterate the spiritual-material dualism which was so basic to LeSueur's discussions of the "moral nature" of man. Against the charge that a "natural" system of morality is impossible since morality is derived from theology, LeSueur replied: "The broad fact that everywhere we see traces, however rude, of moral feeling is precisely the foundation upon which my whole argument is built; men cannot live together unless they are partially moral; unless, in other words, some general good results from their association." (p. 116) He also denied emphatically that the evolutionism of Darwin and Spencer "materialized" the human spirit and involved "caprice in morality, tyranny in government, uncertainty in science" along with "a denial of immortality and a disbelief in the personality of man and of God," and did so on the grounds that Spencer in no way challenged the existence of the world of spirit or mind:

Evolution, as taught by Herbert Spencer, does nothing to weaken the fundamental distinction between subject and object, between mind and matter. If Spencer teaches that both these aspects of existence may, or rather must, find their union and identification in the Unknowable Cause, he does no more than the Christian, who believes that God is the author both of the visible world and of the human spirit. Evolution gives material laws for human thought, only in so far as it shows the dependence of each higher plane of life on those below it. . . .[49]

Nor, he added, did evolutionism *ipso facto* seek to subvert belief in immortality or in a personal God:

The doctrine of evolution is simply a mode of conceiving and accounting for the succession of events on the earth. It is in no sense a metaphysical or ontological doctrine, and lays no claim to the absoluteness with which metaphysical and ontological doctrines are invested. It does not pretend to penetrate to essences or to unveil final causes. If it is regarded by some as solving all mysteries, that is simply because they do not adequately understand it. Mr. Spencer certainly has never given countenance to such an idea. It does, however, as Darwin said of his philosophy, call constant attention to the need for providing all things. It strikes at the idea of authority, always excepting the constitutional authority, as we may term it, of demonstrated truth.[50]

The doctrines of immortality and the idea of God, LeSueur concluded, were undermined only in the sense that modern science had discredited the theological system which served as the authority upon which such doctrines had been taught. Science, he added, does not doubt that such notions may be true; it simply asks that they be given "more conclusive demonstration" by defending them "in the open field of philosophy."[51]

The second chapter of W.D. LeSueur's inner biography was in general an optimistic one. It saw him reject theological systems of morals in favour of the edifice of positivism and, in particular, of Herbert Spencer's attempt to show "the evolution of morality as an objective process." (p.120) History, for Spencer and for LeSueur, was primarily the study of human conduct, and morality was one aspect of that conduct—"developed conduct." History seemed to show that human conduct, if looked at objectively (that is, from a social point of view rather than from the perspective of one's own consciousness), was in a state of constant ascendance from lower to higher, simplicity to complexity. In the long course of human evolution a point beyond the struggle for subsistence had been reached in certain societies, a stage at which the power of ethical choice in human action had become possible. Spencer's view was that the best interest of the individual is generally with obeying the dictates of his "higher" (later-developed) faculties through the voluntary subordination of the "lower." This requires self-control, but subordination of self in this way not only places man in a greater harmony with society but also with himself. (pp. 123-124)

LeSueur drew upon evolutionary science in a way decidedly different from American Social Darwinists such as William Graham Sumner. He used Spencer's naturalism, his organicism, and his universalism as a means of consolidating the social bond, not as a rationalization for the existence or hegemony of an individualistic ethic. In part, this response was due to the dictates of LeSueur's own intellectual and moral premises. But if his life can be seen as one manifestation of what was earlier called the Anglo-Canadian moral imagination—if, that is, it represents part of a continuing tradition in Canadian social thought—then perhaps LeSueur's particular use of Spencer's ideas is a small but not insignificant commentary on the nature of the Canadian cultural experience itself. Late nineteenth century America can perhaps generally be characterized as a country overwhelmingly dominated by Frye's myth of freedom; and Sumnerian Social Darwinism gave reign to such freedom in the sphere of economic action. The myth of freedom in Victorian Canada was compromised significantly by a stronger presence of the myth of concern. Physically in the New World but culturally of the Old, those such as LeSueur drew naturally upon the historical ties and organic evolution of Canadian society.

Herbert Spencer, as LeSueur understood him, had much to contribute to an understanding of such a culture and society. The organic analogy which was the basis of Spencer's thought could be used to criticize a *laissez-faire* society, for it stressed interrelationships and mutual dependence. While Spencer's methodological individualism allowed him to elevate the role of the individual within society (''society existed for the benefit of its members'', not the other way around), his rejection of a mechanistic model of society in favour of the idea of ''The Social Organism'' (as he often called his basic metaphor) equally insisted upon the symbiotic relationship of individual and society:

> The individual citizen [is] embedded in the social organism as one of its units, moulded by its influence and aiding reciprocally to remould it.

> The cardinal truth, difficult adequately to appreciate, is that while the forms and laws of each society are the consolidated products of the emotions and ideas of those who lived through the past, they are made operative by the subordination of existing emotions and ideas to them.[52]

Such ideas could have much meaning for English-Canada, which drew seriously from both the liberal and conservative philosophical traditions and the culture of which was something of a fusion of the two.

While not ignoring the individualistic strand in Spencer's philosophy, LeSueur drew upon the organic aspect of his thought to show the way in which Spencer could provide a naturalistic social ethic for the modern age. ''Let me not hesitate to say,'' he wrote, ''that many in this generation are willing to take their stand, and live their lives, upon such basis of truth as they can discover in nature and in human relations. . . . Human ties are not less tender or precious for the knowledge that we hold our treasures in earthen vessels.'' Here were signs that William Dawson LeSueur, Canada's philosophical radical of the nineteenth century, was ''radical'' for a fundamentally ''conservative'' purpose. As in his writings on criticism, so too in his writings on the scientific spirit was the tension between the modern myths of freedom and concern and the corresponding polarity of liberty and order present. In the second chapter of his internal biography, LeSueur sought to reconcile the spirit of science with the spirit of Christianity,

the concern for enquiry into all things with the concern for the preservation of human community. "What we want," said the exponent of the
critical path, the opponent of Christian doctrine, "is a 'natural piety'
that shall link us in thought and sympathy with both the past and the
future of mankind." (p. 119)

NOTES

1. Sara Jeannette Duncan, "Saunterings—The Age," *The Week*, Vol.
IV (March 3, 1887), pp. 216-217.

2. Prior to 1872, Canadian periodicals were generally of a local nature
and often experienced only a brief existence due to a number of publishing
difficulties. The periodical press from the publication of the *Canadian Monthly
and National Review* (1872-78) on was of a more national scope and while these
periodicals suffered no few publishing problems, throughout the rest of the 19th
century one such journal or another was in existence: *Belford's Monthly
Magazine* (1876-78), *Rose-Belford's Canadian Monthly and National Review*
(1878-82), *The Bystander* (1880—intermittently to 1890), *The Week* (1883-
1896). See R.L. McDougall, "A Study of Canadian Periodical Literature of the
Nineteenth Century" (unpublished Ph.D. dissertation, University of Toronto,
1950), pp. 4-5.

3. W.J.R., "Man Here and Hereafter," *Belford's Monthly Magazine*
Vol. III (May, 1878), p. 757.

4. Fidelis, "The Seen and the Unseen," *Canadian Monthly and
National Review*, Vol. IX (June, 1876), p. 495. "Fidelis" was the pseudonym
that Miss Machar (the daughter of a Principal of Queen's University) used
throughout her life. See Norah Story, *The Oxford Companion to Canadian
History and Literature* (Toronto: Oxford University Press, 1967), p. 488, for
biographical information.

5. Goldwin Smith, "The Immortality of the Soul," *CMNR*, Vol. IX
(May, 1876), p. 408.

6. James DeKoven, "The Gates of the Invisible," quoted in Paul A.
Carter, *The Spiritual Crisis of the Gilded Age* (DeKalb: Northern Illinois
University Press, 1971), p. 16.

7. 'H.', "A Few Words About Nature," *Dalhousie Gazette*, Vol. VII,
no. 3 (December 19, 1874), pp. 17-19.

8. Carl Berger, The Vision of Grandeur" (unpublished Ph.D. dissertation, University of Toronto, 1966), p. 434. LeSueur believed that Fiske's
attempts at such a reconciliation were wholly inadequate. See W.D. LeSueur,
"Evolution and the Destiny of Man," *Popular Science Monthly*, Vol. XXVI
(February, 1885), pp. 456-468.

9. L, "Science," *Dalhousie Gazette*, n.s. Vol. IV, no. 5 (Jan. 25,
1879), pp. 50-52.

10. [anon.], "Is a Belief In Darwinism Consistent With a Teleological
View of the Natural World?" *Dalhousie Gazette*, Vol. XVIII, no. 11 (April,
1886), pp. 141-143.

11. J.E. Creighton, "The Age and Its Tendencies," *Dalhousie Gazette*,
Vol. XVIII, no. 10 (March 27, 1886), p. 123.

12. Berger, *op. cit.*

13. M.A. Jevons, "One Faith in Many Forms," *Rose-Belford's Canadian Monthly*, Vol. 4 (October, 1884), p. 344.

14. "Morality and Religion" [unsigned editorial], Toronto *Mail*, January 10, 1880, p. 2.

15. For an indication of the international debate, see "A Vindication of Scientific Ethics," note 10, below p. 383.

16. See Herbert Spencer, *The Data of Ethics* (New York: D. Appleton and Co., 1883), Ch. II, "The Evolution of Conduct," pp. 8-20, and *passim*; J.D.Y. Peel, *Herbert Spencer; the Evolution of a Sociologist* (New York: Basic Books, 1971), pp. 84 ("The fundamental purpose of Spencer's whole lifework was to provide a scientific morality; The *Ethics* was the culmination of the whole. Years later, in the *Autobiography*, he stated again that the aim of philosophy was to provide 'a basis for a right rule of life, individual and social.' "), pp. 85-86, 97-98, 110-111, 133-136, 150-153. LeSueur's representation of Spencer's philosophy, in his article, "Mr. Spencer and His Critics"/"A Vindication of Scientific Ethics," may be seen as accurate. Spencer, having read the article, wrote to the author: "You have not only given a very admirable exposition of certain of the cardinal principles contained in that work but have very effectively enforced them by arguments of your own." Herbert Spencer to W.D. LeSueur, April 27, 1880, W.D. LeSueur Papers, Vol. I, file 4, PAC.

17. See D.H. MacVicar, "Recent Aspects of Materialism: being A Lecture delivered at the Opening of the Session of 1871-72, of the Presbyterian College, Montreal" (Montreal: J.C. Becket, 1871), pp. 1-11; Rev. James Carmichael, "Design and Darwinism" (Toronto: Hunter, Rose, & Co., 1880), pp. 5; Surena, "Modern Scepticism," *Canadian Monthly and National Review*, Vol. II (August, 1872), p. 173; "Round the Table," *ibid.*, XI (May, 1877), pp. 547-48; 'G.,' " 'The marvels of Scientific Logic'," *Rose-Belford's Canadian Monthly*, Vol. V (October, 1880), pp. 361-371. For an indication of the plight in which men suspended between the worlds of religion and science could find themselves, see these articles on W.H. Mallock by R.W. Boodle: "Modern Pessimism," *Rose-Belford's Canadian Monthly*, Vol. III (June, 1879), pp. 591-601; "Mr. Mallock: A Retrospect," *ibid.*, Vol. VI (February, 1881), pp. 195-203; "Mr. Mallock's 'Romance of the 19th C'—a Review," *ibid.*, Vol. VII (September, 1881), pp. 322-327.

18. Each of these examples is drawn from MacVicar, *op. cit.*, pp. 3-4. In a "Prefatory Note" to this pamphlet, MacVicar noted that "the arguments advanced against Materialism were delivered *in substance* in the Class-room three years ago, and in several respects more fully developed than in their present form."

19. For Tyndall's address and a discussion of the context in which it was delivered, see George Basalla, William Coleman and Robert H. Kargon (eds.), *Victorian Science; a Self-Portrait from the Presidential Addresses to the British Association for the Advancement of Science* (New York: Doubleday, 1970), pp. 436-478. The quotation from Tyndall is drawn from pp. 474-475.

20. *Ibid.*, p. 437.

21. Alexander Johnson, "Science and Religion; an Address Delivered at the Convocation of McGill University, May 1st, 1876, to the Bachelors of

Applied Science'' (Montreal: Dawson Brothers, 1876), pp. 6-7. The address was originally published in the Montreal press at the request of the students.

22. *Ibid.*, p. 7.

23. A Canadian by birth (he was born in Kingston in 1848, the son of Queen's College's Professor of Greek), G.J. Romanes was raised in England, to which his family returned when the father came into an inheritance. Although his many biological writings gave him a reputation as one of the leading scientific naturalists of his day (the *Times* stated in 1886 that ''Mr. George Romanes appears to be the biological investigator upon whom in England the mantle of Mr. Darwin has most conspicuously descended''), he has, perhaps more accurately, been described as one of those men whose philosophies of life hovered ''between science and religion'': ''Romanes was . . . clearly a man of unsettled intellectual convictions who throughout life kept hoping to discover a single set of principles that would satisfy all conditions.'' Hence his book, *A Candid Examination of Theism* (1878), published under the pseudonym ''Physicus,'' saw no validity in the orthodox arguments for natural religion, while his posthumously-published *Thoughts on Religion* revealed that he refused to give up the possibility of a religious interpretation of man and nature. *Christian Prayer and Natural Laws* (1873), written while Romanes was still a student at Cambridge, was an essay which sought a middle way between science and religion. ''The essay, though clearly favouring the possibility of answered prayer,'' wrote F.M. Turner, ''revealed neither zeal for orthodoxy nor firm adherence to naturalistic opinion. Rather, it sought to fend off the dogmatic claims of both positions.'' The above biographical information and quotations are drawn from ''George John Romanes: From Faith to Fatih,'' Ch. 6 in F.M. Turner, *Between Science and Religion* (New Haven: Yale University Press, 1974), pp. 134-163.

24. Other articles which bear directly on the controversy are: John Tyndall, ''Reply to the Critics of the Belfast Address,'' *Canadian Monthly and National Review*, Vol. VII (February, 1875), pp. 183-195; ''Current Literature'' [an editorial note], *ibid.*, Vol. VIII (December, 1875), pp. 549-551; John Tyndall, '' 'Materialism' and Its Opponents,'' *ibid.*, (January, 1876), pp. 56-68; Rev. James Martineau, ''Modern Materialism: Its Attitude Towards Theology,'' *ibid.*, Vol. IX (March, 1876), pp. 223-237; John Watson, ''Science and Religion; a Reply to Prof. Tyndall on Materialism and Its Opponents,'' *Ibid.*, Vol. IX (May, 1876), pp. 384-397; John Watson, ''Professor Tyndall's 'Materialism','' *Rose Belford's Canadian Monthly*, Vol. I (1878), pp. 282-288. It must be stressed that almost every article or pamphlet published in Canada during the 1870s which discussed the relationship between science and religion referred, either directly or obliquely, to Tyndall and the ''materialism'' question.

25. The debate was heralded by a detailed review of Romanes' book in the *Canadian Monthly and National Review*, Vol. VII (March, 1875), pp. 284-286. It was launched, however, by an article by Agnes Maule Machar which reviewed the ''Prayer Question'' as it had evolved in England (and as set forth in an Appendix to Romanes' book entitled, ''The Physical Efficacy of Prayer''): see A.M. Machar, ''Prayer for Daily Bread,'' *ibid.*, Vol. VII (May, 1875), pp. 415-425. This was followed by LeSueur's rebuttal, ''Prayer and Modern Thought,'' *ibid.*, Vol. VIII (August, 1875), pp. 145-155. After the publication

of these two articles the debates proceeded apace: Fidelis, "Prayer and Modern Doubt," *ibid.*, Vol. VIII (September, 1875), pp. 224-236; Fidelis, "Prayer and Christian Belief," *ibid.*, Vol. VIII (October, 1875), pp. 328-334; S.E. Dawson, "Prayer and Modern Science," *ibid.*, Vol. VIII (December, 1875), pp. 512-522; George J. Romanes, "The Physical Efficacy of Prayer," *ibid.*, Vol. IX (March, 1876), pp. 211-221; Fidelis, "The Divine Law of Prayer," *ibid.*, Vol. X (August, 1876), pp. 144-155.

26. See: Goldwin Smith, "The Immortality of the Soul," *Canadian Monthly and National Review*, Vol. IX (May, 1876), pp. 408-416; Fidelis, "The Seen and the Unseen," *ibid.*, Vol. IX (June, 1876), pp. 495-508; Professor J.E. Wells, "Evolution and Immortality," *ibid.*, Vol. X (October, 1876), pp. 291-298; John Watson, "Darwinism and Morality," *ibid.*, Vol. X (October, 1876), pp. 319-326; J.A. Allen, "The Evolution of Morality: A Reply," *ibid.*, Vol. XI (May, 1877), pp. 490-501; John Watson, "The Ethical Aspect of Darwinism: a Rejoinder," *ibid.*, Vol. XI (June, 1877), pp. 638-644; W.J.R. [W.J. Rattray], "Man Here and Hereafter," *Belford's Monthly Magazine*, Vol. III (May, 1878), pp. 757-778; A.W. Gundry, "Spencer's 'Data of Ethics'," *Rose-Belford's Canadian Monthly*, Vol. III (December, 1879), pp. 646-650; Goldwin Smith, "The Prospects of a Moral Interregnum" [a revised version of an article published slightly earlier in *Atlantic Monthly*], *ibid.*, Vol. III (December, 1879), pp. 651-663; G.A.M., "Mr. Goldwin Smith's *Atlantic Monthly* article," *ibid.*, Vol. III (December, 1879), pp. 663-665; W.D. LeSueur, "The Future of Morality," *ibid.*, Vol. IV (January, 1880), pp. 74-82; W.D. LeSueur, "Morality and Religion," *ibid.*, Vol. IV (February, 1880), pp. 166-171; Rev. J.F. Stevenson, "Morality and the Gospel," *ibid.*, Vol. IV (April, 1880), pp. 335-342; Fidelis, "The Source of Moral Life," *ibid.*, Vol. IV (April, 1880), pp. 343-351; W.D. LeSueur, "Mr. Spencer and His Critics," *ibid.*, Vol. IV (April, 1880), pp. 413-422; W.D. LeSueur, "Morality and Religion Again.—A Word With My Critics," *ibid.*, Vol. IV (June, 1880), pp. 642-655; W.D. LeSueur, "Mr. Goldwin Smith on 'The Data of Ethics,'" *Popular Science Monthly*, Vol. XXII (December, 1882), pp. 145-156.

27. One such exception was J.A. Allen, "The Evolution of Morality . . . ," *op. cit.*

28. See Watson's essays, above, but especially his essay, "A Phase of Modern Thought," *Rose-Belford's Canadian Monthly*, n.s. Vol. III (November, 1879), pp. 457-72.

29. See G.J. Romanes' critique of LeSueur's first article on the "Prayer Question," in "The Physical Efficacy of Prayer," *op. cit.*

30. LeSueur's essay criticising Fiske was "Evolution and the Destiny of Man," *Popular Science Monthly*, Vol. XXVI (February, 1885), pp. 456-468; his essay on Lyman Abbott was "Evolution Bounded by Theology," *ibid.*, Vol. XXIX (June, 1886), pp. 145-153; on Porter, "Ex-President Porter on Evolution," *ibid.*, XXIX (September, 1886), pp. 577-594. LeSueur's debate with G.M. Grant began with a discussion of the merits of the theological claims made by the American evangelists, Dwight L. Moody and Ira Sankey, but soon broadened to a full discussion of the place of Christianity itself in "modern culture." LeSueur wrote under the pseudonym, 'Laon,' but by 1885 'Laon' had been identified in print: see William Cushing (ed.), *Initials and Pseudonyms*, rev. ed., 1st series (New York: Crowell, 1885), p. 165. The editor is indebted to

Ms. Marilyn G. Flitton for this last reference. The 'Laon'-Grant debate consisted of the following pieces: Laon, "Messrs. Moody and Sankey and Revivalism," *Canadian Monthly and National Review,* Vol. VII (June, 1875), pp. 510-513; Rev. G.M. Grant, "Laon on 'Messers. Moody and Sankey and Revivalism,' " *ibid.*, Vol. VIII (September, 1875), 250-255; Loan, "Proofs and Disproofs," *ibid.*, Vol. VIII (October, 1875), pp. 339-348; Grant, "Christianity and Modern Thought," *ibid.*, Vol. VIII (November, 1875), pp. 437-441; Laon, "Modern Culture and Christianity," *ibid.*, Vol. VIII (December, 1875), pp. 523-533. For the debate with Bishop John Travers Lewis, see: "Agnosticism—a lecture Delivered in St. George's Hall, Kingston, on the Occasion of the Meeting of the Synod of the Diocese, June 12, 1883, by the Lord Bishop of Ontario," (Kingston: British Whig Steam Presses, 1883), pp. 32; W.D. LeSueur, "A Defence of Modern Thought . . ." (Toronto: Hunter, Rose & Co., 1884), pp. 40; Vindex, "A Criticism of Mr. LeSueur's Pamphlet, entitled 'Defence of Modern Thought' " (n.p., n.d.), pp. 16; W.D. LeSueur's, "Evolution and the Positive Aspects of Modern Thought. In Reply to the Bishop of Ontario's Second Lecture on 'Agnosticism' " (Ottawa: A.S. Woodburn, 1884), pp. 43. The editor has been unable to locate a copy of Lewis's second lecture.

31. W.D. LeSueur, "Science and Its Accusers," *Popular Science Monthly,* Vol. XXXIV (January, 1889), pp. 379, 375.

32. 'G,' " 'The Marvels of Scientific Logic,' " *op. cit.*, p. 361.

33. *Ibid.*, p. 371.

34. LeSueur, "Ex-President Porter on Evolution," *op. cit.*, p. 577.

35. *Ibid.*

36. C.W. Parkin, "Diderot and Materialism," *Rose-Belford's Canadian Monthly,* Vol. VII (December, 1881), p. 642.

37. Alfred North Whitehead, *Science and the Modern World* (New York: The Free Press, 1967), p. 57.

38. Robert M. Young, *Mind, Brain and Adaptation in the Nineteenth Century* (Oxford: Clarendon Press, 1970), p. 2.

39. It was Vogt who had pronounced, in his *Physiological Epistles* (1847), that "the brain secretes thought, just as the liver secrets bile." See ch. 2, "Materialism, Naturalism and Agnosticism," in John Passmore, *A Hundred Years of Philosophy* (Harmondsworth, England: Penguin Books, 1970), pp. 35-47, for background and context.

40. See Daniel Clark, "Physiology in Thought, Conduct, and Belief," *Rose-Belford's Canadian Monthly,* Vol. VI (April, 1881), pp. 363-377; R.M. Bucke, "The Correlation of the Vital and Physical Force," *British American Journal*, Vol. III (May, June, July, 1862), pp. 161-167, 225-238; R.M. Bucke, "The Moral Nature and the Great Sympathetic," *American Journal of Insanity,* Vol. XXXV (October 1878), pp. 229-253. James Horne, "R.M. Bucke: Pioneer Psychiatrist, Practical Mystic," *Ontario History,* Vol. LIX (1967), pp. 197-208.

41. W.D. LeSueur, "The Moral Nature and Intellectual Power," *Rose-Belford's Canadian Monthly,* Vol. III (July, 1879), pp. 104-105.

42. *Ibid.*, p. 105.

43. *Ibid.* LeSueur's italics.

44. Richard Hofstadter, *Social Darwinism in American Thought* (Boston: Beacon Press, 1970), p. 32.

45. See *ibid.*, ch. 2, "The Vogue of Spencer," pp. 31-50, and *passim.*

For a more recent estimate of the rise and decline of Spencer's reputation see Peel, *op. cit.,* ch. 1, "The Man and His Work," pp. 1-32, and ch. 9, "History's Revenge," pp. 224-248.

46. From William Graham Sumner, *The Challenge of Facts,* quoted in Hofstadter, *op. cit.,* p. 59. See Richard D. Altick, *Victorian People and Ideas* (New York: W.W. Norton & Co., Inc., 1973), p. 232, for an equation of "Social Darwinism" (in this sense) with the philosophy of Herbert Spencer.

47. LeSueur, "Evolution and the Destiny of Man," *op. cit.,* p. 467.

48. *Ibid.,* pp. 467-468. Italics in original.

49. LeSueur, "Ex-President Porter on Evolution," *op. cit.,* pp. 589-590.

50. *Ibid.,* p. 591.

51. *Ibid.*

52. The substance of this paragraph is drawn from Peel, *op. cit.,* chapter 7: "The Organic Analogy", pp. 166-191.

5. Science and Materialism (1877)

There is no question that the cardinal fact in the history of the nineteenth century is the prodigious development of natural science. Considering how near at hand, for the most part, are the objects with which natural science deals, it seems wonderful at first sight that the scientific age of the world should have come at so comparatively late a period of human history. The ancient Greeks are, to this day, our masters in art, so far, at least, as sculpture and architecture are concerned; but their scientific attainments were of the most meagre kind. There was no deficiency amongst them of intellectual vigour, or of logical acuteness; while their powers of observation, in all that related to certain aspects of nature, were singularly keen. We must therefore attribute their failure to apply themselves seriously to science, not so much to any want of capacity for that kind of study, as to something in their national character which turned their energies in other directions. The fact is, that the explanation of their backwardness in science is also the explanation of their forwardness in art. Their polytheism peopled the earth for them with gracious ideals; but at the same time it prevented them in a great measure, from realizing the existence of natural laws. Their minds were full of pictures and fancies; and, rejoicing in these, they did not feel the need of any deeper insight into the nature of things than their common experience supplied. Then, just as their superstitions declined, the national genius began to fade. The Romans were not a race to do much for science; their talent was for government; the knowledge they prized was the knowledge of how to deal with men, not how to analyze matter. After the fall of the Roman Empire, a dismal period of barbarism supervened. If we can trust contemporary accounts, Satan—of whom Greeks and Romans to their great happiness had known nothing—would seem to have been let loose for about a thousand years, filling countless minds with the most vivid terrors, and working all manner of mischief upon true believers. If these accounts are true, of course there could be no science where natural law was

SOURCE: *Canadian Monthly and National Review*, Vol. XI (January, 1877), pp. 22-28.

being so constantly broken by this malignant spirit, his emissaries, and his victims; if they are not true, we still see very good reason why natural science should for long ages have made no progress. Aristotle, at the very close of the sixteenth century, was still a standard authority in physics—so much so that Galileo incurred great hostility for proving the master wrong in his assertion that the rapidity of descent of falling bodies was in proportion to their weight. For this inexcusable piece of presumption he was compelled to leave Pisa, where he filled a chair in the University, and where he had taken advantage of the Leaning Tower to make his experiment.

The names of Copernicus, Vesalius, Servetus, Kepler, Galileo, and Toricelli, show us that, in the sixteenth century and beginning of the seventeenth, men had begun to think of the universe as something else than a theatre for the exercise of supernatural powers. A great deal of valuable scientific work had in fact been done when Bacon conceived his great work on the means of advancing science. The merit of Bacon consists not in his own scientific researches, which bear no comparison with those of the men I have named, but in the clearness and vigour with which he grasped the idea of science as a progressive interrogation of nature by means of observation and experiment. Since the time of Bacon, science has, in the main, kept to the true path. Only eight years elapsed between the publication of the *Novum Organum* (1620), and Harvey's immortal disquisition "On the motion of the heart and the circulation of the blood." The same century produced Newton, Boyle, Linnaeus, and a host of other illustrious names; and science henceforth had its recognised place as one of the most important and beneficent branches of human activity.

√ And now where are we? Is it not the case that science, so feeble once in comparison with the strong prepossessions or instinctive beliefs of mankind—science, which formerly but picked up the crumbs that fell from the table of human reason, while metaphysics and theology feasted and lorded it at the board—science, that was persecuted and cast out in the persons of its early professors, its Roger Bacons, Galileos, and Brunos—science, in which men saw no beauty or promise that they should desire it—is it not true that this stone which the builders rejected, has become almost the head of the corner in the edifice of our civilization? Upon what are the eyes of all men waiting, but upon science to heal their diseases, and even cleanse their iniquities? Is it not true that theology itself—I speak now only of what you all know as well as I—is looking to science to place a true interpretation upon its records. "Describe to us," say the theologians,

the physical history of the earth, and whatever you can satisfactorily prove, *that* we shall accept as the true sense of the Mosaic record, no matter what verbal difficulties may stand in the way. You have shown us that we must no longer talk of a six *days'* work in creation; we quite accept your amendment, and shall be prepared to give our best consideration to any others you may propose. As soon as you are quite sure about the doctrine of evolution, we think we shall have no difficulty in finding that, too, in a manner, outlined in our record.

This is an honour to which science in its earlier stages never looked forward. It hoped to unravel progressively the mysteries of nature; but it never expected to be called in to assist in the task of Biblical exegesis. Times have changed since the inventor of the telescope fell into the hands of the tormentors for his speculations on the solar system; or, coming down much later, since Buffon was compelled to pen a very humble retractation of certain errors which the doctors of the Sorbonne asserted they had discovered in his "Système de la Nature." Had he lived in the present day he might have corrected the errors of the doctors.

It would be easy to pursue this line of thought, and to prove by many unimpeachable testimonies the high position that science has won for itself in the modern world; but the easier the task, the less need there is to perform it. Glance at but one sign of the times—the eagerness with which any real master of science—a Huxley, a Tyndall, or a Proctor[1]— is listened to whenever, forsaking the study or the laboratory, he comes before the public as a lecturer. It is not the learned only who flock to hear him; but multitudes of average men and women go to get what instruction they can. They feel their need of it; they know that this is a real world in which they live; they are beginning to have some perception of the immutability of its laws; and, what those laws are, they fain would learn. The gifted scientific teacher occupies indeed a position of great privilege, and, let me add, of great responsibility. He may not succeed in awakening—as of course he does not aim at awakening— those violent emotions which follow upon certain methods of teaching. He neither shouts, nor sings, nor contorts his body, nor heaps up incongruous imagery, nor revels in anecdotes, nor indulges in weak sentimentalism, nor gives way to grotesque violence of language; but he touches the understanding, and shapes opinions, and moulds purposes. It behoves him, therefore, to use his great power with strict conscientiousness for the wisest ends. He must be careful, above all, not to engender a conceit of knowledge on the part of his hearers, nor to illustrate it by anything in his own manner or language. He should caution his hearers against substituting blind deference to his authority, or to any scientific authority, for the blind deference they may have hitherto paid to other authorities. He should speak with certainty only of the known, and with proper reserve of what is only probable or purely hypothetical. He should dwell upon the great truth that emancipation from error means responsibility for a higher mode of life; and that, if it does not result in this, it is valueless, if not worse than valueless in causing truth to be evil spoken of. He should insist strongly on the difference between real knowledge and sham knowledge; between a true insight into facts and grasp of principles on the one hand, and a mere command of phrases on the other. Let him do these things, and abound in doing them, and he will quickly be recognised as the highest type of teacher in this generation.

The function of science is to interpret to man the world in which he lives, and especially the material conditions on which his well-being depends. It explains to him the properties of matter and the constitution of his own physical nature. It is concerned with questions of cause and effect, or antecedence and sequence. It gives him, in regard to many things, a power of prevision which to his ancestors would have seemed simply miraculous. It enables him to wield with ease and certainty some of the mightiest and subtlest forces of nature. It places at his service agencies, such as electricity and magnetism, which as yet far outrun his powers of comprehension. It carries him into regions of the invisible and impalpable, and exhibits to him wonders that utterly dwarf the direct revelations of sense, and seem at times to threaten the fundamental postulates of his philosophy. Science, we may say, is the minister of man's thinking faculty; or we may regard it as the product of that faculty working according to its own laws, just as honey is the product of the instinctive labours of the bee. Manifestly, so long as man thinks, and so long as he has an inexhaustible universe to think in, science must advance; we can set no limit to its conquests. Unless human powers at some point in the future begin to fail, it must continue its beneficent career, giving man wider and wider control over nature, and thus increasing the advantages, and decreasing the disadvantages, of his lot upon earth. Lucretius has drawn a pitiable picture of primitive man roaming naked through the forests, contending at dreadful odds with the inexorable powers of nature, fleeing in terror from wild beasts, and filling his mind with superstitious terrors over and above those which his helpless condition might so well have inspired. The imagination of the poet did but anticipate in this case, as it has done in so many cases, the knowledge obtained from direct observation. We know of tribes at this moment of whom all this is true, and who superadd, what the poet has not thought of placing in his picture, abominable excesses of lust and cruelty. Yet from this lowly origin it is impossible not to believe that the whole human race has sprung; and all that now separates the civilised man of to-day from his savage progenitor shows the work of his thinking faculty, and of those other faculties or capacities of his nature which the power of thought has called into exercise. Primitive man has simply his senses to guide him, and a little superiority in cunning over the beasts of the field; the only force he can wield is that which his muscles supply; the only dangers he can avert—and these of course not always—are such as his senses directly apprize him of; the only benefits he can grasp are such as nature visibly offers. Civilised man uses his senses to guide him to instrumentalities and agencies by which their range is vastly increased. Primitive man grasps a club and feels himself strong; civilised man imprisons fire and water, or mixes a few chemical substances, and he has command of forces that could almost rend the globe. Mr. Spencer expresses the difference by saying that the one has but a very narrow, and the other a comparatively wide and distant, command of his "environment," that is to say, of environing or surrounding objects and conditions. The work of science is, to help us to act not only *here* and *now*, but far away and, as it were, long in the future. When we make provision *now* to fight against an epidemic which science tells us will, in all probability, visit us at a certain time in the future, we are in effect carried forward to that future time, and enabled to deal with its contingencies as if they were present. When, by aid of the telegraph, we receive timely notice of the failure of certain crops in certain places, we make our arrangements to meet, as far as possible, the consequences of the fact. In a thousand ways what we do now has reference, not to the immediate present, but to what we know will be by-and-by. By the aid of science we throw out, as it were, vast feelers—shall I shock you too much by calling them metaphorically *antennae*?—into distant space and time, and regulate our present conduct by what we are thus enabled to perceive. This is having an enlarged grasp of our environment—a somewhat barbarous phrase, perhaps, to those who are unaccustomed to it, but a very useful one to those who feel its force.

As I said some time ago,* we do not come here to discuss mysteries; and I therefore make no apology for these very simple remarks. To some they are the very A. B. C. of knowledge; but others may be helped by them to a more vivid conception than they have hitherto possessed of the nature and function of science. If I can be of assistance to such, I must only crave the patience of the more learned. Now, when we say that *science* gives to man an ever increasing grasp of his environment, we simply mean—what? That the action of man as a thinking being secures him this increasing grasp. Let us now, in the light of this indisputable statement, examine very briefly the question, Whether there is any justification for the prevalent fear that physical science tends to result in materialism.

*i.e. In an earlier part of this address, which as being of merely local interest, has not been reprinted here.

The best definition of materialism I have anywhere met with is that given by Auguste Comte, who speaks of it as a tendency to apply to a higher range of enquiries, the methods appropriate to a lower. He recognizes, accordingly, several kinds of materialism corresponding to the several fundamentally distinct branches of human knowledge. A person conversant with the laws of mechanics, who should insist that these were capable of explaining all chemical phenomena, and who should take a delight in dragging down, so to speak, the more complex modes of action which chemistry reveals, to a mechanical basis, would be, in his way, a materialist. Similarly, a chemist who refused to recognize in the phenomena of life anything but a somewhat obscure chemistry, and who pursued his labours in the same levelling spirit, or as the French would say, *esprit de nivellement*, would also be a materialist. Again, the physiologist, deeply versed in the laws of individual life, whose passion was to show that the various modes of social action were nothing more or higher than the processes of secretion, digestion, nutrition, &c., with which his peculiar studies had rendered him familiar, and who disdained any other preparation than he already possessed as a physiologist for the study of social phenomena, would be the most irrational materialist of the three. What common sense and the best instinctive feelings of our nature resent in the conduct of such men is, their love of vulgarizing, of dragging down to a lower level, what they wilfully refuse to qualify themselves to understand. The materialism, however, which excites the greatest repugnance is that which loves to dwell on the physical basis of mind, and to ignore the utter impossibility of expressing any of the phenomena of mind in terms of matter. We say of a man that he is wise or foolish, just or unjust, brave or cowardly, faithful or false; but what possible application can any one of these terms have to the grey matter of the brain, or to the nervous system as a whole? To banish these words from our daily conversation would be to sentence ourselves to mutism and idiocy; to apply them to anything material would be to imitate lunacy. Professor Tyndall has himself confessed that a transition from matter to thought is absolutely inconceivable, unthinkable. Where then can be the possible advantage, after once settling the point that certain material conditions are necessary—as far at least as our experience enables us to judge—to the existence and activity of thought, in studiously dwelling on those material conditions, and turning our eyes away from all that would reveal to us the radical, immeasurable, unfathomable difference between thought or consciousness and its objects? Surely there is none; but, on the contrary, much disadvantage and loss, as there must always be when we set ourselves in opposition to nature.

Now, if by materialism we understand, with Auguste Comte, a tendency to confound distinct orders in nature, and especially to withhold from the highest of all, the respect that is its due, we may safely say that the tendency of science is *not* in this direction. Not only does science not tend to force all thought down to one plane, but it can only win its way by recognizing the claims, and accommodating itself to the exigencies of each distinct branch of enquiry; and no one knows better than a true man of science, that nerve vibrations and molecular movements in the brain, are no more the equivalent of thought than the pen with which Tennyson wrote, was the equivalent of "In Memoriam." Others may indulge this fancy, but the man who has to advance the boundaries of science cannot afford such trifling. For him, above all others, it is necessary that, leaving the things which are behind, he should press forward to those which are before. The truths of mathematics do not suffice in the realm of chemistry; chemistry fails to interpret the secrets of physiology, and physiology does but darken counsel when it attempts to formulate the conscious activity of man, to express in terms of its own the length and breadth and depth and height of his intellectual and emotional experience. To some it seems as if the reduction of thought to a level of a mere property of matter would cut at the root of a vast body of superstition; but, on the other hand, what superstitions may not be introduced if once we take the false step of joining what nature has sundered, or of pronouncing that there is but one order of phenomena where she has plainly declared there are two. Unless I am mistaken, I already see superstition creeping in by this door. Let us only hope the evil will not go very far. The poet's words are fortunately true in the main, that

> All reason wastes by day, and more,
> Will instinct in a night restore.

Science, as I before remarked, is simply the intellect of man, exercising itself in a certain direction. We are too apt to imagine that our abstract words stand for concrete existences. If science were something *outside* the mind, gifted with an activity of its own, what it might do with mind we can only guess. But seeing that it has no standing-ground in the whole universe except in the mind of man—or some similarly organized being—its triumphs are simply the triumphs of mind. Are we then to suppose that our intellectual powers in the course of their triumphant career will triumph over themselves, and be self-consigned to a lower place in nature than they had before claimed to occupy? I see no shadow of reason for entertaining such a notion. Brain is brain, and mind is mind; and though each may react on the other, it is the merest folly to say that one, in any sense, is the other. Compare the brain of a Shakespeare with that of some very ordinary person, and what difference will you find, except perhaps, in size,—the same kind of difference that exists between two pumpkins in the same market-cart. But compare the mind of Shakespeare with the mind of the ordinary person: the one is an empire the other a parish; we can hardly bring ourselves to regard them as commensurable. Consider again, that we do not set ourselves to improve the mind by improving the brain, except in so far as, by keeping the whole body in good health, we may try to improve the conditions for intellectual labour. The only thing we can possibly do for the brain is, to keep it well supplied with healthy blood, and to draw off the blood in sleep, or at least reduce its quantity, at proper intervals. In this respect, however, the brain receives no peculiar treatment; for arms and legs equally require to be nourished by the blood, and to have their periods of rest. But we act on the mind directly by setting it tasks, by appointing it exercises, by training it to do what surely the brain does not do,—recognize similarities, detect differences, weigh evidence, pronounce judgements. If you say that certain movements in the brain accompany all these acts, I say yes, and movements too, in the heart and stomach. The keen pursuit of an intellectual problem will quicken the heart's action; a sudden surprise will arrest and disturb it; unpleasant thoughts will impede digestion; fear will produce perspiration, and cold in the extremities. All this goes to show that man is a unity; but it does not go to show any identity of nature between mental experiences and their physical accompaniments.

There are many signs that the scientific men of to-day are beginning to realize more than ever the littleness of their knowledge in comparison with what remains to be known, and that they are prepared to accept a reversal of some of their fundamental notions in regard to the possibilities of existence. We are all of us materialists in regard to some things; and the whole scientific world, in its gropings after the beyond, has of necessity to be materialist in this sense, that until some new realm of nature has sufficiently discovered itself for some of its laws to be perceived and understood, investigators have no option but to apply the principles of those regions of knowledge with which they are already acquainted. Sufficient experience has, however, already been gained of the adjustments necessary in passing from one class of phenomena to another, to make it incumbent on our philosophers to be prepared, whenever the occasion arises, to abandon any given mode of thought for another—*any* which a different class of phenomena may clearly appear to require. . . . [When] . . . we take into consideration the number of new conceptions that are crowding upon men's minds, and the necessity that may at any moment arise for an alteration of our point of view, or at least the admission of what had before appeared inconceivable, we shall, I am sure, be led to the conclusion that there never was a time when rash dogmatism was more out of place than at the present. The temper we should all cultivate is one of earnest truth-seeking and patient waiting. Let us use provisionally the highest conceptions to which we can at present rise; but let us not set our faces, as some do, against the very thought that some day these conceptions may be proved inadequate. Then, while we are patiently waiting for higher light upon certain problems, let us be vigorous in attacking all demonstrable errors. There is in every age a work of unbuilding to do as well as work of building. Our very bodies are undergoing constantly a double process of destruction and renovation; and, unless the destruction is vigorously carried on, the renovation must languish, and the health of the whole body suffer. Our systems of belief in like manner require from time to time to be relieved of dead matter; and he who ministers to this end is entitled to no less gratitude than he who provides new materials for assimilation. To hold a consistent, manly course, however, and to be outspoken for what we regard as the truth, calls for courage just in proportion as our opinions diverge from those which society is pleased to take under its patronage. It needs a steady gaze to look the world full in the face, and in that look proclaim your determination to have a mind and will of your own. But do this; disengage yourself from a routine with which you have no sympathy, boldly take up your own position, and you will become a centre of attraction to other minds; like will gravitate to like. I know of no more impressive words on this subject than those of Mr. John Morley,[2] where, in his noble work on "Compromise," speaking of the bondage in which so many men of superior mind are to the smile of the world, he says:

And what is this smile of the world, to win which we are bidden to sacrifice our moral manhood; this frown of the world, whose terrors are more awful than the withering up of truth and the slow going-out of light within the souls of us? Consider the triviality of life and conversation and purpose in the bulk of those whose approval is held out for the prize and mark of our high calling. Let us measure the empire over them of prejudice unadulterated by a single element of rationality, and let us weigh the huge burden of custom unrelieved by a single leavening particle of fresh thought. Ponder the share which selfishness and love of ease have in the vitality and maintenance of the opinions which we are forbidden to dispute. Then how pitiful a thing seems the approval or disapproval of these creatures of the conventions of an hour, as one figures the merciless vastness of the universe of matter, sweeping us headlong through viewless space; as one hears the wail of misery that is for ever ascending to the deaf gods; as one counts the little tale of the years that separate us from eternal silence. In the light of these things a man should surely dare to live his life, with little heed of the common speech upon him or his life; only caring that his days may be full of reality, and his conversation of truth-speaking and wholeness.

These are weighty words, but they are perhaps too sadly solemn for me to leave them with you as a farewell; so I will read you in conclusion a poem by one of the noblest spirits of this century, Arthur Hugh Clough, a poem which speaks of man's power over the universe, and summons him to a career of joyful conquest over all natural obstacles and difficulties:—

Hope evermore and believe, O man, for, e'en
    as thy thought,
So are the things that thou see'st; e'en as
    thy hope and belief.
Cowardly art thou and timid?   they rise to
    provoke thee against them.
Hast thou courage?   enough; see them exulting
    to yield!
Yea, the rough rock, the dull earth, the wild
    sea's furying waters
(Violent say'st thou and hard, mighty thou
    think'st to destroy),
All with ineffable longing are waiting their
    Invader;
All, with one varying voice, call to him,
    Come and subdue:
Still for their Conqueror call, and, but for
    the joy of being conquered,
(Rapture they will not forego) dare to resist
    and rebel;
Still, when resisting and raging, in soft under-
    voice say unto him,
Fear not, retire not, O man; hope evermore
    and believe.
Go from the east to the west, as the sun and
    the stars direct thee,
Go with the girdle of man, go and encompass
    the earth.
Not for the gain of the gold; for the getting,
    the hoarding, the having,
But for the joy of the deed; but for the Duty
    to do.

Go with the spiritual life, the higher volition
    and action,
With the great girdle of God, go and encompass
    the earth.
Go; say not in thy heart, 'and what then
    were it accomplished,
Were the wild impulse allayed, what were
    the use and the good?'
Go; when the instinct is stilled, and when
    the deed is accomplished,
What thou hast done and shalt do, shall be
    declared to thee then.
Go with the sun and the stars, and yet ever-
    more in thy spirit
Say to thyself: It is good; yet is there
    better than it.
This that I see is not all, and this that I do
    is but little;
Nevertheless it is good, though there is
    better than it.

6. The Scientific Spirit
(1879)

The modern world is, in an altogether peculiar degree, under the dominion of physical science, and more of the best thought of our time is being drafted into scientific regions. It would be vain to deny that this phenomenon is accompanied by a great bettering of the conditions of life, throughout a large section at least of society, and that human thought, speaking generally, is in a healthier state than in the days when science was feeble and theology strong. We have, therefore, an evident interest in advancing the boundaries of science, and to this end it is important that the scientific spirit should be cultivated and guarded, if possible, against any weaknesses or errors into which it might have a natural tendency to fall. In the opinion of some thoughtful persons the time has come when a wise direction of scientific discovery, and a wise organization of the present resources of civilized society are of more importance than the mere increase of scientific knowledge. The poet Shelley, in the beginning of this century, wrote:

> We have more moral, political and historical wisdom than we know how to reduce into practice; we have more scientific and economical knowledge than can be accommodated to the just distribution of the produce which it multiplies.

If this was so in Shelley's time, how is it now? Steam was then but in its infancy; the railway was not; the telegraph was not even a dream. One thing is beyond all doubt. We have enough physical science—if that could suffice—to make a very comfortable world of this to all decent people; whereas, for some years past, the amount of distress consequent upon financial confusion and the dislocation of industry, has been something appalling. Our unlimited command over the resources of nature has not enabled us to give bread to the hungry nor clothes to the naked; while the only remedy we can think of for hard times is—idleness. Men must suffer because they have produced too much.

SOURCE: *Rose-Belford's Canadian Monthly and National Review,* Vol. III (October, 1879), pp. 437-441.

Let them therefore stand idle and wait until the surplus products of their industry have been consumed; then, perchance, they may hope for employment and food. Such is the "fix" into which the wisdom of the nineteenth century manages to thrust itself. Surely such a result should be regarded as the *reductio ad absurdum* of something. But of what?

Let us have science then, since science does us good, or at least gives us the means of doing ourselves good; but let us see if we cannot humanise it so as to increase the probability that it will prove of universal, and not of merely partial, benefit. Let us see also that the minds which occupy themselves with science do not waste their powers in unprofitable inquiries, and possibly, by the pursuit of false methods, do themselves more harm than good. Let us try to realise clearly what the true scientific spirit is, and do our best to develop and strengthen *that*.

One of the chief dangers to which science is exposed is that of dogmatism. It is exposed to this danger through its very strength. Theology was once strong—strong in its control of the human mind, strong in the enthusiasm it was able to create, strong in the universality of its claims and its ambition—and it was dogmatic as nothing else has ever been, or probably will ever be. Dogmatism is nothing but the temper of command unreasonably exercised. Science in the present day wields command, and it only too easily falls into the snare of dogmatism. We have heard in our day of an "orthodox" geology, an "orthodox" political economy, and probably other sciences as well have their orthodox schools. Having myself given an account the other day to a scientific friend of the argument of a little work entitled "Scepticism in Geology," [3] which has now reached a second edition, I was surprised at the warmth of indignation with which the attack on the system reared by Lyell was received. A person present having asked my friend whether he would not read the book in question, in order to judge better of the value of its arguments, he answered emphatically "No," he would not, he said, waste time on anything so absurd. Similarly, I have seen people utterly refuse to read so much as a line in defence or explanation of spiritualism; while, in the region of Political Economy, I have known a writer set down as utterly incompetent on the simple ground that he had criticised the views of Adam Smith and John Stuart Mill. Nay more, in the latter case, the writer in question, without an examination of a page of his book was stigmatised as an *inflationist*; whereas, the chief point of his objection to Adam Smith and John Stuart Mill was, that the language held by them in regard to money gave rise to all kinds of inflationist heresies and schemes.* No one, indeed, can mix

*The writer referred to is Mr. H.V. Poor, of New York. His views on the point in question are fully shared by Sir Anthony Musgrave.[5]

much with men who occupy themselves chiefly with science, or who, without being possessed of much scientific knowledge, have a natural predilection for science, without seeing how readily—I speak generally of course—they glide into dogmatism, and assume, not for themselves personally, but for the great Church of Science of which they hold themselves members, an infallibility far surpassing that of the Roman Pontiffs, which, when fully explained, is found to be a very limited thing. For "*Roma locuta est, causa finita est*,"[4] they are quite prepared to say, "*Scientia*," &c., and when once the name of science is invoked, controversy must cease.

Now it is very obvious that there is nothing scientific in dogmatism carried to this point. One can excuse a well-informed man for not caring to discuss matters, on a footing of equality, with an ill-informed one; nor need any one trouble himself with theories which imply complete ignorance of facts on the part of those who put them forward. Coleridge's dictum about "understanding a man's ignorance" before you conclude that he is hopelessly in the wrong comes in here. If we not only believe a man to be ignorant, but, as it were, are able to survey his ignorance, to see all around it, and understand both it and him; then we may, without arrogance, decline to re-open, for his amusement, questions which we have good reason to consider closed. But, in many cases where "science" is appealed to, nothing of this kind can be claimed. The dogmatist simply knows what is current as the orthodox science of the day or hour, and, strong in this knowledge, pooh-poohs any facts that may be alleged in opposition thereto. And yet how very brief is the authority which many scientific theories enjoy! They "have their day and cease to be," and are only referred to afterwards as examples of inconclusive reasoning or over-hasty generalisation. The geologists of to-day have made no satisfactory reply to the attacks made by the physical school upon their mode of computing time; yet how much of geological theory depends upon the correctness of that method! The whole doctrine of "causes now in action" may be said to be at stake; for if the Lyellian school of geologists have proved anything, it is that causes now in action could not have produced the results we see in much less time than has been claimed.

The remedy for dogmatism in science is a recognition of the essentially provisional character of all scientific theories. Every science, it should be remembered, owes its existence to a certain process of abstraction. The universe is a whole, and only as a whole can it be fully comprehended. We light upon a fact or a phenomenon, and discern its relations to certain closely connected facts or phenomena. Apart from these it would have no significance whatever; seen in connection with them it has both significance and interest. But how do we know what its remoter relations may be or what may be its place in the general scheme of things. Any theory we can frame is valid only so far as the discovered relations are concerned; in other words it is a working hypothesis and no more. How unwise therefore to allow a working hypothesis actually to stand in the way of work,—to nail ourselves down to it, as if it were really part of the durable framework of the universe! The doctrine of gravitation itself can only be held to be provisionally true, in regard, at least, to the terms in which it is expressed. The facts on which it is based, and which at present it serves to formulate, will remain unchanged; but the time may come when we shall see them in other relations, and when their whole character, relatively to our apprehension, will be changed. And it will be something in that day, should it ever come, to be saved from the necessity of attributing to the brute earth the power of acting, without any intermediary, upon similar brute masses elsewhere, which is what the theory as at present framed compels us to do. The true scientific attitude of mind is one opposed to all dogmatism, one which regards the work of science as in its nature exhaustless, and which sees that progress consists in ever grasping more and more of the unity of laws and phenomena, and not in pursuing separate lines of enquiry into infinitely minute detail.

Science indeed, to be true to itself, and to do its work in the best way must be nothing less than philosophy; or at least it must be steeped in the widest conceptions that philosophy can supply. It would be idle to decry specialism in the study of science, for it has long been a necessary result of the enormous development of scientific knowledge; but, at the same time, it can hardly be questioned that special sciences are often studied in a very unscientific manner and spirit—that is to say, as a mere matter of curiosity, or perhaps of personal competition, and without any sense of what Comte calls the *ensemble*—without any genuine interest in science in the widest sense of the word. What is the difference between a mania for collecting old books or old tea-pots and a passion for gathering every obtainable plat, insect or fossil in a certain district, unless the latter tasks be undertaken with the distinct object of furthering the general work of science, either by establishing some theory in the particular branch in which the effort is made, or by throwing a side light upon some connected study? It may be said that all these pursuits sharpen the faculty of observation: so they do in the particular region in which the faculty is exercised, but not in other regions; on the contrary the more attention is concentrated on one class of objects the less (necessarily) will it be given to other classes. One master interest has often dwarfed, if not killed, every other. While, therefore, I readily give my sympathy to those whose tastes take them afield and lead them to study nature in any of her forms, I look for some manifestation of interest in science as a whole, some sense of the unity of all truth, something altogether above and beyond the fiddle-faddle dilettanteism of a curiosity hunter, before I congratulate science on the labours bestowed in her service. I have seen a boy turning up words in a Latin dictionary, and I have seen a man turning up plants in Gray's Botany, and I cannot say which of the two processes seemed to me the more scientific.

The true man of science ought, above all things, to be *interesting*. Living in a world whose phenomena he is studying, with whose laws he is every day gaining a wider acquaintance, and seeing the bearing of these upon human life and history, he should be of all men the most companionable and the one from whose intercourse we should derive the most profit. If this be so, there surely must be something wrong with a science that simply enables its possessor to pound general society with long words, and which causes all his interest and enthusiasm to go out towards the infinitely minute and the infinitely unimportant. The entomologist in "The Poet at the Breakfast-Table,"[6] having been invited to look at the stars through a telescope, declined on the ground of pressing occupations. "May I venture to ask," said the Poet, "on what particular point you are engaged just at present?"

> Certainly, Sir, you may. It is, I suppose, as difficult and important a matter as often comes before a student of natural history. I wish to settle the point once for all whether the *Pediculus Melittae* is, or is not, the larva of Meloe.

The Pediculus, concluded the Poet, occupied a larger space in that man's mental vision than "the midnight march of the solar system." When Rousseau came up to Paris to submit certain new musical ideas to the *savans* of the Academy, he found, as he tells us in his "Confessions," that these men enjoyed a great advantage over him, inasmuch as their scientific attainments enabled them to talk continuously without putting any meaning into what they said, and to repel all new ideas by the simple iteration of formulas. Jean Jacques is not an unimpeachable witness in his own cause; but some of us have heard enough perhaps of what has purported to be scientific talk to be prepared to believe that his description may not have been altogether wide of the mark. The fact is that men of science are often dreary in the extreme through the concentration of their interests upon some narrow field of investigation, and the complete absence from their minds of all wider views or aims. We do not go to such men for counsel, for sympathy, or for anything pertaining to good fellowship or social enjoyment. By long gazing at specimens they are well on the way to becoming specimens themselves; and "the unstable and the unlearned," taking them as types of what science does for a man, think but ill of its power to round human life into harmonious completeness.

Many, no doubt, are fitted to engage in the work of scientific observation and classification, whose power of original thought is inconsiderable, and whose metaphysical conceptions, if they indulge in any, will be of a simplicity bordering on rudeness. But the spirit in which these will pursue their studies will depend greatly upon the example set by greater men, and it is, therefore, of vast importance that the leaders in scientific investigation should set clearly before the world where the chief interest and the highest glory of science lies, that they should visibly make it the instructor of humanity to all noble ends, that they should put it forward as the great liberaliser of thought, the enemy of superstition and confusion, the beautifier of life, and that in which man's highest faculties can find unfailing exercise and satisfaction. If science were always exhibited in this light by its foremost representatives, we should get rid of the notion that it is a thing of catalogues and long names; and the rank and file of scientific workers would be more conscious of an object to their labours than they are at present. The opposition so often imagined to exist between science and poetry is due to nothing but the faulty exemplifications which we have of science. Give to it the depth which comes of union with philosophy, and inspire it with the faith which true philosophy teaches, and it will itself catch the language of poetry to express its glorious revelations.

We have in Canada many organizations which are helping forward the work of science in their own several ways. We must all desire that the labours of these should be crowned with success, and that Canada should contribute its share to the scientific achievements of the age. The makers of catalogues will not do much for us if left to themselves; but if a true scientific spirit can be diffused among the intelligent youth of our country, if a spirit of rational inquiry can be awakened, if the work of science can be nobly conceived by us, then we shall be sure in due time to do our part faithfully and well in building up that structure of scientific knowledge which, in the years to come, shall be, as it were, the common home and shelter of humanity.

7. Morality and Religion
   (1880)

The above is the title of an article in which the *Mail* newspaper very courteously refers to my remarks in the last number of the MONTHLY, under the heading of "The Future of Morality."[7] As the whole question at issue is one upon which the minds of all thinking men in this generation are much engaged, I shall not, perhaps, be regarded as pursuing the subject too far if I attempt a few words of reply to my candid and considerate critic.

My position, it may be remembered, was—to put it briefly—that morality is a thing of natural growth, that it consists essentially of the exercise of certain just and benevolent feelings—with their appropriate outcome in action—towards our fellow-beings, and that no system of religion, past or present, can claim to have invented it, or to be alone capable of maintaining it in vigour. No "apostolic doctrine of the cross," I held, was needed to save the world "from becoming altogether corrupt."

What has been the place in history, or what have been the special relations to morality of the great religious systems that have so powerfully swayed men's thoughts, are questions that I did not attempt to discuss; but I may here say that, in the light of the evolution philosophy, it is difficult not to believe that some great conservative purpose must have been served by systems so powerful and widespread. From a naturalistic point of view they have been the product no doubt, to a large extent, of men's needs and of the working of the blind instincts of humanity. Like the governments of the past, they have had their faults, yet, like them also, they have contributed their share to the work of human civilization. They have furnished leading-strings to thought, motives to effort, and stimulus to imagination. They have powerfully helped to consolidate society, and at the same time they have strengthened the individual against society, that is to say, cherished his individual life by introducing him to a region of thought in which social distinctions and the various accidents of time and place

SOURCE: *Rose-Belford's Canadian Monthly and National Review*, Vol. IV (February, 1880), pp. 166-171.

disappear. To believe all this is only to believe in a "soul of good" in all that has been very persistent, and at the same time very potent, upon the earth. To regard religion, as some thoughtlessly do, as having been always and everywhere and in every way the enemy of the human race, is to show a radical incapacity for dealing with historical problems. Once adopt such a view, and farewell to the "scientific method."

The view which the writer in the *Mail* thinks it important to put forward is that, in point of fact, the morality of to day is permeated by Christian sentiment, and essentially founded upon Christian hopes and fears. Supposing we grant that for argument's sake, what follows? That the Christian system of doctrine is true? No such conclusion is legitimate; nor would any one seriously attempt to prove the truth of Christianity from such a consideration. The early propagators of Christianity had to step forth into a world that was *not* permeated by Christian sentiment, and had to gain adherents to their cause by arguments drawn from the nature of what they taught. The position of matters to-day is that, from every pulpit in the land, the cry goes forth that scepticism is making havoc in society; that in fact the work of the early Christian centuries is being undone. What imports it then to know that modern morality bears a Christian stamp, and that even our advanced philosophers are, so to speak, metamorphic with the glow of underlying beliefs? What we are concerned to know is how far the disintegration of belief which we see taking place around us will proceed, and what will happen if it should become complete. Any man who speaks to either of these questions will speak to the times; and, if he is earnest, will have earnest listeners. But a man who simply points to what he holds to be a present fact, without furnishing or attempting to furnish any guarantee that the fact will be an enduring one, does not say what any one particularly wants to hear, unless it be those who particularly want *not* to see the true issue that is before the world. And, after all, there are enough such to make this mode of treating the subject far from unpopular.

I find, however, in the article to which I am referring, not a few confirmations of the leading views contained in the contribution which it criticizes. "As a matter of fact," says the writer, "we know that human morality has always been enforced by religious sanctions of some sort or other." The very word "enforced" here employed, points to the independent origin and authority of morality, for that which enforces cannot be one with the thing enforced. The fact is, as stated in my last article, that morality springs up—a natural product of human relations—and then religion steps in and takes it under its patronage, not in general, without more or less seriously perverting its character; for while it "enforces" certain natural duties, it weakens their authority by associating them with a number of purely arbitrary precepts, and often giving to the latter a decided precedence. Thus, under the Jewish law, a man could be put to death for violating the Sabbath, while he who beat his slave to death, went unpunished, provided only the unhappy victim did not actually die under the lash. Surely, with such an example as this before our eyes, the patronage of morality by religion is not a matter for unmixed congratulation. The founder of Christianity recognised that the true moral law, that which he summed up in two great commandments, had been rendered void by the traditions of men, and that, under the blinding and paralysing influence of priestcraft, human consciences had lost nearly all spontaneity of action: so it has been in countless instances in the world's history—theology has grasped morality, and all but strangled it.

"With the question as to the dogmatic value of the various theologies," says the *Mail*, "we have nothing at all to do here," it is enough to know that morality has always been enforced by religious sanctions of some sort or other. Is this said seriously? For, if so—if the writer is not assuming and taking his stand upon the supreme value and authority of the Christian theology—then I would ask why should not the fate which has confessedly overtaken the other theologies overtake the Christian also? And why should not the world survive the latter catastrophe as it has done former ones of a similar kind? Christianity, we are told, "found hollow and worm-eaten faiths, and their consequence a decaying and utterly debased morality," and it replaced them with something better. But how do faiths, let us ask, become hollow and worm-eaten? What is a hollow and worm-eaten faith? Might we not almost say, modifying a well-known phrase: *si exemplum quaeris circumspice*? [8] Is a faith becoming hollow and worm-eaten when the intelligence of the age is more and more passing it by; when its supporters, as a rule, prefer evasion to argument; when augurs try not to laugh in one another's faces, when a vague sentimentalism succeeds to the rigorous logical processes of earlier times, and all clear statements of doctrine become increasingly unpopular; when it seems a dangerous thing to so much as touch the text of sacred writings, even with a view to bringing it nearer to the exact words of inspiration; when, for everyone who proclaims his doubts or his disbelief on the housetop, scores tell the same tale in private; and, finally, when the whole intellectual interest of the age is with those thinkers who are pursuing their several lines of thought and discovery with the least possible reference to the declarations or assumptions of the still dominant theology? If these are the signs, which of them, I ask, is lacking in our own day?

"Hollow and worm-eaten faiths": surely the words fall with an ominous sound upon the ear. Let anyone think but of the change that has come over society within the last generation in the matter of belief in the miraculous; let any man of mature years compare the intellectual atmosphere of to-day with that which surrounded him as a youth; let him but glance at our literature, and see how it has thrown off the fetters of theology; let him but think of our science with its fundamental assumption of unvarying law, and if he does not conclude that the faith which found other faiths "hollow and worm-eaten" is itself yielding to decay he will be blind, indeed, to the signs of the time. True the land is dotted everywhere with churches and more are rising; but are these churches, or those who minister in them, grappling with the real problems of the age, are they helping to clarify human thought, or to simplify human conduct, or are they, mainly, distracting and enfeebling the minds of their followers by impossible blendings of mundane with ulta-mundane morality, and of a natural with a non-natural order of things? In a chuch which I lately attended, I heard thanks offered for the interposition of Providence in the case of a fireman who had fallen through the roof of a burning house without being kindled, and then a petition—almost in the same sentence—that, inasmuch as in the natural order of things a certain number of firemen would perish in the pursuit of their calling. Divine grace might be extended to them and Divine comfort to their families. Here were two absolutely contradictory ideas presented almost in a breath. If, however, the reverend gentleman who prayed in this wise were to become a life insurance agent, which of the two orders of thought would he adhere to? Would he not confine himself exclusively to the human order, and charge a premium on the lives of firemen (if he insured them at all) that would cover all the risks of their calling, without the slightest reference to the chances of Divine interposition? Would he abate the smallest fraction in his rates on the score of "special providences?" I think not; business is business, the faith of the most sceptical philosopher in the constancy of averages is not more profound or unfaltering than that of the man who, when on other ground, seems to recognise Divine interposition everywhere.

The question then, I say, is—when the vitality of a creed is under discussion— not how many churches that creed has called, or is calling, into existence, but what the churches are doing. If they are in the van of human progress, visibly raising men and women in moral and intellectual stature, reading, with a deeper insight than is elsewhere possessed, the riddles of human existence, carrying whatever is best in human nature to its highest expression, giving to each the highest philosophy of life that he or she can grasp, looking into the eyes of all with a gaze of utter truthfulness and of intensest faith, then, I say, the creed that has called *these* churches into existence is, and must be, the mistress of the world. But if, on the other hand, every line of this description suggests what is wanting rather than what is present, then we may declare that these churches, numerous as they are, are built not upon a foundation of firm, vigorous and vital belief, but upon mere human weakness, and that desire for aggregation that comes of weakness, or, put it at its best, upon a social instinct which finds an ancient tradition a convenient object round which to rally.

It is admitted by the writer in the *Mail*—who in this, of course, only follows St. Paul—that those who have not had the benefit of revelation are "a law unto themselves," a fact which he explains by saying that the Divine Being "has left upon the tablets of their heart the solemn traces of his creative touch." In giving this explanation, however, he shows that he was *not* serious in professing to take up a position of neutrality among the conflicting theologies; for this is an essentially Christian assumption. The broad fact that everywhere we see traces, however rude, of moral feeling is precisely the foundation upon which my whole argument is built; men cannot live together unless they are partially moral; unless, in other words, some general good results from their association. To try and snatch this fact from me by expressing it in terms of a theology is, as the argument lies, a mere *petitio principii*.

We are also told that "break-up in beliefs has always entailed a moral cataclysm," and that this fact may be "gleaned anywhere and everywhere in the history of nations ancient and modern." So it does not matter what superstitions have established themselves in any age or country: once established they are the bulwarks of morality. Surely to prove this, which I think would be difficult, is to prove too much, and the suggested analogy is not pleasant for those who wish to believe that Christianity is more than a superstition. We are threatened with a cataclysm if the dams of orthodoxy burst, and are pointed to the cataclysm that followed when the dams of various ancient mythologies burst. Had an enemy constructed this argument one could understand it; but, when seriously tendered in support of the orthodox cause, it has a distinct Hibernian flavour. If I remember rightly, the early Christian apologists accused the heathen roundly of demon-worship; there was no talk in those days of the salutary moral influence of all religious beliefs whether true or false. That we have landed in such talk to-day is a most significant fact.

It is assumed by many persons, and distinctly so by the writer to whom I am referring, that morality is everywhere purified and strengthened by alliance with theology. The contrary, however, is only too often conspicuously the case. Does devotion to a church always make a man a better citizen?—does it quicken his interest in public questions and make him more conscientious in dealing with them? I have heard men say, with something like a pious shudder at the thought, that they had never cast a vote at an election in their lives; their interest was all in "the second coming of the Lord." I have heard others who were pre-eminent for submission to ecclesiastical authority refusing to condemn the enormous civic offences of such a criminal as "Boss" Tweed. To do them justice, they apparently had no organ or faculty by the exercise of which they could condemn civic misdeeds, though their zeal for religion and reverence for its mysteries were unimpeachable. I have heard religionists confess that they would rather remain ignorant of the arguments that could be brought against their creed; as what they wanted was not truth, but an easy, comfortable frame of mind. There are, indeed, large sections of the religious world where the idea of loyalty to truth has no recognition, and where, therefore, it is enough to condemn any opinion to say that it is an "uncomfortable" one. The most widespread symptom of all, however, and the most disheartening one, among pious people, is the absence of all high idealism, as applied, at least, to the affairs of this world. A moral "rule of thumb" is good enough for them; and they look askance on any one who proposes to use a better.

A true morality, it will be seen more and more as time advances, requires the acceptance of this life, not as something provisional merely, but as the appointed, and, so far as we know, the only theatre of man's activity. We shall never treat life with due seriousness, we shall never make full proof of its resources, so long as we cling to the idea that it is as nothing compared with a life beyond. That detachment from the things of earth which is regarded as so eminent a spiritual grace is, from the point of view of natural morality, simple treason to humanity. Granted that there be a life beyond, surely our business is to make the best of the life that now is. If we are not faithful in that which is our own, how shall we be so in anything else? The servant who had received but one talent despised that, and hid it in a napkin; it was too small a capital, he thought, to work upon. And in the same way many to-day think this life too poor a thing to do anything with; their thoughts, their hopes are all beyond. Health, intellectual vigour, kindly social relations, the beaming faces of children looking out upon the world with a fresh curiosity and minds unwarped by superstition, the joyousness that waits upon a mind freed from all sophistry and full of light from singleness of eye—these are but shadowy or unattainable goods, and not worthy to be compared with some "glory that is to be revealed" hereafter. And so, in the days when consistency was more common than it is now, men fled into deserts or immured themselves in monasteries, that they might give themselves wholly to spiritual things. And there they emaciated themselves and saw visions and wrought miracles, and gave themselves to profound meditations and severe ascetic exercises, but brought little to light for the improvement of human life or the increase of human happiness.

We are asked what we propose to substitute for Christianity. My answer is that no argument which I or any other can use can have any effect upon a mind not fitted to receive it. In so far as we influence men, we influence them individually, and shall the man who feels that what I say is true, turn to me and ask what new belief I propose to give him, as if he were a child whom I had robbed of a toy. Let the man who puts this question—I mean now any man—stand forth, and let me ask him:

Are you convinced, or are you not? If you are not then your question is an idle one, seeing that no one has disturbed your belief. If you are, do you think you can throw upon *me* the responsibility of working into your scheme of life the new truths to which I have awakened you. Surely that is your business not mine. If I tell you that you are on the edge of a precipice, do I thereby incur the whole responsibility for leading you to a position of safety? If I persuade you that the bank in which your money is invested is insecure, must I proceed further and select, on my own responsibility, a new investment for you? Yet you might as well hold to the affirmative in either case, as to say that I must furnish you with a complete set of positive opinions, because I have shown you that certain of your former views were erroneous.

The fact is, however, that no convinced person makes this preposterous demand. It is chiefly used by those who are fighting against conviction, as a means of gaining a little breathing-time; and asked by these, it does not call for an answer.

Let me not, however, hesitate to say that many in this generation are willing to take their stand, and live their lives, upon the basis of such truth as they can discover in nature and in human relations. Nor does the universe become to us "vague, dark and blank," nor is "the kindling fire of the heart" extinguished. Human ties are not less tender or precious for the knowledge that we hold our treasures in earthen vessels, and that our opportunities of ministering to their happiness are but limited. The witchery of beauty in a flower, the fading splendours of a sunset sky, do not penetrate our souls the less deeply because we compare their evanescence with our own; nor shall our hands do less faithfully that which they find to do because we know that the night cometh when no man can work. It has been said of Galileo's discovery that it had the effect of placing the earth among the stars, of making it (in men's thoughts) a heavenly body instead of a mere low-lying plain. What we need now is that some Galileo or Copernicus shall place the life of man in this world at its true level, by encouraging us and enabling us to believe that *here* we may have our heaven. By cherishing such a hope, and working towards its fulfilment, do we cut ourselves off from aught of good that blends itself with the universe? Do we tie our thoughts down to any mere system of negations? Assuredly not. Grant that we have abandoned many things that we formerly held as true, no immanent Divinity we ever recognised can have vanished from the universe. Dagon may fall in its temple,[9] because he was wilfully set up by human hands; and some of the lamentations we hear are lamentations over the fall of a mere idol, cherished because it seemed to lend itself to the gratification, or at least to promise the gratification, of selfish and wholly unspiritual desires. We cannot answer for Dagon; he is falling every day; but we know there is that enshrined in some human hearts that survives all intellectual shocks, and sits ever "Like light in the sun, throned." But time and language would fail us to tell what human life might be, if men but ceased to despise it, and to place elsewhere their highest hopes and aspirations, if they but thought of this earth, humble though it may be in comparison with some distant orb of which we know nothing, as their *home*, if they felt themselves responsible for its moral order and beauty, and did not indolently sigh over its miseries, and comfort themselves with the thought of some great rectification to come. What we want is a "natural piety" that shall link our days together in continuous effort for the advancement of purely human objects, and link us in thought and sympathy with both the past and the future of mankind. Then, in the fulness of time, shall appear

     the crowning race

Of those that eye to eye shall look
   On knowledge, under whose command
   Is Earth and Earth's, and in their hand
Is Nature, like an open book;

No longer half akin to brute
   For all we thought and loved and did,
   And hoped and suffered is but seed
Of what in them is flower and fruit.*

*In Memoriam

8. A Vindication of Scientific Ethics (1880)

Mr. Spencer, in his "Data of Ethics," has not written a popular treatise on morals, nor has he appealed to any lower tribunal than the highest intelligence and the maturest judgment of his generation. The more I think of his book, the more it seems to me a sign that shall be spoken against, but a sign, at the same time, in which, or by which, great victories will be won for the human race.[10] I am far from saying that it tells us everything we might wish to know in regard to the springs of conduct, or the special sources of moral energy; but I contend that it tells us much that is of supreme importance, and that anything we may require to add to the statements it contains will not be found in conflict with the writer's main positions.

Mr. Spencer, it must be understood, undertakes to trace for us the evolution of morality as an objective process. Morality, like everything else, must have a history. What is that history? This is the question to which Mr. Spencer addresses himself. If we can trace the development of morality in the past, we shall be better able to understand its characteristics in the present, and its probably course in the future. Mr. Spencer says truly that morality is a certain aspect of *conduct* in general; it is, as he holds, *developed* conduct; and, in order that we may understand what conduct is, he asks us to examine it in its earliest manifestations, and to follow it through the ages, as it gains in definiteness, in complexity, in range, and in the importance of its reactions upon consciousness. This is a view, the legitimacy of which it seems impossible to dispute. When our attention is arrested by any structure in nature, we, very properly, ask

How has it come to be what it is? Did it spring into existence at once in the form under which we behold it now, or was it shaped by slow

SOURCE: *Popular Science Monthly*, Vol. XVII (July, 1880), pp. 324-337. This article was originally published under the title "Mr. Spencer and His Critics," in *Rose-Belford's Canadian Monthly and National Review*, Vol. IV (April, 1880), pp. 413-422. LeSueur's rebuttal of certain technical objections to Herbert Spencer's *The Data of Ethics* made by Goldwin Smith, Henry Calderwood, and James McCosh have here been omitted.

degrees? If the latter, what were the stages through which it succes-sively passed?

Do not tell us that the same questions cannot profitably be asked in regard to morality until the questions have been fairly put and answered according to the best obtainable knowledge.

The great objection hitherto made to the scientific study of history, or of any moral subject, has been that all calculations based upon general laws of growth or progress are liable at any moment to be thrown into confusion by the appearance upon the scene of forces or of influences of a wholly exceptional character. Thus the birth of some man of transcen-dent abilities may alter, it is said, the whole course of a nation's history. The answer to this objection is two-fold: first, that the great man or hero is himself a product of antecedent conditions, and is born into a society more or less fitted to feel and submit to his influence; secondly, that the effects wrought by exceptional characters are but exceptional, and that the great stream of human development follows its course but little affected by accidents here or there. Mr. Spencer, therefore, and those who think with him, may, without in the least compromising their system, make large admissions as to the influence of certain special agencies. They do not necessarily blind themselves to the course of history in the ordinary sense of the word, because they make a special study of the development of conduct. The line of observation and argument pursued in the "Data of Ethics" is hopelessly antagonistic only to that form of supernaturalism which disbelieves totally in evolu-tion, preferring to regard human history as the theatre of forces having no relation to preceding conditions, and acting consequently as simple disturbers of the natural equilibrium of society. The adherents of this school must only fight the development theory as best they may. The battle is engaged, however, along the whole line, and to defeat evolu-tion, you must defeat it not in ethics only, but in biology and physics as well. As long as the two latter divisions hold their ground, be sure that any victory over the first can be but momentary.

It is obvious that the method pursued by Mr. Spencer must give rise to many misapprehensions. The first thought that suggests itself to even an attentive and earnest reader is, that he has left out of sight, and is prevented by his principles from doing justice to, a number of very important considerations. Our individual consciousness tells us nothing of the dependence of present modes of conduct upon past; but it tells us much of the special motives which influence us from moment to moment. So a wave of the sea, if we could imagine it conscious, might know much of the pressure of adjacent waves and its own adjustments of form in consequence of that pressure, but might know nothing of ocean currents or the attraction of sun and moon. We feel the influence of some potent personality, but think little of the causes that have fitted us to do so; yet, to be able to trace and understand those causes, would give us a far more comprehensive theory of our moral nature than to be able to analyse and measure with the utmost accuracy the special personal influence by which we are so strongly affected. In a word, what may be called the accidents of our life fill an altogether larger space in consciousness than the general laws in virtue of which we are substantially what we are. Mr. Spencer has undertaken to trace those general laws, leaving accidents out of sight as much as possible; and, naturally, consciousness protests. If, however, we only call to mind, and impress upon ourselves, what it is that Mr. Spencer attempts, we shall recall many of our criticisms, and find it better to listen attentively to what he has to say.

Again, with every action there goes a certain accompaniment of individual feeling. We have a sense of its voluntariness, and a consequent sense of responsibility. To us, each action stands and is seen in relation to the sum of our own individual actions, and the proportion which it bears to that sum is very different from the proportion it bears to the whole sum of action in general. It is easy, therefore, to conceive how different the subjective view of action must be from the objective, and how far a history of action such as Mr. Spencer undertakes to write, must be from such an account as we might gather from the dicta of consciousness. But if our individual lives are but links in one great chain of life, which we have learnt in these latter days to extend to the lowest forms of the animate creation, can the individual consciousness, however bright and penetrating we may suppose it, be trusted in its affirmations regarding the genesis of action and the development of moral feeling? What can mere consciousness—apart from knowledge derived from external sources—tell us of our bodily constitution and development? It is occupied almost solely with sensations of pleasure and pain; it knows what are proximate causes of one or the other; but [of] what the laws are that rule the human organization, it is wholly ignorant. We have absolutely no consciousness of the nature of digestion or respiration; we only know in a rough way what creates disturbances in one region or the other, and what promotes comfort. Is it likely that we shall know any better from a simple question of our individual consciousness how our actions are produced, or what is their essential character and true significance? It seems to me that the feelings accompanying moral action are no safer guides to a true understanding of that action than the feelings accompanying digestion are to a true understanding of digestion. The objective method of study, as applied to human conduct, has this great advantage, that, while looking at things from the outside, and grasping the *enchainement* of cause and effect through all past time, it can also take account of the direct revelations of consciousness, so far as these seem to furnish any safe guidance. Mr. Spencer, it may be presumed, knows something personally of the inner life of humanity. He has written this treatise in full view of all that his personal experience has taught him of the motives by which men are swayed and we must suppose that, in his mind at least, there is no contradiction between his philosophical theories and the teachings of life or the affirmations of consciousness. It is well to bear in mind that philosophers after all are men first and philosophers only afterwards.

The adverse criticisms that have been offered upon Mr. Spencer's last work may be said to resolve themselves into two leading objections—first, that he does away with the essential distinction between right and wrong, and, second, that, for regulative purposes, his system is wholly unadapted to human wants. I propose to consider these points separately.

Let us, in the first place, try to understand clearly what Mr. Spencer's view is. Looking at conduct objectively he sees, as we advance from lower to higher forms in nature, an ever-increasing and improving adaptation, first to the preservation of individual life, and next to the preservation of the life of progeny. The lowest creatures in the animal kingdom possess little or no power of self-protection, and are therefore, broadly speaking, wholly at the mercy of their environment. With greater complexity of structure comes greater power of providing for wants and averting dangers; while the interests of the progeny become more and more a care to the parent animals. The time comes, in process of evolution, when the individual acquires the power of choice between opposite courses of action. One sense may prompt to a certain line of action, and another to a different one. Smell, for example, may attract to food, but sight may reveal an enemy of superior power; or certain mental images which the sight of offered food, or of the apparatus in which it is placed, calls up may inspire caution and compel abstinence. Mr. Spencer here shows that the interest of the individual is generally concerned in obeying the higher or more lately-developed sense, instinct or faculty, in preference to the simpler and more primitive impulse; and this distinction between actions inspired by more far-reaching and those inspired by less far-reaching perceptions, he considers as homologous to the distinction which emerges in the human region—and which, as civilization advances, becomes ever more pronounced—between right and wrong. In the one case the individual weighs present gratification against his permanent interests as an individual; in the second he weighs his interests as an individual against those of the social body in which he is included. In either case he does well if he yield to the larger thought—that which summons to self-control, and which promises a continuance and enlargement of his activities. From this point of view the conduct which places a man in harmony with society is simply an extension, a further development, of the conduct which places him in harmony with himself, by subordinating his momentary desires to his permanent interests. In the one case he says,

> I have a larger life to consider than that of this moment; I have all my past, the memory of which I would not wish to extinguish; I have all my future, which I am not prepared to sacrifice.

In the latter he says,

> I have a larger life to consider than that which is made up of my personal pains and pleasures; I have inherited sympathies and acquired attachments; the goodwill of my fellow-man is much to me, and I feel that apart from the support and assistance that they render me, and apart from the activities I exercise as a member of society, I should be a miserably contracted creature. Shall I therefore in the interests of my narrower self make war upon my larger and better self by pursuing anti-social courses of action?

The argument in both cases is the same; the only difference is that in one case length of life is at stake, and in the other breadth of life; but all higher action, it may be assumed as a principle, tends to life. "Do this and ye shall live''; in these words lie all that the evolution philosophy has to teach on the subject of morals; for they summon to right action, and they point to the reward—LIFE.

I fail to see that under this mode of treatment the distinction between right and wrong is in danger of disappearing. Those possibly who have considered it a pious thing not to know why right is right or why wrong is wrong may resent being told that a *rationale* of the antagonism between the two has been discovered. They may insist that they have hitherto done right and avoided wrong from motives far transcending in elevation any regard for perpetuation or improvement of life, their own others'; and it would be ungracious, doubtless, to contradict them. But for all that, as a motive to sway the mass of mankind, the thought that right action tends to life and higher life, that wrong action tends to lower life and ultimately to extinction of life, should scarcely, one would think, be a sterile or inoperative one. Much would depend no doubt upon the mode in which the thought was presented by those who have it in their power to influence public opinion. That the minds of a large portion of the community have been so poisoned by the drugs of a false theology as to be incapable of responding to any teaching based on the pure laws of nature there is only too much reason to believe; but I should refuse to admit as valid against the evolutionist system of morals any argument drawn from their present condition or requirements.

The objections made to Mr. Spencer's explanation of the difference between right and wrong are very similar to those made to the Darwinian theory of the descent of man. In the dispute which raged more violently some years ago than it does now in reference to this question, an angelic character pronounced himself "on the side of the angels," as was but natural. It was thought utterly derogatory to man's dignity to suppose that his ancestry could run back into the brute creation; and so today it seems to threaten the stability of all moral distinctions to connect moral actions, by any process of filiation, with actions which, as we understand morality, present no moral character whatever. But just as no theory of man's origin can make him other than he actually is to-day, so no theory of the origin of morality can affect the fact that in the conscience of the modern civilized man there is a great gulf fixed between right and wrong. But, some will say, upon the evolution theory the highest morality is but self-seeking. Be it so, but if my self embraces other selves, if my personality has globed itself out till it includes a large portion of humanity, I can afford to be self-seeking without any falling away from nobility or disinterestedness. When Jesus said, "He that saveth his life shall lose it, and he that loseth his life shall save it," he meant, as we have always understood, that a careful study and pursuit of narrow personal interests would involve the sacrifice of wider and nobler interests; and that on the other hand by a surrender of our lower selves, we could rise to higher life. From whichever point we view it, he bids us aim at *life*, and so far he might be accused of prompting to self-seeking; but when we once see how life may be understood, and what it may be made to include, we perceive how pointless is the objection. It is indeed difficult to imagine how any person, except one who had been restrained from evil simply by superstitious fears, could feel himself less bound to do right and avoid wrong, because he had been shown that right actions to day are the lineal descendants of all those actions, conscious and unconscious, by which life has been preserved, and improved in the past, and that wrong actions claim their paternity in whatever in the past has tended to disintegration, degradation and death. Who would not rather be on the side of the forces of life, in harmony with and aiding the upward movement of nature, than helping to tear down the good work that the toiling ages have wrought?

Can such a system, however, possess any binding force? Here we find ourselves face to face with the question whether the evolutionist theory of morals is really adapted to take the place of those regulative systems which Mr. Spencer represents as ready to pass away. One thing is certain: it does not act upon the mind in the same way as systems which appeal to supernatural terrors and hold out a prospect of supernatural rewards. It will not awaken as powerful emotions as theology has in the past awakened; for theology has connected with theologically-right action rewards wholly incommensurate with the merit of such action, and with theologically-wrong action punishments equally incommensurate with its demerit; while the natural theory of morals can only point to the natural results of actions and promote as best it can a disposition to respect natural laws. No doubt this is tame work after what we have been accustomed to; but everything grows tame, in a sense, as civilization advances. We no longer torture criminals, nor feast our piety with *autos-dafe*.[11] We no longer thrash knowledge into school-children; and we are so dead to the necessity of cultivating national spirit that we forbid prize-fighting. Upon every hand, the drastic methods of the past are discredited, for we find, in point of fact, that gentler methods are better. Sangrado[12] no longer depletes our veins of the blood needed for carrying on the processes of life; we keep our blood and let nature have her way as much as possible. No doubt there is further progress to be made in the same direction; and who shall say that a system of rational rewards and punishments in *this* life, such as the evolution philosophy unfolds, may not be found more efficacious than the monstrous rewards and punishments of the supernatural sphere. Such a system may not inspire death-bed terrors, but neither will it provoke life-long jeerings; and, if once understood theoretically, its gentle—though not always gentle—pressure would rarely be absent from consciousness. The villain, it may be said, will think little of sacrificing his higher social to his lower personal self; and in his case, therefore, the system would be inoperative. Precisely, and how does Monsieur the villain comport himself now? Does he occupy a front seat at church (something here whispers that sometimes he does, but that is another kind of villain, and there is no use in mixing up matters), and send his children to Sunday School, and show in every way the great influence which theological instruction has had upon his mind? Or we may ask whether, in the "ages of faith," the villain was an unknown character. History tells us that when supernatural hopes and fears— above all fears, which are more potent than hopes—were at their highest, precisely then was there most of violence and crime. And when natural morality finally succeeds to supernatural, it is safe to predict that it will find some heavy arrears of work on hand.

We need not trouble ourselves, then, with considering how the lowest types of humanity will act under the supposed *regime*; what we are concerned with is the effect likely to be produced upon the mass of society. As regards men in general, will natural morality exert a sufficient regulative force? To this question I should be inclined to answer unhesitatingly yes, provided only proper means be taken to bring the new system home to people's understandings. No one will pretend that the theology now in possession exerts all the regulative influence that could be desired. For one thing, it cannot make itself believed by large multitudes; and, in the second place, very many of those who do believe it, or who profess to do so, are far from leading edifying lives. Every leading religious denomination has numerous representatives in our jails and penitentiaries, as official documents show; while, if we turn to the records of the insolvency courts, we shall find ample evidence that men can be at once zealous supporters of a church and sadly inexact—to say the least—in money matters. Why do I mention these things? Surely not to cause any one pain, but simply to show how the question stands. Some people argue as if we had *now* a perfect regulative system, which the new opinions are in danger of disturbing. But no; we have a very imperfect regulative system, upon which it is hoped a great improvement may be made. Theologians have, for some time past, been sensible of the shortcomings of the old teaching, for they have been trying to graft upon it the idea of the *naturalness* of the rewards and punishments to be meted out to right and wrong-doers respectively. We hear now that sinners will not be overtaken by any external penalties, but will be left to the simple and inevitable consequences of their own misconduct. They would not be happy, we are told, in heaven, because their characters are not adapted to that abode of bliss; and upon the whole, therefore, they are better off on the other side of the great gulf. How all this can be reconciled with the teaching of the Bible, where Hell is represented, not as prepared by the sinner for himself, but as prepared by God for the devil and his angels; and Heaven, in like manner, as something specially prepared for the righteous, who there enjoy a felicity with which the sufferings of this present time are not worthy to be compared, it is not for me to say. One thing is clear, however, and that is, that such glosses as these are recognitions of, and concessions to, the principle of development. Heaven, according to this hypothesis, is the developed life of righteousness, and Hell the developed life of moral rebellion; but though theology may dally with this view, it can never do more than dally with it; it can never make on its own, seeing that the text of the Bible so plainly declares the cataclysmal nature of the change which takes place at death. But if theology has to dally with development, how much better founded, and how much better adapted for acting upon men's minds, must a system be which, from first to last, assumes development, and which is not checked in its exposition and application of natural laws by any stereotyped creed or text?

In the new system we really have the reconciliation of self-interest and duty, for we see self-interest merging into duty, and we see duty bringing the highest rewards that self-interest could desire. To say that this system will be powerless for regulative purposes, is to take a thoroughly unnatural view of human nature. It is to assume some tendency in man to evil, over and above the promptings of the self-protective instinct. Now this surplusage of evil in human nature, I, for one, strenuously deny. Every man comes into the world with a problem to solve, upon the solution of which his whole course in life depends; and that problem is the due balancing of higher and lower instincts in the interest of higher life. To suppress the lower at the bidding of the higher, would, as Mr. Spencer shows, be to suppress life itself. This would be casting aside the problem, not solving it. What is important to remember is, that in the lower there is nothing essentially bad, and that the conflict between lower and higher goes on in the region of purely personal desires before it is carried into the region of social relations. An enlightened interpretation of self-interest in regard to personal matters is thus a preparation for enlightened and worthy action in the social region. For example, the man who has strenuously controlled appetite in the interest of health, and who has realized the satisfaction and happiness that comes of doing so, will be better fitted to control selfish, in the interest of social, impulses than one who had never learned to control appetite at all. He comes to this higher test fortified by self-conquest, and with an increased sense of the dignity and worth of life,—prepared moreover to believe that the path of true happiness is an ascending one. Let these truths—for they *are* truths—be believed and taught; let men see the path along which their moral development has lain in the past, and along which it must lie in the future, and we shall have little reason to regret the lures and terrors of the old theology. Either this, or there is some radical flaw in the constitution of things, by reason of which they tend to corruption,—a belief which some may hold on theological grounds, but which I venture to say would never commend itself to any unbiased intelligence, irreconcilable, as it is, with the actual existence of good in human nature and human institutions.

The questions, however, may finally be asked whether a naturalistic system of morals will ever excite the enthusiasm, ever create the same intense longing after purity of heart, that has been produced under the influence of the Christian creed. Will it ever show us the "quick-eyed sanctity" which Dr. Newman mentions as a peculiar fruit of the spirit? Will it ever call forth such a pleading for fuller and higher spiritual life as we find in Charles Wesley's hymn:

> I want a principle within
>   Of jealous, godly fear,
> A sensibility to sin,
>   A pain to feel it near.

> I want the first approach to feel

Of pride or fond desire,
To catch the wandering of my will,
    And quench the kindling fire.

Quick as the apple of an eye
    O God, my conscience make!
Awake my soul when sin is nigh
    And keep it still awake.

We have in these verses the expression of a passionate desire for conformity to a Divine ideal, and the question is, whether we can expect any approach to the same earnestness in pursuit of such excellence or elevation of character as the evolution philosophy indicates as attainable. If allowance be made for the solemnity imparted to the above utterance by the momentous character of Christian beliefs, I see no reason why the moral enthusiasm of humanity should not flow in as full tide through the new channel as through the old. After all, there are but few in every generation who are fired by an intense desire for the highest holiness; and some, it must be remembered, who appear to have very lofty spiritual ambitions, give occasion for the remark that they might better have aimed at humbler achievements. We may, therefore, reasonably hope that, when once it is understood where the hopes of humanity lie, there will be no falling off, to say the least, in the number of those who will strive after nothing short of the highest ideal their minds are capable of conceiving. . . .

The gist of Mr. Spencer's teaching, in so far as it assumes a moral character, might I think be summed up in these words. Taking the book as a whole, and looking, as we are bound to do, at its inner sense, it must, I think, be acknowledged that, while it does not deal with motives or the subjective aspect of morality, the view which it presents of the connections of moral action, the width of its survey over nature, the conclusive manner in which it demonstrates the healthfulness of what is right and the rightness of what is healthful, should tend to confirm in right determinations even those who miss from it what they deem of most importance. To those, on the other hand, who have long been wistfully looking for an exposition of the natural laws and sanctions of morality, it will be a word spoken with power, and in many ways a help towards higher life. There is but little scandal after all, if we come to think of it in supposing that action which we call moral may be a developed form of action to which the name cannot be applied: but there is great edification in the thought, now brought home to our understandings, that, by every truly moral act, we help to build up and improve the life of the world and make ourselves co-workers with the principle of life everywhere.

9. Materialism and Positivism (1882)

Materialists and positivists are commonly classed together by those who have never well understood what either materialism or positivism really is. Positivism is supposed to be materialistic because it fails to call in spiritual existences in explanation of phenomena—because, in other words, it stops short at facts, and does not seek to search out ultimate causes. The people who draw this inference take for granted, apparently, in their ordinary thinkings, that all facts must be facts of matter, and that those who confine themselves to facts must consequently be materialists. There is, therefore, really a fundamental materialism in the very criticism that fastens upon positivism the charge of materialism. Let us, however, look a little more closely into materialism considered as a mode of philosophical belief.

What do we mean by matter? First of all, it is obvious that we mean something that is objective to the mind or thinking faculty—something the mind finds upon its path, as it were, and that is the source to it of certain definite impressions. All impressions made upon the mind do not, however, equally connect themselves with the idea of matter. Some, of course, do not so connect themselves at all. When we are struck by the generosity or baseness of an action, or feel the influence of character, or experience the pleasure of harmonious or the pain of discordant relations, our consciousness is in no way concerned with matter. There might be no such thing as matter in the world, for aught we know or care about it at such moments. Yet our impressions have the very highest degree of definiteness. But even impressions made directly on our physical senses do not all, with equal force, bring the conception of matter before the mind. The word "phantasm" bears witness that visual impressions do not always convey a belief in the existence of the external reality called matter. It means, literally, "an appearance"; but it has come to mean an appearance void of all substantive reality. There is the same implication when we speak of "rubbing our eyes" to make sure that we see a thing. The sense of hearing is, in like manner, sometimes distrusted; and it may be said

SOURCE: *Popular Science Monthly,* Vol. xx (March, 1882), pp. 615-621.

that, if we lived in a world in which our only knowledge of objective existence was through sights and sounds, our idea of matter, if we had one at all, would be very different from what it actually is. There is, however, another sense, the testimony of which is held to be surer than that of any other, the sense of touch. Sight may deceive, hearing may deceive; but what we can touch and feel is real. Here we find the true basis of the popular idea of matter—that which can be *felt*; that which resists our muscles. It is true that in this case, also, we are thrown back upon subjective impressions, or, in other words, upon mental experiences; but these experiences have at once a certain breadth and a certain intimacy about them, which leads us in general to give them the preference, and to make what seems to be the source of them our very type of reality, to which we apply the special name of *matter*.

Considering the subject further, we perceive that sight and hearing are, strictly speaking, specialized forms of the sense of touch—forms so specialized that their fundamental similarity to touch is commonly lost sight of. There is, therefore, no good reason for treating their revelations as less founded on reality than those which we owe to muscular sensation; yet, for all that, matter, to the popular mind, will always be something which directly appeals to the sense of touch.

We may now begin to see what materialism is. Materialism is a form of belief, or mode of thought, which in all things prefers to rest on the evidence of the broadest impressions of physical sense, and which suspects, where it does not deny, the reality of aught that can not be brought to the test of sense-impression. It objects to advancing beyond the primary elements of consciousness; and any steps which it takes in the region of mental or moral phenomena it takes grudgingly and with a constant dread lest it should be led to recognize as real anything that can not be *felt* as we feel sticks and stones. The materialist has to live as other men, and, where his theories are not at stake, he will use ordinary human language as freely as others. He will talk of hope and fear, of love and hatred, of ambition and apathy, of honor and disgrace, of character and motive and principle, as if he knew what he meant, and as if the words he used answered to certain realities of human life. But, once touch his theory, and he will seek to drain these words of all meaning, or else fall back upon vague talk about "modes of matter."

Materialism is the refuge of minds that have been immaturely freed from spiritualism, or perhaps we may more fitly say, spiritism. By spiritism we mean that undeveloped condition of the mind in which hypothetical existences are required at every turn to account for observed phenomena, in which the mind can not bear to be left alone with facts. The child learning to walk holds by its mother's finger; the mind learning to think uses such hypotheses as it can construct, and for physical acts it frames spiritual antecedents. The child who thinks it can walk before it really can, and leaves its mother's finger, finds itself compelled to creep along by the wall. In like manner the materialist who has let go his spirit hypotheses is compelled to creep along by the wall, to rest upon something *hard*, in order to steady his steps. Divert his attention, and he will walk for a while with his hands free; but, remind him where he is, and he totters back in a moment to his tangible support.

The positivist, on the contrary, is a man who has learned to walk alone. He asks only support for his feet; and *that* he finds in the instinctive confidence in his physical and mental powers, with which, in common with other men, he is endowed. To the positivist a fact is a fact, wherever and in whatever guise he meets it. And all facts stand to him upon an equal level in point of authority. Having learned to dispense with the spirit hypothesis, he has learned to dispense also with bad metaphysics, particularly with the bad metaphysics that lie at the foundation of materialism. He repudiates the idea that a superior degree of reality attaches to *hard* things, and he bewares of drawing the metaphysical conclusion that tangible things constitute the stuff of the universe. A hard thing is well in its way: so is a soft thing; so is an impalpable thing. What the universe is ultimately made of he does not inquire, because he knows the inquiry is vain. He is content with facts, and to him a fact is *whatever produces a complete and definite impression upon the mind.* He does not make his own mind the measure and test of all possible existence, but he holds that it is the measure and test of all things that concern him. There may be things of which he knows and can know nothing, but he indulges in no speculations in regard to these—his duty being, as he conceives, to apply himself assiduously to the knowable order.

To the positivist, I have said, all facts are of equal authority; and, in order to decide what is a fact, and what therefore he should treat as a reality, he merely asks, Is it capable of definitely affecting my mind? Whatever stands definitely related to the mind is a fact, and has all the reality that can be discovered in anything whatsoever. All we can say of a piece of granite is that it definitely affects the mind; we know it as so-and-so. Whether it be, as Mr. Herbert Spencer maintains, but the representation of an unknowable reality, the positivist does not inquire: enough for him that he is able to cognize it under certain definite forms. But what we here say of a piece of granite, which would be the materialist's choice illustration of real existence, we may say equally of an action, a word, a thought, an impulse, a characteristic, a tendency. These are all facts, capable of definitely affecting the mind, and often affecting the mind more intimately and powerfully by far than tangible objects. What is it in my friend that is of most concern to me? His bodily frame? By no means. He could not exist without a bodily frame, any more than he could walk without ground to walk on. But his bodily frame may have nothing in it to please the eye, or in any way to arrest attention. The color of his hair, his weight, or even his stature, might change materially, and the difference to me would be little more than if he had changed his clothes, provided the disposition of his mind, those mental and moral qualities that had won my regard, had remained unchanged. In this case, disposition, a thing wholly impalpable, is of vastly more account to me, as an element in my environment, than the whole assemblage of physical properties and qualities represented by my friend's bodily structure. Now, the difference between the materialist and the positivist lies just in this, that the former is embarrassed at the decided effects which he sees produced by impalpable things, while the latter escapes such embarrassment entirely, simply by not having set up any arbitrary standard of what constitutes reality. The materialist does not want to recognize anything as real that does not more or less resemble his piece of granite, that does not affect the tactual sense; while the positivist is content to recognize all things as real that reveal their existence to the mind by affecting it in a definite manner. He cordially admits that the piece of granite does this, but he says also that a thousand things that have no analogy with it whatever do it as well.

Some people, chiefly materialists, will heedlessly say that this is idealism. But they are totally mistaken. Idealism consists in affirming reality of the mind and denying it to objective existence, or in affirming that the apparent distinction between subject and object is unreal and illusive. The positivist does neither the one nor the other. He simply abstains from setting up an arbitrary standard of reality. He talks neither of mind-stuff nor of world-stuff; such talk, indeed, he can not help regarding as *all* stuff. He *knows* that he knows and that he feels, and that there are certain definite sources of knowledge and feeling. He perceives that he has an environment upon which he can act, and which reacts upon him. That environment is a very complex one, answering to the complexity of his own nature. There is nothing within him, indeed, that has not some answering element without. Regarding him first as an animal, he has a nutritive system, which has its answering external realities; he has a nervous and muscular system, to which the outward frame of things in like manner responds. Taking a higher point of view, he has intellectual faculties which lay hold of the relations of things in the outer world; he has an emotional nature, with moods that vary according to the nature of the stimulus they receive; he has social faculties and propensities that find exercise in the domain of society; he has powers of moral judgment that recognize, apart altogether from the verdict of society, the essential moral qualities of actions. To each range or level of function in the individual man there are corresponding realities in the outer world; and it is to be observed that what are realities to one set of functions are not realities in the same sense to any other. The nutritive quality of an apple is not a reality to the muscular sense, nor is the weight of the apple which is cognized by the muscular sense a reality to the nutritive function. The test of reality is, we thus see, the existence or non-existence of definite relationship. To illustrate the same form further, we may observe that the physical properties of bodies are not realities to the intellectual faculty that investigates their spatial or numerical relations. The weight of a statue, or the chemical composition of the marble or bronze of which it is made, is not a reality to the aesthetic sense. The emotional nature finds its realities in the things that kindle emotion, not in those that furnish matter for intellectual exercise or for physical sensation. Who can ever forget those exquisitely simple words of the poet Tennyson?—

> And the stately ships go on
>   To their haven under the hill;
> But oh, for the touch of a vanished hand,
>   And the sound of a voice that is still!

The vanished hand, the silent voice, are here but symbols of a thousand clustering associations dear to the heart in past times, and dear to the heart still. The physical sensation is the *nexus* of things that no physical methods could possibly enable us to understand, things known only to the emotional nature. The touch or the voice that thrills one human being will be wholly indifferent to another—will, in fact, rank only as a mere physical sensation. The heart of a mother would be rent by the cry of her child in pain or in danger; but what would that cry be to a devouring beast? It would have no relation, except as a definite volume of sound, to anything in the beast's nature, and therefore, in all the elements that would speak to a human—to say nothing of a mother's— heart, would be non-existent.

It is, however, when we consider man in society that the range of impalpable realities becomes widest, and embraces facts of the deepest import; and just as society becomes more complex does this truth assume deeper significance. In a society like ours, at every step a man takes through life, he encounters forces as real as those of physical nature, but whose seat is in social institutions and in the dispositions of individual men. There are ambitions, interests, customs, prejudices, conventionalities, and a thousand intangible forms of social force, that all react upon the individual man like so many conflicting winds and currents. The individual can and does react against these, and herein he differs from a wave-tossed vessel; but, steer his course with as firm a hand and as steady an eye as he may, the great composition of social forces will powerfully affect the line of his movement.

The great practical defect of a materialistic philosophy is that it leads its adherents to underestimate all forces and influences that can not be reasoned about as we reason about the laws of matter. The materialist rests by preference on a relatively low plane of thought; and he is at a great disadvantage when he has to deal with matters that lie in a higher plane. But many are materialists in this way who would utterly repudiate materialism in theory. In other words, there are many whose methods of judgment are wholly unsuited (through excess of simplicity) to questions involving the higher human motives, or the less obvious conditions of human happiness. Many a man has made a disastrous business failure through a too materialistic way of looking at things. He wants money, let us say, for his business; he finds a partner who has money, and the importance which he attaches to this obvious and, so to speak, palpable condition, leads him to overlook the less obvious but equally important conditions of character, compatibility of disposition, and business aptitude. He finds to his cost in a short time that these things should not have been overlooked. Men, again, who have unlimited faith in the power of statute law to work moral reforms are so far materialists. Their trust is really in physical force. The whole school of political economists have helped to cultivate materialistic modes of thought, by making abstractions of all the influences that modify the working of their so-called economic laws. The truth of the matter is, that the moral condition of society at any given time profoundly modifies the whole course of business. Paralyze confidence between man and man, and the whole commercial and industrial world falls out of gear. Restore confidence, and the wheels of exchange once more begin to move. In a thousand ways, that people with materialistic modes of thought are apt to overlook, tangible results depend upon intangible causes, or are governed by intangible conditions. A true philosophy bids us always to try and rise in our speculations to the level of the phenomena with which we have to deal, and always to beware of denying or ignoring the complexity of a problem merely to indulge our intellectual indolence. Materialism, according to Comte's definition, is essentially *that habit of judging things from too low a plane*, and this is the sense in which I use the word throughout this paper. To suppose that any particular grossness attaches to matter is a conception worthy only of the moles and bats of philosophy. Before we could affirm grossness or anything else of matter we should have to get some of it, and compare it with something that was not matter, but which yet could be legitimately compared with it. Until this feat is accomplished, it would be well for all sensible people to refrain equally from praise and from abuse of matter. What there can be no risk of error in assuming is, that the exercise of certain faculties gives us the conception we have of matter, and that the exercise of other faculties gives us mental experi-

ences of quite a different order. The materialist insists upon the conver-
tibility of all experiences of the latter kind into experiences of the
former kind. The positivist, on the contrary, feels under no obligation
to perform any operation of this kind; and fails to see how he would be
advantaged if he could or did perform it. He is content to believe that we
are in no less real a world when we are dealing with human affections
and passions, with social laws and forces, and with spiritual results in
general, than when we are occupying ourselves with things that appeal
directly to the outward senses, and that give us our impressions of form,
color, and weight.

It has thus, I trust, been made apparent why the positivist would
refuse to be called a materialist, and why he would equally object to be
spoken of as an idealist. He is the only man, as it seems to me, who
takes the world exactly as he finds it; and who, upon principle, abstains
at once from unfounded affirmations, unsupported judgments, and
unanswerable questions. His business, as he conceives it, is to regulate
his life, and help others to regulate their lives, by *realities*; and a thing
to be a reality to him does not need to be a stone-wall.

10. A Defence of Modern Thought (1884)

. . . From the point of view of the present writer, there are good reasons for believing that a general readjustment of thought is now in progress, and that it is destined to go on until old forms of belief, inconsistent with a rational interpretation of the world, have been completely overthrown. This progressive readjustment is not a thing of yesterday; it is simply that gradual abandonment of the theological standpoint which has been taking place throughout the ages. As a modern philosopher has remarked, the very conception of *miracle* marks the beginnings of rationalism, seeing that it recognises an established order of things, a certain "reign of law," with which only supernatural power can interfere. The progress beyond this point consists in an increasing perception of the universality of law, and an increasing disposition to be exacting as to the evidences of miracle. No candid person can read the history of modern times without arriving at the conclusion that the whole march of civiliation illustrates, above every-thing else, this gradual change of intellectual standpoint. Man's power keeps pace ever with his knowledge of natural law, and his recognition of the uniformity of its operations. What we see to-day is simply the anticipation by thousands of the conclusion to which all past dis-coveries and observations have been pointing, that the reign of law is and always has been absolute. This is really what "agnosticism" so called means. It means that thinking men are tired of the inconsistencies of the old system of belief, and that they desire to rest in an order of conceptions not liable to disturbance. The great Faraday, who had not brought himself to this point, used to say that when he had to deal with questions of faith he left all scientific and other human reasonings at the door, and that when he had to deal with questions of science he discarded in like manner all theological modes of thought. The region

SOURCE: *Popular Science Monthly*, Vol. xxiv (April, 1884), pp. 780-793. A longer version of this article had earlier been published under the same title, with the addition: "In Reply to a Recent Pamphlet, by the Bishop of Ontario [John Travers Lewis]." The last paragraph of the essay as published here is from the original version.

of science was one region, that of faith was another; and between these he placed a wall so high that once on either side he could see nothing that lay on the other. He did not attempt to reconcile faith with science as some do; he separated them utterly, feeling them apparently to be irreconcilable. Thus he virtually lived in two worlds—one in which no miracles took place, but in which everything flowed in an orderly manner from recognised antecedents, and another in which the chain of causation might be broken at any moment by supernatural power. Since Faraday's time, however, men of science have grown bolder. They have renounced the attempt to live a divided life. They do not believe in insuperable barriers between one field of thought and another. They believe in the unity of the human mind and in the unity of truth. They have made their choice—those of them at least whom the Bishop of Ontario designates as agnostics—in favour of a world in which cause and effect maintain constant relations. In doing so they do not act wilfully, but simply yield to the irresistible weight of evidence. Miracle is a matter of more or less uncertain testimony, while the unchangeableness of natural law is a matter of daily observation. Miracles never happen in the laboratory. Supernatural apparitions do not haunt the museum. Distant ages and countries or lonely road-sides reap all the glory of these manifestations. What wonder then that the man of science prefers to trust in what his eyes daily see and his hands handle, rather than in narratives of perfervid devotees or in traditions handed down from centuries whose leading characteristic was an omnivorous credulity. There is nothing negative in this attitude of mind. On the contrary, it is positive in the highest degree. The true man of science wants to know and believe as much as possible. He desires to know what *is* and to adapt his thoughts to that; and the universe is to him simply an inexhaustible treasure-house of truths, all of more or less practical import.

It is right, however, before proceeding further, to examine this word "agnosticism" a little, to see whether it is one that is really serviceable in the present controversy. That some have been willing to apply the term to themselves and to regard it as rather *ben trovato*,[13] I am quite aware; but I think there are good reasons why serious thinkers should decline to call themselves by such a name and should object to its application to them by others.

A question proposed for discussion either can or cannot be settled; it either lies within or beyond the region in which verification is possible. If it lies within that region, no man should call himself an agnostic in regard to it. He may withhold his judgment until the evidence is complete, but suspension of judgment is not agnosticism which, if it means anything, means a profession of hopeless and, so to speak, invincible ignorance in regard to certain matters. But if it would be absurd for a man to profess himself an agnostic in regard to problems admitting or believed to admit of solution, is it not idle for any one to accept that designation because he believes that there are other problems or propositions which do not admit of solution? All one has to do in relation to the latter class of problems is to recognise their unreal or purely verbal character. It is the nature of the problem that requires to be characterized, not our mental relation thereto. The latter follows as a matter of course from the former. Moreover, why should anyone wish or consent to be designated by a term purely negative in its meaning? It is what we know, not what we do not know that should furnish us with a name, if it is necessary to have one. The little that a man knows is of vastly more consequence to him than all the untrodden continents of his ignorance. The chemist calls himself so because he professes to have a knowledge of chemistry: he does not invent for himself a name signifying his ignorance of political economy or metaphysics. Why then should any man adopt a name which defines his relation not to things that he knows or to questions to which he attributes a character of reality, but to things that he does not know and to questions which, so far as he can see, have no character of reality? Let others give him such a name if they will, but let no man voluntarily tie himself to a negation.

There are some, as I believe, who have adopted the appellation of agnostic thoughtlessly; some through indolence, as appearing to exempt them from the necessity of a decision in regard to certain difficult and, in a social sense, critical questions; and some possibly for the reason hinted at by the Bishop of Ontario, namely, lack of the courage necessary to take up a more decided position. Whatever the motive may be, however, I am persuaded that the term is a poor one for purposes of definition; and I should advise all earnest men, who think more of their beliefs than of their disbeliefs, to disown it so far as they themselves are concerned. If it be asked by what appellation those who do not believe in "revealed religion" are to be known, I should answer that it is not their duty to coin for themselves any sectarian title. They are in no sense a sect. They believe themselves to be on the high road of natural truth. It is they who have cast aside all limited and partial views, and who are opening their minds to the full teaching of the universe. Let their opponents coin names if they will: they whom the truth has made free feel that their creed is too wide for limitation.

The Bishop of Ontario stands forth in the pamphlet before us simply as the champion of the two great doctrines of God and Immortality. In reality, however, he is the champion of much more, for he does not profess that these doctrines can stand by themselves apart from a belief in revelation. The issue between the Bishop and those whom he styles agnostics is not really as to these two abstract doctrines, but as to the validity of the whole miraculous system of which his Lordship is a responsible exponent. If we can imagine a person simply holding, as the result of his own individual reasonings or other mental experiences, a belief in God as a spiritual existence animating and presiding over the works of nature, and a further belief in a future existence for the human soul, I do not see that there would necessarily be any conflict between him and the most advanced representatives of modern thought. No, the trouble does not begin here. The trouble arises when these beliefs are presented as part and parcel of a supernatural system miraculously revealed to mankind, and embracing details which bring it plainly into conflict with the known facts and laws of nature. To detach these two doctrines therefore from the system to which they belong, and put them forward as if the whole stress of modern philosophical criticism was directed against them in particular, is a controversial artifice of a rather unfair kind.

We are reminded by the right reverend author that no chain is stronger than its weakest link, and we are asked to apply the principle to the doctrine of Evolution, some of the links of which his Lordship has tested and found unable to bear the proper strain. The principle is undoubtedly a sound one; but has it occurred to his Lordship that it is no less applicable to the net-work of doctrine in which he believes than to the doctrine of Evolution? Some links of that net-work are snapping every day under no greater strain than the simple exercise of common sense by ordinary men. It is a beautiful and well-chosen position that his Lordship takes up as champion of the doctrines of God and Immortality against "agnostic" science; but it would have argued greater courage had the banner been planted on the miraculous narratives of the Old and New Testament. A gallant defence of the Scriptural account of the taking of Jericho, of the arresting for a somewhat sanguinary purpose of the earth's rotation, of the swallowing of Jonah by a whale, and his restoration to light and liberty after three days and nights of close and very disagreeable confinement, of the comfortable time enjoyed by Shadrach, Meshach, and Abendego in the fiery furnace, of the feeding of five thousand men with five loaves and two fishes and the gathering up of twelve basketsful of the fragments—a gallant defence, I say, of these things would be very much more in order; for *these* are the links that criticism has attacked and which the common judgment of the nineteenth century is daily invalidating. Modern philosophy in its negative aspect is simply a revolt against the attempt to force such narratives as these upon the adult intelligence of mankind—against the absurdity of assigning to Hebrew legends of the most monstrous kind a character of credibility which would be scornfully refused to similar productions of the imagination of any other race. Let there then be no misunderstanding: science is not concerned to prove that there is no

God, nor even that a future life is an impossibility; it simply obeys an instinct of self-preservation in seeking to repel modes of thought and belief which, in their ultimate issues, are destructive of all science.

One has only to reflect for a moment, in order to see how much theological baggage the orthodox disputant throws away, when he confines his arguments to the two points of God and a Future Life. Were it thrown away in sincerity argument might cease; but no, the manoeuvre is first to make a formidable demonstration as champion of two cardinal doctrines which in themselves arouse little opposition, even where they do not commend assent, and then to apply the results of the proceeding to the benefit of those parts of the system which had been kept in the background. It is not the interest of a simple theistic belief, unconnected with any scheme of theology, that the Bishop of Ontario writes: what he has at heart, I venture to say, is that men may believe as he does. The theism of Francis Newman, or of Victor Hugo, or Mazzini—all convinced theists—would be very unsatisfactory in his eyes, and it may be doubted whether he would take up his pen for the purpose of promoting theism of this type. It should therefore be thoroughly understood that while his Lordship is professedly combating agnosticism, he is really waging war on behalf of that elaborate theological system of which he is an exponent—that system which bids us look to the Bible for an account of the creation of the world and of man; and which requires us to believe that the Creator found it necessary in former times, for the right government of the world, to be continually breaking through the laws of physical succession which he himself had established. In arguing against the doctrine of Evolution, he labors to establish the opposite doctrine of the creation and government of the world by *miracle*.

The question therefore is:—Can science be free and yet accommodate itself to the whole elaborate scheme of Christian orthodoxy? The great majority of those who are most entitled to speak on behalf of science say No: and it is this negative which his Lordship of Ontario converts into a denial of the two doctrines above-mentioned. But let those who are at all familiar with the course of modern thought ask themselves if they recall in the writings of any leading philosopher of the day arguments specially directed against the hypothesis of God or even against that of a possible future state of existence for humanity. What every one can at once remember is that the writers who are called "agnostics," the Spencers, Huxleys, Tyndalls, and Darwins, plead for the universality of nature's laws and the abiding uniformity of her-processes. That is what they are concerned to maintain, because it is upon that that all science depends. Scientific men in general are but little disposed to disturb any one's faith in God or Immortality, so long as these doctrines are not associated with, or put forward as involving others which really invade the domain of science and tend to cast uncertainty upon its methods and results.

In seeking to account for "the modern spread of agnosticism," the Bishop finds that it is to "the widely spread popularity of the theory of Evolution, leading as it does to materialism," that the phenomenon is to be attributed. Consequently the theory of Evolution must be destroyed. The episcopal edict has gone forth, and the episcopal batteries are raised against this later Carthage of infidelity. But, alas! it does not sufficiently appear that the right reverend director of the siege understands either the nature of the task he has undertaken or the significance which would attach to success could he achieve it. To take the latter point first: science was making very rapid progress before the evolution theory had acquired any wide popularity, before in fact anything was known of it outside of one or two speculative treatises; and already the opposition of science to a scheme which makes this earth the theatre of miracle-working power was well-marked. Twenty-two years ago, when "The Origin of Species" was but two years old, and had still a great deal of opposition to encounter even from men of science, before even the term Evolution had any currency in the special sense it now bears, a leading prelate of the Church of England, Bishop Wilberforce, discerned a sceptical movement "too wide-spread and connecting itself with far too general conditions" to be explained otherwise than as "the first stealing over the sky of the lurid lights which shall be shed profusely around the great Antichrist."* To charge the present intellectual state of the world therefore on the doctrine of Evolution is to ignore that general movement of thought which, before the idea of evolution was a factor of any importance in modern speculation, had already, as the Bishop of Oxford testified, carried thousands away from their old theological habitations, and which, with or without the theory of evolution, was quite adapted to produce the state of things which we see to-day in the intellectual world.

The doctrine of evolution is simply the form in which the dominant scientific thought of the day is cast. As a working hypothesis it presents very great advantages; and the thinkers of to-day would find it hard to dispense with and the aid it affords. But supposing it could be shown that the doctrine, as at present conceived, was untenable—what then? Would men of science at once abandon their belief in the invariability of natural law and fly back to mediaeval superstitions? By no means. If there is any class of men who have learnt the lesson that the spider taught to Bruce, it is the class of scientific workers. Destroy one of their constructions and they set to work again, with unconquerable industry, to build another. In fact they are always testing and trying their own

---

*Vide Preface to "Replies to Essays and Reviews."

constructions; and we may be sure that if the evolution theory is ever to be swept away it will be by scientific not theological hands. It holds its ground now, because it is a help to thought and investigation; if it should ever become so beset with difficulties as to be no longer serviceable it will be withdrawn from use, as many a theory has been before it, and as many a one will be in the days to come. Amongst contemporary men of science there is probably none who believes more strongly in the doctrine in question than the Editor of the *Popular Science Monthly*, Prof. E.L. Youmans; yet in a recent number of his magazine he has marked his attitude towards it in a manner which for our present purpose is very instructive. "It is undeniable," he writes,

that the difficulties in the way of the doctrine of evolution are many and formidable, and it will no doubt take a long time to clear them up; while the solution of still unresolved problems will very possibly result in important modifications of the theory as now entertained. But the establishment of the doctrine of evolution, as a comprehensive law of nature, is no longer dependent upon its freedom from embarrassments, or that absolute completeness of proof which will only become possible with the future extension of knowledge. Notwithstanding these drawbacks the evidence for it is so varied, so consistent, and so irresistible, as to compel its broad acceptance by men of science, who, while disagreeing upon many of its questions, find it indispensable as a guide to the most multifarious investigations.

We come now to the further question of the validity of the criticisms directed in the pamphlet before us against the doctrine of evolution, in discussing which the competency of the critic for his self-imposed task will necessarily come more or less under consideration. Let us first notice the quotations which his Lordship brings forward, remembering that the doctrine of evolution in its present shape may be said to be the work of the last twenty years. Well, his Lordship quotes three leading scientific authors, Owen, Agassiz and Lyell;[14] but it is noticeable that, in no case, does he give the date of his quotation, and in the case of the first two does not even mention the work in which the passage he refers to is to be found. The quotations are intended to show that these eminent authors rejected the doctrine of the "origin of species by natural selection." As regards Agassiz, who died ten years ago, every one knows that this was the case; and most are also aware that the great Swiss naturalist left behind him a son, a naturalist almost equally great, who supports the Darwinian theory as strongly as his father opposed it. Owen, though not a Darwinian in the full sense, held views which were clearly in the direction of natural selection. It is, however, when we come to Lyell that we have cause for astonishment. Here we have the most eminent of English geologists, whose adhesion to the Darwinian theory, announced for the first time in 1863—the date of the publication of the first edition of his "Antiquity of Man"—created such a sensation in the scientific world, quoted, at this time of day, as an anti-Darwinian! What are we to think of this? I cannot and do not believe, nor would I wish to suggest, that the Right Reverend the Bishop of Ontario was carried so far in his zeal against evolution as deliberately to misrepresent Sir Charles Lyell's attitude towards that doctrine. The only other hypothesis, however, is that of extreme ignorance. Of this his Lordship must stand, not only accused, but convicted. The fact of Sir Charles Lyell's conversion to the views of Darwin on the origin of species was one of which the whole reading world took note at the time, and which has been known to every tyro in general science from that day to this. His Lordship, quoting from the "Principles of Geology," but without any mention of edition, represents Sir Charles as holding "that species have a real existence in nature, and that each was endowed at the time of its creation with the attributes and organization by which it is now distinguished." That these *were* Sir Charles Lyell's views when the earlier editions of his "Principles" were published everyone is aware; but it is a most extraordinary thing that anyone should have quoted them as his full twenty years after he had distinctly abandoned them. The preface to the fourth edition of the "Antiquity of Man" opens as follows:—

> The first edition of the "Antiquity of Man" was published in 1863, and was the first work in which I expressed my opinion of the prehistoric age of man, and also my belief in Mr. Darwin's theory of the 'Origin of Species' as the best explanation yet offered of the connection between man and those animals which have flourished successively on the earth.

In the 10th edition of his "Principles," published in 1868 he says (page 492) that

> Mr. Darwin, without absolutely proving this (theory), has made it appear in the highest degree probable, by an appeal to many distinct and independent classes of phenomena in natural history and geology.

Darwin himself would not have claimed more for his theory than this. Professor Huxley would not claim more for it today. Enough for either of them the admission that, by arguments drawn from many quarters, it had been rendered "in the highest degree probable." In his "Antiquity of Man,''* Sir Charles Lyell expressly acknowledges the inconclusiveness of the arguments he had used at an earlier date to prove that "species were primordial creations and not derivative." His reasonings, he frankly confesses, could not hold their ground "in the light of the facts and arguments adduced by Darwin and Hooker." As regards the "descent of man," after quoting a passage from Darwin to the effect that "man is the co-descendant with other mammals of a common progenitor," he observes that

> we certainly cannot escape from such a conclusion without abandoning many of the weightiest arguments which have been urged in support of variation and natural selection considered as the subordinate causes by which new types have been gradually introduced into the world.

On every point, therefore, the real views of Sir Charles Lyell, as formed in the light of the facts adduced by Darwin and of his own maturer reasonings, were totally opposed to those quoted in the Bishop's pamphlet. Is it not remarkable, such being the case, that not one member of the reverend and learned clergy of the Diocese of Kingston, by whose special request this document was given to the world, should have suggested a correction on this point? Was there not a lay delegate who could have done it; or were they all—Bishop, clergy, and laymen—equally in the dark? It would really seem so. Who can wonder that the doctrine of evolution does not make much progress in certain quarters?

Sir Charles Lyell unfortunately is not the only author misrepresented. Huxley is said to "discredit" the origin of life from non-living matter. Huxley does nothing of the kind; he simply says that the experiments heretofore made to show that life can be so developed have not been successful. On the page of the pamphlet immediately preceding that on which this statement is made in regard to Huxley, we are informed, correctly, that the same great naturalist professes "a philosophic faith in the probability of spontaneous generation." Surely his Lordship could not have understood the force of these words, or he would not have said, almost immediately after, that "the origin of life on earth . . . is not only discredited** by Huxley but by many other

---

*See 4th edition, p. 469.

**His Lordship means "discredited not only by Huxley, but by &c." The inaccuracy of expression observable here is paralleled in many other passages of the pamphlet. For example, his Lordship says, page 5: "They are not content to speak for themselves, but for all the world besides." A Bishop should write better English than this.

great scientists.'' A writer who finds such comparatively simple language beyond his comprehension is not, one would judge, very well fitted to enter the lists against the leading thinkers of the day, except perhaps for strictly diocesan purposes.

That his Lordship is really hopelessly at sea in discussing this question is evident by many signs. Such sentences as the following speak volumes for the mental confusion of their author: ''Agnosticism takes refuge in Evolution in order to get rid of the idea of God as unthinkable and unknowable.'' Here again inaccuracies of language. An idea may be unthinkable in the sense of not admitting of being *thought out*, but can an idea be said to be ''unknowable?'' What is an unknowable idea? An idea must be known in order to be an idea at all. But this mere verbal inaccuracy is not the worst. We had been told that Agnosticism was a form of opinion according to which nothing could be known of God. Now it seems that Agnosticism has to fall back on Evolution, ''in order to get rid of the idea of God as unthinkable and unknowable.'' Now the so called Agnosticism could not have been agnosticism in reality, otherwise it would not have required the help of evolution in such a matter. If we ask how Evolution helps Agnosticism to regard ''the idea of God as unthinkable and unknowable,'' we shall only find the confusion growing worse confounded. Evolution has nothing to do with such questions: it is a simple theory as to the mode of generation and order of succession of different forms of existences.

It is, however, when his Lordship comes to discuss the doctrine of the survival of the fittest that his sad want of acquaintance with the whole subject shows itself most conspicuously. Let me quote:

> By some means or other 'the survival of the fittest in the struggle for existence' is assumed to be a law of nature, and if it be so our faith is severely taxed. Survival of the fittest—fittest for what? If the answer be, fittest for surviving, we argue in a circle, and get no information whatever. The only rational answer must be, they survive who are fittest for their environments in size, strength and vigour.

Let me here ask what sense the learned author can possibly attach to these last words except the very one he had just discarded as meaningless—''fitness to survive.'' How is fitness to environment proved except by the actual fact of survival? Do environments always require ''size'' as an element of fitness? By no means, they sometimes require smallness. When a mouse escapes into a hole, where the cat cannot follow, it survives not by reason of its size, but by reason of its smallness. Strength again is one element of adaptation to environment, but only one; and it may fall far below some other element, swiftness, for example, or cunning, in practical importance. The fact however that the learned author sees no meaning in the answer "fitness to survive," tells the whole story of his own unfitness for the special environment in which he has placed himself in attempting to discuss the doctrine of evolution, and rather tends to create doubt as to the survival of the work he has given to the world. This is a matter in which no aptitude in quoting Horace is of any avail. The road to an understanding of the terms and conceptions of modern science lies in a careful study at first hand of the works in which these terms and conceptions are expounded. His Lordship assumes that, if we say that those survive who are fit to survive, we utter a barren truism. It is a truism we may grant, but not a barren one, any more than the axioms of geometry are barren. The simple word "fitness" implies a definite external something, adaptation to which is the price of existence. The definiteness of the mould involves the definiteness of that which is moulded; and all the miracles of life and organization we see around us are in the last resort merely examples of adaptation to fixed conditions of existence. "Born into life we are," says Matthew Arnold, "and life must be our mould." By "life" understand the universe and we have a poetical version of the doctrine of the survival of the fittest. It so happens, and this is a further truth which it would not be well to pass over, that adaptation does more or less imply excellence even from the human standpoint. All those adaptations that favour human life and happiness we of course call excellent, even though they may not be favourable to the life and happiness of other living creatures. And as man has thriven mightily and prevailed, adaptation *in general* presents itself to him in a favourable light. Occasionally, when his crops are destroyed by some insect pest wonderfully adapted for its work, or when his cattle are infested with deadly parasites, or when some germ of disease is multiplying a millionfold in his own frame, he sees that *all* adaptations are not yoked to his especial service.

His Lordship seems to suppose that the believers in the doctrine of the survival of the fittest are bound to show that there has been a steady improvement of type from the first dawn of life. To show how gross and inexcusable a misunderstanding this is, I need only quote two sentences from Sir Charles Lyell's "Antiquity of Man":—"One of the principal claims," observes the great geologist,

of Mr. Darwin's theory to acceptance is that *it enables us to dispense with a law of progression* as a necessary accompaniment of variation. It will account equally well for what is called degradation or a retrogade movement towards a simpler structure, and does not require Lamarck's continual creation of monads; for this was a necessary part of his system in order to explain how, after the progressive power had been at work for myriads of ages, there were as many beings of the simplest structure in existence as ever.*

Writing thus in ignorance of what the law of the survival of the fittest, as formulated by Darwin, and accepted by modern men of science, really means, his Lordship is able to ask such pointless questions as whether the law is illustrated in the slaughtering of the flower of a nation in war, and whether it is the fittest who survive famines, pestilences, shipwrecks, &c. His Lordship evidently does not himself believe there is any provision for the survival of the fittest in the Providential government of the world; yet, strange to say, he taunts evolutionists with this lack in the general scheme of things. If it be an embarrassment to their theory how much more should it be to the Bishop's theology? The evolutionist might, however, turn round and instruct the divine out of his own pocket Bible, where it is expressly stated that the wicked shall not live out half his days; and then out of the newspapers which continually show us what happens to the violent and bloody man, to the intemperate and to various other classes of evil doers. The evolution philosophy does not guarantee, as has been already shown, continuous progress in what, from the human standpoint, may seem the best directions; but evolutionists are able to note, and do note with satisfaction, that the qualities which the moral sense of mankind most approves do in point of fact tend to the survival of their possessors. War itself illustrates the principle; seeing that the most important element of strength abroad is cohesion at home, a condition which must depend on a relatively high development of social justice. To take an example from our own history: English arms would not have been so successful as they have been abroad, had there not been an united country behind them. It was the virtues, not the vices, of the Roman people that enabled them to conquer the world. It was their vices not their virtues that led to their fall. Fitness to survive is a quality the import of which varies according to circumstances. In shipwrecks (to pursue his Lordship's illustrations) the fit to survive are those who can swim, or who have readiness of resource or strength of constitution. In famines and pestilences the physically stronger will as a rule survive; though here prudence and self-control become also most important elements of safety. Let it always be remembered that the problem with which evolutionary philosophy has to grapple is not how to account for a perfect world, or a perfect state of society, but how to account for just such a mingling of good and evil (accompanied by general tendencies towards good) as we actually witness. This once

*Fourth edition, 4th page 459.

settled, most of the objections of the theologians would be seen to fall wide of the mark.

To persons unfamiliar, or but slightly familiar, with the present subject, it is possible that the Bishop of Ontario may appear to have touched a weak point in the doctrine under discussion where he says;—

> Laws of nature should be obeyed and co-operated with, not fought against and thwarted; and, if the survival of the fittest be one of those laws, we ought to abolish all hospitals and asylums for the blind, the deaf, the drunkard, the idiot and the lunatic, and we ought to expose to death all sickly, puny and superfluous infants.

A word therefore in regard to this objection may not be thrown away. The first observation to make is, that there is nothing whatever in the law of the survival of the fittest, as understood by men of science to-day, which could possibly be converted into a rule of conduct. The scientific world is not aware that nature has any ends in view, or is capable of having any ends in view, which she needs the help of man to enable her to realize. Science does not attribute purpose to nature. Science has simply obtained a glimmering of how, in point of fact, nature works. It sees that survival is a question of fitness, in other words a question of the fulfilment of the conditions on which continued existence depends. In some cases, as is well known, superiority of type becomes an impediment, not a help, to the preservation of life; and in a vast number of cases the differentiations on which survival depends imply neither progress nor retrogression.* What moral guidance, therefore, can possibly be found in a simple perception of the fact that in the realm of nature there are conditions attached to survival? We may ask, in the next place, whether there is any single law of nature which men "obey," or ever have obeyed, in the sense in which his Lordship bids us obey the law of the survival of the fittest. When a conflagration rages, do we "obey" and "co-operate" with nature by adding fuel to the flames? When pestilence is abroad, do we try to increase its deadly activity? When we stumble, do we make a point of yielding to the law of gravitation and throwing ourselves headlong? When the winter winds are howling, do we throw open doors and windows that we may feel all the force and bitterness of the blast? Or do we, in these and all other cases, seek to modify the action of one law by that of another—a process his Lordship calls "thwarting"—in order that their combined or balanced action may yield us as nearly as possible, the results we

*Vide Spencer, "Principles of Sociology," Vol. I. pp. 106-7, and Haeckel, "History of Creation," Vol. I. p. 285.

desire. We throw water on the fire. We use disinfectants and prophylactics against the plague. We set muscular force against that of gravitation. We oppose warmth to cold. In none of these cases do we ask what nature wants: we are content to know what *we* want. We don't really believe that nature wants anything; so we have no hesitation or compunction in letting our wants rule. In the matter of the weak and sickly, they might perish if unconscious forces alone were at work, or even in certain conditions of human society; but it does not suit *our* interests, for very obvious reasons, to let them perish. To do so would strike at all human affections, and would so far weaken the bonds of society and render the whole social fabric less secure. Moreover a sick man is very different from a sick animal. The latter is inevitably inferior as an animal, whereas the former may not only not be inferior, but may be superior as a *man*, and capable of rendering much service to society. Two instances occur to me as I write—that of the late Professor Cairnes in England, and of the late Professor Ernest Bersot in France, both smitten with cruel and hopeless maladies, but both fulfilling, in an eminent degree, the highest intellectual and moral offices of *men*. What the well do for the sick is of course obvious and attracts sufficient attention; but what the sick do for the well, not being so obvious, attracts less attention than it deserves. Yet how many lessons of patience, fortitude, and resignation—lessons that all require—come to us from the sick bed, or at least from those whom weakness of constitution or perhaps some unhappy accident has robbed of a normal activity and health. At times we see superiority of intellectual and moral endowment triumphing over the most serious physical disabilities; as in the case of the present Postmaster-General of England, who accidentally lost his sight when quite a youth. The late M. Louis Blanc, a man of splendid talents, never advanced beyond the stature of a child. The ancient Spartans might have exposed one of so feeble a frame on Taygetus; for with them every man had to be a soldier; but, in modern life, with its greatly diversified interests, many a man too weak to be a soldier can yet render splendid service to the community. It will, therefore, I trust, be sufficiently obvious, first, that nature has no commands to give us in this matter; and secondly, that there are excellent reasons why we should not treat the sick and weakly, as the lower animals commonly, but not universally, treat the sick and weakly of their own kind.*

There is, however, another view of this question which should not be overlooked. While human beings in civilized countries manifest, and always have manifested, more or less sympathy with the physically

*See Romanes, "Animal Intelligence," pp. 471, 475, as to the sympathy exhibited by the monkey towards their sick.[15]

afflicted, their steadfast aim has been to get rid of physical evil in all its forms. No care that is taken of the sick has for its object the perpetuation of sickness, but rather its extirpation. We do not put idiots to death; but when an idiot dies there is a general feeling of relief that so imperfect an existence has come to an end. Were idiots permitted to marry, the sense of decency of the whole community would be outraged. Public opinion blames those who marry knowing that there is some serious taint in their blood; and commends on the other hand those who abstain from, or defer, marriage on that account. There is probably room for a further development of sentiment in this direction. We need to feel more strongly that all maladies and ailments are in their nature preventible, inasmuch as they all flow from definite physical antecedents. As long as our views on this subject are tinged in the smallest degree with supernaturalism, so long will our efforts to track disease to its lair and breeding grounds be but half-hearted. How can we venture to check abruptly, or at all, the course of a sickness sent expressly for our chastisement? Is it for us to say when the rod has been sufficiently applied? How do we dare to fortify ourselves in advance against disease, as if to prevent the Almighty from dealing with us according to our deserts? We vaccinate for smallpox, we drain for malaria, we cleanse and purify for cholera, we ventilate and disinfect, we diet and we exercise—and all for what? Precisely to avoid the paternal chastenings which we have been taught are so good for us, and the origin of which has always been attributed by faith to the Divine pleasure. Evidently our views are undergoing a change. We all wish to be fit to survive, and all more or less believe that it is in our power to be so and to help others to be so. We believe in sanitary science; and, if we attribute any purpose in the matter to the Divine mind, it is that all men should come to the knowledge of the truth, as revealed by a study of nature, and live. . . .

There are two great practical problems with which men of intellect may grapple to-day. One is how to *put back* the thoughts of men so that all that was credible to their forefathers may be credible to them. The other is how to *put forward* men's thoughts so that they may harmonize with the new knowledge the world has acquired—so that a new intellectual and moral equilibrium may be established. At the first of these tasks the priesthoods are labouring, with many helpers from the ranks of the laity. In regard to many of these, both priests and laymen, one must testify that they have a true zeal for human welfare. Still, in spite of all the reactionary efforts made by men who are true, and by men who are not true, the intellectual standpoint of the world is shifting. Men do not believe as they once did, they cannot believe as they once did; though they may religiously utter the old formulas, and close their eyes harder and harder against the growing light. The second cause has as yet but few avowed helpers. There are scoffers enough in the world in all conscience. Those who confess to one in private that they have ceased to believe what the churches teach are to be met everywhere; they seem at times almost to outnumber the professors of orthodox opinions. But, when it is a question of openly advocating what they hold to be the truth, the great majority decline a responsibility so fraught with chances of social and public disfavor. One great reason for this timidity is, that hitherto it has not been seen how a new construction might rise upon the ruins of the old. To see this, however, all that is needed is to study closely the framework of things, and mark how society is actually put together, and how it has grown together throughout the ages "by that which every joint supplieth." These pages have not been written solely for a controversial purpose. They have been written in the hope that some may be moved to assert for themselves a larger intellectual liberty, and that the great cause of putting forward men's thoughts, and preparing the new equilibrium, may in some humble measure be advanced.

PART THREE
On Morality and Politics

To criticize is to judge conduct or policy in accordance with an ideal standard.

—Nicholas Flood Davin, "London and
Canadian Press," *CMNR* (February, 1874)

To live worthily we must set before us an ideal, and that ideal must be something more than mere worldly success. The love of the beautiful and the true must enter into it in some measure, or it is no ideal at all. . . . These considerations are of equal applicability in the wider sphere of our national affairs.

—W.D. LeSueur,
"Old and New in Canada"(1875)

Introduction

The third chapter of W.D. LeSueur's inner biography has a background which will be generally familiar to most readers. The three decades following Confederation were years of the consolidation and expansion of that essentially political achievement. The individuals who dominated the Canadian landscape—Macdonald, Blake, Mercier, and Laurier—were political animals; the great organizational achievement of the period was the growth of two national political parties; the scandals and the successes were political; even the scaffold from which Louis Riel was hanged was as much a political platform as it was a structure for execution. Political and material expansion went, with the force of nationalism lending to its dynamic, hand in hand. The National Policy, one Canadian historian has written, was "a materialistic policy for a materialistic age."[1] The spike driven at Craigellachie, the "infant industries" of an industrializing Ontario, and the men in sheepskin coats who at the turn of the century found themselves at the wood-frame Dominion Immigration Hall in Winnipeg were all to become part of the Canadian historical experience because of the gradual articulation of a conception of the national good filtered through the lenses of political necessity.

There is a side to the political history of these years which is, however, less well known. The reaction by intellectuals in Canada to the political ethos of their age forms this more specific context for the third major area of W.D. LeSueur's social concern and criticism, for the political atmosphere of the Canadian nation in the final third of the nineteenth century was by no means without critical commentators. The general tone of this intellectual response to the age of Macdonald and Laurier was captured by the sensitive Ottawa public servant and poet, Archibald Lampman, in "The Modern Politician":

> What manner of soul is his to whom high truth
> Is but the plaything of a feverish hour,
> A dangling ladder to the ghost of power?
> Gone are the grandeurs of the world's iron youth,
> When kings were mighty, being made by swords.
> Now comes the transit age, the age of brass,

When clowns into the vacant empires pass,
Blinding the multitude with specious words.
To them faith, kinship, truth and verity,
Man's sacred rights and very holiest thing,
Are but the counters at a desperate play,
Flippant and reckless what the end may be,
So that they glitter, each his little day,
The little mimic of a vanished king.[2]

To each of these lines, which mirror the disappointments and unease of an age, could be added a half-dozen sermons, speeches, and articles which echoed the poet's sentiments. The age was one of unquestionable "progress" in a number of ways; yet even so, something was happening in the process, it was believed, to the moral core of the nation. Political morality, like religious authority, seemed to be in decline and the question of the age was 'why?' W.D. LeSueur was a major voice among many who grappled for an answer.

I

Disaffection with the course of political events and with the state of political culture in general was a major factor giving the "Canada First" movement of the 1870s its semblance of cohesion. Goldwin Smith, its intellectual mentor if not its actual leader, lamented the sad state of political affairs for decades. "Corruption grows by what it feeds upon," he wrote on the eve of the Pacific Scandal.

It will increase, and increase in an ever accelerating ratio, while the moral resistance will become continually weaker, till among us, as in other countries, bribery becomes a jest, and corruptionist a name hardly more odious than that of politician. . . . How is the evil to be checked? This cry is loudly raised to-day by the still unextinguished morality of the nation. Tomorrow it will be heard no more, and the thought of reform and purity will be derided as an impracticable dream.[3]

The dreams embodied in the Confederation agreement seemed, to Canada Firsters, to have taken an ironic turn. Had not the federal union been possible, W.A. Foster asked, "because it offered a prospect of relief from that sickening political squabbling which party spirit carried to the greatest extreme and opened up a new arena in which statesmanship might win prizes worth contending for?"[4] Privately, Goldwin Smith revealed the same convictions as to the moral vacuity of Canadian political life. "In Canada," he wrote to a correspondent in 1876, "we are giving to the world a specimen of party government when there is no longer any question upon which a party can be rationally or morally formed. The result is the alternate ascendancy of two gangs, calling themselves by party names without the shades of distinctive principle." For Smith, one such "distinctive principle" was to put national before party ends, for his next sentence read: "Confederation without nationality is no bond."[5] This was, in part, the meaning of the phrase "Canada First." As Colonel George T. Denison recalled, many years after the demise of the movement: "we believed in the sentiment of putting the country above all other considerations, the same feeling that existed in Rome, 'When none was for a party; when all were for the State.' This idea we were to preach in season and out of season."[6]

Condemnations of the lack of moral or political principles within the political system in Canada were not confined to the pages of the *Canadian Monthly* or to supporters of the "Canada First" movement. They also found their way into the assembled bodies of churches and universities. Here the loudest and most persistent voice was that of G.M. Grant, a leading Presbyterian divine of ecumenical bent and the Principal of Queen's University from 1877 to 1902. As early as 1867 Grant had been unable, when speaking on the subject of "Reformers of the Nineteenth Century" to a Y.M.C.A. audience in Halifax, to include politicians among "moral and spiritual Reformers": the subjects of his address were Coleridge, Wordsworth, and Carlyle.[7]

As Grant observed political life around him during the 1880s and 1890s, he had even less reason for doing so. It was utterly necessary, he insisted, to establish the relationship of religion to the secular life, for without a religious backing the citizen will lack an understanding of true liberty; and without liberty the religious life is impossible. The greatest threat to this liberty, he warned his Halifax audience, was political allegiance. "As regards politics, the citizen's difficulty is not with the nation, but with his party." It was necessary, therefore, for the citizen to remain free of the restrictions imposed upon his liberty of thought by party affiliation. "Party organization," he told an 1880 gathering of North America's Presbyterians in Philadelphia, "may be thought incapable of allowing such liberty, because party aims at immediate and definite results. He that will not submit to its platform must be read out of his party."[8]

For the remainder of his life Grant reiterated these concerns. "Political partyism," he told a Toronto congregation in 1887, was worse than clericalism.

It offered to our young men a faction or machine identified with dead issues, and filled with living rancour. . . . It made one-half of our people look upon the other half as enemies against whom they must ever be on the watch; against whom every trick, stratagem and fraud was allowable.[9]

Such warnings were a staple in the intellectual diet of Grant's students at Queen's. "There are two extremes against which you should be on your guard from the outset," he told its 1899 graduates: "the standing aloof from the general life, and on the other hand identifying yourselves with a party machine, and becoming soiled . . . with the debasing aims and practices of those whose motto is—Our party, right or wrong."[10]

This widespread concern by Canadian intellectuals over political morality was intensified by the fact that it was obvious that the problem was not really a Canadian one. It did not lie in the origins of Canadian political parties or in the personal morality of the country's politicians. In the United States between the end of the Civil War and the turn of the twentieth century, middle class reformers voiced complaints of their own government and legislators similar to those of Goldwin Smith, G.M. Grant, and W.D. LeSueur. American politics in the Gilded Age were the politics of hollowness, when noise and histrionics won office. The political tone of the Gilded Age was perhaps set by the member of President Grant's cabinet who, summing up his philosophy of executive-legislative relations in 1869, said: "You can't use tact with a Congressman! A Congressman is a hog! You must take a stick and hit him on the snout!"[11]

Little wonder, given such attitudes, that foreign observers such as Moisei Ostrogorski could write of the age that "ideas, convictions, character, disqualify a man from public life."[12] Little wonder, too, that political commentators such as E.L. Godkin, editor of *The Nation*, were repelled by what they saw around them, and called for an "awakened [public] conscience" and for political reform. Such reform, Godkin wrote to a friend as early as 1867, "ought to be set on foot everywhere, having for its object the hunting down of corrupt politicians, the stoppage of unscrupulous nominations, the exposure of jobs, of the sale of franchises and votes, and the sharpening of the public conscience on the whole subject of political purity. If this cannot be done," he concluded, "the growing wealth will, you may rely on it, kill—not the nation, but the form of government without which, as you and I believe, the nation would be of little value to humanity."[13]

Godkin's priorities, as revealed in this letter, reach the heart of the matter and strike to the centre of W.D. LeSueur's concern for the relationship between morality and political culture. It was not with personal morality or even with the national well-being in themselves that Godkin, LeSueur and other critics wished to direct their major attention. These were but the specific manifestations of problems that seemed inherent in popular self-government in an increasingly democratic age. It is not insignificant that the years between 1872 and 1901, which mark the publication of LeSueur's first and last articles on morality and politics, also witnessed the appearance of Sir Henry Sumner Maine's four essays on *Popular Government* (1885), James Bryce's massive study, *The American Commonwealth* (two volumes, 1893), and W.E.H. Lecky's equally-thorough examination of *Democracy and Liberty* (two volumes, 1896).[14]

These men differed significantly from each other in their evaluation of the nature, workings, and ramifications of popular government, and in their judgements on the relative merits of democracy. But they were united by a common commitment to the theory of progressive development, to evolution as a principle that could help to explain the process by which certain nations "progress" while others do not. They also shared an historical approach to the studies which they undertook. Each was an evolutionary social critic concerned not so much with determining how to ameliorate specific social problems as with focussing in upon ethical problems raised within the specific political cultures which they examined.

Contemporaries of W.D. LeSueur, each of these men lived in an age of constant change and social malaise, whether in W.E. Gladstone's England, Grover Cleveland's America, or John A Macdonald's Canada. It was the bewildering and perplexing reality of this transformation which drove them to large-scale social analysis. As J.W. Burrow states, in *Evolution and Society*:

> The fact of historical change, its speed and its terrible apparent autonomy and indifference to individual human desires and actions, was something of which no thoughtful mid-Victorian could remain unaware. It is understandable that men involved in such a transformation should become aware of the impersonal character and immense possibilities, exhilarating and terrifying, of social change, and only natural therefore that they should become preoccupied, not merely with the existence of sociological laws, as distinct from laws of individual human nature, but particularly with the question of social change, as opposed to the less spectacular problem of social stability. They knew that their society was travelling, and they wanted to know the route and destination.[15]

The concerns of these Victorian social critics thus reflected the needs of their age, which Burrow rightly insists "can only be understood in terms of the collapse or modification of the certainties, religious, ethical and political, of the earlier part of the nineteenth century."[16]

II

The essays and addresses which document this chapter of the biography of W.D. LeSueur's mind reflect virtually all the political problems which disturbed contemporaries such as Goldwin Smith, G.M. Grant, and Henry Sumner Maine. In November, 1872, for example, while Sir John Macdonald feared that Sir Hugh Allan was in the process of blackmailing his government and that publication of the facts of the "corrupt bargain" between Cartier and Allan's railway interests could topple his ministry,[17] LeSueur published "Party Politics" in the *Canadian Monthly*. It was his first article on the subject of prevailing political morality, and the fact that he was a federal civil servant was probably sufficient to make him seek the security of the pseudonym, "A Radical." "Party," he wrote, "may . . . be defined with absolute correctness as a body of men whose interest in supporting one another is greater than the interest they have in giving a right direction at all times to public policy." (p. 178) Six months later, when Lucius Seth Huntington read his long and solemn indictment of the Macdonald ministry's involvement with railway interests in the House of Commons, thus beginning the chain of events which unravelled the facts of the "Pacific Scandal," LeSueur might well have felt fully satisfied that he had chosen to use a phrase as unequivocal as "absolute correctness" in his definition.

In "Old and New in Canada" one not only reads of the disaffection of a generation with contemporary political morality, political parties, and the partisan party press, but also senses the stirrings of a hope that the growth of a non-partisan public consciousness willing to speak out on vital issues might affect some changes in this state of national affairs. "What we really require," he had written in 1872, "is not closer party organization . . . but a general awakening of the political consciousness of the country." (p. 179) The "Canada First" movement seemed to represent just such a national awakening. It was, to be sure, a shift of opinion experienced and given expression only by a few—but it *was* a beginning, a sign of hope, an indication that perhaps a "real faith in liberty and truth" (p. 183) might, after all, prevail if the critical spirit could be applied to political life. "Philosophical speculation," LeSueur claimed, could have as salutary an effect on the discussion of important political issues as it did in other, more abstract, realms of the mind.

But the current state of political life mitigated against this necessary questioning. The party system gave to the modern public "the permanent spectacle of two bodies of men professing to speak the truth upon public questions, and yet, with monotonous regularity, contradicting one another on every point." The main problem was not that 'grosser immoralities' such as the Pacific Scandal would go unnoticed. Such obvious wrongs would be discovered and corrected. Political partyism had a much more insidious effect, for it produced an "intellectual and moral confusion," a "desolating scepticism" which slowly permeated the public consciousness and led people to suspect "both . . . men's motives and . . . the validity of all logical processes." (p. 187) What was *needed* was a "faith in reason as applied to public affairs"; what *existed* was a national culture that was for the most part oppressive and uniform. (p. 187)

Early in the twentieth century, in the last of his essays on the subject of political culture, LeSueur wrote: "It would really be a great thing if some one from a position of advantage could talk plainly to people about the actual facts of current politics. It is not ornate phrases that are wanted, but honest grapplings with realities." (p. 239) Having found no such leadership forthcoming from those with "positions of advantage" (presumably he meant the politicians themselves), LeSueur had sought to perform this task. His writings on "Partisan Government" (1881), "The Anarchy of Modern Politics" (1883), "Problems of Government in Canada" (1895), and "The Problem of Popular Government" (1901) were the most perceptive commentaries on the nature, growth and consequences of the development of representative government that Canada had yet produced. They surpassed in depth of analytic penetration the writings of Goldwin Smith, which seldom went beyond Madisonian and Burkean discussions of "faction" in government, and were to be bettered only by the broad sweep of André Siegfried's observations in *The Race Question in Canada* (1907).

LeSueur's writings on morality and politics took as their compass the Anglo-American world, not Canada alone. While often eloquent in expression, they were for the most part without the "ornate phrase" and were laced with an ironic wit which sought to draw out fully the nature and implications of certain words and phrases which were then passing into the political folklore of the English-speaking nations: "representative government," "popular government," "democratic government," and "public opinion."

It was, however, a double-edged irony, turning in the end upon the author himself. The critical spirit could work with the dimension of time in two ways. It could, on one hand, seek to liberate the mind from dogmatic restrictions to intellectual and social freedom imposed by the past; but it could, on the other, also warn when necessary that the very effort to ensure the progress of civilization by removing traditional practices or institutions could destroy in the process certain important elements which had hitherto helped to preserve social stability. When working in the name of progress, the critical spirit, in short, insisted that questions be asked of the consequences of the indiscriminating swath cut by the very idea of "progress". In his attempt to assess the political shibboleths of his day, W.D. LeSueur transformed himself in the public eye into a defender of the values and traditions of a by-gone age. The infidel who had challenged the religious orthodoxy of the nineteenth century in Canada was a political reactionary in the twentieth. Yesterday's 'Radical' had become today's 'Tory.'

LeSueur's attention to the political ethos of his age was thus part of his more general concern with the obvious discrepancy, observed by many, between material and moral progress.

> It is not too much to say that there are few thoughtful persons to whom at odd times a doubt does not present itself as to whether modern civilization is developing 'in a right direction,' whether the movement in society is still an upward one; whether the forces of construction and organization are still gaining upon those that tend to disorganization and dissolution.

So he wrote in 1881. Individuality, enthusiasm, and sincerity seemed all to be in decline, and evidences of these tendencies could be found in pampered children, lowered education standards, an unthinking and increasing reliance on the ability of science and technology to solve social problems and to bring about the good life, and above all in the general popular contentment to "move about in a haze of half-thoughts and half convictions," to "rush through life, feeding on the trifles of the moment, but never asking any news of their own inert selves; and never knowing what it is to trust even for a moment to any profoundly apprehended truth, to any comprehensive and unifying principle."[18] Six lines from Arnold's "Empedocles on Etna" seemed to capture perfectly the prevailing social mood:

> The Gods laugh in their sleeve,
> To watch man doubt and fear,
> Who knows not what to believe
> Since he sees nothing clear,
> And dares stamp nothing false where
> He finds nothing sure.

"It is when these things come home to us with force," LeSueur concluded,

> that we are led to ask ourselves whether a hollow is not forming in the very heart of our civilization; whether the superficial lives of so vast

a portion of the community can co-exist for any length of time with such an observance of social morality as is requisite to give cohesion to the fabric of society; whether a fatal blindness to all important facts may not be the accompaniment of our devouring eagerness for facts that are not important.[19]

A civilization had seemingly lost its moral bearings. It triumphs were those of the ethic of freedom; its defeats were those of the ethic of concern. Its ambiguous prize was not only material progress through social innovation, but also social and moral drift. Its loss was social cohesion, its sense of community, a loss which Lampman had mourned in ''The Modern Politician.'' Lampman's lament of the passing of ''the grandeurs of the world's iron youth'' was not a declaration of the inherent superiority of monarchy or a wish to romanticize a feudal past. It was a bitter commentary on the disintegration of certain essential virtues which, he believed, had helped in the past to cement and give meaning to the social bond: ''faith, kinship, truth and verity,/Man's sacred rights and very holiest thing.'' This was also the essential point which LeSueur sought to make in all his articles on politics and morality, and it went far beyond the necessity of having honest politicians in office. He wished to stress the necessity of bringing about a reconciliation between the twin imperatives of ''Progress'' and ''Order,'' between the tension-ridden ethics of freedom and concern.

It is impossible here to explore in detail the various ways in which LeSueur attempted to make his readers aware of the discrepancies between the political vocabulary of his day, couched in the language of freedom (through the use of words such as ''popular,'' ''democratic,'' and ''responsible''), and the compromising realities of political practice. The reader will wish to do that himself. In doing so, he will note that LeSueur invoked the positivist ideal not as a panacea for modern problems but as a means of asserting his vision of the state of society toward which men must strive. ''The polity to which the future belongs,'' he insisted, ''is one that will not set order against progress and progress against order, but that will make equal provision for both, and make each contribute to the other; so that order shall facilitate progress, and progress strengthen order. This is the positivist ideal.'' (pp. 206-207) It will also be noted how, in LeSueur's view, political parties subvert this ideal, even though nominally they are committed to it, by elevating party interests—which should be the means by which the end of the national good is achieved—to the state of an end. Having no principles of their own, modern political parties, like the ''stationary'' school of governing, ''[subsist] wholly upon contradictory borrowings from the two antagonistic doctrines'' of reaction and revolution. The inevitable result had been ''the confusion, skepticism, and apathy which are such marked characteristics of the political thought and action of our time.'' (p. 207)

The reader will also wish to follow the connection which LeSueur made between representative institutions, public opinion, democracy, and political parties. Unlike Henry Sumner Maine and W.E.H. Lecky, both of whom he took to task, there is little sign of crankiness or negativism in LeSueur's analysis of these phenomena. His sole aim was that the public be made aware of the weaknesses as well as the strengthens of modern political evolution. His hope was that, thus enlightened, the public conscience would insist upon necessary corrective measures. Hence his focus upon the key words in contemporary political discourse. Of ''representative institutions'' he asks, 'representative of what, by whom, and to what end?' 'What,' he also asks, 'do terms such as ''democracy,'' ''public opinion,'' and political ''responsibility'' truly mean within the context of contemporary political practice?' His own words make the sequences of relationships between these shibboleths clear and put forward a judgement decidedly different from those then dominant:

Representative institutions mean simply this: that the people are summoned to govern themselves. The question then at once arises: How are the people to do this? They can only do it through some individuals chosen for the purpose. Who are these to be? Manifestly the men who can best give expression and effect to the will of the people. What is the will of the people? What is the dominant sentiment of the hour? Upon this point the most opposite opinions may prevail among sagacious men. Every one inclines to think that his own opinion must be widely prevalent; and some are bold enough to believe that if their opinion is not prevalent, they can make it so. There are, therefore, of necessity, rival candidates for the honor and advantage of giving expression the national will. One is carried to power; the rest are swept into opposition: parties are established. (p. 195)

This is not an entirely inaccurate description of the facts of modern political life; yet very much in evidence between the lines is LeSueur's assertion that the popular values ascribed to each of these facts undermined the ultimate end toward which the whole process should be directed: the good of the social whole. Although lauding ''the public'' in his speeches, in private the ''modern politician'' gives that public little credit for any real intelligence. ''The common idea among politicians is that the people can be stampeded by a word, a phrase, some unguarded expression or trifling act which in any way touches . . . a popular prejudice.'' (p. 238) And despite this low estimate of the public, politicians shift with popular whims or appeal to local issues that will ensure re-election. The result is an abrogation of true leadership, the growth of a delegatory form of political leadership, the impairment of parliament as a deliberative body, and a general situation throughout the country in which "the representatives of the dominant party" become "little present deities for the purveying of government favour to their several localities." (p. 218) 'Given this popular conception of political leadership and followership,' went the broad question that dominated LeSueur's critique, 'can it be said that the national interest is truly served or a common sense of national purpose really achieved, even if this is the age of "democratic government"?'

The problem of popular or democratic government was a simple one to state: "how to make each individual a helpful, not a retarding or an opposing influence in the work of good government." (p. 229) But it was not an easy one to solve, for the democratic ideal, based upon what LeSueur called "the pride of individualism" (p. 212-13), contained within it an imperative which made the necessary equilibrium between progress and order a difficult one to achieve. Democratic government, went LeSueur's definition, was one "under which the sovereign power of the State . . . was distributed, as the lawyers say, 'per capita'." Its basic flaw was that it presupposed an "absolute equality between man and man," an assumption which had the effect of divorcing the notion of equality from the moral or intellectual qualities of individuals. (p. 227) The result, in the long, historical transition from divine and monarchical to democratic government, had been an assertion of freedom of individuality without a corresponding increase in the sense of social responsibility:

> The idea that the power once possessed by one, or by a limited class, is now divided amongst the whole people is familiar enough; but the idea that each man should try himself by the rule which he applies to the monarchs and oligarchs of the past is not a familiar one. We condemn the rulers of the past because they did not consider themselves the mere trustees of power, and study at all times the good of the whole people. And yet, I fear the common idea to-day is that each man's vote is his private property, to be used as may best suit his private ends. It was for a precisely similar misuse of power that some monarchs have lost their heads in times past. (p. 229-30)

These were not words which were easily palatable in Canada in the second year of the twentieth century. They had been spoken to an audience of students at the University of Toronto, where only a half dozen years earlier another "generation" of students, without a representative body in which to express their discontent over the exercise of arbitrary authority by senior members of the university administration, had gone on strike. "Responsible Government" had not yet reached the venerable halls of the provincial university. One of the leaders of the student rebellion of 1895 had been William Lyon Mackenzie King, who even as a senior undergraduate believed himself to be the inheritor of the burden of upholding the liberal-democratic tradition in Canada. "If there's anything that makes my blood boil, it's tyranny," he had proclaimed at one of the student rallies.[20] But tyranny, "Responsible Government," and Mr. King belong in the final chapter of the "inner biography" of William Dawson LeSueur.

NOTES

1. R.C. Brown, "The Nationalism of the National Policy," in Peter Russell (ed.), *Nationalism in Canada* (Toronto: University of Toronto Press, 1965), p. 162. For an assessment of the ethos of the period, see P.B. Waite, "Sir Oliver Mowat's Canada: Reflections on an Un-Victorian Society," in D. Swainson (ed.), *Oliver Mowat's Ontario* (Toronto: Macmillan, 1972), pp. 12-32; for general background see Waite's volume, *Canada, 1873-1896: Arduous Destiny* (Toronto: McClelland and Stewart, 1971).

2. Archibald Lampman, "The Modern Politician," reprinted in K. Wilson and E. Motheral (eds.), *The Poet's Record; Verses on Canadian History* (Winnipeg: Peguis Publishers, 1975), p. 52.

3. Goldwin Smith, "Political Corruption," *Canadian Monthly and National Review*, Vol II, no. 4 (October, 1872), p. 366. For other examples of Smith on political morality, see his "Political Struggles on Both Sides of the Line," *ibid.*, pp. 263-73, and "A Bystander," "The Dominion Parliament," *ibid.*, pp. 56-67, and "Colonel Gray on Confederation," *ibid.*, pp. 182-83. On the transatlantic context of this concern, see the following articles by Smith: "The Organization of Democracy," *Contemporary Review*, Vol. 47 (1885), pp. 315-33; "The Decline of Party Government," *Macmillan's*, Vol. 36 (1877), pp. 298-306; "The Failure of Party Government," *The Nineteenth Century and After*, Vol. 45 (1898), pp. 729-32; "The Disintegration of Political Party," *ibid.*, Vol. 164 (1897), pp. 753-54. See also Elisabeth Wallace, *Goldwin Smith: Victorian Liberal* (Toronto: University of Toronto Press, 1957), esp. Ch. x: "Democracy in Canada," pp. 226-252.

4. W.A. Foster, *Canada First: A Memorial*, p. 89; quoted in Carl Berger, *The Sense of Power* (Toronto: University of Toronto Press, 1970), p. 69. See also A.G. Bailey, *Culture and Nationality* (Toronto: McClelland and Stewart, The Carleton Library, No. 58, 1972), pp. 130-176.

5. Smith to Rogers [initials unintelligible], Feb. 3, 1876. Goldwin Smith Papers, microfilm reel #2, copy in Douglas Library, Queen's University, Kingston, Ontario.

6. Colonel George T. Denison, *The Struggle for Imperial Unity* (1909); quoted in F.H. Underhill, *The Image of Confederation* (Toronto: CBC Publications, 1967), p. 15.

7. Rev. G.M. Grant, "Reformers of the Nineteenth Century" (Halifax: James Bowes & Sons, 1867), p. 32.

8. Principal G.M. Grant, "The Relation of Religion to Secular Life" ["A paper read before the Council of the Reformed Churches holding the Presbyterian System, at . . . Philadelphia, Sept. 23, 1880"], *Rose-Belford's Canadian Monthly*, Vol. v, no. 6 (December, 1880), p. 622.

9. "Political Partyism—Rev. Principal Grant's Denunciation of the Machine.—Two Brilliant Sermons—He Shows the Danger to Which the Country is Exposed by Violent Partisanship—Independent and Honest Men Required for the Service of the State," *Toronto Mail*, Monday, Feb. 14, 1887. Clipping in G.M. Grant Papers, Vol. 25, Public Archives of Canada.

10. "Principal to Students—Baccalaureate Address to the Graduates of Queen's—Duty to Caesar, and Duty to God—The Scholar in Politics—Reform Organizations—Law and its Limitations—Importance of Knowing God—The Need of the Age." *The Kingston News*, Monday, April 24, 1899. Clipping in *ibid*. For an address by a prominent leader of the Methodist Church on the subject of political parties, see Nathaniel Burwash, "The Evolution and Degeneration of Party,—A Study in Political History," *Transactions of the Royal Society of Canada*, Section II (1903), p. 3; for a nineteenth century journalist's opinion of partyism, see Nicholas Flood Davin, "London and Canadian Press," *Canadian Monthly and National Review*, Vol. v, no. 2 (Feb. 1874), pp. 121-122.

11. Quoted in J.A. Garraty, *The New Commonwealth, 1877-1890* (New York: Harper & Row, 1968), p. 225. For a general survey and estimate of the state of American political culture between 1877 and 1890, see pp. 220-258.

12. M. Ostrogorski, *Democracy and Political Parties*, II; quoted in *ibid.*, p. 222.

13. *Life and Letters of Edwin Lawrence Godkin*. Edited by Rollo Ogden (New York: Macmillan, 1907), Vol. I, pp. 299-300. Godkin's correspondent is not identified. For other examples of Godkin on the political culture of his day and on the alienation of the intellectual from political life, see Vol. I, p. 313, Vol. II, pp. 113, 184-185. See also John G. Sproat, " *The Best Men*": *Liberal Reformers in the Gilded Age* (New York: Oxford University Press, 1968); Stow Persons, *The Decline of American Gentility* (New York: Columbia University Press, 1973), ch. IV; "Gentry Politics," pp. 131-178.

14. "Democracy," Maine wrote, "is commonly described as having an inherent superiority over every other form of government. It is supposed to advance with an irresistible and pre-ordained movement. It is thought to be fully of the promise of blessings to mankind; yet if it fails to bring with it these blessings, or even proves to be prolific of the heaviest calamities, it is not held to deserve condemnation." *Popular Government* (London: John Murray, 1885), p. viii. For the comments of Maine, Bryce, and Lecky on American "partyism," see *ibid.*, p. 31; James Bryce, *The American Commonwealth*. New Edition (New York: Macmillan, 1914), Vol. II, pp. 3-250; W.E.H. Lecky, *Democracy and Liberty*. New Edition (London: Longmans, Green and Co., 1899), pp. 85-86.

15. J.W. Burrow, *Evolution and Society: a Study in Victorian Social Theory* (Cambridge: Cambridge University Press, 1970), pp. 99-100.

16. *Ibid.*, p. 93.

17. D.G. Creighton, *John A. Macdonald: The Old Chieftain* (Toronto: Macmillan, 1955), pp. 146-147

18. W.D. LeSueur, "Is Civilization Declining?" *Rose-Belford's Canadian Monthly* Vol. vi, no. 1 (January, 1881), pp. 95-97. See also Arnold Haultain, "A Revolutionary Epoch," *The Week*, Vol. iii (July 1, 1886), pp. 493, *passim.*, for a catalogue of contemporary political events which suggested to the author that "a strange if not dangerous condition of things" existed, wherein "the very soul of society . . . has been cast down and disquieted within us."

19. *Ibid.*, p. 97.

20. R. MacGregor Dawson, *William Lyon Mackenzie King: Volume One, 1874-1923* (Toronto: University of Toronto Press, 1958), p. 34.

11. Party Politics
(1872)

A friend of ours was once a good deal puzzled in attempting to explain to a young lady of an enquiring turn of mind the nature of a Parliamentary Opposition. Government she understood and Parliament, as a deliberative and legislative assembly, she understood; but the idea of a party of men, whose sole function was to *op*-pose what others *pro*-posed, seemed to be beyond her grasp. If it could have been explained to her that this so-called Opposition was a mere temporary organization for a temporary purpose—the government of the country having fallen into bad hands and it being very desirable to harass them into an abandonment of their position—the thing would have been more easily intelligible; but no, the truth had to be told, that this "opposition" was as permanent an institution as Government itself, and that the eagerness and bitterness with which it pursued its ends, bore no assignable relation to the merits or demerits of the holders of authority. However faultless an Administration might be, there must still be an Opposition, or the British Constitution would fall to pieces. "Why don't they content themselves with opposing what is wrong?" was asked, with simplicity. "Well, of course, that is what they profess to do," was the answer.

Then there is no particular reason for calling them Opposition, for everybody professes the same thing. I am Opposition, and you are Opposition—we are all Opposition together, if that is what it means.

The difficulty in which our young friend was involved was one which, in some shape or other, presents itself to everybody. Even grown men, tolerably familiar both with the theory and the working of the Constitution, find themselves wondering how the thoroughly artificial distinctions which prevail in the political arena came to acquire

SOURCE: *Canadian Monthly and National Review*, Vol. II (November, 1872), pp. 447-455. The essay was originally published under the pseudonym "A Radical." In his 1881 article entitled "Partisan Government", also published in this volume, Le Sueur admits that he had written the article (see p. 200).

such force and persistence; wondering too, whether no new page of political history will ever be turned, and the monotonous see-saw of party strife—Oppositions becoming Governments, and Governments becoming Oppositions, and each, with ever change of fortune, displaying most, if not all of the faults of those whose places they take—be succeeded by something more in accordance with reason, and more favourable to true progress. The subject is one which a little honest thought will do a great deal to clear up; for, to tell the truth, the difficulties that seem to surround it are mainly the creation of those who think they have an interest in the perpetuity of the present state of things. It is commonly assumed for example, by the defenders of party, that those who are disposed to regard it as out of place in this advanced stage of human culture and reason, are bound to devise a complete new set of institutions for the government of nations; and, having devised them, to demonstrate their practicability. This assumption we entirely repudiate, for reasons which will sufficiently appear in the course of our argument. What we have to do, is to try and render a true account of party to ourselves, to ascertain what it is and what the conditions are that call it into existence. As we pursue the investigation we shall see that the conditions which give it its greatest vitality have passed away, and are little likely to return; and that party, if limited to its natural and legitimate development in these days, would be a very different thing indeed from what we now witness.

We cannot do better than take our departure from Burke's well-known definition. "Party," says the great philosophic statesman, "is a body of men united for promoting, by their joint endeavours, the national interest, upon some principle in which they are all agreed."[1] Party, in this sense of the word, is something every one can understand: it calls for no justification, any more than any other form of association for a worthy object. It will be observed, however, that, according to Burke's definition, party is but a means towards an end, and a means which is only available in certain defined circumstances. The end is the national interest, and the condition necessary to give vitality to party, is the agreement of all its members in "some particular principle" which they wish to see applied in the government of the country, and to which, of course, another party in the State is opposed. Burke says not a word to justify the opinion that parties are essential to the well-being of the State, under all circumstances: for that would be simply tantamount to saying that no country could be prosperous in which there were not those radical differences of opinion upon political subjects, which alone afford a rational basis for party organization. Nearly all the talk we hear in the present day on the subject of parties really involves the absurd proposition that, *unless* a country is divided against itself, it cannot stand. Because parties were once a necessity of the times—the natural expression in Parliament of real and lamentable antagonisms that existed throughout the country, therefore parties must exist for ever; and if we have not real antagonisms to support them, we must get up sham ones! The Chinaman, in Charles Lamb's charming apologue, set his house on fire, in order to have, indirectly, some roast pork. Our roast pork is the party system; and, in order that we may taste the savour again and again, we set the State on fire with all kinds of false and factitious issues.

In Burke's time, and almost down to the present day, in England, there have never been wanting more or less serious causes of division among parties; moreover, in a country like England—the continuity of whose political history has never been broken by revolution, and where, consequently, many institutions exist, simply because they *have existed*, and not because they are peculiarly adapted to the present time—there will always be a certain opposition between those who wish to preserve what time has handed down, and those who, imbued with the spirit of the present, aim at bringing everything as much into harmony with that spirit as possible. Even in England, however, there are unmistakable signs that the palmy days of the party system have passed away for ever. It is in politics, in these days, very much as it is in war: men see the inevitable much sooner than they used to do; and, when they see the inevitable, they yield to it. This arises simply from the greater sway that reason has over the minds of men, and, particularly, over the minds of those fitted by nature to lead.

The truth of these remarks may be seen signally illustrated in the policy of the Conservative party, led by Mr. Disraeli and the late Lord Derby, on the question of Parliamentary Reform. Everyone remembers what a nagging opposition they offered to Earl Russell's seven-pound-householder Reform Bill of 1867; and everyone remembers still better what kind of Reform Bill the same party, after their nagging had worked them into power, left on the statute book,—a bill which virtually amounts to what was once the cry of the extreme Radicals, household suffrage. Another illustration, almost as much to our purpose, may be seen in the very feeble opposition offered in the House of Commons to the Ballot Bill recently passed.[2] In former times such a measure could only have become law after the most convulsive and dangerous struggles; but, men now-a-days see what is coming and, even if they don't like it, try at least to reconcile themselves to it. Very much of the violence of former times was due to the blind prejudice with which even able men, and of course still more ordinary men, approached the consideration (if consideration it could be called) of all political questions. In these days educated men do not like to think themselves the victims of prejudice, and are, therefore, led to seek some solid ground of reason which to base their opinions. In former times the interest of their party or their class was all that most men felt under any obligation to consult. In these days even average men have a certain feeling that the interest of the state is something greater and more important than that of any party or class whatever; and that it is both unreasonable and selfish to expect the higher interest to yield to the lower. All these causes tend to make the contrast of opinions far less sharp, and differences of political aim far less profound, than formerly. In other words, the ground is cut away, to a great extent at least, from under the feet of parties; and if we see them still arrayed against one another, it is simply that the interest of certain professional politicians is concerned in their preservation.

The political circumstances of Canada are very different from those of the Mother Country. *There*, where so much exists which it interests one class to maintain, and which it seems to interest a much larger class to destroy, there will, for a long time to come, probably, be some real significance in the terms "Conservative" and "Liberal," or "Tory" and "Radical," though there is every reason to hope that the political struggles of the future will be mitigated by the influences to which we have just referred. In Canada, however, when the same terms are employed, nothing can exceed the sense of mockery they bring to the mind. In olden times, when a knot of infatuated men thought they could govern the country for their own private interest, the political designations that had been borrowed from the parent State were not so entirely out of place. But in the present day, you who call yourselves Conservatives, do tell us, for heaven's sake, what it is you wish to conserve that anybody else wishes to destroy? And you also, who call yourselves Liberals, where are we to find proofs of your liberalism or liberality, or whatever it is you pride yourselves upon? Or, if you prefer to call yourselves Reformers, what is it that you wish to reform? Your political creed, if we credit your own professions, is one of the intensest conservatism, regarding all the established principles of the constitution. You find fault with nothing, so you say, in the political framework of the State, and only complain of a few abuses of executive authority on the part of a set of men whom you hope soon to consign to perpetual oblivion; and yet you dub yourselves Reformers; just as if there was work to be done for a generation or a century, in the redressing of abuses, the removal of anomalies, and the general reconstitution of a disordered commonwealth. When you have acceded to power and have wrought such improvements as you are able or disposed to do in the management of public affairs, what will there be to hinder you from adopting the title of "Conservatives," now appropriated by and to your opponents? Nothing in this wide world. And what will there be to hinder them, after you have committed a few blunders, as you are sure to do within a short time, from seizing, if they choose to do it, for political effect, upon your special name of "Reformers," on the plea that they are going to put to rights all the things that you have put wrong? Surely you are both to be congratulated on the peculiar felicity of party designations so chosen that you might make an impromptu "swap," and look neither wise nor more foolish in your new colours than you do at present. ✓

We shall be reminded here perhaps that, in talking of "Conservatives," we are altogether behind the age, inasmuch as the Administration and its friends are known, we have a party name chosen expressly to suit the times, and one therefore which ought, if party names are worth anything, to possess an altogether peculiar degree of appropriateness. What, however, does the recent election teach us? Why that in the Province in which the sentiment of Union and the spirit of Progress are the strongest, the Union and Progress Government has experienced a signal defeat.[3] Take it all in all, there can be no doubt that in Ontario there is a stronger sense of the advantages of the present union, and a more enterprising and progressive spirit, than in any other Province of the Dominion; and yet precisely in Ontario has the Union and Progress cry proved a failure. Viewing things from the common stand-point of the Ministerial press, we should have to conclude that a majority of the electors, in a majority of the constituencies in Ontario, are hostile to Union and Progress; but where shall we find a Ministerial paper sufficiently severe or consistent in its logic to state such a conclusion? No, the Union and Progress cry meant nothing, or next to nothing, from the first; it was a mere piece of election clap-trap; and the proof that it was such lies in the fact that no one now has the hardihood to argue that since Ontario has shown itself opposed, on the whole, to the "Union and Progress" Government, it is therefore hostile to the great principles the Government professes to represent.

It is not the *bitterness* of political discussion that seems to us the worst result of the party system; it is its amazing *hollowness*. A reasonable man is simply lost in wonder as he reads day after day, in ably-edited journals, whole columns of writing in which there is hardly the faintest gleam of sincere conviction to be discerned. Day after day the same miserable evasions, the same varnishing up of unsightly facts, the same reiteration of unproved charges against opponents, the same taking for granted of things requiring proof, and proving things that nobody questioned; the same hypocritical appeals to the good sense of the electors whom every effort is being used to misinform and confuse; the same dreary, unmeaning platitudes: in a word the same utter abuse of man's reasoning powers, and of the privileges and functions of a free press. Of course so long as both sides indulge in this kind of thing, each can make out at least a partial case against the other; and so a constant crossfire is kept up in the exposure of misrepresentations, and the rectification of all that has been set down in malice on one side or the other. To-day a good point perhaps is made by the Opposition; to-morrow it will be returned to them, if possible, with interest. Such is the party system of political warfare—a system which ought to have won the admiration of Archdeacon Paley, since it possesses the attribute that was wanting to that celebrated watch of his—the power, namely, of perpetually reproducing itself.[4] Looking simply at the wordy strife between two such organs say as the *Globe* and the *Mail*, what is ever to bring it to an end? There is no termination to their arguments, any more than to a repeating decimal, which, truth to tell, they very much resemble.

"Like everything good," says the former of the two journals we have just mentioned, "party may be abused."[5] We should like very much to know where the proper use of party ends and its abuse begins. The abuse, we suppose, is when men do things in the interest of their party that are not for the interest of the state; when, for example, the supporters of a Government convicted of some reprehensible act rally around it to save it from just condemnation; or when an Opposition, knowing that the Government is dealing with a very difficult and dangerous question, walking, to use Horace's metaphor, on hot cinders lightly covered over with ashes, seek to hamper and distress it by every means in their power, even at the risk of fanning the smouldering fires into open conflagration. But if this is abuse, it is of the very essence of party politics. Either the interests of the country or the fortunes of their party are to dominate in men's thoughts: if the former, then all party tactics are at an end; if the latter, then it is simply absurd to talk of party being "abused." It is all abuse from first to last. You might as well talk of selfishness being abused, or dishonesty being abused, or of hypoc-risy being abused.

Let us, however, hear a little more about party from that thorough believer in it whom we have just quoted:—"All the essential charac-teristics of party," he proceeds to say,

enter into the very idea of free popular government, and when they are eliminated, such a government is not only impossible but incon-ceivable. Who is to say what is really for the good of the nation? All may be equally patriotic, all equally anxious to lay aside self-seeking and everything mean and unworthy, but they may have different ideas how this greatest national good is to be secured; nay they will have if they think freely and intelligently. And with what result? Why, with the formation of more or less distinctly opposing parties, with more or less keenness in their discussions, and more or less divergence in their eventual courses of action. The whole history of the past tells of this; while the 'national principle' would at best but give us something like the slumberous stillness of a sultry summer noon—quiet and peaceful, but at the same time stagnant, and the fruitful parent of injurious miasmata.

Here let us draw breath. Who would have imagined, had we not let out the secret, whence this charming picture of party politics was taken? There is a touch of idyllic tenderness and sweetness about it which the great Sicilian poet himself could scarcely have surpassed. "More or less keenness in their discussions"—of course; but then each side is so "anxious to lay aside everything mean and unworthy"—among other things, all mean and unworthy suspicions of their opponents—that really their divergences of opinion serve only to procure for those who take part in politics a reasonable and healthful amount of intellectual exercise. Under the "national" system we should all stagnate and be choked by noxious miasmata; while under the party system we are braced and vivified by the pure powers of free discussion. What a happy, golden dream, one cannot but exclaim, for a writer to have who was penning an article for the same columns that contained "What wants me?" Not more fancy-free was Colonel Lovelace in his prison[6] than is this editor in his sanctum. He cannot for a moment assume the patriotism of his particular political opponents—*they* are tricksters, corruptionists, deceivers—everything in fact that is morally execrable; but when he wants to draw a picture of the party system at work, why, all at once the political atmosphere becomes pure if not altogether calm; there is equal patriotism on both sides, and men are only divided by theoretic differences which do not in the least impair the profound respect they entertain for one another.

Now the truth of the matter is that what this enthusiastic advocate of party has been here describing is not party at all; but that very "national" system, the application of which to popular institutions he pronounces to be sheerly "inconceivable" (thought not *too* inconceivable to allow its miasmatic results to be clearly foreseen). No one pretends that if men could be induced to give up the conscious imposture and rant and gibberish that are now dignified with the name of party controversy, they would forthwith all be of one mind. The great difference would be that men would endeavour to make their opinions triumph by legitimate means; and further, that the expression of all opinions would be very much freer than at present. As things are now a man is not at liberty at all times to utter the thought that is in him; he has to consider how his party will be affected by what he may say. In this way truths that would be eminently reasonable, so far as the country's interests are concerned, are suppressed as being unreasonable from a party point of view. The credit that a man would, personally, feel inclined to give his opponents for something he knows them to have done well, he withholds out of consideration for his party who would be seriously compromised by an admission in favour of those whom they are steadily trying to undermine in popular favour. It is the rarest thing in the world at present to see a man get up in Parliament and seem to utter his real and innermost conviction on any important question. You note his place in the chamber, and before he speaks you know almost all he has to say. Such is the party system. Instead of stimulating thought and teaching intellectual honesty, it does just the reverse—puts a ban on the free exercise of a man's mind, and leads people to conceal or misrepresent their real opinions.

We fancy that when people try to realize to themselves what the political situation would be like, in the absence of party organization and party strategy, a vague idea too often takes possession of their minds, that there would no longer be any available means of dislodging an unworthy Government from power. They forget that it is party that keeps such a Government in power at all. What is it that for years past has kept the special object of Opposition censure—Sir George Cartier, surrounded by that compact band of immortals, and made him, altogether, the most powerful man, personally, in the whole country? The answer is simply—party. It must not then be lost sight of that a relaxation of party ties, and a more honest and independent devotion on the part of every member of Parliament to the public good, while it would shield the Administration from factious assaults, would also compel it to rely not on the support of an interested party, but on the honest approval of the people's representatives. There is not only a connection—there is a direct proportion between rigour of party discipline and political corruption. The one varies with the other and necessarily. When we speak of "a strict party vote," what do we mean, except a vote in which the merits of the question were put out of sight, and party interests were alone consulted? And what do we mean by "party discipline," except that species of control, partly internal and partly external, which compels a man to support his friends *per fas et nefas*, or as we say in English, "through thick and thin"? It may not always be a money consideration, immediate or prospective, which leads a man thus to surrender independence and conscience into the hands of others, but whatever the motive, it is a corrupting one. Unless we are mistaken, a leading Canadian "statesman" once said to a member of Parliament, who professed himself ready to support him whenever he was in the right, "That is not what I want; I want my friends to support me when I am wrong as well as when I am right." And are they not both, at this moment, members of the Dominion Ministry? The friend who once wanted to limit and condition his support found, no doubt, substantial reasons for making it unlimited and unconditional—the kind in fact that was wanted. This is an illustration of the party system, if you like: one that everybody will recognize who knows the real article. As to that beautifully-coloured picture of the *Globe*'s, exhibited under some other name, it might do very well; but as "A Study of Party Politics," it can only be laughed at.

The great difficulty in arguing the thesis that the public interest is not promoted by an arbitrary division of the legislature and of all those who take an interest in politics, into two opposing camps, is to avoid saying things that are self-evident. It is perfectly clear that a party would not be a party, as the word is commonly understood, if it were actuated only by a desire for the public good, and if it followed out a strictly honourable line of action towards its adversaries. Such a body would not and could not display what is called party spirit; and as to party discipline, it would be lost in the higher and nobler discipline of duty. The agreement that existed amongst its members at any moment, however perfect it might be, could not be held to guarantee their agreement on any new issue; for *ex hypothesi* every man, as often as a new question came up, would shape his course upon it, not with a view to improving the position of his party, but to promoting the advantage of the State. It is understood now that those who act together to-day will act together to-morrow and next day. Why? Simply because *they mean to do so*; that is all about it: they have determined that their opinions shall not differ. For how could they ever hope to gain party triumphs without party organization and party orthodoxy? If the country does not thrive under such a system; if the vices of government are not cured; if the people are not educated to disinterestedness and high-mindedness: in other words, if patriotism and public spirit are not encouraged—so much the worse for all the interests, moral and material, involved. The British Constitution of which party-government (we are told) is the noblest tradition, cannot be allowed to fall through merely because a nation threatens to go to ruin.

When we are told that party is absolutely essential to free, popular government, we cannot help thinking what a vast amount of government is done, and what vast interests are successfully managed, without any help from the party principle. Look at our municipalities; look at our banks, our railways and other public enterprises; look at our churches. Would it really be well to see our city corporations, and our county and township councils divided between two parties, each trying to hamper the other to the utmost of its ability? Who would care to hold stock in a bank or a railway, whose affairs were made the sport of party struggles? Whenever party spirit has shown itself in connection with the latter class of corporations, it has been the product of, as it has in turn ministered to, the very grossest and most shameless forms of corruption and robbery. We see party here assume its final and perfect development as the *ring*—an association of robbers who have agreed to aid in filling one another's pockets. When however, (as fortunately is most often the case) this horrible disease has not fastened upon a great public company, its administration is a fair type of what the administration of a country's affairs might be, if the organized selfishness of party were to pass away. Every shareholder knows that the value of his property depends on the successful administration of the company's affairs, and the maintenance of its credit before the world. His great anxiety, therefore, is to have the right kind of men as directors, and, when the right men have been found, it generally rests with them to say how long they will remain in the responsible positions assigned to them. Men get thanks for conducting the affairs of a company or association prudently and successfully; they get none for doing their duty by the State: they get interested and formal praise from their supporters, and unvarying depreciation and abuse from their opponents. The praise affords them no satisfaction, and the abuse, in the long run, hardens them and takes the edge off all finer feelings. The great difference between a member of a joint-stock company and a member of Parliament is, that while the former would lose more than he would gain by pursuing an obstructive course, or in any way trifling with the interests of the society, the latter may pursue a similar line of conduct, and profit by it. His interest as a private citizen in sound legislation, and effective administration may easily be overcome by those special inducements which party leaders can offer. That is precisely the position, and hence it is that party is possible in the Legislature and *hardly any where else*. Party may therefore be defined with absolute correctness as a body of men whose interest in supporting one another is greater than the interest they have in giving a right direction at all times to public policy. [We] should scarcely call this, however, a good thing *per se*.

What becomes then of Burke's definition of party as "a body of men united for promoting by their joint endeavours the national interest upon some principle in which they are all agreed?" Is it of no application at all in our day? Certainly; as often as a body of men honestly agree in a particular principle, let them unite their efforts to make that principle triumph, and if they choose to call themselves a party, why let them do so. No harm will result from that. Harm results when men take a license to themselves to do, as a party, things that are not for the national interest at all, and that, in their own consciences, they know are not for the national interest. It is certainly a strange thing that, because a number of men have got hold of one sound principle through which they hope to triumph, they should feel themselves excused in giving their sanction, if not their active support, to a number of evil ones. Yet this is precisely what our parties do; they have one end in view which perhaps they sincerely think a good one, and this end they allow to justify or sanctify the most scandalous means. Such is the party system; and if any one hints that a system, which not only permits but erects into a code the loosest moral practice, may not be worth perpetuating, he is pronounced at once an enthusiast, a dreamer, a doctrinaire, a person whom all sensible, practical men may complacently laugh at, without troubling themselves in the least to enquire into the value of his ideas.

We are very far indeed from thinking that the age of political conflict has passed away in Canada. On the contrary, there is sharp work to be done at the present moment, and we only wish we could see a clearer prospect of its being done efficiently and speedily. What we really require is not closer party organization (the great specific of the "Grit" press) but a general awaking of the political conscience of the country. It is of little avail for a party to be in the right on some main issue if it is constantly putting itself in the wrong on a number of minor questions, and, in a general way, pursuing just as weak and temporizing a course as if its moral foundations were altogether unsound. Where we see a party acting in this way, and deriving no inward strength, apparently, from its espousal of the better cause, we may safely conclude that it has espoused that cause simply as a matter of expediency, a matter of party tactics. No wonder if truth triumphs slowly through such advocacy.

The unexpressed idea in the mind of every man who tells us that party-government must be eternal is this: that men in general are too selfish and too corrupt to accept any other system; the main thing in politics must always, it is held by these highminded individuals, be a strife for place and power, and the State must e'en take her chance between contending factions. If people who think this (and they are many) would only utter it openly, instead of darkening counsel by their sophistical platitudes about party and its abuses, we should be in a much fairer way of rising above our present low level of political morality. Party is such a venerable institution that, like the heathen temples of old and the Christian sanctuaries of the middle ages, it can give shelter and asylum to all kinds of crimes. But let men cease to talk about party in the abstract, or as an institution, and say what they mean, namely, that there is no use in looking for honesty and disinterestedness in politics, and then perhaps this very enlightened age will begin to feel a little ashamed that such injurious allegations should be so openly made. We do not share the opinion of these cynics; we hold that a great portion of the evils from which we suffer are due to a defective political system, and to that confusion of mind on political subjects which the current language in regard to party is so well calculated to produce. The heart of the people is not so unsound as some would have us believe; and if the people make up their minds to it, they can have honest men to serve them—men who will prefer honour to office, and the sense of duty performed to personal triumphs however flattering. To preach the cessation of party strife is no doubt, at present, like crying in the wilderness, but our hope is that, like other preaching that has begun in the wilderness, it will end by converting the multitude. Stripped of all verbiage and of all subtleties, the question is simply one between good and evil; and the good must either gain on the evil, or the evil on the good. The precise equilibrium we see established at present has no warrant of perpetuity; it is simply the creation of the public opinion of the moment. In which direction then will public opinion change? Shall we see parties taking to themselves a wider and wider license than ever, and, in their senseless animosities, trampling on the best interests of the State? Or shall the change be towards purer and more rational methods of government? Shall we see the press of the country becoming what a *free* press ought to be—just, outspoken and independent, dealing with public questions in a broad, national spirit, and with public reputations with that respect which *self*-respect invariably inspires? Or, shall we see the reverse of all this in a further development of the wretched system of "organs"? These are questions which the future has to decide, and upon the decision of which a vast amount of national prosperity may—nay must—depend. The country in which a high tone of public feeling prevails, in which government is administered with purity, and public affairs are discussed with reason, enjoys already the best kind of prosperity; and only where these moral elements of well-being abound can the material possessions and advantages of a community be turned to their best account.

12. Old and New in Canada (1875)

Few acts that we perform bring with them more of inward admonition than the changing of the date as we enter upon a new year. How often by force of habit we write mechanically the old familiar figures, only to be reminded, as we correct them, of days that are no more. The feelings excited within us, as we think of the year that has gone, vary with our individual experiences; but to all, except the very young or the very thoughtless, reflections are suggested that ought to be, and no doubt are, in a greater or less degree wholesome. The flight of time leaves us all something to mourn over, or, at least, regret. Our standard of duty and our aim in life must have been low if we have fully realized either the one or the other. There is no sense in undue self-depreciation, and when a man has, upon the whole, done well, he ought to acknowledge the fact to himself, though he need not boast of it to others. But who that has done well does not feel that he might, and therefore ought, to have done better? It is the most elevated characters, as a rule, those whose lives are the worthiest, that know least of the pleasures of self-complacency.

Not a few, perhaps, as they review the past, will confess to themselves that they have *not* done well; but, however sadly the confession may be made, the advent of the New Year, with all its accompaniments of social and family rejoicing, should inspire in such a manly trust that, in the future, the errors of the past may be atoned for or retrieved. Who indeed does not feel nerved at this time for more serious and worthy efforts? Who does not hope that the New Year will be better than its predecessor? Too often, alas, such hopes are illusory; but it is well that they should come and shed at least a transitory gleam over our lives, and raise us, though it be but for a moment, above our ordinary selves. There are cases, however, in which but a little quickening or encouragement is needed to lift a man decisively into a higher plane of life, and this, the advent of a new year, with its opening vista of hopes and possibilities, is as likely as anything else to supply. The past has indeed

SOURCE: *Canadian Monthly and National Review*, Vol. VII (January, 1875), pp. 1-9.

borne away with it many precious opportunities; but has it not also borne away our errors, and left us in present possession of experience? Let us then, at such a time as this, endeavour to realize rather the advantages of our present position than the extent of our past failures; let us enter bravely on the advancing year, not boasting ourselves of victories yet unwon, but inwardly resolving to fight a good fight, and make the very best of what life has yet in store for us.

"The healthy sense of progress," says Ruskin,

> which is necessary to the strength and happiness of men, does not consist in the anxiety of a struggle to obtain higher place or rank, but in gradually perfecting the manner, and accomplishing the ends, of the life we have chosen, or which circumstances have determined for us.

To live worthily we must set before us an ideal, and that ideal must be something more than mere worldly success. The love of the beautiful and the true must enter into it in some measure, or it is no ideal at all, and our lives, guided by none but vulgar and selfish motives, will be thoroughly prosaic and unlovely. What, therefore, taking any high view of human nature and its destiny, it chiefly concerns every one to know is, what character he is building up or has built up for himself— what in fact he is, essentially, leaving accidents of fortune and position out of sight. These considerations are of equal applicability in the wider sphere of national affairs. Our trade returns give us a measure of the country's material prosperity, but they do not furnish an answer to the question of most interest to every high-minded citizen—in what direction the national character is developing itself from year to year? We know there are multitudes of men who could scarcely by any possible effort raise themselves to the level of such a question as this; but none the less shall we venture to treat it as *the* question of the hour and of every hour. We believe with the poet, that "there is a higher and a lower," and we desire that each may be recognized for what it is. It is well that the country should thrive commercially and industrially; but unless we are to accept once for all the doctrine that it is better of a man to be successful than honest, we must hold, and hold strenuously, that a nation's highest interest is its character. In the present stage of our country's development a weighty responsibility rests upon all who have, in any measure, the direction of public opinion. There are alternative courses open to us, and we have even now to choose upon which we shall enter. Shall we as a people show that we have inherited the best qualities, and are prepared to emulate the best achievements of the great historic races to whom we trace our origin; or shall we ignobly content ourselves with just enough of public virtue to save the state from disintegration? Shall we realize fully our responsibilities as a self-governing people, and make our example one that shall strengthen the cause of good government throughout the world? Shall we have the courage to look within us rather than without us for solutions of our political problems, judging of questions less with reference to what others may have done, or attempted to do, before us, than with reference to what seems best in view of our own circumstances and capabilities? Shall ours be the timid creeping temperament that waits for others to risk an experiment, shunning all initiative even in matters calling loudly for action; or shall we feel that, not only individually but as a nation, we should be prepared to quit us like men, and bear our part bravely in the struggles and chances from which no life, individual or collective, can ever be free? Shall we have real faith in liberty and truth, or shall we listen to the treacherous suggestion that the opinion of the majority should in certain matters be exempt from criticism? Shall every citizen be free to utter his sincere opinion on any and every subject, or shall we adopt the maxim propounded some time ago by a most influential authority, that the proper answer to certain arguments is to knock the speaker's hat over his eyes? In a word, shall we be a high-minded or a low-minded people? Shall it be our aim to occupy in due time a dignified place among the nations, bearing our own burdens and running our own risks, or shall we be content to slink through history in obscure dependence, caring only that for us an adequate supply of butter be spread upon an adequate supply of bread?

These, and such as these, are the practical issues which it is given to the Canadian people to decide. We study the signs of the times with an earnest desire to ascertain, if possible, what they promise for the future. Some of them, unfortunately, are only too discouraging. An eloquent French writer asked with astonishment, some thirty years ago, how it was that, among so many clever things that had been said on the subject of popular education, no one had thought of saying that the real education of a free country lay in the permanent spectacle of its politics. This thought has been expressed often enough, in one shape or another, of late years, but even so, we do not give it the heed that it deserves. A corrupt administration of public affairs exercises a directly corrupting influence on the country at large; and an administration which, without being in the full sense of the word corrupt, is characterized by party narrowness, and by a general absence of high or generous principle, exerts an influence perhaps scarcely less injurious, because it gives a kind of sanction to the most prevalent vices of society. Of late our politics have not been gaining in dignity or nobility, but whether the people take much to heart what has been amiss is extremely doubtful. Constituencies welcome back to their bosoms representatives whose elections have been cancelled for dishonest practices. It would indeed seem as if there was a general disposition to sympathize with men who have been put to serious trouble simply because they, or their friends for them, would buy votes right and left. Localism, too, is rampant everywhere: the man elected by his fellow-citizens to Parliament or to a Provincial Assembly, knows that the special interests of his constituency, not the general interests of the country, are those over which he has to watch with the greatest vigilance, and for his dealings with which he will be held to the strictest account. It may be said that party, whatever evils it may bring with it, tends to check this spirit of sectional selfishness, inasmuch as we find certain constituencies steadily returning Opposition representatives, and so, to a great extent, cutting themselves off from such advantages as the Government of the day may have at their disposal. There would be more force in this argument if it were not tolerably well known that the constituencies practising such political heroism are looking forward to a good time coming when the loaves and fishes will be distributed upon a different principle, or, more correctly, upon the same principle differently applied. With such a prospect in view, it only needs a little tenacity in clinging to familiar associations to nerve a constituency for enduring the cold shade of opposition for a term of years. At the same time there is a *little* virtue in not going over incontinently to the winning side; and, if party is the cause of this, let party have the credit, for it needs it, goodness knows.

In a free country, the newspaper press reflects, perhaps with greater fidelity than anything else, the morals and culture of the people. We have no wish to disparage the press of Canada. In point of talent and enterprise it is a credit to the country. We have seen in Canadian newspapers many an article by no means unworthy, in vigour of thought or in literary execution, of the best journals of London or New York. There are brains enough among our writers to make the press all that it ought to be, and a much greater power for good than it really is. What we miss, as a general thing, is that outspoken sincerity which gives language its chief force. Our writers, ranged as they are on opposite sides of the great political battle-field, are not free to utter what they think or if they are free, do not care to use their freedom. Their articles are the pleadings of so many professional advocates, not the sincere declarations of men desirous only to lay the truth before their readers. Here and there, and now and then we see exceptions. It is hard for a man of any native independence of character not to throw off the livery of party sometimes, and boldly speak the word that he feels to be true and reasonable. When this happens, the more orthodox members of the party pronounce their erring brother eccentric and dangerous, very much as the older heads of a church pronounce sentence upon some young and ardent divine who has begun to show immoral doubts as to Noah's Ark or Jonah's whale. There are shakings of the head, and expressions of regret, and predictions of loss of influence, &c.; what really troubles these sage authorities being a horrible doubt as to the prospects of party government should the practice of telling the truth in the papers ever become at all general. That such assertions of independence are not more frequent is really a significant fact. If the public, as is generally the case, is pleased to find a man discussing a public question with impartiality, why is not the thing oftener done? The reason we believe to be this: newspaper men feel that society is, in some rough, ill-defined way, divided between two parties, and that every journal must place its chief dependence on one or the other. It is very well to indulge now and then, at distant intervals, in a little bit of brilliant criticism at the expense of the party with which you habitually act, but the thing must not be carried too far, or nobody will know where to find you. The serious question will arise as to whether you are a Conservative or a Reformer; and if you are found to be neither one nor the other, you must have rare merits not to be cast off entirely by the very community it is your object to serve. As yet, unfortunately, people in general can only think of an Independent in politics as a kind of nondescript, a man of no settled views, whom it is not safe to trust. Newspaper editors and proprietors know this, and consequently it is but seldom and fitfully that the banner of independence is flung to the breeze. In fact hitherto there has been no steady breeze to fling it to—nothing but an occasional puff, so that the noble piece of bunting has hardly had time to show its pattern before it has fallen in limp disgust around the supporting flagstaff.

Another defect of our press, akin to that we have already mentioned, is the extreme conventionality of its tone in dealing with fundamental questions to which the restrictions of party politics do not apply. In England the highest statesmen in the land express, without the least reserve, their opinions in favour of, or against, the retention of the colonies; and many of the most eminent of both political parties have expressed themselves decidedly in favour of an early severance of the union, at least with Canada. Here, how many precautions our writers and speakers take! How many apologies are offered for the least concession to the opinions of those who favour separation! What copious professions of loyalty! How the necessity for discussing the question at all is deplored, and how ready every one is to move a hoist of a thousand years! When Venus has made half a dozen more transits, the question may then possibly come up for discussion in some practical shape; but at present no one but a revolutionist, or a theorist, which is the same thing, could possibly wish to regard it as a "live issue."

Now there is no question on which, as we think, dogmatism is more out of place than this one of the future relations of the colonies to Great Britain. No one can, with any shadow of reason, pretend that all the arguments are on one side; and therefore whatever view any particular thinker takes, he ought to remember that there are other and contrary opinions quite as much entitled to a respectful hearing as his own. But what we contend for at present is that there is no justification for the timid and (to repeat the word we used before) conventional manner in which the question is dealt with by the Canadian press. If English statesmen, like Lord Derby, Mr. Gladstone, Sir Charles Adderley, Mr. Bright, Mr. Lowe, and Mr. Ayrton, can express themselves freely in favour of an early separation of Canada from Great Britain, there is surely no reason why a stigma should be attached to a Canadian who shares the same views. To grow hysterical, as some of our newspapers do, whenever the subject is mentioned, betokens at once weakness and insincerity, and is very little suggestive of faith in the destinies of this great Dominion. In England a writer like Mr. Frederic Harrison can discuss the institution of monarchy itself with a freedom which here would have exposed him to insults on every hand: there he was simply criticised, for the most part with great good temper and moderation. In England the well-known historian, E.A. Freeman, could speak of the rejoicings over the recovery of the Prince of Wales as "an extraordinary outburst of flunkeyism." Whether the phrase was entirely justifiable we are not in a position to say; but it illustrates, at least, the freedom of speech which Englishmen hold themselves entitled to. The *Pall Mall Gazette*, at the very time when the papers were filled with reports of the ceremonies gone through on that auspicious occasion, and when the ultra-loyal were boasting of the unshakable hold the monarchy had upon the affections of the English people, took occasion to point out how, very short a time before the deposition and imprisonment of Louis XVI, all parties in France were vying with one another in bepraising their sovereign, and proclaiming how indispensable he was to the welfare of the state. Instances like these might be multiplied *ad infinitum* to show that what nobody would dare to utter here is freely uttered in the mother country, and that not by obscure or ignorant people, but by men of mark whose words command the attention of the most influential classes. Why should this be so? We boast sometimes that, though we are Canadians by residence, we are Englishmen by race and citizenship: then why not be Englishmen in temper and courage.

The same timidity that marks every expression of opinion in this country upon fundamental political questions, manifests itself not less strikingly in the region of philosophical speculation. We are not now advancing any opinions of our own upon philosophical topics; nor do we, in the most remote way, wish to claim for any set of opinions a position of advantage over any other. Our purpose is simply to call attention to the astonishing uniformity with which the newspaper press of Canada gives forth the safest of all possible opinions whenever the utterances of any "advanced thinker," like Tyndall or the late John Stuart Mill, are under consideration. Is there really such absolute agreement among all the leaders of opinion upon such matters? It seems to us that in private life men are occasionally met with who do not look with a very severe eye on either philosophical or theological heterodoxy; but, somhow or other, their opinions do not find their way into print.* The opinions of the masses in these matters constitute a law that no one seems disposed to question. We must look to the mother country again if we want to see signs of the most characteristic intellectual movement of the present age. Here we are all of one way of thinking. The infallibility of Pope Public Opinion has been tacitly decreed, and those who do not assent to the dogma are wise enough to hold their tongues.

Are there no indications, however, of a revolt against the somewhat oppressive uniformity of our national culture? Fortunately there are, or it would be impossible not to conclude that Canada was making a very poor start in the race for national greatness. A new generation is springing up, to whom the history of the Double Shuffle is like a tale of little meaning, however strong the words may be in which it is told—a generation who do not find that their views, as to what is desirable for the country, are adequately represented by either of the existing parties, and who have resolved that their influence shall be devoted to securing for Canada a higher type of government than she has ever hitherto enjoyed. The giants of party warfare laughed to scorn at first the striplings, as they deemed them, who stood forth and challenged them to combat; but more than one well-directed pebble has smitten the foreheads of the boasters, and given them cause, at least, for serious and painful reflection.

The great service which, as we believe, the new claimants for political influence will render the country, will be the raising of the general standard of political morality, and inspiring what is so much lacking in the masses—faith in reason as applied to public affairs. The immoralities of a grosser kind which are incident to partizanship in politics, are known to every one, and have been sufficiently discussed in the pages of this Magazine; but what is not so thoroughly understood is the intellectual and moral confusion, the desolating scepticism, both as to men's motives and as to the validity of all logical processes, produced by the permanent spectacle of two bodies of men professing to speak the truth upon public questions, and yet, with monotonous regularity, contradicting one another on every point. Is it any wonder that, under such a system, true and false, honest and dishonest, should

---

*Certain letters that have lately appeared in the "Nation" form a startling exception to this statement.[7]

come to be regarded as words empty of meaning; since what is false to one party is true to the other, while the patriots and heroes of the one are the intriguers and corruptionists of the other? It is only necessary to talk to half a dozen average voters in succession to find how little they feel the force of any appeal to conscience or reason in connection with politics, and how very feebly, if at all, they identify the interests of the country with their own. You seem, in fact, if you try to discuss these things with them seriously, like a bringer-in of strange doctrines—a man from whom it is advisable to sheer off at the earliest possible moment.

The Party of the Future, therefore, if we may venture to call it so, has not made its appearance a day too soon. It would be a mistake, however, to suppose that it has suddenly spring out of nothing. *Ex nihilo nihil* is a maxim no less rigorously true in regard to political organizations than in regard to the visible forms of creation. There have been men in the country at all times who have been disposed to regard the exercise of their political functions as a high and important trust, and who, though they may have co-operated to some extent with one or other political party, have steadily refused to reconcile or adapt themselves to the prevailing tone of political morals. These, however, have been scattered in different places, and their voices have, for the most part, been all but lost amid the noisy strife of factions. That they have not entirely failed of influence was happily proved when the country was summarily called upon to decide whether or not it would condone the misdeeds of the late Government in the matter of the Pacific Railway Charter. We have heard the action of Sir John A. Macdonald warmly defended by men of rather more than average understanding and character. Over and over again it has been pleaded that he did nothing more than any other politician would have done in his place, and that, believing this continuance in power a necessity for the country, he was justified in using any and every means for securing that end. Why was it that these sophistries, only too readily welcomed by many, failed to decide the issue? It was because nearly all honest minds rejected them, because nearly the whole influence of the intelligent and uncorrupted portion of the community was thrown against the immoral doctrines which, to save a party leader, were being so openly preached. Before, good men had been more or less divided between the two political parties; but the facts suddenly laid before the country bore to the generality of honest minds but one construction, and hence the immediate disturbance of the balance of parties. What degree of disapprobation of Sir John Macdonald's proceedings was felt by the average voter, there might perhaps not be much satisfaction in knowing with exactness.

It is well that a country should possess virtue enough to take a right course in great crises, but it is far better that its ordinary politics should bear the stamp of high principle. There is little merit in merely avoiding great crimes, but there is much in guarding day by day against common temptations, and conscientiously performing common duties. The question remains to be answered: How did the country get into the state which rendered the Pacific Railway Scandal a possibility? Through what multiplied omissions of duty, through what multiplied yieldings to improper suggestions did the constitutencies of this country bring themselves into the condition that encouraged Sir John A Macdonald to employ such means as he did for perpetuating his power?

The advantage of a live party whose one great object is to promote a healthier political life in the country is that, if it is properly energetic, its influence will be felt not occasionally only, at critical periods, but from day to day; and it will thus prevent the moral tone of the body politic falling to that low point which is so favourable to the breaking out of virulent maladies. It is a great encouragement, besides, to those who are in favour of honest and good Government to know that they have active sympathizers whose efforts united to their own are likely to be productive of marked results. A third point not less important than either of these is, that when once an influential organ has begun to discuss public affairs impartially and dispassionately, the old hypocritical pretence that truth in regard to political matters cannot be had, ceases to be tenable. There are a great many persons in the world who want to do wrong but who require a pretext; if you utterly destroy their pretext there is a chance that they will not face the naked, undisguised sin. Reason may thus be made a valuable ally of conscience.

The political movement here adverted to was, at the outset, undoubtedly, an intellectual movement.[8] It was the revolt of educated and thoughtful men against the inanity and worse than inanity of what was offered to them as political discussion. It was, we may also reasonably believe, a direct product, in some measure, of that higher culture which the universities and colleges of our land are steadily promoting. In part it was the work of one eminent and generous mind who, in proportion as his disinterested and enlightened zeal for the good of the country won him the hatred of the leading party journals, found himself gaining the esteem and confidence of all the better portion of the community—the portion, to wit, whose moral and intellectual perceptions had not been hopelessly blunted by the evil principles and methods of our politics.[9] To say that the movement is one which attracts young rather than old or middle-aged men, is simply to say that it is one which substitutes for the cynical maxims which so largely govern men in later life, principles that appeal to generous and uncorrupted feeling. It is a matter, we think, for no ordinary rejoicing, that the youth of Canada do begin to show a lively interest in public affairs, and that they seem conscious of ideas and aspirations different from those of their predecessors. As Quinet has eloquently said, "Every generation before them has accomplished its work, and they have also theirs, the sacred type of which they bear within themselves."* The men in actual possession of power tell them they have come too late to accomplish anything new or great, that political institutions have assumed their final shape, that society has settled down into unalterable habits; in a word, that the thing that hath been is the thing that shall be: but those who feel that in them the spirit of the world has renewed itself, will not be silenced or subjugated by such discourses. They have their own share of original creative energy, and must bear their own distinct part in rearing the edifice of civilization. It does not follow that because men are young they will despise experience. A great deal is offered, however, as experience, that is not experience at all in the true sense of the word. Numbers of men will tell you now, "as the result of their experience," that there is no use trying to prevent bribery at elections; and it is certainly true that the older men grow the more disposed they are to tolerate abuses—the more readily they conclude that all kinds of evils are irremediable. It is the glory, not the weakness, of youth to reject the experience that lends a sanction to wrong, and to resolve—even though it be without a full appreciation of the difficulties to be overcome—that the experience of the past shall not be the experience of the future.

We want, as has already been hinted, more originality in this country. The way to be original is, not to make a point of differing from other people as much as possible—that, in an individual, means simple affectation and vanity—but to guard against the habit of adopting from others customs and habits without any examination of their suitability in our own case. If we only copy others in so far as it is clearly for our own good that we should do so, and in all other cases adopt a line of action of our own, we shall be as original as there is any need to be. The same thing applies of course to opinions; there are some that we must take on trust, if at all, because we are not competent judges of their subject matter, but there many which we are quite competent to examine, and yet take on trust all the same. The habit of Canada in the past has been to look to England for the initiative in everything. How long, does any one suppose, we should have gone on trying controverted elections before Parliamentary Committees, if Mr. Disraeli had not shown us a more excellent way? The ballot is not an institution we particularly admire, but here again Canada follows scrupulously in the wake of the Mother Country, the Australian colonies having long preceded her in the same path. If England had not, early in the century, relaxed the stringency of her laws on the subject of Trades' Unions, it is

*"Le Christianisme et la Revolution Française," p. 13.

extremely doubtful whether Sir John A. Macdonald would have had the courage to come forth two years ago as "the working man's friend." As a previous writer in this Magazine has pointed out, the costly broad gauge which our Canadian railways have just abandoned after so much inconvenience, was adopted from England with little or no thought as to whether it was suitable to the requirements of this country. It is high time that we began to trust our own motherwit a little more, and not look abroad for precedents and examples before we dare move hand or foot. No one but a fool will make light of experience, but when for the sake of profiting by other people's experience we forego all independent movement of our own, we turn that which should be a blessing into a bane; and, in our extreme carefulness to avoid small mistakes, run a serious risk of committing enormous ones.

It rests with the rising generation in Canada to show what is in them of original impulse, to show how they have learnt the lessons of the times, and how they understand the country's needs. We must profess our faith in that "Modern Culture" which a leading English Review has lately so seriously impeached.* We believe that the heart of the present generation is in the right place, and that the chief tendencies of the time are in a right direction. And, because such is our belief, we are intensely desirous that Canada should keep well abreast of the most progressive communities in all that relates to her intellectual and moral, as well as political, life. Let every one then bring to the common weal his own appropriate contribution. "Let every one," as the great Apostle has said, "minister according to the proportion of faith." A high order of faith is what we need in order to be truly useful to the State, that faith in right which comes, as the poet has told us, of self-control, or in other words, of the daily practice of right in our own lives, and the harmonizing of our individual desires with the general good. This is the faith that overcomes the only dangerous materialism of the age, that, namely, which consists in asserting and believing that selfishness is the *primum mobile* of human society, and that money is the one lever that can move the world. Its appropriate expression is not national self-glorification, but strenuous devotion to all worthy causes. The man who tries to work himself into a persuasion that the country he inhabits must necessarily be great, and glorious, and powerful, is a mere simpleton; but the man who feels deeply his own responsibility to the State, and tries to discharge that responsibility faithfully, is the type of a good citizen.

The New Year is now before us. It will bring much work for each one of us to do: to some it will offer opportunities of important public usefulness; to some it will present critical alternatives of right and

*London *Quarterly Review,* Oct., 1874.

wrong; to every one it will bring some righteous cause to vindicate, some evil principle to condemn. The page before us is white and stainless: let us endeavour so to act that when snatched away, its record full, it may tell of lives not entirely devoted to personal objects, of good intentions not wholly unfulfilled, or worthy aims not quite unrealized. Familiar as they are, why not quote again the solemn verses translated from Goethe by one whose own laborious and noble life has been one of the grandest lessons of the age:

> Heard are the Voices,
> Heard are the sages,
> The worlds and the ages;
> 'Choose well, your choice is
> Brief and yet endless;
>
> Here eyes do regard you
> In eternity's stillness;
> Here is all fulness,
> Ye brave to reward you;
> Work and despair not.'

13. Partisan Government (1881)

No occasion is more favorable to reflection than the morrow of a great crisis. While the crisis is impending, all thought are given the practical question, how to meet it. The time for philosophizing is not then; it is a time for making the best use of whatever wisdom, whatever insight, whatever moral firmness past experience has wrought into our characters; but, the crisis over, we can think whether we were as well prepared to meet it as we might have been, and we can re-examine with much profit the ideas and impressions by which our action was shaped. An important matter of consideration and study for every intelligent citizen of a free country is the relation which it behooves him to sustain toward the political parties which, under one name or another, he is sure to find established in the state. How far is the existence of parties justified by circumstances? What are their methods, and how far do they really seek to promote the national welfare? Is one more national and less selfish in its aims than the other, or then any other? Is there danger in strict party allegiance? On the other hand, is an independent attitude likely to lead to loss of influence? The answers to be given to these questions will differ somewhat according to the country in which they are asked; but it has occurred to us that there are certain general considerations on the subject of political parties which are likely to be more or less helpful anywhere, and which are not unsuited to the pages of this review.

Of late years the party system has not been the subject of much eulogy; more evil by far than good has been said of it, though it has not in general lacked for defenders when attacked. Sir Erskine May, author of "The Constitutional History of England," endeavors to hold the balance even in awarding to party the praise and blame that are its due.[10] "In the history of party," he says,

> there is much to deplore and condemn, but more to approve and commend. . . . We see the foremost of our fellow-countrymen contending with the bitterness of foreign enemies, reviling each other with cruel words, misjudging the conduct of eminent statesmen, and pursuing them with vindictive animosity. We see the whole nation

SOURCE: *North American Review,* Vol. CXXXII (January, 1881), pp. 52-63.

stirred with sentiments of anger and hostility. We find factious violence overcoming patriotism, and ambition and self-interest prevailing over the highest obligations to the state. . . . But, on the other side, we find that government without party is absolutism. We acknowledge with gratitude that we owe to party most of our rights and liberties. . . . We glory in the eloquence and noble sentiments which the rivalry of contending statesmen has inspired. We admire the courage with which power has been resisted, and the manly resolution and persistence by which popular rights have been established. . . . By argument and discussion truth is discovered, public opinion is expressed, and a free people are trained to self-government. We feel that party is essential to representative institutions.

It is a little hard to harmonize some of the statements of the eloquent author. "We glory," he says, "in the eloquence and noble sentiments which the rivalry of contending statesmen has inspired." But he had spoken of these eminent statesmen as "contending with the bitterness of foreign enemies, reviling each other with cruel words, misjudging and pursuing one another with vindictive animosity." He tells us that "by argument and discussion truth is discovered"; but the kind of argument and discussion he had previously described is far more likely to blind men to the truth than to open their eyes to it. Lastly, he speaks of the noble way in which oppositions have vindicated popular rights; but this is not, strictly speaking, an illustration of the working of party. When people are hurt they will cry out; it needs no party organization to bind together men who have a common grievance. Oppositions have shown the spirit and normal working of party far more in the obstacles they have thrown in the way of government than in the pleading of popular causes.

Sir Erskine May traces the origin of party, in its modern and legitimate form, to "the bold spirit of the Puritans," who, in the reign of Elizabeth, "spoke out in the House of Commons in support of the rights of Parliament and against her prerogative in matters of church and state." A very respectable origin this, but, upon the whole, a fanciful one. One scarcely recognizes even the germs of party in any such protest for conscience' sake. Sir Erskine himself tells us that throughout all changes of governmental arrangements "patronage has been the mainspring of the organization of parties. It has ever been used," he proceeds, "to promote the interests and consolidate the strength of that party in which its distribution happens to be vested." This is intelligible, and it harmonizes with much that falls under our observation from day to day. It seems, however, to have but little relation to "the bold spirit of the Puritans" under Elizabeth.

It is, as we think, an error to discuss the party system as if it were a special contrivance of modern government,—something which might either be or not be, according to circumstances, and susceptible, if retained, of indefinite modification. If this view of the matter were correct, it would be impossible to explain the universal prevalence of the system wherever representative institutions have been introduced. "We feel that party is essential to representative institutions," says the able authority we have quoted, and herein he is undoubtedly right. Representative institutions mean simply this: that the people are summoned to govern themselves. The question then at once arises: How are the people to do this? They can only do it through some individuals chosen for the purpose. Who are these to be? Manifestly the men who can best give expression and effect to the will of the people. What is the will of the people? What is the dominant sentiment of the hour? Upon this point the most opposite opinions may prevail among sagacious men. Every one inclines to think that his own opinion must be widely prevalent; and some are bold enough to believe that if their opinion is not prevalent, they can make it so. There are, therefore, of necessity, rival candidates for the honor and advantage of giving expression the national will. One is carried to power, the rest are swept into opposition: parties are established.

Scarcely any other general course of events than this is conceivable. But once place a party in power, and it has the strongest reasons for wishing to remain there. It will at times sacrifice the very principle that caused its triumph, rather than part with the honors and emoluments of office. Even when it is not prepared to go as far as this, it will seek to consolidate its strength by the means already hinted at, and by other means still less edifying. It is not necessary, perhaps, to dwell on this aspect of the subject, as even wayfaring men, though fools, are not very apt to err therein. It is of more importance, probably, to emphasize the view that some form of political organization for the ascertainment of public opinion is a matter of necessity; and that, as political parties fulfill this function in a certain measure, they must be allowed to have their utility. It is of importance to do this, because, unless we make allowance for the services that parties, with all their drawbacks and defects, render to the state, we shall rail at them "not wisely, but too well." And here we might add, with a slight touch of pathos, "*crede experto*"; for even so did we rail in the days when Manlius was consul, and all controversies seemed simpler to a somewhat more youthful enthusiasm.*

The point to which we are now drawing attention has nowhere been better brought out than in one or two of the admirable essays on

*Vide "Canadian Monthly and National Review," November, 1872.

government, embodied in Mr. Frederic Harrison's work entitled "Order and Progress."[11] The pure democratic theory is that a nation with free institutions governs itself; and when, in a general election, we witness the vast and striking phenomenon of an entire people casting their votes for the men who are to represent them, we are apt to overlook the means by which matters were brought just to that point,— means in the absence of which a general election, or any election, would be an impossibility. The voting of the multitude Mr. Harrison calls "the cooperation of the governed" in the decision of the special issues placed before them. "We are accustomed," he says,

> to turn our attention so exclusively on this cooperation, that we unconsciously grow into the notion that numbers could cooperate by direct identical action. We might as rationally suppose that an army of one hundred thousand soldiers would simultaneously raise the right foot and march in a body upon a given point, or go through a collective campaign, by independent free purpose of each individual soldier, without any officers or any word of command. Practically it is impossible that societies should act in the pure democratic or universal equality way. The real government or personal organ is disguised, or ignored, or almost smothered under forms, which seem to make the civic cooperation an automatic act of each citizen; but, so far as any real government exists, or any real action results, there is somewhere a person, a mind, and a will which originates it.*

In another place the same author remarks:

> Acting individually, neither a million of men nor fifty millions of men could make a law of the simplest kind, if they toiled for a century. Nor even could a thousand or even a hundred men together make a law. It would always be, *quot homines, tot leges*, if they tried forever, so long as the real individual thought of each citizen acted in honest independence of purpose.**[12]

Again:

> Our public life has become so completely one of polls, assemblies, committees, and boards, so habitually do we fix our attention on the combination of many opinions and many wills which they present, that we are apt to forget how completely all these conform to the same law, how much they screen from us the same inner truth, that

---

*"Order and Progress," page 50.
***Ibid.*, page 45.

all combined action of many implies a personal organ as its agent. Parliaments in the aggregate do not really make laws any more than nations as an aggregate do; committees delegate their action virtually to individual members; boards apportion within them the actual work; so that, in the ultimate reality, what is done in the collective name of the body is the work of one, or, at least, each substantive part is the work of one; *what is left undone is that at which many work without effacing their differences*.*

In the case of *plebiscite* everything depends upon who frames the question, and how it is framed. The government of the day, guided by some one ruling spirit, propounds, in its own interest, the particular question to which the people are to say yes or no. In an election there can be no voting until the candidates are reduced to one or two groups; and, as Mr. Harrison remarks,

it is difficult to conceive how few may be the persons who really do often force a candidate on a constituency; very often it is a single person, not even himself a voter.

But not only in politics do we witness the ascendancy of certain individual wills. "In any way," to quote this author again,

in which forces can be tested, we find this result, and we expect to find it; the collective action of any community, be it club, association, constituency, city, nation, will be determined by those members who, relatively to the rest, are not the cleverest or the best, but the strongest and the most tenacious of their own aims, and most apt to lead others to their aims.**

The reason why voting, as commonly practiced, furnishes the basis for a fair estimate of political forces, is because the voting has been preceded by the usual contest and agitation, in which the leading actors on either side have put forth their powers of attraction and persuasion, have developed their capacity for leadership, and effected a division of the community corresponding to the strength of the sentiments they have severally succeeded in evoking.

That political parties are in some sense a necessity, may indeed be deduced from a law with which Mr. Spencer has rendered us familiar, "the instability of the homogeneous." It is one of the commonplaces of practical politics that what a party gains in mass, beyond a certain

Ibid., page 48.
**Ibid.*, page 72.

point, it loses in cohesion. On the one hand, danger from the enemy being less, discipline is less rigidly enforced, one vote more or less counting for comparatively little; on the other hand, the rewards which the party has to bestow on its followers being (on account of the numbers) relatively fewer, the expectation of favors to come is less lively, and party attachments consequently feebler. If, then, we suppose one party to have completely absorbed its opponents, we should have at once a *régime* of pure individualism, which Mr. Harrison has so well shown to be incompatible with any kind of political action or movement.

It is a use of parties, so to speak, to focalize opinions, and thus to establish centers of gravity for the political system. To say that they do this at the cost of considerable refraction of the scattered rays they receive, is to say that they do it in the only conceivable way. There is, therefore, no use, at present, in quarreling with parties, as if it were in our power to stamp them out of existence. What we may do is to criticise them, to contrast their professions with their practices, to point out the debasing nature of the tyranny they seek to exercise over the nation, and to show how this tyranny may be resisted. It does not follow that, because the initiative in political matters must be taken by somebody, it therefore should be taken by the precise men who now take it. It does not follow that, because opinion must be organized, because aims must be concentrated, before there can be determinate political action, the work should be done precisely as we see it done now. The power which Mr. Harrison declares to reside in the mass of the poeple is *the power of veto*; they cannot arrange the plan of a campaign; but, if the plan has been very badly arranged by those who have taken it in hand, the people can, in a decisive manner, show their disapprobation. They can veto the policy, they can discard the candidate proposed to them by their party leaders. They can, in the same way, show their disapprobation of the methods by which party ends have been pursued.

If space allowed it, many signal instances could be cited of the exercise by a nation of its reserved powers in a very unexpected manner. Two of the most striking are furnished by recent English politics. In the year 1874, Mr. Gladstone made a sudden appeal to the people, and, in an address to the electors of Greenwich, struck the lowest note he had ever struck in his whole political career—that is to say, claimed the support of the nation on the ground, chiefly, that he had reduced taxation, and would, if returned to power, probably reduce it still more. The people answered, in the most emphatic way, that there were things they cared more for than a low rate of taxation, and that Mr. Gladstone was not the man they wanted just then at the head of affairs. Mr. Disraeli was borne into power by an immense majority, and ran for six years a career which was generally thought a very distinguished one. At the height of his prestige, and while the stamp of the mint was yet fresh on his brilliant coinages, ''Peace with Honor,'' ''A Scientific Frontier,'' ''*Imperium et Liberatas*,'' he also appealed to the people, and got a reply that he little expected in an almost contemptuous rejection by the nation he was supposed to have dazzled out of all its wits.

The capital charge which must be brought against party is that being professedly merely a means to an end, that end being the national welfare, it becomes an end to itself, and leads the nation a ridiculous dance to the ridiculous airs of the party managers. ''The moment,'' says Mr. Harrison,

> any machinery is required to appeal to voters,—and in every complex and large society some machinery is required,—skill in using the machinery acquires so important a place as very often to outweigh every other fact; and the result is determined, not by the influence of eminent character, not by the real wishes of the voters, but by the technical mastery of those who work the canvassing apparatus. The more complex the body, and the more elaborate the voting appartus, the more important becomes skill in managing the apparatus. Where the electing body, as in an English or American city, is both huge and unorganized, it can only be reached by expedients which develop special ingenuity, and usually demand immense resources.

Here again we find ourselves face to face with a fact which we may not like, but which there is no getting rid of. The ''machine'' in politics is a phenomenon of evil omen, suggestive of all that is dark and sinister and tricky; but it makes things go, and something is required for the purpose. We should not, however, regard it as a phenomenon peculiar to the field of politics. Wherever there is organization there is a ''machine''—that is to say, a headquarters of influence and command, an inner circle of men to whom the organization as it exists is a matter of prime importance, and who have the technical knowledge necessary to enable them to work it in their own interest. Every profession is more or less controlled by a machine. Literature itself is not free from a *soupçon* of the same influence. There are machines educational and machines ecclesiastical; and the further we look, the less occasion we shall find to wonder that the machine has taken possession, almost bodily, of our politics. But because machines have to be, and because they have interests that are not those of the public, it does not follow that the public must helplessly accept their dictation. There is a portion of the community which stands outside the sphere of their influence, and the community at large does not absolutely shut its ears to the voice of reason. The practical problem, therefore, which should engage our efforts is not how to banish the machine from politics, but how to force it to do decent work, how to teach it a certain measure of respect for the public intelligence.

The latter is the great point. When the party leaders on both sides have a really intelligent public to deal with—a public that resents as an insult such travesties of political discussion as fill the partisan press, a public that abhors the policy of slander, a public that loves the truth and rates the "campaign liar" just as it does any other liar, a public that repudiates the pestilent maxim that in politics, as in war, everything is fair that tends to success—when, we say, the party leaders have such a public as this to deal with, they will modify their tactics to suit the times. They will look to their nominations, lest they be too suggestive of a mere chase after spoils; they will look to their platforms, lest perchance some of the planks be too rotten to bear an honest man's weight; they will look to their methods, lest having done other things well, they turn public sentiment against them at the last moment. "But will this ever be?" some may ask; "are there any signs that such a condition of things is at all possible in any future with which we need concern ourselves?" We answer that he is the best citizen who is willing to work for the remotest future—who casts into the ground the seed of an honest word and a good example, without troubling himself too much as to whether *he* will ever see any fruit from it. We answer further, however, that there *are* signs that such a change as we have described is now in process of accomplishment, and that the agencies which favor it are daily gathering strength.

In an article already referred to as written some years ago, we expressed ourselves as follows, on the subject of party journalism:

It is not the bitterness of political discussion that seems to us the worst result of the party system; it is its amazing hollowness. A reasonable man is simply lost in amazement as he reads, day after day, in ably edited journals, whole columns of writing in which there is hardly the faintest gleam of sincere conviction to be discerned. Day after day the same miserable evasions, the same varnishing over of unsightly facts, the same reiterations of unproved charges against opponents, the same taking for granted of things requiring proof, the same proving of things that nobody questions, the same hypocritical appeals to the good sense of electors whom every effort is being used to misinform and confuse, the same dreary, unmeaning platitudes,— in a word, the same utter abuse of the reasoning faculty and of the functions and privileges of a free press. Of course, so long as both sides indulge in this kind of thing, each can make out at least a partial case against the other; and so a constant crossfire is kept up in the exposure of misrepresentations and the rectification of all that has been set down in malice or unduly extenuated on one side or the other. To-day, a good point is made by the opposition; to-morrow, it will be returned to them, if possible, with interest. Such is the party system of political warfare—a system which ought to have won the admiration of Archdeacon Paley, since it possesses the crowning attribute which was lacking to that celebrated watch of his, the power, namely, of perpetually reproducing itself.

Now, in so far as this language is applicable to the political controversies of to-day,—and few will deny it a certain applicability,—it becomes the duty of all who have it in their power to influence public opinion independently of party, to call attention in season and out of season to the utter insincerity of the whole performance. If people answer that they do not look for sincerity in political journals, and that for their own part all they want is to hear all possible good of their own side and all possible evil of the other, nothing more can be said; they must die, if they are determined to do so, in their sins. Some, it must be allowed, though they are not likely to make such an avowal, might do so with truth; for there are misguided individuals in the community who outdo in party bigotry the most violent of their leaders, just as there are lay devotees who far outdo their priests in superstition. On the other hand, there are many who have a tincture of fair-mindedness, and some respect for their own understandings, and who would be inclined to resent any deliberate attempts to befog and befool them. To these an appeal on behalf of rational and decent methods in political discussion may hopefully be made; not in the expectation, as we have before said, of doing away with parties and caucuses, with managers and wire-pullers, but of leading these to recognize some limit to their powers.

That party controversy is in general the merest parody of anything like legitimate and serious political argument is easily shown to any one who is not himself a hopeless thrall to party; and not less demonstrable is it that the systematic depreciation and abuse of public men tends to poison the whole political atmosphere and to educate the rising generation in a sickly cynicism by robbing them of all opportunity of recognizing and admiring public virtue in their own land and time. Let genuine, unmistakable corruption be exposed and lashed; and, if possible, let the operation be performed by some one who hates corruption in a friend even more than in a foe; but let not errors of judgment receive the denunciation due only to deliberate misdoing. Where public services have been rendered, let them be cheerfully and unstintedly acknowledged; and where a man has won a general character for uprightness, let his character be reckoned the property of the nation, and not a foot-ball for faction. Is not our country's richest inheritance to-day the *character* of the men who laid the foundations of her national greatness? And shall it be said that the United States have ceased in the beginning of the second century of their independence to lay up this particular form of wealth? It is sad to think to what a trade calumny has been reduced, and that instead of a growing faith in those who are called to the service of the republic, there should be an established conventional tone of mockery and distrust. Yet who is there practically conversant with public affairs who does not know that, many as are the evils that fasten themselves on government, the general state of things is not as bad, or nearly as bad, as is conventionally represented, that public men in general are far more honest than they get the credit of being, and that we are really, to a large extent, walking in a vain show of political wickedness, produced wholly and solely by the persistent falsifications of unscrupulous party journals? A vain show in one sense, for wickedness in the measure alleged does not exist; but a most serious reality in another, for this constant talk about evil *begets evil by begetting despair of good*.

To dwell, however, on all the weak points of political parties would take a book rather than a magazine article. The only remedy—and that but a partial and gradual one—for the evils we decry is the education and development of the enlightened and independent element in public opinion. Fortunately the agencies required for this important work are not altogether lacking. Some of the most influential journals of the day are honorably independent in their political judgments. The higher journalism, indeed, is constantly tending to throw off the trammels of party, and to view national questions from a national stand-point. It would be well, it seems to us, if the independent journals would unite in exhorting the parties to throw aside the hypocrisy which makes them pretend to more principle and more *principles* than they really have. In the absence of all differences of political principles, it is conceivable that one party, or one following, might yet propose better candidates than another; and, if distinctive principles are lacking, it would be better that the fact should be acknowledged, and that the electoral contest should turn simply on the merits of the candidates. There would then be vastly less of misleading and illusory argument than there is at present. Under no possible circumstances can hypocrisy do any good. That it would be well, also, to remove in part the temptations to mere party greed by some permanent organization of the civil service, seems also obvious; but this is a practical question of great difficulty, upon which we cannot undertake to offer any further remarks. That parties are beginning to recognize the necessity of putting respectable candidates in the field, would seem to be indicated by the nominations for recent Presidential elections; and that even the staunchest adherents of a party can be recalcitrant when the managers push management too far, has also been signally illustrated by late events. There is no reason, therefore, to despair of the political situation; there remain some things to the nation which it is quite worth while to try and strengthen. We shall make war best on the excesses of party strife by seeing that we understand thoroughly what parties are; by making due allowance for the conditions under which they work; by showing even a large degree of charitable tolerance for those who do the drudgery of actual organization and who cannot always be expected to be patriots of a high order; and, finally, by exerting all the influence we possibly can in promoting fair, candid, and broadly national views of public questions. This involves, of course, making direct and vigorous war upon all the palpable moral abuses and nuisances of party strife, particularly the wholesale traducing of character, which has hitherto been its most conspicuous accompaniment. And, in doing all this, let us remember for our comfort this saying of Burke's: "Plain good intention, which is as easily discovered at the first view as fraud is surely detected at the last, is of no mean force in the government of mankind."

14. The Anarchy of Modern Politics (1883)

In the Editor's Table of the April number of this magazine, there appeared what seemed to me some most excellent remarks on "The Hindrances to the Science of Politics." One of the chief of these the writer declared to be the wide-spread skepticism as to the possibility of such a science. "In no country," he added, "was this skepticism so pronounced as in the United States." Members of Congress and of the State Legislatures would all alike agree that the idea of constituting such a science was wholly chimerical. It was also stated, and pretty conclusively shown, that popular forms of government "favor and foster states of mind that exclude all considerations of a scientific nature," by calling into ascendency in a special degree

> the incalculable element of personal caprice. . . . In a country where everybody is eligible to office, where the incentives to office-seeking are universal, where politics has become such a natural pastime that the whole scheme of public education is subordinated to it, personal aspirations and the interests of selfish ambition will dominate unrestricted in the management of public affairs.

Offices being filled by partisans, whose lives have largely been spent in intrigue and the practice of vicious arts,

> the first presumption in regard to an officer-holder is, that he is unfit for the place. . . . These of course are not the men to appreciate the scientific elements and aspects of governmental affairs.

As I read all this, I could not help thinking how closely the writer's diagnosis of the conditions of modern political life resembled that given by Auguste Comte in the first chapter of the fourth volume of his "Philosophie Positive." But as Comte analyzes these conditions in greater detail, and treats the whole subject from the point of view of his own systematic philosophy, it occurred to me that something like a

SOURCE: *Popular Science Monthly*, Vol. XXIII (August, 1883), pp. 444-453.

paraphrase of his views might not be unwelcome to the readers of the "Monthly," to whom the subject in its general bearings has been so well opened up in the article from which the above quotations are made.

The main *motif* of the "Positive Philosophy" is the importance, or rather the absolute necessity, if a stable and satisfactory condition of society is ever to be attained, of applying to social and political affairs those scientific principles and methods which have proved their efficacy in the physical domain. The circle of the sciences, he holds, can never be complete until there is a duly constituted science of society. So long as there exists a region, the phenomena of which are not recognized as subject to law, human thought can not assume a really integral character; while, in that outlying region, a more or less hurtful confusion must prevail. Theology has in the past assumed to rule human life, and has done so, according to a synthesis of its own. The feudal and ecclesiastical organization of society in the middle ages was the perfect exemplification of this rule. Now, however, the power of theology has been broken; it has its spokesmen still, who in its name issue mandates to the modern world; but the civilized nations have no mind to return to what would now be a house of bondage—though in its day it may have been, and in Comte's opinion was, a house of shelter. But, meantime, what are the civilized nations doing? What guidance, if any, are they now following? Comte recognizes, looking chiefly at the European nations, three doctrines, or schools, as striving for the mastery in our day—the reactionary, the revolutionary, and the stationary. The first, as its name imports, would fain bring modern society back under the theological *régime*, placing morality and government on a supernatural basis, and using the lures and terrors of another world as a means (supplemented, of course, by the hangman, in whom reactionists always have a fervent and affectionate belief) of repressing disorders in this. On this continent we have, perhaps, no school which openly avows these aims; and yet there are movements visible from time to time which show that Comte could at least find the rudiments of a reactionary party even in this land of liberty and light. Governor Benjamin F. Butler's recent Fast-day proclamation was a singularly impudent attempt to browbeat the Commonwealth of Massachusetts into a more pious observance of the day than the eminent official thought would be likely to be made in the absence of such pressure. The efforts of those who wish to inoculate the constitution with a particularly pure theological virus tend in the same direction, and would make the father of Positivism smile were he alive.

The revolutionary doctrine, according to Comte's nomenclature, is that which proclaims liberty in its widest sense—an unlimited right of free inquiry, and an unlimited freedom for the people of political action. As Comte well points out, this school offers to society no definite guidance whatever—simply proclaims that all principles are to be examined and all experiments tried. That, after a certain amount of examination and experimentation, some set of principles might emerge, which society could accept as final, the revolutionary leaders are careful not to hint, lest they should be suspected of having some such set of principles in their mind, and so being at heart *doctrinaires* and perhaps even partisans of order. No, the revolutionary ideal is the negation of all trammels, change for the sake of change, a constant bubbling of the social caldron, so that no unit may remain long at the top, or long at the bottom, or long anywhere. But society can not live on change; and, in the absence of any definite doctrines of their own, the revolutionary school, when they are at the head of affairs, are compelled to make use of the principles and habitudes they find established, and even to fall back on rags and tatters belonging by right to their reactionary opponents. Thus the free-thinkers who now control the government in France are dogmatically teaching theism in the public schools. They want to give *some* kind of support to ideas of duty; and, having no coherent views of their own on the subject, they adopt, as a temporary make-shift, a theory and a synthesis which some of them would individually reject, and which none of them probably would care to be called on to expound.

The "stationary" school is that which erects into a doctrine a permanent principle of political action—the necessity of balancing reaction against revolution; holding out to society no prospect beyond that of an eternal seesaw of opposite tendencies. Disdaining all Utopias, it yet proposes to itself, as Comte observes, the very wildest of Utopias—that, namely, of securing social well-being by playing off the instinct of order against the instinct of progress. Having no principles of its own, it subsists wholly upon contradictory borrowings from the two antagonist doctrines. While it acknowledges that neither the one nor the other is fit to preside over social and political action, it thinks that, if *both* can be applied at once, all will go well. What has chiefly given vitality to this school, according to Comte, has been the example of England—which, however, has been, he asserts, an eminently misleading one; the stability of the English polity having been due to altogether exceptional circumstances, which are not and can not be reproduced in the numerous countries to which English institutions are sought to be applied. This "essentially loyal *régime*," he further says, is approaching its end even in the country to which it is native; and English authorities, as I may have occasion to show before I close, are not wanting who share the same opinion. The polity to which the future belongs is one that will not set order against progress and progress against order, but that will make equal provision for both, and make each contribute to the other; so that order shall facilitate progress, and progress strengthen order. This is the positivist ideal.

On this continent political parties can not be said to be constituted on the lines here marked out. Owing to the absence of political privilege and the comparative unifromity of social conditions, we do not as yet see any party, of sufficient importance to be taken into account, to which the term revolutionary could be applied. For the same reasons we have no distinctly reactionary party. At the same time, taking a wider view of things, and looking rather at the constitution of *opinion* than at the structure of parties, we shall probably see that the two opposite schools mentioned by Comte are sufficiently well developed, and that the third or "stationary" school comprises a very large section of the entire population. The forces are at work, though, as the politicians say, they may not yet be "in politics." All three concur in creating and continually intensifying the confusion, skepticism, and apathy which are such marked characteristics of the political thought and action of our time. What now remains is to study the results of these general conditions in a little more detail.

By reason of their greater complexity,* and also on account of their closer contact with the whole range of human passions, social questions ought to be reserved more scrupulously than any others for intelligences, necessarily few in number, that by a severe preliminary training have been gradually prepared to work them out to satisfactory results. That this is the normal state of things we have abundant historical evidence to prove; and when, in an epoch of revolution, the situation is changed, we can only regard the case as pathological; though, possibly, as already explained, provisionally inevitable and indispensable. What, then, must have been the ravages of this social malady in a time when all individuals, however inferior their intelligence, however destitute of all suitable preparation, were summoned indiscriminately and by the most energetic modes of appeal to decide day by day, with the most deplorable levity, and without guidance or check of any kind, the most fundamental questions of political. Instead of being surprised at the alarming divergence of views produced by the universal propagation during the last century of this anarchical tendency, should we not rather experience a gratified wonder at discovering that, thanks to the natural good sense and intellectual moderation of men in general,** the disorder is not more complete, and that, beneath

---

*From this point onward I shall, for the most part, be giving what at the outset I proposed to give, namely, a paraphrase rather than a translation of what Comte has written on this subject. (See "Philosophie Positive," first edition, vol. iv, p. 118 *et seq.*)

**This touch is very characteristic of Comte. He was no flatterer of "the

the decomposition of social maxims, certain rallying-points for humanity may still be dimly discerned? The evil has now reached such a point that all political opinions, though traceable to one or other of the sources mentioned, assume an essentially individual character, owing to the infinite number of variations produced by the intermingling of these three vicious principles. Except in cases where men are carried away by their interest in some common object or measure—which, however, each generally plans to turn to his own especial advantage—it becomes more and more impossible to get even a small number of individuals to adhere to anything like an explicit programme, or one in which vague and ambiguous language has not been employed to produce an illusory appearance of a really unattainable harmony of opinion. In the countries in which this intellectual disintegration has been, as it were, consecrated, since the commencement of the revolutionary era in the sixteenth century, by the political preponderance of Protestantism, diversities of thought, without being less intense, have been much more numerous, the popular mind having given itself over, in the absence of any energetic spiritual authority, to the indefinite discussion of religious opinions, which, of course, are at once the vaguest and the most discordant of all. No country has better verified this tendency than the United States of America, where Christianity is represented by some hundreds of sects radically at variance with one another, and daily undergoing further subdivision into shades of opinion which at last become almost purely individual. The countries that were not brought to a stand by the false "Halt!" of Protestantism do not present so great a total of vagaries; and the false opinions which have taken root in them, being more definite in their character, can be more hopefully dealt with.

The inevitable result of such an intellectual epidemic has been the gradual demolition of public morals. Such is the eminently complex character of social questions that, even when deliberate sophistry is absent, either side can be defended by extremely plausible arguments; seeing that there is no institution whatever, no matter how really indispensable to society, that has not many and serious drawbacks; while, on the other hand, the most extravagant Utopia always presents some undeniable advantages. We must not, therefore, be surprised if we see nearly all the great principles of public morality undergoing attack; their defects being generally very obvious, while the facts that justify them, though in reality far more decisive, lie sometimes far

---

people," and yet in the people he saw a reservoir of all the forces and all the virtues needful for the happiest regulation of the social state. The greatest philosopher, the mightiest leader of men, was in his view simply an organ of society, drawing all his strength and efficiency from the general life of society.

below the surface, and are only brought to light by a careful and delicate analysis. But to abandon the rules of social action to the blind and arbitrary decision of an incompetent public, is really to destroy their authority. Before, therefore, there can be that convergence of opinion in relation to such matters which is indispensable to social well-being, there must be a voluntary and intentional abdication by the majority of their sovereign right of judgment—an abdication which they would probably be very willing to make if they could only find suitable organs for the exercise of the function. In the wretched routine of our political struggles, it is common to find the most judicious and honorable men accusing one another of folly or of wickedness, on the strength of the vain antagonism of their political principles; while, in every important crisis, the most opposite political principles are habitually defended by partisans of apparently equal respectability. How, then, is it possible that the influence of this double spectacle, essentially incompatible as it is with any deep and permanent conviction, should not destroy all true political morality in the minds of those alike who take part in it or who view it with admiration?

Private morality depends, fortunately, on many other general conditions besides fixity of opinion. Here, in ordinary cases, a true natural sentiment speaks much more powerfully than it does in regard to public relations. The disorganizing forces have, moreover, been counterbalanced to a great extent; partly by a progressive softening of manners, the result of more general intellectual culture, bringing in its train a greater familiarity with and a juster appreciation of the fine arts, and partly by the unceasing development of industry. It must be added that the rules of domestic or personal morality, as they depend on simpler conditions, and admit of easier demonstration, are naturally less endangered by the incursions of individual analysis. And yet the time has undoubtedly come when, in the private as well as in the public sphere, we are called upon to witness the lamentable results of the general unsettlement of opinion. Whether we consider the relations of the sexes, or of different ages and conditions, we shall find that the necessary elements of all satisfactory social life are directly compromised, and are daily becoming more so, by the action of a corrosive discussion, dominated by no real principles, which delivers up to hopeless uncertainty every idea of duty. The family, which the fiercest blasts of the revolutionary tempest in the last century had left untouched, is, in our day, radically assailed in its two essential foundations, marriage and inheritance. We have seen even the most general and obvious principle of individual morality, the subordination of the passions to the reason, flatly contradicted by certain would-be reformers, who, without stopping to consider the teachings of universal experience, rationally sanctioned as they are by the scientific study of human nature, have tried to establish, as the fundamental doctrine of their improved morality, the systematic domination of the passions!

As a necessary and direct result of such disorder in the intellectual region, we see corruption erected into a recognized and indispensable means of carrying on government. So powerless have general ideas become, into such discredit have they fallen, that they no longer avail to prompt any course of action; and governments find themselves, therefore, without any other resource for securing such union of individuals as is necessary to the maintenance of a rude material order, than an almost open appeal to purely personal interests. But, were men animated by profound convictions, such a means of influence would never have to be resorted to. Even in characters of the least elevation, human nature seldom debases itself so far as to follow out a line of conduct in direct opposition to any set of convictions. We see this proved in the case of men of science: in politics, where the reign of law is not yet established, they frequently exhibit the most shameful tergiversation; while they stand firm against all temptation to abandon their anti-theological opinions for which they believe they have a scientific warrant. We thus see that the prevalent intellectual confusion not only allows the development of political corruption, but absolutely renders it necessary as a means of government, which of course can not be carried on unless a certain number of individuals can be brought to act in harmony. This fact, however, does not excuse the governments of our time for showing such a preference as they do for this particular means of influence; nor for using it, as they do, almost exclusively in their own personal interests. Bad as the *instrument* is, it might be used to better *ends* than is commonly the case, if the "practical politicians," instead of casting scorn on all attempts to establish a science of politics, were to lend such aid as they could to its elaboration. They could lend some aid by a mere change of attitude.

The political corruption of our day is not confined, however, to the direct offer by governments of material inducements for political support. We see a form of it in the awarding of distinctions and titles; and, taking a wider view, we see that all our institutions work together to call into activity the selfish ambition of all the more energetic members of the community. In this most important respect, the existing condition of society itself may be said to be eminently corrupting. At the same time that the prevalent intellectual anarchy has dissolved any public prejudices that stood in the way of unlimited individual self-assertion, the inevitable decomposition of the ancient social classification has likewise thrown down the barriers to private ambition, which is now, in the name of progress, invited to take the very highest flights. Carried along by an irresistible current, governments have had to try and meet the new demands of the time by an extravagant multiplication of public offices, by making access to these as easy as possible, and by changing the incumbents as often as possible. Yielding in the first place to an evil necessity, they have afterward converted that necessity into a general resource of government, by trusting, as a regular thing, to the interested support of energetic and ambitious men with whom they divide the profits arising from the management of the public business. How dangerous such an expedient is from the point of view of the governments themselves, it is almost needless to point out; since it must necessarily call forth far more claims than it can satisfy, and consequently excite against the established *régime* passions far stronger than any it can evoke for its support.* If we just look at the selections for a generation or two past for the most eminent political functions, is there any reason why the great majority of our aspiring men should not conceive the hope of climbing in their turn to similar positions? Another marked feature of the times is the disposition to trust to material agencies or mere acts of legislation for the removal of evils that have their root in men's ideas and in social customs. An amendment to a constitution or a charter is proffered as a plan of political salvation; or, worse still, we are asked to rest our hopes on the substitution of this man for that in a cabinet. Meanwhile, the absence of any clear or comprehensive conception of the social future affords a career only to the most vulgar kind of ambition. At no former epoch, probably, were such chances ever offered to a presuming and adventurous mediocrity. The quality chiefly required in public life is fluency of speech, above all, a fluency which suffers no abatement if it is suddenly called on to change sides on a question. In a time of weak and wavering convictions there has naturally been a demand for representatives characterized by the vagueness of their intellectual habits and an habitual lack of fixed opinions. Unless we could hope that such a condition of things would be but transitory, it would really constitute the most shameful social degradation. That hope we may, however, entertain. If there are forces of decomposition at work, there are also—though their action may not be so conspicuous—forces of regeneration; and what is needed to give these a decisive victory is the formulation and application of a true political philosophy.

Such was the view taken by Comte, over forty years ago, of the then political situation in France and other countries enjoying constitutional *régimes*. Matters have not mended since his day: principles are more than ever discredited in political affairs; parties no longer even profess them; and government and legislation are carried on at mere haphazard. The great object with party managers is to get all important

*How exactly this applies to the existing situation in France, and how nearly it describes the situation here, no reader will fail to remark.

questions taken "out of politics," so that there may be nothing to embarrass the scramble for offices. The New York "Sun" lately reminded the Democrats that their business was "to elect a President," not to reform the tariff. Seek first, it says, to "elect a President," and all good things will be added unto you; but grapple with a great question like the tariff, and your opponents will surely get the better of you. Another leading organ observes that, now that the offices are no longer generally available, owing to the passage of the Pendleton civil-service bill, for the reward of political services, there remains nothing for a victorious party but "a damned barren ideality."[13] The strength of the language, which we reproduce with absolute faithfulness, may be taken as a gauge of the disgust which the average politician feels when he sees nothing before him but a chance of doing his duty, without any special reward therefor. The novel, "Democracy," about which so much has been said, does not overstate the case in the least.[14] When Mrs. Lee, in that lively story, tells the senator, who pays her the compliment of consulting as to the best course to take in a certain complication, to do "what is most for the public good," her counsel falls utterly pointless and abortive, simply because "the public good" had nothing whatever to do with the matter in hand. The senator himself could not pretend to tell her at what point the two things came into any kind of relation with each other. The questions involved were questions purely of self-interest, and, whatever course was taken, the country had nothing to gain.

If we turn to England, signs are not wanting that there too the absence of political principles is leading up to a crisis. "The notion," said the London "Times" recently,

> that any particular set of men are in possession of principles especially calculated to promote the national well-being, or that any particular trick of government could add appreciably to the sum of happiness, is one which nowadays finds remarkably few advocates. Moreover, there is a pretty general feeling that [it] is [of] very little use to rely upon principles of any kind. . . . At the present time we are not proceeding upon any principle known to either political party; and it is that fact which explains the hollowness of all political discussion, and the marked incredulity of the intelligent public toward all political professions. The fact is, that our political principles are worn out, and that the conflict which raged around them while they were vital is being mechanically carried on by men whose business it is to fight about something.

When remarks like these can be made by the "leading journal," it would certainly seem as if Comte was not far wrong in his prediction that the English system would before long reveal its essential weakness. The question then arises, Can government be permanently carried on under these conditions? As Comte has remarked, the absence of principle in public life reacts upon private life; and certainly, in the latter sphere, the disorder we now witness is not what might have been expected in an age of such general enlightenment. It would seem as if, before long, those who now profess to take things as they come, and make light of all attempts to construct a philosophy applicable to human affairs, might be compelled to humble themselves to believe that Science may have a word to say in regard to the highest order of phenomena just as she has had in regard to all orders up to the highest. If the pride of individualism should ever have such a fall as this, there is no doubt, in the mind of the present writer, that Science will respond nobly to the new call upon her, and will show how order and progress can be reconciled, and a moving equilibrium be established which shall be the proper manifestation and expression of a normal and healthy social life.

15. Problems of Government in Canada (1895)

The problems of government in Canada are those incident to political institutions essentially democratic in character. A Canadian does not need to be a very old man in order to remember the time when it was generally supposed that the copy we had made in this country of British institutions was an effectual safeguard against the evils of democracy. We looked across the border; and, according as our thoughts reverted more naturally to Scripture or to the classic poets, we would either thank God that we were not as those republicans or murmur after Lucretius,

> Suave mari magno turbantibus aequora ventis
> E terra magnum alterius spectare laborem.[15]

This mood of self-gratulation has not wholly passed away even yet; but later political speculation, confirmed by not a little practical experience, has taught us that the essentials of democracy may lurk under forms of government professedly nondemocratic, and may even work more wide-apread mischief owing to their not being recognized in their true character. The readers of Sir Henry Maine's well known work on "Popular Government" will remember that, in one most important respect, he finds the English system of government more democratic than that of the United States.[16] In the latter country most elaborate precautions have been taken against any sudden or ill-advised change in the law of the constitution; whereas in England a constitutional change requires no more formality, no more discussion, no more delay than the passing of any ordinary act of Parliament.

What is the essential principle of democracy? Professor Sidgwick, of Cambridge, discussing this question, says that the fundamental principle of democracy is that government should repose on the active consent of the governed; and this principle he says he accepts. He adds, however, that the advocates of democracy generally put forward explicitly or implicitly another principle which he does not accept,

SOURCE: *Queen's Quarterly*, Vol. II (January, 1895), pp. 198-209.

namely "that any one self-supporting and law-abiding citizen is on the average, as well qualified as another for the work of government."[17] It seems to me that there is yet another principle widely held in democratic communities, which constitutes a still more serious corruption of that true democratic principle which Professor Sidgwick accepts; and that is, that the powers of the government should be locally exercised by representatives of the dominant party in the interest of that party.

If it be a part of democratic doctrine that the will of the majority should be able to find swift expression in legislation, then few countries are, in this respect, so little democratic as the United States, while few, if any, are more democratic than Great Britain and her colonies. It would probably be held, however, by thoughtful believers in democracy that the true democratic principle is not infringed by mere checks upon hasty legislation, so long as those checks have approval of the people at large, and so long as there is no exercise of veto power by a non-popular or anti-popular chamber. The representative of democracy might say:

> We know we are but human, and therefore liable to error; and we do not object to having the legislative projects we put forward from time to time referred back to us for further consideration, provided the powers that do this are constitutional powers, and are themselves popular in their origin. What we could not stand would be to have an individual or a chamber representative, not of the nation, but only of a limited class within the nation, sitting in judgment on the mandates of the people.

If we look at the matter closely, the essential idea of democracy will be found to involve no more than the fundamental principle which Professor Sidgwick says he accepts, "that government should rest on the active consent of the citizens." A system of government embodying and consistently applying this principle, free from contamination by such illegitimate adjunct principles as are mentioned above, may, in a useful sense, be described as "pure" democracy; while one which drags in the latter, and gives them equal authority with the true principle on which they are foisted as corollaries, may be designated as "impure" democracy.

The most advanced ideal of government, if we adopt these definitions, is therefore "pure" democracy; but the ideal does not exist in concrete shape: what we find actually existing is "impure" democracy. Probably the government of Great Britain makes as near an approach to pure democracy, in the sense defined, as is now to be seen in the world; that is to say, it is the system of government in which the fewest false accretions attach themselves to the true principle, "that government should rest on the active consent of the citizens.'' It is evident that, in some states of society, government cannot rest on the active consent of the citizens; it *must* assume a tyrannical or, under improved conditions, a monarchical form, owing to the fact that the mass of the citizens would not otherwise be disposed to submit to any political control. Monarchy, therefore, in so far as it implies the control by one of an unwilling many, has its proper place in communities that have not yet developed a sufficient amount of internal cohesion to fit them for free institutions in the full sense. Of course, as in England, the form of monarchy may be retained, long after its coercive function has ceased. It then becomes a kind of historic adornment to an essentially democratic state, and by keeping the people in touch with their past may serve a very useful purpose. It may, and in all probability does, serve the further purpose of symbolising in an efficient manner the unity of the state, and bringing home to the mind of jarring factions the conviction that there are paramount and permanent national interests which in their restless strife they must be careful not to touch. The maxim that the King can do no wrong is but another way of saying, that while individual men may err, and parties adopt wrong politics, the State as a permanent organization has no responsibility for such divagations, but remains the unfailing source of good to its subjects, the true creator of their liberties and protector of their civilization.

If we consider the position of Canada, we shall find that it has many points of natural and, so to speak, historical advantage. To be closely bound by political and social ties to a country enjoying so high a type of political liberty as England is no small advantage in itself. To England we look, or at least may look and should look, for our examples of statesmanship. The ideals that rule English public life ought to be, and to some extent doubtless are, influential here. It is to English public opinion—the most honest that exists in the world—that we are most interested in commending ourselves and our methods. The relations existing between Canada and the Mother Country are honorable to both. The writer of these pages has met intelligent and fairly educated Americans, who were surprised to learn that Canada did not pay taxes to England, and who had some difficulty in understanding what the relations between the two countries could be, if Canada was not, in some way, made tributary to England's wealth and greatness. It is to our advantage, again, that we have adopted the strong English system of cabinet government, instead of the weaker system, existing amongst our neighbors, of government by committees of the legislature.

To turn to another class of considerations, our population, as compared with that of the United States, is more homogeneous in character. Such foreign elements as we possess exist in assimilable quantity, and are not inaccessible to the ordinary currents of public opinion. The

French-Canadian question does not, after all is said and done, present any serious hindrances to our political development. Our fellow-citizens of French origin know they have to live with us, and we know that we have to live with them; and all that is wanted to make things run smoothly is a spirit of equity and, if possible, of common patriotism on both sides. It might indeed be plausibly argued that the present division of our population into two widely-differing elements, one certainly predominant in numbers and influence, but the other large enough and important enough to be able to stand firmly on its rights, is favorable to the development of political intelligence, and especially of that spirit of moderation which is the chief safeguard of political institutions and of national life.

The character of our climate may fairly be reckoned a further point in our favor. It is a climate which tends to produce a hardy, industrious, energetic and resourceful race. The Canadian summer is genial and bounteous; the Canadian winter is bracing and not to be trifled with. A more salubrious climate, on the whole, is probably nowhere to be found, nor a healthier or more vigorous race. These facts are not without their political significance; for, if we want the best political results, we should have the best natural conditions and the best human material to begin with. Without flattering ourselves unduly, we may say that in both respects we have as good as the best.

Assuming the foregoing facts as data, we may proceed to enquire what the actual direction of our political development has been and is, and what the immediate prospects before us. If we go back sixty or even fifty years in the history of Canada, we shall find its government still, to a large extent, in the aristocratic stage. Sixty years ago, what is now known as "responsible government" had not yet been conceded. There was a system of popular representation; yet in may ways the people were governed in the old-fashioned sense by administrators who assumed to know what was good for them better than they did themselves. The situation is well described in Sir Francis Bond Head's "Narrative," which shows in a very instructive manner how popular personal government may be when characterized by fearlessness and disinterestedness. The forces of democracy, however, were advancing like a rising tide; and in what seemed the very hour of his triumph the unbending champion of conservatism was obliged to make way for a more pliant successor. The full establishment of responsible government did not at once dispel the idea that, in the matter of appointments to the public service, a Governor might act upon his own convictions of what was best without consulting his Ministers. The last Governor to maintain this position was Sir Charles Metcalfe. What he plainly saw was that the reason his Ministers wanted to be consulted was in order that they might use the "patronage" to strengthen their political position; and to his straightforward mind it seemed an abuse that appointments should be used for such a purpose. To be sure, he was imposing severer conditions on his Ministers in Canada than had, for many a long year, been imposed upon Ministers in the Mother Country; but he doubtless perceived that the political exercise of patronage in a country like Canada was very much more serious in its effect on the balance of parties than in a country like England. Be this as it may, the position was practically untenable, and we do not hear of its having been taken up by any of his successors.

But how the spirit of democracy has ripened since that time! Not the spirit of pure democracy, but of impure democracy—the spirit which says that one man is about as good as another for a legislative or administrative position, that every smallest exercise of executive power is to be availed of for party purposes, that the expenditure of public money is as much as possible to have a similar destination, and that throughout the country the representatives of the dominant party are to be converted into little present deities for the purveying of government favour to their several localities. Can it be denied by any serious man, be he conservative or liberal, that this is the spirit that rules to-day? If any man does deny it, it can only be because he is not in touch with public affairs, and does not know the facts.

The idea that one man is about as good as another for any legislative or administrative position antedates, it must be admitted, the great democratic development of modern days. Monarchies have on the whole done more to shelter incompetency in office, and even on the field of battle, to the deadly peril of the national interests, than democracies. Monarchies, too, have systematically created sinecures to an extent that democracies have not ventured on doing. When we think of the Grand Monarque and his beggarly courtiers rioting on the taxes of a starving nation, we feel that a day of vengeance had to come; and when we think of the useless pensions which formerly loaded down the Civil List in England, we have reason to congratulate the Mother Land on the good fortune which enabled her to avoid a revolution once or twice impending. Speaking of the reign of William the Third, Hallam says:

> A system of infamous peculation among the officers of government came to light in this reign through the inquisitive spirit of Parliament; not that the nation was worse and more corrupt than under the Stuarts, but that a profligacy, which had been engendered and flourished under their administration was now dragged to light and punishment. Long sessions of Parliament and a vigilant party spirit exposed the evil, and have finally in a great measure removed it.

As lately as the beginning of the reign of the present sovereign considerable resistance was made to a proposal for the appointment of a committee to enquire into the pension list; and, when finally the committee was granted, the member of Parliament, Mr. Harvey, who had been foremost in urging its appointment, was excluded from it, because he had announced his intention to make public the evidence obtained.

There is a difference to be noted, however, between the view taken of these things under a monarchical and under a democratic regime respectively. Under a monarchy, the money taken to reward favorites or pay party tools is more or less recognized as stolen, and efforts are made to conceal the iniquity. Under a democracy the idea is that it is the people's money voted by the representatives of the people, and spent by the men whom those representatives keep in power. Ergo, there can be no stealing about it; and a sufficient answer to any criticism as to the way in which it is spent is that the people are willing to have it so. The late Sir John Macdonald is credited with having said that, if the people were bribed, it was with their own money; as if that settled the whole question, and completely established the innocence, if not the excellence, of the practice. The hollowness of the sophism is, however, visible at a glance. It is never *the people* that are bribed: it is *sections* of the people, who, if they conduct themselves well politically, get an undue share of the money of the *whole people*. You can never bribe a man with what is absolutely his own money; not even the genius of the late chieftain would have been equal to that. Under the system in question men can be appointed to important offices who have no qualification for them, and no intention whatever to fulfil, or attempt to fulfil, the duties supposed to appertain to them. To all intents and purposes they are appointed to sinecures, and the duties which they are nominally paid for performing are discharged by subordinates. The real purpose which such men serve is either to exercise a watchful care over party interests in their localities, or to furnish shining examples of what a party in power can do for those who render, or have rendered, it service. These are the prize-winners in the great lottery of politics, and their success is expected to have a powerful influence in disposing others to take their chances on the same side.

Sometime the prize-winner is not, taking everything into account, so great a prize-winner as appears at first sight. He may have impoverished himself through politics, and an office is given to reward him for his "sacrifices" for the party. Would it not be much better, however—seeing the people approve of such things—to take a parliamentary vote to reward Mr. So and So for his sacrifices for such and such a party, instead of putting him into an office the duties of which he will never fulfil and where he more or less interferes with the full authority and responsibility of the real executive officer? It would certainly cost the country much less in the end; and possibly, by making the people more distinctly realise that party battles were being fought with public money, would evoke a condemnation of the principle. "There is no act," says John Stuart Mill,

> which more imperatively requires to be performed under a strong sense of individual responsibility than the nomination to employments. The experience of every person conversant with public affairs bears out the assertion that there is scarcely any act respecting which the conscience of the average man is less sensitive.

If the conscience of the average man is so lacking in sensitiveness what shall be said of the conscience of the "local committee"? But imagine talking about the conscience of a local committee! Were ever terms more mutually contradictory, more utterly exclusive of one another, ever brought into conjunction? Yet it is the local committee that generally has the decisive word in any question of local patronage.

There was a great political convention held in the capital of the Dominion about a year and a half ago, in which a number of important questions were discussed, and a party platform was constructed.[18] The time was eminently seasonable, one would have thought, for the declaration of sound principles in regard to appointments to public office and the general exercise of ministerial responsibility in the expenditure of public money, because the convention followed upon the lamentable exposures of the sessions of 1891 and 1892—exposures which had led the government of the day to promise a thorough investigation and, as far as might be necessary, reorganization of the Dominion civil service. Yet, strange to say, the convention in question, though deploring in general terms "the gross corruption in the management and expenditure of public moneys which has for years past existed under the rule of the Conservative party," had no distinct word to say on the subject of the abuse of patronage or the necessity for a divorce between the public service and party politics. This silence was the more remarkable inasmuch as certain independent journals had called attention to this question, as one in regard to which the convention should certainly not the lose the opportunity of placing itself on record.

England for many years past has had an entirely non-political civil service. The permanent civil service cannot to-day be used by any minister for the purpose of augmenting in the very smallest degree his political influence. First appointments are given strictly and solely to those persons who are certified by the Civil Service Commissioners as having gained the highest stand in an open competitive examination. As regards promotion, that is governed by seniority, other things being equal or nearly so; but when other things are not equal merit determines the choice. Were any Member of Parliament to attempt to interfere in a question of promotion, his intrusion would be resented as a gross impertinence. In the United States, a steady advance is being made towards a similar system. Some years ago (1883) a large part of the Civil Service was placed under the control of a Commission, and from time to time other portions of it have been placed on the same footing. Quite lately, as the New York "Nation" of November the 8th informs us, President Cleveland "has made a wholesale extension of the competitive system," and has thus brought within its operation "all the minor offices in the departments now omitted, all of the employees in Custom-houses where they number as many as twenty, 1,500 of the 2,300 places now excepted in the postal service," and has put a stop to a flagrant abuse which before existed, by which a person appointed, as a matter of patronage, to an "excepted" place could be transferred to one not excepted, so as to create another vacancy in the former place.

What are we going to do about it in Canada? There is our democratic neighbor dealing blow after blow at the spoils system, and across the ocean we see the Mother Country rejoicing in a public service absolutely free from all taint of political interference, while we content ourselves with a Civil Service law which simply prescribes a very elementary qualifying examination, as a condition of eligibility, and then hands over all appointments to the politicians and their committees. Worse than that, we do not even rigorously exclude political influence from the higher walks of the service, when promotions are in question. To their honour be it spoken, many Members of Parliament are too high-minded and honorable to wish to force their favorites over the heads of other men; but that such abstinence is not general may be judged from the fact that experienced officers may be heard declaring that the only escape from a political interference, which would throw everything into confusion, is to follow absolutely the rule of seniority, even when it involves promoting a decidedly inferior man to a position the duties properly belonging to which he will never be able in any adequate manner to fulfil. Personally I do not accept this position; on the contrary it seems to me that, for reasons which could be stated, had I space at my disposal, the distinct recognition of superior merit as a ground for promotion, would, even as things are, help to ward off, rather than invite, political interference. The question, however, is: How long is Canada going to remain democratic in this unworthy sense? How long will it be before the people of this country arrive at the common sense conclusion that, if they want efficient service in return for their very liberal outlay upon the civil list, they must see to it that the civil service is not allowed to be a preserve for party politicians.

It is not appointments only that furnish grist to the political mill. The most minute expenditure of public money must be conducted into the right political channel or there will be trouble. "Idem sentire de republica," or, in plainer English, to vote the right ticket, is a test that is imposed no less on the glazier who replaces a broken pane, and the grocer who provides a bar of soap for a public office, than on the recipients of more important favors. How much of envy and jealousy is bred throughout the country by the sharp line of distinction thus drawn between those who may, and those who may not, look for government patronage, is not only easy to imagine, but is probably familiarly known to most readers of these pages. A still worse result is the connection established in so many minds between the exercise of the franchise and personal profit. The life of the average Member of Parliament is certainly not in all respects a happy one. He is, if he belongs to the party in power, the channel of government favors to his locality; and this may be flattering to his pride and self-importance; but, on the other hand, he is never able to meet half the demands made upon him, and thus stands in jeopardy every hour of losing the votes of the patriots whom he fails to satisfy. Another and very grave aspect of the matter is that departmental action is seriously weakened, as well as obstructed, through the necessity, now generally recognized, of consulting the wishes and interests of local politicians. The powers of the executive are supposed to be wielded for the benefit of the whole country; yet how is it possible under our present system that they should not be made to a great extent partisan in their operation? A member of the popular branch of the Dominion Legislature was, not so long ago, heard expounding his view of the theory of government. "If," said he,

I had a son who cheeked me, do you think I would go out of my way to do anything for him? Not much. Well, what claim can an Opposition constituency have upon the government for public buildings or anything else the government has it in its power to bestow?"

This gentleman spoke with the air of one uttering a truth everlasting enough for Thomas Carlyle himself. He evidently felt that he had got down to the bed-rock of political philosophy. But if such is the state of mind of a man of position and influence, what is likely to be that of the average elector?

"But is not the credit of Canada good?" it may be asked. Yes, the credit of Canada is good; and that shows that we have among our public men, some who are laboring to keep in check tendencies, which, if unchecked, would ruin the financial standing of the country and seriously imperil its political future. That much firmness and skill and watchfulness must be exercised by certain members of the executive in the public interest cannot be doubted; otherwise, things would be worse than they are. But why struggle with a defective system when a little resolution might put an end to it? Why allow ourselves to be outstripped in controlling the abuses of patronage by the democratic nation to the south? If we admire England and are proud of our connection with it, why not import English ideas of Civil Service organization, so far as they are applicable to this country? Are Canadians so morally inferior a race that they cannot do without a "spoils system,"—that their whole interest in politics would die out if considerations of gain did not stimulate them to political activity? It would certainly be painful to any true patriot to have to adopt that conclusion. The American revolutionary statesman, Alexander Hamilton, is said to have expressed the opinion that when corruption ceased in England, the British constitution would fall to pieces. Possibly, the gentleman who likened an opposition constituency to a cheeky son might entertain similar apprehensions as to the result of the disappearance of corruption in Canada; but as corruption has practically been brought to an end in England, and as the British Constitution survives, the rest of us may be allowed to cherish better hopes. What is wanted in Canada is a change in public opinion. Nothing has been more discouraging hitherto than the lack of interest on the part of the average citizen in any suggestions for the purification of our politics; but, judging by the increase in the number and influence of the independent journals, and the somewhat higher tone of political discussion, as compared with, say, twenty years ago, in the more important party journals, there is some reason to hope that the times are ripening for an onward and upward movement in our political life. That movement must find a voice, it must find a leader. Who among the statesmen of the day has confidence enough in himself and faith enough in the people of Canada to place himself at its head? Or must a new man arise before the new time can be born?

16. The Problem of Popular Government (1901)

There are many distinct problems of popular government, but the one great and comprehensive problem which it presents is: how the best results may be obtained from it—how it may be made to work for the highest good of the community in which it is established. Popular Government, or Democracy, is now an almost universal datum throughout the western world, in which, of course, we include western Europe. Early in the last century, as we must now designate the nineteenth, the philosophical De Tocqueville somewhat sadly proclaimed its coming, bidding the world prepare for a *régime* under which privilege, precedent, personal authority, the sagacity of the statesman, the wisdom of the philosopher, and the erudition of the scholar would alike be swept out of sight by one vast wave of popular domination. He mentions in his correspondence that, in America, he had found manners and ideas uniformly commonplace; and what he feared was that Democracy everywhere would simply mean the reign of commonplace. To a refined and sensitive spirit the prospect was not encouraging; but a robuster philosophy might, perhaps, have enabled him to feel that there was still hope for the world—that, however mediocrity might assert itself for a time, the finer fruits of the human spirit would flourish again in due season. Some, however, of De Tocqueville's contemporaries were not disposed to acquiesce in the opinion that the universal triumph of democracy was inevitable. They saw the foe advancing, and armed themselves to give him battle. Our own annals afford a conspicuous example of this political temper in the person of Sir Francis Bond Head, who, sixty-three years ago, was administering in this city the government of the Province of Upper Canada. "The British Constitution," he says in one of his despatches to the Colonial Office, "has nothing to dread from its low-bred antagonist (democracy) in America if His Majesty's Government will

SOURCE: *University of Toronto Monthly*, Vol. I (April, 1901), pp. 229-241; (May, 1901), pp. 257-263. A lecture delivered in the Chemical Building, University of Toronto, February 23, 1901. Also published in pamphlet form (n.p., n.d., copy in the Public Archives of Canada).

not avert from us its support." He was greatly scandalized to hear that instructions had been given to the Lieutenant-Governor of New Brunswick to endeavour to place in his Council "gentlemen representing the various interests which exist in the Province, and possessing at the same time the confidence of the people at large." It seemed to him, and he said as much to the Colonial Secretary (Lord Glenelg), that this was neither more nor less than giving the highest official countenance to anarchy. He speaks in another despatch of "the repeated repulses which the American people have met with whenever they have attempted to invade Canada for the purpose of forcing upon us their loathsome institutions." That Sir Francis was a high-minded man—a much more high-minded man than some of the Reformers with whom he had to contend—no impartial reader of his "Narrative" can doubt: but he was on the losing side. He was a man of great force of character, and he had in fact rallied a large portion of the Province to his views; but the Colonial Office clearly saw that a cause which depended on personal force of character could not be permanently sustained. He was informed that "His Majesty's Government looks to no transient results or temporary triumphs." Finally, as you are aware, he sacrificed his office rather than obey the instructions he had received to restore a certain person to office whom he had thought it proper to remove.

I do not know whether the conflict between the two irreconcilable ideas of personal government and popular government can be better studied than in the volume to which I have been referring. It is almost impossible not to sympathize with the champion of the dying cause; and yet the very heroism which he throws into the fight gives foreboding of failure. His opponents did not require to be heroic, nor yet uncommonly straightforward. They only needed to unite on a policy, and pursue it with persistence. What they wanted above all things was control of the patronage; and that they got through the establishment of what was called "responsible government."

At the time that Sir Francis was waging his hopeless contest in this Province the Reform Bill (1832) had already been passed in England. That bill, as it proved, contained in germ the whole democratic system of government; but this was not perceived at the time by its authors, nor even, for the most part, by its opponents. It contained the principle of Democracy in this respect, that it gave *substantial* representation to the masses of the people; the play of party politics did the rest. So long as there is an untouched reservoir of political power anywhere, so long will it attract the covetous glances of the party most likely to profit by tapping it. It is difficult for the practical politician to pass by a mass of possible votes *irretortis oculis*.[19] At the same time many were the declarations made that there was no intention, or even thought, of democratizing the Constitution of England. Lord John Russell declared in 1837 that, so far as he was concerned, the settlement of 1832 was final. "Having," he said,

> only five years ago reformed the representation, having placed it on a new basis, it would be a most unwise and unsound experiment now to begin the process again. . . . I say, at least for myself, that I can take no share in such an experiment.

As we all know, however, that indefatigable statesman did in later years take part in several such experiments. In 1854, and again in 1859, he made unsuccessful attempts to carry further measures of reform. On the latter occasion he is recorded to have said:

> I wish to disclaim entirely any intention to frame a new Constitution. I disclaim such a project for two reasons. One is that I have no wish to alter the Constitution of this House; the other is that, if any such alteration were sought, I should feel totally unable to propose anything that would stand in the place of the ancient and glorious Constitution of the country.

This sentiment was echoed and reinforced by Mr. Disraeli on the other side of the House. "We think," he said,

> that the English Constitution is not a mere phrase. We believe that we live under a monarchy, modified in its action by the authority of estates of the realm. . . . Under a democracy we do not live, and I trust it will never be the fate of the country to live.

In 1859 Lord Palmerston was at the head of the Government; and it was an open secret that he was far from enthusiastic for the cause of Reform. In reply to some one who was maintaining that, even though the suffrage were extended, the same class of men would continue to be elected to Parliament, he is reported to have said: "Yes; I dare say the actors will be the same, but they will play to the galleries instead of to the boxes." We all know the course which Parliamentary Reform followed in England: how Lord Russell was again unfortunate with his bill of 1866, and how Lord Derby and Mr. Disraeli put their heads together to "dish the Whigs" with their more radical measure of the following year, which became law. It was at the latter date that Delane, the celebrated editor of the *Times*, said, as quoted in a letter of Lord Houghton's, that "the extreme party for reform are now the grandees; and the dukes are quite ready to follow Beale into Hyde Park." Disraeli had educated his party with a vengeance—all except the three recalcitrants, the Earl of Carnarvon, General Peel and Viscount Cranbourne, now Lord Salisbury. The Whigs, however, were not so completely "dished" as had been hoped, for they came back into power with a rush in the first election held under the new Act. Still, the name "democracy" remained in disfavour. Even in 1884, when Mr. Gladstone brought in and carried his last Reform Bill, he disclaimed any intention "to call into existence a majority of working class electors." With the dexterity that characterized him, and made him so extraordinary a "Parliamentary hand," he added the significant words: "I cannot say I think it would be attended with any great danger, but I am sure it is not according to the present view or expectations of Parliament." In spite of all disclaimers, however, the Constitution of England was by these successive measures being steadily democratized; and at this moment, in the opinion of no less an authority than Sir H.S. Maine, it rests on a more dangerously democratic basis than that of the United States.

If I might be allowed to give my own definition of Democracy, I should say it was a system of government under which the sovereign power of the State—the great "Leviathan" of Hobbes—was distributed, as the lawyers say, "per capita." Let a be the sovereign power of the State in its totality and η the varying number of citizens, then $\frac{a}{\eta}$ represents each man's share of power. This formula takes no account of moral or intellectual force, which cannot be severed from the individual possessing it. This, alas! is the fly in the precious ointment of pure and unadulterated Democracy, or Democracy conceived as absolute equality between man and man. If a man has money we can take it from him. If he has physical force, he can be overpowered by numbers; but if he has intelligence and force of character we cannot seize upon these. Democracy, let me hasten to say, has its foundations deep in human nature. The whole philosophy of it is summed up in a single line of Aeschylus, on which my eye casually fell the other day, and which, in this place, I may venture to repeat:

$$\text{'Ἑκὼν γὰρ οὐδεὶς δουλίῳ χρῆται ζυγῷ—}$$

the English of which is simply, "No one willingly bears a servile yoke." In a State, the power of which is made up of the aggregate strength of all its members, no man likes to think that, while contributing strength and helping to make the arm of the law effective, he has no voice whatever in public affairs. Political Economy and the Bible, it has been said, have been the two great preachers of Democracy— Political Economy by concentrating attention upon what is to the common advantage, and taking no account of political privilege; the Bible, by proclaiming the essential equality of all men, and basing all social relations on the Golden Rule. However this may be, Democracy has come, it is with us now, and there is every appearance that it is going to stay. Even were we opposed to it, we might well exclaim in the words of a great poet:

> Far other bark than ours were needed now
> To stem the torrent of descending time.

But no reasonable man will oppose himself to that which he sees to be inevitable. Rather, perceiving it to be inevitable, he will seek out the causes and conditions which, in making it so, make it also best suited on the whole to the age in which it has appeared.

How much obloquy has been heaped upon popular government it would weary you to tell. Those of you who have read Sir Henry Maine's work entitled "Popular Government" know with what dignified irony he treats the hopes which Democracy has inspired in its champions and advocates. Those of you again who have read Mr. Lecky's volumes have not failed to recognize his evident desire to place popular government in the worst possible light.[20] No doubt both these eminent writers say many things that are true; they point out real flaws and weaknesses in popular government; but they do not attempt to show how the tendency of the times in the direction of Democracy is to be reversed. I cannot help agreeing with the verdict of Mr. John Morley, on the first of these writers. "Sir Henry Maine," he says,

> is a bureaucrat who cannot bear to think that Democracy will win. . . . His tone is that of a political valetudinarian, watching with uneasy eye the ways of rude health.

Mr. Lecky, too, is a writer who, as his later writings have particularly shown, and, I may add, as he is exhibited to us by no mean judge of character, "Punch," is more or less disgusted with life, and consequently with Democracy. No despondent man, however, can be a safe guide. The men to trust are those who, if they have to recognize evil, think at once of the remedies that can be applied, or look beyond the evil to the good that may eventually be evolved from it. Say what we will of Democracy it means political life of a certain kind for everybody except those who turn aside from the boon because they are obliged to share it with so many quite plain people.

Let us admit that Democracy is open to much criticism, that its ways are not the ways of the philosopher or the saint, that there is a terrible flavour of average humanity, and sometimes of inferior humanity, about its doings; all that does not prove that it is not in theory, or that it is not destined to become in practice, the best form of human government. When a child is learning to walk we do not feel like deriding its hesitation and timidity, or exulting over its falls. Popular government, to my mind, is very much in the position of a child learning to walk. The child is born unable to walk, but it *must* learn to walk; its whole future development depends on the acquisition of that accomplishment. Human societies, in like manner, are born unfit for self-government; but their complete development depends on their becoming fit for it. That seems to me to be the case in a nutshell. The stage of imperfect attempts, marked by many lapses and many more or less ungainly movements, has to be passed through. We are yet in that stage, and clever writers, if they are so minded, can find much to satirize in our performances. But, looking at the main question, who can deny that a community in which each individual contributed some grain of wisdom or moral force to the general direction of affairs, would constitute a higher political type than one in which a few ruled and the rest submitted to their dictation, however benevolent that dictation might be. The problem of popular government is precisely the problem how to make each individual a helpful, not a retarding or an opposing, influence in the work of good government. The historian Grote has well said that

No system of government, even supposing it to be very much better and more faultless than the Athenian democracy, can ever pretend to accomplish its legitimate end apart from the personal character of the people, or to supersede the necessity of individual virtue and vigour.

Democracy comes to the individual citizen without respect to social rank and says,

The time has come for you to assume a share in influencing and directing the government of your country. You may not at present have all the qualifications required for that duty, but you cannot begin earlier; and it is necessary that you, a citizen, should acquire the education of a citizen. Therefore begin now, follow your best judgment, try to rise superior to purely selfish interests, and in due time you will find yourself doing fairly well.

Unfortunately this is not the prevalent conception of the meaning of Democracy or of the nature of its appeal. The idea that the power once possessed by one, or by a limited class, is now divided amongst the whole people is familiar enough; but the idea that each man should try himself by the rule which he applies to the monarchs and oligarchs of the past is not a familiar one. We condemn the rulers of the past because they did not consider themselves the mere trustees of power, and study at all times the good of the whole people. And yet, I fear the common idea to-day is that each man's vote is his own private property, to be used as may best suit his private ends. It was for a precisely similar misuse of power that some monarchs have lost their heads in times past. That a man's vote is not absolutely his own to do what he likes with is proved by the laws against bribery. Unfortunately, the laws against bribery cannot reach all forms of bribery, cannot touch, for example, the shameless offers often made of vote and influence in return for some favour or other from the government of the day. There is something very discouraging, it must be admitted, in the willingness of the people, as the phrase is, to be bribed with their own money—in such a phenomenon, for example, as the monotonous regularity with which bye-elections go in favour of a government with a strong majority.

In this respect it can hardly be claimed that the wealthier classes show an example of singular virtue to their humbler fellow-citizens. Look at this portly gentleman, dressed in irreproachable English tweed, with a decided dash of social culture, who comes forward to address an audience of electors in a mining town. Being the person of the most weight in the community, he has been elected chairman of the meeting; nevertheless he ventures an opinion of his own. "Gentlemen," he says,

> as chairman I have not much to say to you on this occasion. I shall just say this, however, that the question you have to consider is, in my opinion, a very simple one; namely, whether the party in power or the party out of power is likely to do most for the business interests of this locality. We need not wander beyond that.

Here was the keynote struck by a man possessing all the advantages of education, social position and pecuniary independence, which go to make up a typical specimen of what used to be called the "ruling classes." A discussion follows, and some very plain citizens seem to think that certain other questions, more remote from their own local interests, might properly be taken into consideration. The great man, however, speaks again, and makes it clear that he looks with great disfavour on all such divagations. I dare say many of you have witnessed scenes very similar to this. My own sketch is drawn from life, and it seems to me to cast a somewhat doubtful light on the influence exerted by those so-called higher classes who, fifty years ago or so, were thought to be the only safe depositaries of political power. Is Democracy, it may be asked, having a fair trial when men of wealth and influence are doing their utmost to hold it down to the most inferior conceptions and practices? There is worse than this, however; there is the fierce contempt which men conducting large enterprises sometimes show for political issues of all kinds, and their avowed willingness to throw all their influence on the side of any government whatever with which they can make an advantageous deal.

Everyone remembers Montesquieu's dictum about the different forms of government and their respective fundamental principles. Absolute governments must repose on fear, monarchies on honour, aristocracies on moderation, and republics on virtue. To someone who cited the remark as to republics to Alexander Hamilton, the latter replied that, in his opinion, what republics most depended on was corruption. Montesquieu, however, was perfectly right in postulating public virtue as a condition of the permanence of republics. If the electorate as a whole is corrupt, republican institutions will be of short duration. On the other hand, Hamilton was not altogether wrong in his fling as to the necessity of corruption. There is no absolute contradiction between the two views; the one refers to the conditions for the *existence* of a republic, the other to the conditions necessary as things are to the carrying on of the work of government. The more public virtue there is, the less need will there be for resorting to Hamilton's prescription for keeping the machinery of government going. Raise the level of public virtue and certain things which are now only done from interested and selfish motives will be done from disinterested and unselfish ones. Raise the level of public virtue and better laws will be passed, and once passed will be observed, not evaded. Raise the level of public virtue and the whole political system will work with greater power towards better ends. But meantime many compromises that would not look well in broad daylight have to be made.

Sir Henry Maine speaks with great severity of the abject flattery administered to the multitude by those who would win its favour. To whom, however, is this mainly a reproach? It is indeed to be regretted that the populace should not have a more delicate taste in this matter than the monarchs and other great ones of the past before whom men of intellect used to debase themselves; but what are we to think of more or less educated gentlemen who purvey the stuff? If the people would take a true measure of themselves they would be aided by referring to a book that never flatters, and that knows nothing of party views. They would there find such utterances as these:

Why do . . . the people imagine a vain thing?
Where no counsel is, the people fail.
Where there is no vision, the people perish.
The people that know their good shall be strong.
The people that do not understand shall fall.

I do not imagine that in relation to the problems of to-day "the people" of to-day enjoy any advantage over "the people" of the times of Daniel or Hosca. In simpler times there were simpler problems; the problems of our time tax the wisdom of the wisest; so that now, as ever, the people need to take heed against imagining vain things and against acting without counsel or vision. To believe in their own infallibility is a sure way of falling into hurtful errors. Yet something like this state of mind does exist, there is reason to fear, in democratic communities. "No observer of American politics," says a very able writer, Mr. E.L. Godkin,[21]

can deny that, with regard to matters that can become the subject of legislation, the American voter listens with extreme impatience to anything which has the air of instruction; but the explanation is to be found not so much in his dislike of instruction as in his dislike, in the political field, of anything which savours of superiority. The truth seems to be,

he continues

that, with regard to all matters within the field of politics, the new democracy is exceedingly sensitive about any doubts of its competency. It will not suffer any question, or sign of question, of its full capacity to deal with any matter which calls for legislation.

Other testimonies can be cited to the same effect. The late James Russell Lowell, in his essay on Abraham Lincoln, written in 1864, expresses surprise that,

in a country which boasts of its intelligence, the theory should be so generally held that the most complicated of human contrivances, and one which every day becomes more complicated, can be worked at sight by any man able to talk for an hour or two without stopping to think.

Again, Senator Hoar, of Massachusetts, in an article written only a few months ago, says:

Some people never seem to learn that the task of governing a great people is a serious and difficult task, and that the task of governing itself, by a great people, is more serious and difficult still.

The psychology of the case is not, I think, hard to understand. We are all familiar with the adage, "Every man to his trade." Negatively, it means that nobody should dabble in a trade that is not his and that he does not understand; and, positively, it means that very man is assumed to understand *his own* trade. The expansion of free institutions has thrown the work of government into the hands of the people, therefore government has become *their* trade; therefore they must know all about it; or, if they do not, they must refuse to acknowledge the fact. They must not let any college-bred man, or other superior person, affect to teach them their trade. The average voter does not like to think that there are any technicalities in the art of government or of administration which any plain man is not capable of dealing with. As to the government service, it is filled with *our* clerks, and of course, like other employers, we are all quite capable of telling *our* clerks what to do. A well-disposed village blacksmith in the neighborhood of Ottawa once offered me a "lift" in his buggy. As we drove along we passed the house of a prominent civil servant, when my friend enquired what salary the gentleman in question had. I said I was not sure, but thought about two thousand dollars; whereupon, turning to me, the man of muscle said very earnestly: "No man can earn two thousand dollars a year at a desk." He was himself earning at least that amount in his forge and carriage shop; but he did not think the feat could be honestly performed at a desk. My friend was a man of more than average intelligence and business ability, and his blunt declaration gave me a measure of the importance attached by the people to the work of the public departments. It must all be very simple, because theoretically, it is all such work as the humblest voter could, if necessary, either perform or direct. In the United States the theory is now freely advanced that the President does not need to be a man of any special ability; if he only does what the people tell him he will be clever enough. In this country I imagine that the only ability that is distinctly recognized as necessary is the ability to outwit opponents in the political field.

We seem here to be face to face with a paradox. On the one hand government is committed to the people; and it is so far assumed that they are capable of performing the political duties thus devolved on them. On the other hand it is a matter of certainty that the majority of the voters are not very good judges either of the larger questions of politics, or of the details of administration. They are very mediocre judges of what constitutes their own interest in many matters. A nation may want to hold silver in unlimited quantities at par with gold in some arbitrarily chosen ratio; but it does not follow from their wanting it that the thing is feasible, or that the bare attempt to carry it into effect would not be fraught with disaster. A nation may want a high tariff, or government ownership of railways and telegraphs, or a system of old age pensions, or compulsory arbitration, or an elective judiciary, or a strict prohibitory liquor law; or it may hanker after a foreign war, or experience a sudden yearning for a vigorous policy of colonial expansion; but it would be fatuous to imagine that any one of these measures would be secure from failure because it had been demanded by a popular majority. Mr. Frederic Harrison says that "Very plain men know who wish them well, and the sort of thing that will bring them good." To the first half of this statement I am ready to give a general assent; but in regard to the latter half I am far from certain. All depends upon the complexity of the question under consideration, and many of the questions of politics are most complex.

What, then, is the solution of the paradox? The solution seems to me to lie here: the suffrage is not a privilege, but a trust, and universal suffrage does not signify that all men are equally and fully capable of interest in the wise decision of such questions. The art of government is not any man's trade or mystery; it presents an inexhaustible problem in the solution of which we may all co-operate. The fact that a certain section of society may cast a majority of votes does not confer upon them any special competence in dealing with political issues. It may give them power, but as Horace says:

Vis consili expers mole ruit sua.[22]

It is too narrow a view to take of the suffrage to regard it merely as a means of protection for each member of the community. Without questioning the maxim that taxation without representation is tyranny, we cannot consider it as summing up the whole philosophy of the suffrage. The late Mr. Lowe (Lord Sherbrooke) talked most mischievously when he insisted, as he did, upon the necessity of "educating our masters." In a free state no man is master of any other, nor is there any need that he should be. What Mr. Lowe was really afraid of was that the mastery previously possessed by a limited class should pass out of their hands.

In the present day we are accustomed to make a broad distinction between legislation and government; but in point of fact, legislation is one of the two great divisions of government, the other being administration. Parliament makes laws; the duty of the executive is to administer those laws faithfully and honestly, without respect to persons and with a sole view to the public good.

As regards legislation an important point to notice is the altered position of the legislator as compared with that which he occupied under a more limited suffrage. If we go back a little over one hundred years, we find Edmund Burke addressing the electors of Bristol as follows:

If we do not allow our members to act upon a very enlarged view of things, we shall at length infallibly degrade our national representation into a *confused and scuffling bustle of local agency*.

Burke wanted a strong and enlightened Parliament to stand up against an encroaching court; and he did not think Parliament could be strong if its members were reduced to the rank of mere delegates—echoes, not voices. It is impossible not to be struck with his foresight when he speaks of the danger that Parliament may degenerate into "a confused and scuffling bustle of local agency." I think the words describe something with which we are not wholly unacquainted in this country, and which exists in great perfection across our border. I must, however, quote a few words more to show the distance we have travelled since Burke's time. Referring to the course he had held in regard to the troubles in Ireland, he says:

> I conformed to the instructions of truth and nature, and maintained your interest against your opinions with a constancy that became me. A representative worthy of you ought to be a person of stability. I am to look indeed to your opinions, but to such opinions as you and I must have five years hence. I was not to look to the flash of the day. I knew that you chose me with others to be a pillar of the state, and not a weathercock, on the top of the edifice, exalted for my levity and versatility.

In a former speech he had said:

> Your representative owes you not his industry only but his judgment, and he betrays instead of serving you if he sacrifices it to your opinion. . . . Parliament is not a congress of ambassadors from different and hostile interests. . . . It is a deliberative assembly of one nation, with one interest, that of the whole, where not local purposes and local prejudices ought to guide, but the general good. . . . You choose a member indeed, but when you have chosen him, he is not a member of Bristol, but a member of Parliament.

A generation or more later, when the Reform Bill of 1832 was being introduced, Sir Robert Inglis, the member for Oxford, took a very similar stand. "The House," he said,

> is not a collection of deputies as the States General of Holland, and as the assemblies in some other countries. We are not sent here day by day to represent the ideas of our constituents. Their local rights, their municipal privileges we are bound to protect; their general interests we are bound to consult at all times, but not their will, unless it shall coincide with our own deliberate sense of right.

More explicit still, if possible, is the following declaration of the same speaker:

> We are not sent here for the particular spot we represent, but to consider the affairs of the country and the good of the church. When a member is returned to this House he ceases to be responsible to his constituency. It is at the end of the period for which he has to serve them in Parliament that he again comes before them and it is then only that he is accountable to them.

We may come forward another generation still, to the date of the publication of Mr. Mill's "Representative Government," and find the same principle not yet extinct. "A man of conscience and known ability," says that philosopher,

> should insist on full freedom to act as he, in his own judgment, deems best, and should not consent to act on any other terms.

Since that time the doctrine in question has been less and less heard of; and to-day the "delegate" theory of parliamentary representation may be said to be thoroughly established. Where could we find a constituency in Canada that would elect either Burke or John Stuart Mill on the conditions they lay down? If one is to be found, I should be disposed to look for it in the Province of Quebec, where the voters have not yet been educated into jealousy of superior talents, or into distrust of wider views.

The effect of the change has undoubtedly been to impair the character of modern parliaments considered as deliberative bodies, as well as their ability to deal with great measures. There can be no true deliberation without a certain amount of openness to conviction. As things are to-day each member feels bound to carry out the understanding he had with his electors and support the party he undertook to support. An atrophy of the deliberative function of representative bodies has thus set in. How far it will proceed, and what modern parliaments will be reduced to, remains to be seen. How a political structure intended to have a distinct use of its own may undergo complete atrophy we may observe in the case of the college of so-called Presidential Electors in the United States. According to the Constitution these electors were to exercise a real choice of their own; but to-day, and indeed for long since, the college has dwindled into a purely formal device for registering the popular vote. Much is heard nowadays of the machine in politics. It is not much praised in public, though I believe it is sometimes "hugged" in private. Delicacy would of course prescribe privacy for so affectionate an operation. An enterprising newspaper was proposing some time ago to "smash the machine," and, if there were two—of which there was more than a suspicion—to "smash them both." How it was going to be done was not explained, nor who was to be the smasher; and, so far as I can learn, the feat has not yet been accomplished. The fact is that the machine is an absolutely necessary accompaniment of universal suffrage in the present condition of society. It is a kind of primary school of politics, an institution in which raw, untutored minds get their first introduction to political ideas and methods. If there were any possibility of getting into a blue book a representative selection of the correspondence of the local machines throughout the country, with a few samples of the higher epistolary style of the Provincial and Dominion staff officers, I think the country would start back at the revelation. It would not want to hug either the machine or itself. It is wonderful how ugly a little daylight makes some things look. At the same time good comes out even of this seething mass of evil. The primary school does not give a finished education, but it educates up to a certain point those who have any capacity to learn. The member of the local committee is trained to a certain sense of responsibility. He learns what can be done and what cannot be done. He finds out that men are not always governed by their lowest motives. He finds his more disreputable proceedings encountering the reprobation of the decent part of the community. He gets disgusted with the unmitigated self-seeking of some of those with whom he has to deal, and possibly has some useful fits of reflection on his own doings. If his party is in opposition he may learn some lessons of disinterestedness. We may further say this for the machine, that it is a contrivance for getting work done that would not otherwise be done. After its own fashion it keeps alive an interest in politics; it greatly helps to "bring out the vote" in a general election.

It is a somewhat singular thing that the framers of the Constitution of the United States do not seem to have any prevision of the difficulty there would be in getting the people as a whole to act in political matters. The explanation may, perhaps, be found in the fact that they had been accustomed chiefly to town meetings, in which, the subjects discussed being of local interest, decisions were easily arrived at. The Constitution, however, had not been long in operation before there was found to be a missing link—a device for getting the people interested and bringing them to the polls. It was to meet this need that the machine may be said to have been invented. As an impelling and controlling force it has since been brought to great perfection; and yet it cannot be said that the machine itself has either a clear insight into large political questions or any great interest in them. It does not, in fact, look upon great questions with favour. Its saws are not adapted to cut such lumber. It does not argue the question of the tariff, or of grants to higher education, or of Imperial federation, nor yet of prohibition; it approaches the elector with personal solicitation, and with arguments addressed more or less directly to his self-interest. The highest note it ever strikes is local interest: it sometimes reaches that. It does not make the issues that are presented to the country. These are hammered out in the press and, to a much less extent, in Parliament; but it gives many a shrewd hint to the party leaders as to what questions should *not* be allowed to grow into issues. The instinct of the party politician is to fight shy of all large questions; he always sees in them more of danger than of safety, more chances of loss than of gain.

We strike here an ugly feature of the party system. Why do practical politicians shrink so much from dealing with large questions? Simply because they know that unfair means will be tried to embarrass them in carrying such measures through. To bring forward some large measure of legislation is to deploy in the open before an entrenched enemy. The theoretical justification of a parliamentary Opposition is that the acts and measures of every Government require criticism. True, but criticism does not imply deliberate misconstruction and misrepresentation. What should we think of a literary critic who, sitting down to the examination of a book, professedly allowed himself to be dominated by a desire to create as much odium as possible in the mind of the public against the writer? And yet we all know that this is precisely the line an Opposition in Parliament and in the press usually takes in regard to the measures of the Government of the day. The thing is done by each side in turn, so that it is difficult for either side to feel any very genuine indignation when their own methods are retorted on them. What a common thing it is to see this or that casual and really harmless remark of some public man converted by party malice into a studied insult to some sect or class in the community! What a ready recourse there is to charges of want of patriotism! What sad use has been made in more than one emergency of the appeal to national and religious prejudice!

It is impossible to associate much with politicians without being struck by their extraordinary and, as it seems to me, morbid sensitiveness to what they call public opinion. What they are really afraid of is less public opinion than public silliness. If the public only knew how little common sense they are credited with by the very men who, on the hustings, load them with every kind of flattery, they would feel far from complimented. The common idea among politicians is that the people can be stampeded by a word, a phrase, some unguarded expression or trifling act which in any way touches, or might be so misinterpreted and twisted as to appear to touch, a popular prejudice. It is, of course, taken for granted, and rightly as things go, that opponents will do their utmost to make mischief out of the word, phrase or act; but where is that confidence in the superior judgment and sterling common sense of the masses of the people of which we hear so much on certain occasions? Can the voters be at once so wise as we are told, and also so strongly resemble a herd of buffaloes with their snouts in the air ready for a whirlwind dash at the faintest scent of danger? I do not readily reconcile the two conceptions.

There was a politician once, a true man of the people, who did not believe in the buffalo herd theory. That man was Abraham Lincoln. Of him James Russell Lowell, in his celebrated essay,[23] has said:

> This was a true Democrat, who grounded himself on the assumption that a democracy can think. Come, let us reason together about this matter, has been the tone of all his addresses to the people. . . . He put himself of a level with those he addressed, not by going down to them, but only by taking for granted that they had brains, and would come up to a common ground of reason. And Accordingly,

adds Mr. Lowell, speaking for the people of the United States,

> We have never had a chief magistrate who so won to himself the love, and at the same time the judgment, of his countrymen. To us that simple confidence of his in the right-mindedness of his fellow-men is very touching, and its success is as strong an argument as we have ever seen in favour of the theory that men can govern themselves.

Time flies; it is thirty-six or thirty-seven years since that essay was written, and a change may have passed over the spirit of democracy; it may be that there is a "facilis descensus"[24] for self-governing as well as for autocratically-governed communities; but, for my own part, I should be inclined still to have faith in Lincoln's method. One, however, who would walk in Lincoln's footsteps needs to have Lincoln's simplicity, sincerity and strong human sympathy. Of him it may be said that he was a true shepherd of his people, and that the people knew his voice.

What are the voices that people ordinarily hear in the political controversies and discussions of our time? Broadly speaking, are not all the voices merely repetitions of one voice—the voice of Codlin strenuously warning us that *he* is the friend, not Short?[25] In Codlin we must put our trust if all our interests are not to be wrecked. It is at our own risk if we have any dealings with Short. The great trouble with Codlin is that he is not disinterested. If he is in power he wants to stay there; if he is out of power he wants to get there. I do not say, and I am far from thinking, that there is no disinterestedness amongst public men; but I do say that parties *as parties* are not disinterested. Their primary object is power, not the good of the country. To get power they will do many things that are not for the good of the people; to retain power likewise. In saying this one merely repeats the unceasing criticisms of the parties on one another. But is it really possible, one may ask, for a party either to gain or retain power by acts that are not for the good of the people? It is not necessary for my present purpose to maintain that it *is* possible; it is enough to say that political parties *think* it possible sometimes, and act accordingly. But as I am not here to flatter any one, but simply to offer my humble contribution to the discussion of a great subject, I will venture to go farther, and say that parties *may* climb into power on false issues, and may retain it for a time by specious but really hurtful legislation. This is but another way of saying that the people may at times be imposed upon. But, as Abraham Lincoln remarked, they cannot be imposed upon ''all the time.''

It would really be a great thing if some one from a position of advantage could talk plainly to people about the actual facts of current politics. It is not ornate phrases that are wanted, but honest grappling with realities. The question should be put fairly and squarely to the people: How far they think it is right for any man to have pecuniary motives of a personal kind for supporting this or that candidate or party. Bribery by means of five dollar notes is punishable by law; but what moral difference is there between bribery of this kind and bribery by the promise of petty offices and the thousand and one advantages which a party in power can deal out, and does deal out, to its supporters? It is an accepted principle of politics that constituencies returning Government supporters shall be more favoured than those returning members of the Opposition. ''If I had a son,'' I once heard a member of Parliament say, ''that cheeked me, do you think I should feel like doing anything for him? I rather think not. Well, neither should a Government do anything for constituencies that go against it.'' This was several years ago; but much more recently a bright young man, a political worker in one of the newer parts of the country, remarked to me that a new constituency should always side with the Government of the day, as otherwise its growing interests would be in danger of being overlooked. Is it not time that *some* one should say to the people of Canada:

Come let us reason about this matter. Is the suffrage in this country free or is it not? What do you understand by a free suffrage? You mean, do you not, that every citizen is at perfect liberty to vote according to his views and convictions of public duty? But can a man be said to be at *perfect* liberty to vote in that way if certain very material disadvantages attach to his exercising the suffrage in opposition to the Government of the day? You know, of course, such a speaker would add,

that no man who has voted against a Government candidate has the remotest chance of any public employment unless he recants his political opinions, and promises to reverse his vote on the next occasion. Is this freedom? If so, what would you understand by restraint? You have heard of "pulls," have you not? The way to get a "pull" is to "swing" votes—that is the up-to-date expression. The more votes you can swing, the stronger your pull. By means of a pull a man can exert a deflecting influence on Government action. A Government left to itself will generally want to do the right thing. The head of a public department gets interested in his work, and devises many things for the public good. But what does the man with the pull care about the public good? What are laws and regulations, or the rights of individuals, or the efficiency of the public service to him? Such ideas are foreign to all his ways of thinking. All he knows is that he did his work, and that he wants his reward. You complain sometimes that the public service is not what it ought to be; but under such a system how can it be what it ought to be? Yet it is *your* service; it is your money that goes to maintain it; and in whose interest should it be run but in yours? Why should any man have it in his power to cause that to be done which is not in your interest?

An earnest appeal to the public on these lines could hardly fail of producing some good effect. There are other points of view which might be taken. Surely it is somewhat undemocratic that in each locality there should be a boss who more or less commands the avenues of approach to a Government that is supposed to exist for all. Why should one man be more readily listened to than another upon a matter of public business? Do we not all pay taxes alike? Why should one man have to go and put himself under obligation to another, whom the business in hand does not in the least concern, and with whom he may, perhaps, strongly object to come into contact? It is for the people to remedy this evil. It is for the people to seize the idea that the present system deprives them of a free suffrage, and that it tends to corrupt the suffrage by giving men all kinds of mercenary motives for supporting one part rather than another. In the jargon of party politics those who vote against the party to which we belong are spoken of as "our enemies." Why "our enemies?" Is it not a hateful thought that we must make an enemy of a man who differs from us on some question of public policy, or in his appreciation of certain public men? Under the present system a Government is supposed to be greatly beholden to its supporters. The understanding is,

Put us in office, or keep us in office, and we will show you special favour. We want office and you want favours; let us do business on that basis.

Well, the basis is not a good one, and it says something for human nature and inspires a certain amount of confidence in the larger currents of influence that make for good in the general economy of things, that, upon such a basis, government should be as well carried on as it is.

The fact is that there is a higher public opinion abroad in the country with which politicians have to reckon; and it is this higher opinion which forms the strongest support of the public man who desires to do his duty to the whole country. The machine even feels its force at times, as we see by some of the men it brings forward. A "strong" man is wanted to contest a certain constituency, and the strength of the strong man sometimes—not unfrequently—lies in the fact that he is a good man—a man with a reputation for honesty and fair dealing, for kindliness of nature and public spirit. The sense of public duty grows rapidly upon such men; and, when they come into contact with the administrative system of the country, they perceive the iniquity of trying to twist it out of shape in order to serve their own private purposes. They recognize that "business is business" in a sense far different from that in which the phrase has sometimes been used. If patronage is forced upon them—and in a certain position a man cannot escape it—they exercise it with moderation, and, as far as possible, with an eye to the public good. But as to patronage in general, they sympathize with the feeling Sir Robert Peel had on the subject when, in a letter to Cobden, he spoke about "the odious power of patronage." Men of this character are not those whom the machine likes best to deal with. There are meannesses to which they will not stoop; there are vengeances they will not perpetrate; there are enmities they will not recognize. When men of superior character are forced, as they sometimes are, out of public life, it is this that breaks their spirit, the everlasting cropping up in their correspondence of paltry suggestions and impossible, if not iniquitous, demands.

The lesson I draw from these facts is that more trust should be reposed in the people, and that the people should put more trust in themselves. A recent writer has spoken of a certain course of education as tending to "substitute for those warm, wholesome sympathies which are the safest guides in understanding our fellows and regulating our conduct towards them, a cold, critical demeanour of superiority." I trust that such an education is not imparted by any institution of learning in this country. There is something, however, even worse than the "cold, critical demeanour of superiority," and that is a cold, calculating intention to exploit our fellow-men for our own personal advantage. This is a feeling which, I fear, is not unknown among the rising generation of to-day. It is a very serious question at every epoch: What are the young men thinking of? Or to put it more precisely: What are their plans for the future and with what eyes do they look on the world in which they are shortly to play their part? Is each resolving to play solely for his own hand, or are some of them wondering how they can best serve their fellow-men? Surely in a civilization the religion of which is founded on the idea of self-sacrifice, there should not be wanting some volunteers for the cause of public righteousness. If any may look forward to a public career, I would say: Let disinterested and high-minded regard for the progress and honour of the country which has nourished you be the basis of all your action. Refuse to believe those who tell you that guile and finesse are the chief resources of the statesman, for nothing can be less true; they are the resources of the man who is too weak, too deficient in courage and in large views of public policy, to be a statesman in the best sense. Over three hundred years ago the greatest of English poets summed up the political wisdom which he imagined to have come to the mighty Wolsey from his long conversance with affairs, and also from his later misfortunes, in these memorable lines:—

> Love thyself last, cherish those hearts that hate thee;
> Corruption wins not more than honesty.
> Still in thy right hand carry gentle peace
> To silence envious tongues. Be just and fear not.
> Let all the ends thou aim'st at be thy country's,
> Thy God's and truth's.

It requires courage, it requires faith, it requires enthusiasm, to lay out one's life on this plan; but are these qualities dead in this Canada of ours? The times call loudly for men who will apply themselves to politics with the high purpose, not of leading a party to victory, and sharing in the spoils of party triumph, but of raising the public life of the country to a higher plane, and quickening throughout the land the sense of public duty. An excellent writer, the late Sir Henry Taylor,[26] has said that a statesman should have such a disposition that "he may *sun out* all the good in men's natures." Here is a much better clue to the true nature of statesmanship than any that a cynical philosophy can afford. There is also a saying of Burke's that I greatly admire: "We have no other materials to work with than those out of which God has been pleased to form the inhabitants of this island." This means that we should not wait for the millennium to take our stand on the side of justice and truth in national affairs, but, accepting the world as it is, we should do it now. If we wait for the millennium, we shall wait till our valuable assistance is no longer required. But if we fear that circumstances may now and again be too strong for us, let us consider this saying of a great writer whom I have already quoted, James Russell Lowell:

It is loyalty to great ends, even though forced to combine the small and opposing motives of selfish men in order to accomplish them, that we demand in public men.

It seems to me that in these three sayings we have the outlines of a whole scheme of statesmanship. There is no nobler ambition than political ambition if, high above every personal aim, is kept the thought of public service. All cannot hope to occupy a central place in the political arena, but there is useful work to be done by every one who believes in his heart that the public life of the nation should be based on equity and truth, and upon whom the conviction has been forced that every taint of interested motive in the support of a candidate or a party contains the promise and potency of full-blown political corruption. To act steadily upon these views in the humblest private sphere is to render the state most honourable service.

PART FOUR
The Critic as Historian

Myth narrates a sacred History; it relates an event that took place in primordial Time, the fabled time of the "beginnings." In other words, myth tells how, through the deeds of Supernatural Beings, a reality came into existence, be it the whole of reality . . . or only a fragment of reality—. . . a particular kind of human behavior, an institution.

Mircea Eliade,
Myth and Reality (1968)

The fact is that history and criticism to-day are continually at war with the myth-making, legend-forming, tendencies of mankind. It is not what is true that takes the strongest hold on the popular mind; it is what is cast in a mould to fit popular needs; and when the people want to believe a thing it is very hard to prevent their doing so.

W.D. LeSueur,
"History: Its Nature and Methods"
(1913)

Introduction

W.D. LeSueur neither lamented nor resisted the coming of the democratic age. "No reasonable man," he had stated in "The Problem of Popular Government" (1901), "will oppose himself to that which he sees to be inevitable." (pp. 227-28) The Canadian exponent of the critical spirit could see only one solution to the problems of popular government, and it was one that had previously been expressed by Arnold and Mill: "the education and development of the enlightened and independent element in public opinion." (p. 202) LeSueur had attempted to achieve this philosophically in his defence of critical enquiry; in his application of scientific principles to the religious life; in his search for a "natural" system of social ethics based upon evolutionary principles; in his writings on the political culture of his day. But there remained another way by which an enlightened public opinion might be brought into being: the method of historical enquiry.

Popular government had come to stay and there was no use in resisting it. "Rather," LeSueur concluded, the reasonable man, acknowledging this, "will seek out the causes and conditions which, in making it so, make it also best suited on the whole to the age in which it has appeared." (p. 228) Within the context of Canadian history, "popular government" meant "responsible government." If Canadians were to face successfully the problems involved with popular government it was necessary that they be made aware of its origins and of the ambiguous nature of of their political heritage. LeSueur's energies thus gradually turned to Canadian history, and this shift of attention opened the final—tragic—chapter in the life of his mind.

I

When LeSueur delivered his lecture on "The Problem of Popular Government" to his University of Toronto audience in 1901 he had reached sixty years of age and was on the verge of retirement from the federal civil service. After that retirement, the following year, he was free for the first time in his life to devote more than evenings and

week-ends to reading and writing. It was to the study of history that he
now turned. He had always shown an historical perspective in his
writings, but in his essays on politics and morality this had especially
been the case. Several times in those articles references to the Canadian
past had been made. In "Problems of Government in Canada" (1895),
for example, he had written: "Sixty years ago, what is now known as
'responsible government' had not yet been conceded. There was a
system of popular representation; yet in many ways the people were
governed in the old-fashioned sense by administrators who assumed to
know what was good for them better than they did themselves." (p.
217) The most forceful example of these colonial administrators had
been Sir Francis Bond Head, to whom LeSueur also devoted considerable attention in "The Problem of Popular Government" (pp. 224-25),
and whose *Narrative*, LeSueur claimed, "shows in a very instructive
manner how popular personal government may be when characterized
by fearlessness and disinterestedness." (p. 217)

While, as later events were to reveal, Francis Bond Head and his
enemies continued to occupy LeSueur's mind as symbols of the basic
attitudes that could be taken toward popular government, for the first
few years of the twentieth century he wrote nothing on the subject.
Having been asked by George N. Morang to write a biography of Count
Frontenac for Morang's "Makers of Canada" series, LeSueur
familiarized himself with the work of his predecessors, especially that
of Francis Parkman and Henri Lorin, and spent much of his time
consulting original materials on the history of New France in the Public
Archives of Canada. LeSueur's *Frontenac* was published in 1906. It
was an eminently readable book, and remains one of three volumes of
the "Makers" series that has been reprinted[1]); yet it added little to what
was already known about Frontenac and provided little in the way of a
new historical interpretation of the period under study.[2] As such, it was
perfectly suitable for the series for which it was written. LeSueur's
work for Morang as an author, in addition to his already established
reputation as a literary authority, was nevertheless sufficient to have
Morang add his name to those of Pelham Edgar, a young professor of
English at Victoria University, Toronto, and Duncan Campbell Scott, a
leading poet of the day, as an editor of the series. One of the tasks the
new Editor was given was to read a manuscript life of William Lyon
Mackenzie by Ontario Inspector of Schools, Thomas L. Hughes.

LeSueur found no merit whatsoever in the Hughes manuscript. It
glorified Mackenzie's life and actions even more than the two volume
biography of the Upper Canadian reformer written by his son-in-law,
Charles Lindsey, in the year of Mackenzie's death; at the same time it
vilified the "Family Compact." "I have serious doubts as to whether
Hughes could, even if he were willing, re-write the book from a

different point of view," LeSueur wrote to Morang. "Declamation much more than historical analysis or careful research is his forte. Another Ms. and my notes might make a book of it."[3] As a result of reading LeSueur's comprehensive and critical notes on Hughes' manuscript, Morang rejected it. He asked LeSueur to do the volume himself, but the latter refused since he had been instrumental in having Hughes's manuscript rejected and would therefore have been placed in a self-seeking prosition. Professor G.M. Wrong of the University of Toronto was then approached to write Mackenzie's biography, accepted the offer, and then, for reasons that are not entirely certain, withdrew his consent.[4] Morang's appeal to LeSueur was renewed and with some hesitance LeSueur accepted. There was at the time an effort being made to erect a monument to Mackenzie in Toronto, and LeSueur was certain that "a good deal of glorification" would be made of him. "I feel as if my book would not be quite in key with it all," he wrote in his letter accepting the offer to write the book. "However I will try my best to do justice to him and to view such faults as he had with charity."[5] These faults were spelled out by LeSueur under the cloak of anonymity in his letter to the Editor of the "Mail and Empire" in March, 1906. The letter is reprinted here.

The story of LeSueur's Mackenzie biography, its research, writing, and the author's attempts to publish it, is perhaps the most interesting chapter in the history of Canadian historical writing, and may constitute the most lamentable episode in the history of critical intellectual enquiry in Canada. It is not necessary here to place the biography within the context of Mackenzie historiography except in the most general sense: that is best reserved for the time when the book itself can be published. It is sufficient to examine the extent to which LeSueur's biography embodied the critical spirit in the active writing of history and to detect and evaluate different assumptions and perspectives which produced the biography as it was written and prevented it from seeing the light of day.

Through a mutual friend, T. C. Patteson of the Toronto Post Office, LeSueur established contact with Charles Lindsey, in whose possession were the Mackenzie papers. After a personal interview with Lindsey, an arrangement was made whereby LeSueur was to live in the Lindsey home in Toronto to examine at his leisure Mackenzie's correspondence and newspaper writings. During the interview with Lindsey, LeSueur indicated that his biography was to be part of the "Makers of Canada" series; but he did not mention that he had been responsible for the rejection of Thomas Hughes' book. The interview was satisfactory for all parties. Despite the fact that the mutual friend had informed the Lindseys that LeSueur was a "Tory" (a label which LeSueur later disavowed in court) the family was satisfied that he would write a "fair" biography of its forebear. From April to September, 1906, while the Lindseys were on vacation in Fernie, B.C., LeSueur lived in the Lindsey family home and steeped himself in the life and times of William Lyon Mackenzie.

Beginning in October, 1906, LeSueur returned to his Ottawa home to write his life of Mackenzie. The task was to take him until April, 1908, a full year more than he expected. Not all the reasons for this delay were related directly to problems involved in the writing of the biography. As an Editor of the "Makers" series, he was given the responsibility of overseeing, among other things, Stephen Leacock's collective biography of Robert Baldwin, Louis Hippolyte Lafontaine and Francis Hincks. Leacock's book had puzzled the critic. While conservative in many of his opinions, Leacock had written a volume which was extremely "partisan" in favour of the liberal interpretation of Canadian history, especially on the question of Responsible Government. Why, LeSueur had asked himself, the ideological shift? Later, however, he solved the puzzle. "Since leaving Toronto," he wrote Morang in a letter marked 'CONFIDENTIAL',

> I have learned in a way that I cannot hint at, for the information was very confidential—and I hope that you will regard as confidential even my reference to it—that Mr. L's. views *were* conservative, but that in a very deliberate way he decided to give his book a liberal character.
>
> The influences [he continued] which led him to do this are a matter pretty nearly of certainty, and are to be sought in a very high quarter.
>
> Well this makes me mad. To think that I have been tugging away at difficulties springing not from a man's erroneous, but independent and sincere convictions, but from a deliberately adopted bias![6]

The following day LeSueur received Leacock's reply to the notes on the latter's manuscript. "I am much obliged for the views you express in regard to the best way to deal with Responsible Government," Leacock wrote, "and am sorry that I cannot agree with your point of view. I am sure, however, that you will not take it any 'personal' sense that I prefer to stick to the beaten track and view the establishment of responsible government as a great triumph in our history."[7]

LeSueur's reply to Leacock, which dwelt upon missed opportunities, is reprinted here. Throughout the winter of 1906-07, editor and author vied with each other regarding the meaning of Responsible Government, and it was not until the end of April, 1907, that Leacock's book was ready for the press. By then, Leacock was thoroughly disgusted with LeSueur's editorial "interference" and LeSueur concluded his last letter to his publisher with the words: "Don't send any more Leacock's my way."[8]

While time-consuming, LeSueur's difficulties with Leacock's volume were part of an editor's necessary responsibilities. LeSueur's real problem lay not with Leacock but with the "influences" which had apparently convinced Leacock to adopt the historical interpretation reflected in his book. The powers emanating from "a very high quarter" were nothing less than the spectre of William Lyon Mackenzie himself, abroad once again in the corridors of power in the guise of William Lyon Mackenzie King, Deputy Minister of Labour in the Laurier ministry and grandson of the rebel of 1837.

"William Lyon Mackenzie and the liberal tradition," the official biographer of Mackenzie King has written, had always been "integral parts of the family environment" in which King was raised.[9] His mother had made certain that young King was well aware of the accomplishments of his radical grandfather. But the significance of this family connection was brought full-force upon Mr. King when, only four months after his involvement in the University of Toronto students' strike, he first read Charles Lindsey's two volume *Life and Times of William Lyon Mackenzie* (1861). His diary for June and July, 1895, graphically records the impression made by the grandfather's life upon the twenty year-old. "I felt quite inspired and intensely interested," he wrote after having read only Lindsey's introduction and first chapter. "I imagined I could feel his blood coursing through my veins. . . ."[10] Five days later he was well into the first volume:

After coming home I read quite a lot of Mackenzie's life. . . . I never remember a week when I have experienced such inward desires, ambitions, hopes etc. as this past one. Reading the life of my dear grandfather I have become a greater admirer of his than ever prouder of my own mother and the race from which I am sprung. Many of [*sic*] His principles I pray I have inherited. I feel I have I understand perfectly the feeling that prompted his actions I can feel his inner life in myself. I have greater desire to carry on the work he endeavored to perform, to better the condition of the poor, denounce corruption, the tyranny of abused power and uphold right and honorable principles. . . .[11]

About a month later he neared completion of the second volume:

. . . spent most of my time reading Mackenzie's life. As I read of his many marvellous escapes from death the thought occurred to me why should this man escape the many many attempts made to end his life, suffer imprisonment, experience poverty in its worst form, be exiled from his native country, that to him a young child should be born, the 13th & last of a large family, who should have of [*sic*] son to inherit the name of his grandfather W.L. Mackenzie surely I have some great work to accomplish before I die.[12]

Filled with this sense of purpose and identification with his grandfather, Mackenzie King had set out to live up to the burden of his liberal heritage and to fulfil the logic of the tradition of "Responsible Government" which, he believed, his maternal grandfather had largely brought into existence. He had not been amused, therefore, when after a 1903 luncheon at the Rideau Club, sponsored by Post-Master General and Minister of Labour, Sir William Mulock, he found himself conversing alone with Mulock's only other guest, former civil servant William Dawson LeSueur, on the subjects of democracy and Responsible Government. "There are three things I remember distinctly," King later testified under oath.

First of all he said that Mackenzie had impeded rather than aided progress. I thought he must have felt very strongly on the matter to mention it to me in that way. . . . He thought that the Family Compact was the constructive element and Mackenzie the destructive element. The third thing astounded me because I had not even heard that even the Family Compact made the claim that was that Francis Bond Head was the man who ought to get the credit for responsible government.[13]

Little wonder, then, that when Mr. King discovered two years later that this same man was about to write a biography of Mackenzie he was furious. Late in December, 1905, Pelham Edgar wrote to LeSueur from Toronto that "Mr. Mackenzie King has been buzzing angrily into the ears of a few influential people here endeavouring to convince them that you are singularly unfitted to be the biographer of his grandfather."[14] According to Edgar, King had spent two hours with George Morang, the publisher. He had also spoken to Byron E. Walker, a member of the series' Advisory Committee, on an evening when Edgar had been visiting the latter. After Edgar had assured both King and Walker that LeSueur's biography would not be written in a hostile spirit, the "irate grandson" had left. The next day in Ottawa LeSueur was visited personally by King, who charged that LeSueur was incapable of writing a sympathetic biography.

"A biography should only be written," King had stated, "by someone in sympathy with the subject." The biography should therefore be put into the hands of some such person.

" 'That is all right,' " replied the prospective biographer. " 'You are perfectly free to make any representations . . . you like; but I am dealing with Mr. Morang, and if he wants me to write that book, I will write it.' "[15]

King's reply was that if the biography, when published, was "unfair to Mackenzie" he would "do all in his power, and spend any amount of time, in putting the matter in a right light."[16] A day later, LeSueur, incensed at the thirty year old King's impertinence, wrote to Morang offering to call the whole arrangement off. "I wonder," he added in a 'P.S.', "if King thinks this business comes under his blessed department of labour."[17] Morang refused LeSueur's offer to foresake writing the biography of Mackenzie. Acknowledging King's conversations with himself, Byron Walker, and adding the name of J.S. Willison, editor of the Toronto *News*, to the list, he concluded: "I think that we would make ourselves ridiculous now if we yielded to the will of this bumptious young King. Go on and do the book and I am sure that when it is published King will come to me and apologize for what he said. . . .[18]

II

LeSueur thus embarked upon his research and writing of Mackenzie's life with the memory of the Lindsey family's general wish that no injustice to Mackenzie be done, with Mackenzie King's various intrigues, and with a knowledge of the "liberal" orientation of the "Makers of Canada" series on his mind. The first could be countered by his own intention to come honestly to grips with Mackenzie; the second he could only ignore. But as an intellectual he was immensely troubled by the third problem, the "liberal" orientation of the "Makers" series. All his life he had been committed, in whatever arena, to the principle of critical intellectual enquiry, and in his writings on political culture he had insisted that the public not be satisfied with words which only superficially spoke the language of freedom. It would not do for Canadians to utter perpetually that they enjoyed "Responsible Government": they must be made aware of just what that term meant in the practice of politics. As he studied the period in which William Lyon Mackenzie had lived, LeSueur became intensely aware of the fact that the Mackenzie biography offered him the opportunity to do just that.

Meanwhile, the lobbying of Mr. King was taking its desired effect. "How are you getting along with Mackenzie?" Morang wrote in June, 1907.

I have been warned by several of your friends that it will not do to look down on the movement for Responsible Government. The people, rightly or wrongly, Willison says, are for Responsible Government, and it would be a great calamity if we should try and belittle the movement in any volume issued in the MAKERS SERIES. We must not give young King, who has gained much newspaper notoriety of late, any chance to further advertise himself.[19]

LeSueur's reply attempted to assuage Morang's obvious anxiety on the question of Responsible Government. The biography would not deal very much with the period when Responsible Government was "an active working system." It would concentrate, instead, on "simply showing that the form of government which *preceeded* 'responsible government' was not as has been commonly represented."[20] Whether Morang realized it or not at the time, he had just been warned that LeSueur was about to use the Mackenzie biography to launch his soon-to-be-infamous "defense" of the Family Compact.

But LeSueur had more to say to his publisher on the subject of "Responsible Government":

> What I shall make clear is that 'responsible government' is a name that has been given to *party government*. The people have *party government*; there is no question about that. They choose to call it—having picked up the name from the politicians—"responsible government." Well and good—they can call it what they like. I have nothing to say about it except here and there as occasion offers, to indicate what it really is, and that, not by an expression of my own opinions, which will be kept discreetly in the background, but by simple exposition of facts.

As for any fears the publisher might have that "Responsible Government" might be "belittled" in the "Makers of Canada" series, LeSueur assured him (not without a touch of sarcasm) that there need be little fear of that occurrence:

> The series as a whole will do full justice, if not more than justice, to r/g. Leacock glorifies it; Hannay chuckles over it; Bourinot applauds; Decelles accepts it; and Shortt can be trusted to speak of it appropriately and sympathetically. You need not fear, after all this advocacy, that 'Mackenzie' is going to do it much harm.[21]

Despite LeSueur's assurances, George N. Morang's fears only increased as LeSueur wrote to him about the progress he was making. "I want to get a very exact and comprehensive knowledge of the whole subject," LeSueur had written to James Bain of the Toronto Public Library when first embarking upon his research, "which I do not think has yet been set in such a light as to do full and impartial justice to all parties concerned."[22] This was the cardinal sin which the book was ultimately to embody. Had it libelled Mackenzie, as J.C. Dent's *Story of the Upper Canadian Rebellion* (1885) had done,[23] its offending passages could easily have been excised. LeSueur's was the far greater offense of putting forward a general interpretation of Upper Canadian history which ran counter to the orientation of virtually every other book in the "Makers" series. LeSueur's aim was not to lament the coming of democratic, "responsible" government to British North America, but to show that there had existed a vision for the Canadian experience which was not found within the history of the Liberal tradition. Mackenzie's significance was also altered:

> The story to be unfolded in the following pages is the story of a personality and a period. The period was in itself a critical one, and the personality was eminently adapted to render it more so. Had William Lyon Mackenzie never come to Canada, the old system of government would none the less, through the action of general courses, infallibly have given place to government of a more democratic type.[24]

Those were the first three sentences of LeSueur's book, three short sentences which said concisely what the remainder of the lengthy book sought to document in Mackenzie's own words and actions: that social and political conditions made the advent of Responsible Government inevitable and that Mackenzie merely prolonged its coming.

Elsewhere and often in the biography LeSueur readily declared Mackenzie's good intentions. "It is clear that Mackenzie had an instinct to do justice," he wrote in the third chapter. "It was a misfortune that he so often allowed that instinct to be silenced by the blasts of passion."[25] Abundant examples were provided to show the manifest ways in which these intentions wrought contrary results. But there existed the other side of the Upper Canadian political coin. The actions of the "Family Compact" and colonial administrators, it was universally recognized, had also often brought about unfortunate results. Yet their motives were seldom viewed with anything except suspicion. George Bryce's popular book, *A Short History of the Canadian People* (1887), for example, began a typical discussion of the "Family Compact" by noting that it was comprised of those who sought "to rule Upper Canada, heedless of the rights or wishes of its people. We have admired the patriotic, heroic, and sentimental side of U.E. Loyalism; but plainly, as related to civil government, its political doctrines and practices were tyrannical.''[26] LeSueur's book, insofar as it *was* a "defence" of the "Family Compact," was an attempt to reveal the essential illogic of such a position as that of Bryce. The Loyalists were such precisely because they had valued "liberty," in its British and monarchical forms, not because they sought to perpetrate tyranny. If this was the case, could it have been that such members of the "Family Compact" as John Strachan and John Beverley Robinson were, like Mackenzie, well-intentioned individuals with a genuine concern for the future well-being of British North America in mind? Readers of the "Makers of Canada" did not find out, for biographies of neither Strachan nor Robinson found a place in the series, despite LeSueur's concerted attempts to have them included.[27]

As in all his other endeavours, LeSueur's objective in writing the Mackenzie biography was to steer a critical path between competing dogmatisms, whether of orthodox Christianity and extreme scientism, partisan exponents of Liberal and Conservative partyism, or the ill-intentioned, tyrannous "Family Compact" and the liberal seekers of liberty through self-government. As always, his aim was to strike a balance. In the historical context of William Lyon Mackenzie's life-time, it would be a balance of intention. If Mackenzie's attacks on the "Family Compact" and his actions in 1837 revealed his willingness to undermine social order and stability in his genuine concern for the achievement of political progress as he conceived it, it was necessary also for someone to assert the contrary, and no less genuine, concern of Mackenzie's "Compact" enemies that political liberty in the tradi-tional English sense must be preserved by the maintenance of those institutions and practices which hitherto had preserved social order and stability. Thus, after listing in his biography Mackenzie's well-known list of grievances, LeSueur wrote:

No country in the world has yet enjoyed either a perfect govern-ment or perfect social conditions, and there were doubtless flaws in the state of Upper Canada when Mr. Mackenzie took its affairs in hand. What is difficult to understand is how it could have been very different from what it actually was, considering its origin and politi-cal constitution. Yet the whole period has come down to us laden with an odium largely the creation of the hostile criticisms of a few men. If the present age should hereafter be judged by the criticisms of those who to-day take the least favourable view of its public life, what will its repute be? It is easier to create a tradition of evil than one of good. . . . To rejoice not in iniquity, but to rejoice in *the truth* is one of the marks of a very superior grace. And so it comes about that historical criticism has found much more to do in the vindication, or partial vindication, of character unduly blackened than in the darkening of character too highly portrayed.[28] ✓

It was after reading passages such as this that George Morang gradually discovered that his original offer to LeSueur had created, in the words of later trial records, a "monster" which had "out-Heroded Herod," a book that, if published, "instead of helping with a moderate Tory twist," would instead "destroy the usefulness of the rest of the series."[29] By September, 1907, he was seeking assurances from LeSueur that "safe [interpretive] ground" would be taken in case "King and his friends want to have a row."[30] He had by then solicited, at LeSueur's suggestion, Adam Shortt's opinion of Mackenzie's influence. Shortt had replied: "By his extravagant and reckless agitation and revolutionary schemes he did more than all the enemies of reform to discredit the cause and to retard the accomplishment of those liberal measures which the conduct of the Family Compact Party had rendered indispensable." Scarcely reassured at having had LeSueur's general thesis reiterated by the man who was on the verge of publishing the biography of *Lord Sydenham* for the "Makers" series, Morang wrote to LeSueur of Shortt's comment: "I do not believe that it would be judicious to say more than suggest that this was the case, which can be done by quoting documentary evidence here and there."[31] Little did he know at the time that LeSueur was doing precisely that, except that "here and there" meant that the case would be made over and over again in Mackenzie's own words—the rhetoric of vitriol and inconsistency—throughout a manuscript that in page-proof form ran over 550 pages. Like the prospective biographer of William Lyon Mackenzie, the publisher also was more than aware of the ominous presence of the twentieth century spectre of the red-headed rebel of 1837. "I do not mind telling you," Morang concluded the letter in which he had quoted Shortt's opinion of Mackenzie's influence, "that I have promised two or three of my friends who are deeply interested in your book, to let them read it before it goes to the printer. King has worked up considerable interest in it here and I feel that some of our friends think that you intend to slaughter Mackenzie King's distinguished grandfather."

The last of W.D. LeSueur's chapters, the twenty-first, reached George Morang in Toronto late in April, 1908. It was dutifully circulated to LeSueur's "friends": to George Goldwin Smith Lindsey, the son of recently deceased Charles Lindsey, to John C. Saul, the editorial reader, and possibly to J.S. Willison and Byron Walker. As the book neared completion the author was clearly pleased with what he had written, and believed that the book was going to be released "at a good time":

I am not hinting at a conservative reaction in the party sense, but there is a conservative reaction in a wider and deeper sense which the book will just hit. People are becoming aware that they have placed altogether too much faith in the mere theoretical perfection of their political institutions; and that it takes more to make a government responsible than merely to call it responsible. I believe a feeling of real alarm is taking possession of the country. . . . I suppose you read Willison's News more or less. You see queer things there about the doings of ''responsible government.'' Now my book, without quoting any modern instances, forces reflection upon the political situation of to-day and meets a certain rising tide of thought and opinion. It will make people see that for real responsibility they will have to depend on character—the *mere machinery* will never give it. [32]

When he sent the later chapters to Toronto, LeSueur speculated upon George Lindsey's reaction:

The book cannot in all respects be pleasant reading for Mr. Lindsey, and yet I think he will see that while I have shown the failings of M's. character I have tried to do justice to his virtues. That his virtues should have been so largely overshadowed by his faults is not my fault.

I may say that every effort has been made to make my book as new as possible by using hitherto unused sources of information, and by treating questions which other writers have passed over; I try to answer two questions. First:—What were the issues in M's. time, and second:—What part did he play in the working out of those issues and in the history of the country? [33]

Eleven days later, George Lindsey, as well as George Morang, had finished reading the completed manuscript and Lindsey met with Mackenzie King for lunch. King's diary recorded the verdict. ''. . . LeSueur's life of grandfather,'' King wrote on April 28, 1908, was

. . . a vile production. George says it begins by saying Canada wd. have been better off without Mackenzie, & is full of all the unkind things that could be sd. It justifies the family compact, attributes great suspicion to Mackenzie & what not. He says that Morang turned down the book on reading the first few chaps. He also says LeSueur wrote Morang saying now is a good time to bring it out, it wd. serve as a campaign document for the Tories.

But LeSueur was not the only enemy that William Lyon Mackenzie King, it seemed, had to face: "Geo. also gave me extracts from Sydenham's life by Shortt," he added, "which scarcely do justice to grandfather's part in constitut'l reform. I will take up the matter with Shortt."[34] Four days later, on May 2nd, Morang wrote to LeSueur expressing grave misgivings about the book because "according to your version, Mackenzie could hardly be called a 'Maker of Canada,' " and this was followed on the 6th of May with a long letter of rejection. Both Morang's reasons for his decision and LeSueur's reply of 11 May are reprinted in this volume.

III

LeSueur's troubles with the Mackenzie biography had just begun. Now sixty-eight years old, he had just devoted two years to the writing of a book the sole longhand copy of which he had submitted to his publisher. After Morang's rejection of the manuscript for use in the "Makers" series LeSueur offered an immediate return of the $500.00 paid to him as a contributor in return for his biography. Morang refused to relinquish control of the manuscript, and this refusal was followed quickly by a demand by G.G.S. Lindsey that all documents, notes, and papers obtained by LeSueur while the author had lived in the Lindsey house must be returned to the family. LeSueur returned all borrowed materials, but refused to give up the notes he had taken. ". . . [A] great mistake has been made," wrote George Lindsey, "a mistake which I am bound to avoid the consequences of as far as I can." With that he withdrew the family sanction for any book on Mackenzie which LeSueur might write using knowledge or materials gained while he had access to the Lindsey collection of Mackenzie's papers and correspondence.[35]

It is unnecessary to discuss in detail the five court cases which followed. The first three, culminating in a decision made in the Supreme Court of Canada, involved a suit by the author against his publisher to recover the manuscript. LeSueur had won the legal right to his manuscript in the first case; two subsequent appeals by the publisher, aided financially by the Lindsey family,[36] failed. Late in 1911, LeSueur, now in his seventies, recovered what he considered to be the fruits of the major intellectual endeavour of his life. He was then taken to court by the Lindsey family in an effort to obtain an injunction that would prohibit the publication of the original Mackenzie biography or anything else which LeSueur might write on the subject. By this time, Mackenzie King had read all of the correspondence related to the writing of the biography. "It was quite clear," his diary recorded, "that there was a conspiracy to which Morang, thro' the influence of Christopher Robinson & LeSeuer [*sic*] thro' prejudice were parties to have Mackenzie written down instead of up."[37] The grandson, still "irate," spent part of January, 1912, in the Public Archives of Canada reading materials related to Mackenzie. He discovered in the colonial office despatches, in the Durham papers, and in the Elgin-Grey correspondence much which re-affirmed his conviction that Mackenzie had been an able reformer and a selfless hero; he also found the Dominion Archivist, Arthur Doughty, to have been "a bit of a sneak & is party to a conspiracy with Lesuer [*sic*] & others to injure Mackenzie's name & fame."[38] LeSueur, it appeared to King, had been trusted by Doughty to edit the Durham papers.

The *Lindsey v. LeSueur* trial occupied the months from September, 1912, to January, 1913. It was the talk of the city. University professors, Members of Parliament, and many members of the legal profession daily packed the court room. Mackenzie King and Thomas L. Hughes attended regularly. No fewer than forty-seven articles, most of them lengthy, appeared in the main Toronto newspapers during the major week of the trial.[39] The judgement of Justice Britton, delivered on January 10, 1913, in the King's Bench division of the Ontario High Court of Justice, stated that LeSueur was guilty of a breach of contract and good faith.[40] The defendant had received permission to use the family's papers in order to write on Mackenzie for a series about the "Makers of Canada." While he had told the family *that*, he had *not* told them that he had previously been directly responsible for the rejection of a manuscript precisely because the author had portrayed Mackenzie as just such a "Maker." One passage in the LeSueur manuscript used by the plaintiff's counsel to prove the contention that the biographer had no intention of writing about Mackenzie as a "Maker" of Canada had made large headlines: "There were qualities in Mackenzie which in a happier combination might have made him an admirable, not merely a notable, character, a pillar, not a puller-down of the State."[41]

There was, however, a fundamental contradiction in the logic of the verdict. Judge Britton insisted that it was not LeSueur's portrayal of Mackenzie that was at issue. "It does not . . . make any difference," ran the judgement, "whether Mackenzie was a man of high aims and unselfish purpose, contending against real wrongs permitted by bad laws and perpetuated by unjust administration; or a mere adventurer willing to point where he would not lead, a mere inciter to rebellion against laws that were just, and administered by men able and honest."[42] The plain, legal fact, it was claimed, was "that the defendant improperly obtained access to the collection" and then "made an unfair use of the privilege."[43] Yet the main item of evidence that had been used to prove this breach of faith had been that LeSueur had exhibited prior *animus* not to write about Mackenzie as a "Maker" of Canada. The problem rested with the very value-laden title of the series, for it presupposed prior to an author's research and writing of any given volume that he would portray his subject as such a "Maker." In doing so, it undermined the fundaments of historical scholarship. Two years before his death LeSueur wrote a preface to his book which contained a paragraph challenging the logic and the wisdom of the decision in this respect. After citing the passage of the judgement quoted above, he wrote:

That is to say, *Mackenzie might have been all that the latter part of the paragraph* [that part of Britton's judgement, quoted above, which begins, ". . . or a mere adventurer . . ."] *describes*; but if I had ventured to say so, or anything like it, no matter how the evidence might have been forced on me, I should have violated my contract with the owner of the papers. What kind of contract would that have been which bound a man to disregard evidence and give a false version of facts? It seems strange that his Lordship could have penned that sentence and not had a word to say against the immorality of manufacturing historical opinion by contract. As a matter of fact, my book, as anyone who peruses its pages will see, is very far from depicting Mackenzie as a "mere adventurer": no term could indeed be more inappropriate to the character in which he is presented. And as to "pointing where he would not lead," I have expressly credited him with readiness to lead, as well as to incite, and, so far, repelled the charge of cowardice which some have brought against him. Let the book, however, speak for itself.[44]

When the book is published it *will* speak for itself and for one man's sustained commitment to scholarly enquiry. But it was justice, not free enquiry, which reigned when Justice Britton's decision ordered LeSueur to deliver to the Lindsey family the manuscript it had taken him three court cases to repossess. In addition, the author was told that he must surrender all other materials, including notes and copied matter, which contained "information avowedly obtained from the Mackenzie collection." LeSueur appealed the decision, but a year later the Honorable Sir William R. Meredith, Chief Justice of Ontario, sustained the original verdict.[45] Sadly disappointed yet undaunted, LeSueur, now almost seventy-four and recovering from an accident which had resulted in the fracture of two ribs, set out to do the only thing he could in order ever to publish his book on Mackenzie: to duplicate virtually all of his research so that none of his source material would rely on the Mackenzie holdings of the Lindsey family. The undertaking took until early 1915. Meanwhile, after the failure of LeSueur's appeal in the Appellate court, a telegram was received by George Lindsey:

Ottawa 5 Dec. 13.

Accept heartiest congratulations on a splendid victory am delighted.

Willie[46]

IV

This last chapter in the life of the mind of William Dawson LeSueur draws near its conclusion. It is not a tale of bitterness or jaded perspectives. If anything, the critic-turned-historian was now more committed than ever to the necessity of engaging in critical enquiry in the historical realm. The essential nature of history, he wrote to readers of the Montreal *Gazette*, is that it "is not affirmation but enquiry." (p. 285) His Presidential Address to the Royal Society of Canada on "History: Its Nature and Methods" was an open repudiation of the assumptions of those who sought to use history to create or to articulate political or social mythology. Erudite, rich in allusions to conceptions of the craft of history from the time of classical antiquity to the twentieth century, the address was delivered in the midst of LeSueur's battle with the heirs of Mackenzie. While nowhere were Mackenzie and the issues connected with the writing of the biography mentioned in the address, it may be safely said that as the speech was delivered they were nonetheless constantly present both for the author and his learned audience.

LeSueur's last years were scarcely ones of declining powers. Indeed, they were among the most productive years of his life. In them, he returned to his studies of Canadian history. He translated certain of the writings of Champlain and LaVerendrye, published after his death in the Champlain series. He completed a book-length "History of Canada" from its beginnings to 1763. Never published, the book, in typescript, rests—probably read only by its creator—among his papers in the Public Archives of Canada. "In history," its introduction concluded, "we are led to see the connection of events, and, in proportion as we do so, our studies, instead of merely burdening the memory, yield us the pleasure and profit which always accompany expanding intelligence."[47] Personal pleasure and profit there must have been for LeSueur in these last days. After the history of Canada to 1763 was completed, he began what appears to be a thematic outline for the volume which was to succeed it. Entitled "The Political Development of Canada, 1763-1841," the 97 page manuscript is a hurried and sweeping account of Canadian history, written perhaps with the sense of impending death. Had it been expanded, a comprehensive treatment of the political ethos of William Lyon Mackenzie's Canada would have been available to Canadians. Its first few sentences indicate the general aims of its author:

From heaven, Jeremiah says, came the motto, "Know thyself!" Less valuable dicta by far have had the same high origin assigned to them. If self-knowledge is important for the individual, not less important, perhaps even more important, is it for the nation. The nation that does not know itself in some more or less real sense is likely, not only to stray as to the policy and ideals it ought to pursue, but also to lack the true spirit of corporate unity. Until a nation knows itself and has found itself, there is always a possiblity of an outbreak of internal strife. With true self-knowledge comes the spirit of appeasement, of national cohesion founded on mutual comprehension, leading to sympathy, between class and class, and element and element in the population.

The history of Canada is one which has readily lent itself to misinterpretation and consequent misrepresentation; and the result is seen in the imperfect blending to-day of certain of the constituent elements of the Canadian people. Those who read that history aright, and tell the tale of past efforts and struggles in a spirit of unswerving justice, with true historic insight and broad human sympathy, will, in my opinion, render our Canadian state a service of the first magnitude.[48]

In the end it was not the Lindsey family, nor Mackenzie King, nor the courts which brought about the troubles that plagued W.D. LeSueur's later years. No man enquires after "truth" from a vacuum of assumption or conviction, and in the twentieth century W.D. LeSueur was a victim of his own assumptions and convictions. It was seen earlier that LeSueur's critical thought was given direction and cohesion by "a basic commitment to a progressive view of man and history, an organic conception of social reality, and a universalistic conception of life in general." (p. 21) These were philosophical tents fundamentally antagonistic to the cultural currents of the twentieth century.

Like John Stuart Mill, Matthew Arnold, and the American "genteel reformers" who were his contemporaries, LeSueur was part of a middle-class intelligentsia which attempted to extend the ethical norms of its class to society at large.[49] Epistemological dualists who insisted upon the inviolable separation of the "spiritual" and the "material," while at the same time men who as a "class" were increasingly alienated from the growing urban, industrial, "mass society" around them, they revealed this dualism in their rigid distinction between the "higher" and "lower" forms of life, between "culture" and "commonplace." In so doing, they helped to deepen the already widening rift between the intelligentsia and the general public. As Stow Persons has recently written: "The successor to the nineteenth century gentleman is the alienated intellectual."[50]

By the twentieth century, W.D. LeSueur was one such "intellectual," alienated not only by his commitment to "culture" in an Arnold-dian sense but also by his root assumptions. His belief in the existence of a universal moral order may have helped to set personal or cultural standards in the nineteenth century, but it seemed to many a questionable proposition in the fragmented age of Freud and Einstein. An organic conception of social reality may have helped LeSueur to understand the perspectives and concerns for the social good of various Tory members of the Family Compact; it may, indeed, have been the assumption which made him undertake to write a history of Mackenzie's Canada that would strike a balance between the Liberal and Conservative traditions, between the ethics of freedom and concern. But it, too, was a difficult idea to defend in the pluralistic, regional, and racially-divided Canada of Laurier and Borden. Finally, it was now difficult to be a believer in the essentially malleable nature of man by which a nation of rational men could be created through the development of an "enlightened public opinion." In the year that LeSueur's manuscript was rejected by its publisher, Graham Wallas wrote *Human Nature in Politics*. "Whoever sets himself to base his political thinking on a re-examination of the working of human nature," the book began, "must begin by trying to overcome his own tendency to exaggerate the intellectuality of mankind." This was a tendency which LeSueur and many "intellectuals" of his generation failed to overcome. In the context of the major political and military events of the twentieth century, John Stuart Mill's *On Liberty*—which posited a "universe of discourse" in which rational men are informed and persuaded by intelligent discussion and truth prevails through informed debate—may well be viewed as a kind of utopian document.[51]

It remains for the reader, however, as he or she reaches the conclusion of W.D. LeSueur's inner biography, to assess the man, to determine the measure of his achievement, and perhaps to wonder how many other forgotten Canadian ancestors may yet exist for enquiring minds to rediscover.

NOTES

1. The others are A.G. Bradley, *Lord Dorchester* (1907) and H.R. Casgrain's *Wolfe and Montcalm* (1905), both reprinted by the University of Toronto Press in their Canadian University Paperbook series. For a more general background of the "Makers of Canada" series, especially with respect to its "Whig" orientation, see Kenneth N. Windsor, "Historical Writing in Canada to 1920," in Carl Klinck *et al., Literary History of Canada* (Toronto: University of Toronto Press, 1973), pp. 225-232.

2. See Henri Lorin's review of *Count Frontenac* in *Review of Historical Publications Relating to Canada.* George M. Wrong and H.H. Langton (eds.), (Toronto: Morang & Co., 1907), pp. 38-45.

3. LeSueur to G.N. Morang, 16 October, 1905. Lindsey Papers—Lindsey Section, Volume Five, "Lindsey *vs.* LeSueur: Evidence at Trial," Public Archives of Ontario. Unless otherwise noted, all correspondence cited is from this source. For further evidence of LeSueur's reticence, see LeSueur to Morang, 20 October, 1905.

4. In a 1915 "Preface" to his own life of Mackenzie, LeSueur wrote that he eventually "learnt . . . that the gentleman in question [Wrong] . . . had been dissuaded by friends from entering on a subject which he could hardly hope to treat quite independently without exciting partisan feeling and criticism, which might be hurtful to his influence as a teacher." W.D. LeSueur, "Preface" to *William Lyon Mackenzie* (microfilm), W.D. LeSueur Papers, Public Archives of Canada.

5. LeSueur to Morang, 7 December, 1905.

6. LeSueur to Morang, 10 October, 1906.

7. Stephen Leacock to LeSueur, 11 October, 1906.

8. LeSueur to Morang, 28 April, 1907. For Leacock's viewpoint, see Leacock to Morang, 19 October and 3 November, 1906.

9. R. MacGregor Dawson, *William Lyon Mackenzie King; Volume One, 1874-1923* (Toronto: University of Toronto Press, 1958), p. 13.

10. Mackenzie King Diary, Monday, 17 June, 1895. The editor is indebted to Dr. John Kendle for references to the King diary.

11. *Ibid.,* Saturday, 22 June, 1895.

12. *Ibid.,* Thursday, 18 July, 1895.

13. "Did Not Make Bargain to be Friendly to W.L.M.—Ottawa Author Says Such Arrangement Does Not Agree With His Conception of History . . . ," *Evening Telegram* (Toronto), 13 November, 1912. Lindsey Papers—Lindsey Section. Vol. 4/Scrapbook.

14. Edgar to LeSueur, 29 December, 1905.

15. LeSueur to Morang, 31 December, 1905.

16. *Ibid*. The conversation, as recalled by LeSueur, may be viewed as accurate. King, who testified as a witness, did not challenge the veracity of LeSueur's reconstruction of the meeting.

17. *Ibid*.

18. Morang to LeSueur, 2 January, 1906. See also Morang to LeSueur, 8 January, 1906.

19. Morang to LeSueur, 6 June, 1907.

20. LeSueur to Morang, 8 June, 1907.

21. LeSueur's references are to these volumes in the "Makers" series: Stephen Leacock, *Baldwin, Lafontaine, Hincks* (1907); J.G. Bourinot, *Lord Elgin* (1903); Alfred D. DeCelles, *Papineau-Cartier* (1904); Adam Shortt, *Lord Sydenham* (1908).

22. LeSueur to James Bain, 13 January, 1906. Henry Sproat Collection, Scrapbook, Vol. I, p. 107. University of Toronto Library, Rare Book Division.

23. Dent variously described Mackenzie as "ill-balanced," "heartless and selfish," "erratic," "unstable" and "the veriest shuttlecock in the hands of fate." For these and other of Dent's views on Mackenzie, see J.C. Dent, *The Last Forty Years*, Carleton Library Series, No. 62, ed. Donald Swainson (Toronto: McClelland and Stewart, 1972), p. xii. Swainson's introduction provides an excellent treatment of the significance of the Rebellion of 1837 in nineteenth century historiography.

24. W.D. LeSueur, "William Lyon Mackenzie" (original typescript), Lindsey Papers—Lindsey Section, Public Archives of Ontario.

25. *Ibid*.

26. Rev. George Bryce, *A Short History of the Cadian People* (Toronto: W.J. Gage and Company, 1887), p. 357.

27. LeSueur attempted especially to have a condensed version Col. C.W. Robinson, *The Life of Sir J.B. Robinson* (Edinburgh, 1904), included. See LeSueur to Morang, 14 July, 8 and 27 August, 2 October, 1907. LeSueur was directly responsible for Stephen Leacock's moderate descriptions of the "Family Compact" in *Baldwin, Lafontaine, Hincks,* pp. 4-12, and for the last paragraph of George Parkin's, *Sir John A. Macdonald* (1908), which balances Parkin's earlier praise with a recognition of Macdonald's shortcomings.

28. LeSueur, "Mackenzie" (original typescript), *op. cit*.

29. "Feared Book Would Destroy the Series—Publisher's View of LeSueur's Work, According to Lawyer . . . ," Toronto *Globe*, Friday, 15 November, 1912.

30. Morang to LeSueur, 5 September, 1907.

31. *Ibid*.

32. LeSueur to Morang, 23 March, 1908.

33. LeSueur to Morang, 17 April, 1908.

34. W.L. Mackenzie King Diary, 1908-14. Tuesday, 28 April, 1908.

35. LeSueur to Lindsey, 20 May, 1908; Lindsey to LeSueur, 26 May, 1908; LeSueur to Lindsey, 31 May, 1908; Lindsey to LeSueur, 2 June, 1908; Lindsey to LeSueur, 17 June, 1908; LeSueur to Lindsey, 25 June, 1908.

36. "Did Not Make Bargain . . . ," *op. cit*.

37. W.L. Mackenzie King Diary, 1908-14, Wednesday, 27 December, 1911.

38. *Ibid.,* Thursday, 11 January, Friday, 12 January, 1912.

39. Lindsey Papers—Lindsey Section, Vol. 4/Scrapbook: ". . . Press Comments on Trial," Public Archives of Ontario.

40. *Lindsey v. LeSueur* (1913), 27 *O.L.R.* 588 (H.C.).

41. "Says Mackenzie Was Not a Pillar But a Puller-Down," Toronto *Daily Sun*, 12 November, 1912.

42. "Copy of Judgement of Britton, J., delivered 9th January, 1913," p. 3. Lindsey Papers—Lindsey Section, Public Archives on Ontario.

43. *Ibid.*, p. 5.

44. "Preface" (1915), "William Lyon Mackenzie," p. 19 (microfilm copy). W.D. LeSueur Papers, Public Archives of Canada.

45. *LeSueur v. Lindsey* (1913), 29 *O.L.R.* 648 (App. Div.).

46. Lindsey Papers—Lindsey Section. Vol. 4/Scrapbook. On LeSueur's illness see *Ottawa Journal*, 13 March, 1912.

47. "History of Canada to 1763," p. 6. Typescript in W.D. LeSueur Papers, Vol. II, file #10, Public Archives of Canada.

48. "The Political Development of Canada, 1763-1841," pp. 1-2. W.D. LeSueur Papers, Vol. II, file #9. Public Archives of Canada.

49. John L. Tomsich, *A Genteel Endeavor* (Stanford, Calif.: Stanford University Press, 1971), pp. 73-74, *passim*.

50. Stow Persons, *The Decline of American Gentility* (New York: Columbia University Press, 1973), p. vii.

51. Graham Wallace, *Human Nature in Politics* [1908] (Boston: Houghton Mifflin Co., 1919), p. 21. Howard Mumford Jones, "Introduction" to P. Appleman, W.A. Madden, and M. Wolff (eds.), *1859: Entering an Age of Crisis* (Bloomington: Indiana University Press), pp. 16-17.

17. William Lyon Mackenzie (1906)

W.D. LeSueur to the Editor of "The Mail and Empire"—March 21, 1906

Sir,—A correspondent of *The Mail and Empire*, styled "Historicus," commends the action of the Laurier Club in seeking to obtain a conspicuous place on the walls of the provincial building for the portrait of William Lyon Mackenzie, and recommends to that body the project of erecting a monument by which his name and fame may be blazoned forth to posterity. In dealing with the relation of moral standards to temperament and environment, Lord Macaulay states, by way of illustration, that to an Italian audience of the fifteenth century, Iago, and not Othello, would have been the hero of the play. Perhaps to some such perversion of the understanding is attributable the tendency to glorify a character like Mackenzie. It would appear that to be under the ban of the law, human or divine, creates a sure claim to sympathy in certain morbid natures. Thus to boys and others of undeveloped reasoning powers Captain Kidd and Jesse James are real heroes, beings of immense force and daring, with whose crimes they feel no particular concern. The bold outlaw plays the most sensational role in history, to omit which would be fatal to the play. Thus for the exigencies of our national drama the sword of Hotspur or of Monmouth is buckled on the meagre form of W.L. Mackenzie. The downstairs spectators laugh at the travesty, but the gallery is mightily impressed. Bottom felt promptings of the true dramatic instinct when he asked for "a part to tear a cat in, to make all split."

Mackenzie's character and aims have been described by those bound to him by natural ties, and by others who, being accessory to his designs, or his political heirs, have sought their own vindication in defending him. By these he is held up as a disinterested champion of justice and popular rights against the forces of tyranny and corruption. On the other hand he is depicted in the correspondence of Sir John Colborne, and Sir F.B. Head and elsewhere, as an unscrupulous

SOURCE: W.D. LeSueur Papers, Vol. I. Public Archives of Canada. This letter was written under the pseudonym "Simplex."

demagogue, an inveterate liar, who kept himself before the public notice by the libels published in his newspaper, an instrument of Yankee intrigue, and the head of an anti-British faction, composed chiefly of adventurers and outcasts from the United States. We may decide according to our views of the comparative credibility of the witnesses. We know without resort to *ex parte* evidence that Mackenzie progressed from agitation to sedition, and finally conceiving himself to be the Moses who was to lead the people of Upper Canada from under the "baneful domination" of Great Britain, he launched his opera bouffe rebellion, fled incontinently at the first shot, leaving his lieutenants to expiate on the gallows the crime which was chiefly his own, and from the security of the neighboring Republic completed his efforts on behalf of the Canadian people by organizing bands of ruffians to raid and murder them. They had failed of Liberty, he would give them Death. "Historicus" thinks coming generations ought to know of this man. If so let them know the truth.

But, Mackenzie's admirers will tell us, whatever his character, we are under a heavy debt to him, we owe him "the blessings of responsible government." Without pausing to examine this remarkable though familiar idea, it may be affirmed with certainty that if Mackenzie was the father of responsible government he unnaturally repudiated his offspring. I have before me a curious little work with the portentous title:

An almanac of Independence and Freedom, for the Year 1860, Containing a Plea for the Relief of the Inhabitants of Canada from a State of Colonial Vassalage and Irresponsible Rule; and their Early Entrance upon a Prosperous, Happy Career as Educated, Self-governed Freemen; together with considerations with reference to the position in which Upper Canada stands toward the American Republic, and a review of the proceedings of the Convention which met in Toronto on the Ninth of November, 1859

Underneath this is the following reassuring extract from the *Times* of Nov. 28, 1859:

The people of Canada may, if they please, separate themselves from the Dominions of her Majesty—and whenever they please to do so, not a sword will be drawn, not a trigger will be pulled on our part, for the purpose of preventing them.

The author is William Lyon Mackenzie and the purpose to revive the movement which gave birth to the Annexation Manifesto. This famous document is printed verbatim, and considering its supposed Tory origin (which is such a comfort and delight to Grit politicians when their loyalty is under examination) it is interesting to observe among the signatures L.H. Holton, C. Leberge, and A.A. Dorion, all three of whom were afterwards members of George Brown's Government. At the end of the list the editor adds: "L.J. Papineau highly approved of it," and quotes expressions of Papineau that a future generation would insist on regarding them as men whose love for Britain was qualified only by a passion for responsible government.

The original matter in the Almanac shows the mental condition in which a man would go from Dan to Beersheba and cry, "tis all barren!" The country was politically and commercially ruined. There was still far too much British connection to suit him, and too much Popery. The representatives of Royalty worried him.

> Old, poor, needy, broken down knights, pensioners, and baronets obtain an asylum as our colonial governors; have we not better black walnut among ourselves? Did you ever hear of a native colonist trusted to rule the smallest British colony? Not in this country. But let a miserable Irish parasite of power like F. Hincks betray his trust here, England has at once a Governorship and $25,000 a year ready for him.

The pages bristle with admonitions like the following:

> Encourage Free Education—Free Schools. Beware of the Pope and D'Arcy McGee, who seek to destroy Free Schools.

> Contend against all political alliances with Lower Canada.

> Get institutions that will check adventurers and knaves when fools from Europe choose such.

He speaks of the

> degradation of having our statute books searched for any acts which the whim of lords and dukes in the Old World might seek to nullify.

He gives extracts from speeches by British public men to show that Britain was in the humor to get rid of Canada, and, indeed, they fairly stand that construction. There were not a few both in England and Canada who thought responsible government as applied by Lord Elgin meant the abandonment of Canada. Perhaps it is over soon to say they were mistaken.

Mackenzie in 1860 displayed no love for his old allies the "Moderate

Reformers,'' who had used him when it suited their ends and abandoned him when he proceeded to carry his designs to their logical conclusions. He vilifies Ryerson and prints with great glee Ryerson's denunciation of Brown. When we consider he was at this time an old man, on whom misfortune, exile, imprisonment, and a narrow escape from the gallows might be expected to have worked a subduing effect, we can only wonder what his language was like in the early days. But it must be remembered that Mackenzie never came under those influences which in our times are so potent in quieting the clamors of the people's champions. Had it been his lot to pass into the serene atmosphere and emoluments of the bench, or to dream away the afternoon of life amid the Lotus Eaters of the Senate, his fretful spirit might have yielded to the whisperings of the still small voice which says whatever is is right. But he had returned to Canada only to find the country had outgrown him, that his occupation was gone. He was forgotten in his own lifetime, and probably the Laurier Club and ''Historicus'' could do him no greater kindness than to imitate the generation who knew him best.

18. LeSueur, Leacock, and Responsible Government (1906)

W.D. LeSueur to Stephen Leacock—October 26, 1906.

. . . A few words now on the question of Responsible Government. I quite recognize that a book can be written on the lines of yours that will give satisfaction to a large section of the public, but my feeling was that, in dealing with Baldwin, Lafontaine and Hincks, an opportunity was afforded for doing something a little better than repeating that twice told tale, however skillfully the retelling might be done. I was hoping for a book that would make, or if that is impossible, would at least invite people to think dispassionately and unconventionally on the course of Canadian history. Considering the point at which we have arrived in our political development, and the many evils which have fastened themselves on our political system, the time is ripe for a very critical treatment of our political conventions and catch words. The note of your book, on the other hand, is the note of finality. "It is finished—we have Responsible Government." Yes we have "responsible government" and corruption has so enlarged itself that witnesses in the box almost jeer at the magistrate who enquires into their inequities, and a horrible cynicism in regard to every profession of political virtue has taken solid possession of a very large portion of the community. Is this the time to persuade people that their welfare is accomplished, and that they may sit down in peace under Responsible Government as under a combination vine and fig tree? I do not say you distinctly say so in your book, but I do say that you have done it negatively by missing a great opportunity of presenting certain questions as open questions, instead of as eternally settled ones. It is the note of enquiry, that note of what Balfour[1] calls "philosophic doubt," that I miss in a book that gave exceptional advantage—far more than the book I am writing—for introducing it. . . .

SOURCE: W.D. LeSueur Papers, Vol. I. Public Archives of Canada.

---

19. A Rejected Manuscript
   (1908)

A. *George N. Morang to W.D. LeSueur—May 6th, 1908*

Dear Dr. LeSueur:—

 . . . I had not intended writing you at any length in regard to the Life of Mackenzie for some days yet until I had more fully considered the matter, and until Mr. Saul had finished his re-reading of your MS, but I think I must answer your letter at this point in order that you may understand some of the reasons for my hesitation in regard to the MS. From my reading of the history of the anti [*sic*]-rebellion and post-rebellion times as contained in histories proper, in the newspapers and political press of all periods, and in some of the volumes of the present series, and from expressions of opinion which I have read or heard in a variety of ways, and from many sources, since our publications have been announced, I cannot but feel that Mackenzie should be included in the "Makers of Canada" Series. He was more than "an historic character" and the series certainly would be incomplete and open to strong criticism were a fair review of the events in which he figured, and a fair review of his character and career as a public man, omitted. But the estimate must be fair in every sense of the word.

 It seems to me that no man who bore the conspicuous part that Mackenzie did in the period covered by his life both as a "journalist and parliamentarian," could, with any degree of justice, be left out of the list of "Makers of Canada." Political movements and transitions—and the rebellion marks a period of transitions—are nearly always the result of popular agitation. Mackenzie was admittedly a great agitator, if he was nothing else, and whatever may be said about his methods in that particular he was in the opinion of the great majority of Canadians an earnest, honest, and successful agitator against what the weight of both past and present opinion in Canada regards as a vicious system of government. I do not think it is possible to change public opinion in that

SOURCE: *Mackenzie-Lindsey Papers*—Lindsey Section, Vol. v, Public Archives of Ontario. File: "Lindsey vs. LeSueur—Evidence at Trial."

respect and any attempt to defend, much less to justify, that system—which your book seems to do more especially in the latter chapters—would, I am certain, call down both upon the author and the publishers a species of criticism that would be hostile and injurious in the highest degree. You are probably quite ready to accept the responsibility but I do not see how we as publishers could afford to do so. The period in question is full of elements of controversy and a fierce controversy (which must, if possible, be avoided) would certainly be provoked by the publication of a volume in which the system of government typified by the "Family Compact" is palliated, defended and even justified, and moreover, in which the principal character in the narrative is dealt with in a way which would I am inclined to think be regarded as neither generous nor fair. When I say that, I mean that scant justice is done to Mackenzie's virtues—to his highest and best qualities of head and heart—and as much as possible made of his imperfections and weaknesses. That is not the spirit in which any of the "Makers of Canada," or in which any public man who suffered and sacrificed as Mackenzie did in what he believed to be, and in what is generally regarded, as a just cause, should be treated. I am quite satisfied that that is the judgment which would be passed upon your book as it now stands if it were published. Cartier, Howe, Sir John A. Macdonald, Brown, and others that might be named in the series, two or three of them annexationists at one time, have not been treated in that way. Readers would naturally ask why should Mackenzie be singled out and what justification could be offered for so doing? At the present writing I do not know how I could answer this point. . . .

Whatever may be said about the Rebellion—and I am not so sure that even that event is not an arguable question—can there be any doubt that it hastened Responsible Government? It certainly, and without question, brought about Durham's mission, his Report, and the Union Act which was founded on it. I admit that for the time being the Rebellion hurt the Reform party but you will not find many students of that period who are not of the opinion that the Rebellion or rather "the spurt of Civil War" as Goldwin Smith calls it, hastened very materially the dawn of a better system of government and administration. You will remember that Mr. Joseph Chamberlain when Colonial Secretary in his place in the House of Commons, took the same view; in fact, he justified the Rebellion.

Returning to the question of Responsible Government, and the manner in which it is dealt with in your MS, I do not see how any one can, at this late date, afford to belittle the endeavors which Mackenzie, and those who acted with him, made to obtain that boon. Call it what you like, the object aimed at was the same in all the Provinces, viz., the executive responsibility to the people through the Legislature. Howe,

Wilmot, Cartier, Papineau, Ryerson and the others were all striving for the same thing. In Upper Canada Mackenzie bore the brunt of the struggle prior to the Rebellion. Keeping in mind what is said on the subject in the other volumes of the "Makers of Canada" series, I am forced to the conclusion that your book is entirely out of accord with the statements of the case as there made.

When again, in your criticism of Durham and his Report you also come into conflict with Bourinot in "Elgin," Leacock in his "Baldwin, Lafontaine and Hincks," and Burwash in his "Ryerson" and with his estimate and that of Bourinot, of Sir Francis Bondhead [sic.] Furthermore, I may say to you that you are quite out of accord with Shortt's "Sydenham" which cannot as I see it now, stand consistently with your book in the series.

I regret exceedingly to be obliged to write to you in this strain in regard to your MS. in which you have certainly put an immense amount of labor and research and the literary style of which is unexceptionable. I have always understood that there is an unwritten canon in the writing of biography, which demands from the biographer a certain amount of sympathy with the subject of the narrative. This I am afraid is entirely wanting in your estimate of Mackenzie in his struggle with the admittedly evil system of government which then prevailed. I desire above all things to avoid opening up a controversy in regard to these matters because it cannot fail to be injurious to the whole series of biographies comprised in the "Makers of Canada." . . .

I shall be glad to hear from you.

Yours very truly,
Geo. Morang

B. *W.D. LeSueur to George N. Morang—May 11th, 1908*

Dear Mr. Morang:—

I confess I am disappointed at the tenor of your letter, and in no small degree surprised. On the fifth of September last you wrote me enclosing Professor S' [Adam Shortt's] letter, and saying that "we all realize now what will be considered safe ground, and if K. [W.L.M. King] and his friends want to have a row I think we shall be prepared for them." You proceeded to quote a portion of S's letter, and added that you did not think it would be judicious to "any more than suggest that this was the case, which can be done by quoting documentary evidence here and there." Well this is precisely the course I have followed. I do not give it as my own opinion that Mackenzie's action was retardatory rather than promotive; but I show in what a hopeful state things were just before the rebellion and I quote Mackenzie's own opinion that he had thrown things back and his very earnest caution to his friends some years later not to imitate his methods for fear of further delaying things. I do not see how I could more fully have fallen into line with your suggestion about not blurting out the truth in the form in which S. had given it to us; though it says little for the freedom of speech and thought which we enjoy in this land of liberty that the conclusions arrived at by serious scholars on pure questions of history cannot be openly proclaimed. . . .

You speak of my criticism of Durham's report. The only part criticized is that relating to Upper Canada, and the criticism is not mine, but that of an Oxford scholar, wholly remote from our controversies, who made it the subject of a University thesis, and who shows an intimate acquaintance both with the report itself and with the politics of the day in Canada.[2] Is there a Durham myth, too, that must not be criticised, as well as a Mackenzie myth? Time was when it was not considered sacrilege to criticise Durham. He was criticised, and severely, in his own day by Haliburton the Nova Scotian, by Dr. Henry of Quebec, by J.A. Roebuck a fellow radical of the British Parliament, and by many others; and within the last three months W.L. Grant and his colleague Egerton of Oxford have reprinted in their "Canadian Constitutional Development" (a book which is in the hands of all students of Canadian history) the reply made to his report by the Legislative council of Upper Canada. In spite of all our political advancement the document is one which may be read with much advantage to-day. The editors evidently think so, for they say that "Their (the Council's) point of view is expressed with much force." It is hardly possible to express with much force a point of view that is hopelessly weak.

And here let me remark that you may not be fully aware of the amount of work that is being done just at this moment, the necessary effect of which will be a considerable recasting of historical judgments. Garneau's history, which has hitherto been a kind of political Bible in Lower Canada, is being carefully re-edited by his grandson who, on many points, is rectifying his grandfather's statements.[3] The demand is more and more being made that works pretending to be historical shall be based on independent research, and what on earth is the use of independent research if you are predestined to arrive at the conclusions of the multitude every time? If that is the case those writers of the series who simply hashed up the opinions they regarded as prevalent and did not trouble themselves to look deeper took far the wiser part. They did no delving or sifting or wrestling, and their books went all right and are now held up to me as the type to which mine should have conformed. No, thank you!

You speak of its being impossible to change certain popular opinions. Let me give you a right up-to-date example. Vaudreuil, the last Governor of French Canada, was up to a couple of years ago, a kind of idol of the French Canadians, whom it was heresy, or worse, to criticise. One man has changed all that—and how? Simply by producing documentary evidence that the man was incapable and treacherous, and probably corrupt.[4] The evidence was resisted at first and decried, and many hard things were said against the man who brought it forward,—but the facts could not be gainsaid and they won their way. Today Vaudreuil is excluded from the pageants that are to be given at Quebec in July. The Canadians won't have him. . . .

It would be a perfectly unnatural, and in my opinion, a most undesirable thing if all the books of the series had the air of being written under the compulsion of some average opinion—the opinion of the so-called man in the street. The only justification for writing history at all is to shed some new light on events and characters; and in really critical quarters, it is in strict proportion as this is done that books are valued.

I have shed new light on my subject, and I refuse to be brought to the bar of a public opinion formed without any reference to the facts and proofs which my book contains. Did the public of Canada ever before know:—

1. The nature of the attack made by Mackenzie on the Robinsons and Boultons; which led to the wrecking of his printing office.

2. The full extent of the brutality of his general attacks on public men not in Canada only but in England.

3. His mania—for it was nothing less—for assigning corrupt motives to people.

4. His recklessness of statement.

5. The opinion expressed of him and his Grievance Report by Peter Perry the leading reformer in the Assembly; and the opinions attributed (without contradiction) to such reformers as Bidwell and Ketchum.

6. His threat of confiscating the lands of those who opposed the rebellion he was organizing.

7. His efforts to stir up war between England and the United States.

8. That damnable letter of June 1840, inciting to the firing of Canadian frontier towns, and gloating over a $50,000 fire at Kingston which he said was the work of a "patriot"; this, nine months after Sydenham had arrived to put into operation, as far as might be, the ideas of Durham.

9. His even greater dissatisfaction with the system of government which he found in operation under Lord Elgin than with that which he had formerly denounced in Upper Canada.

10. His negotiations with Rolph for an office of emolument which was not to vacate his seat in Parliament, preceding by a few months only an attack of the greatest cruelty and virulence against the same individual.

11. The scheme for sowing religious discord which was carried out with his knowledge by a couple of his leading political supporters in Haldimand.

12. His reversion—this I have not mentioned but should have—it was noticed in a letter to the "Mail and Empire" a few years ago—in almost the last year of his life, after all his expressions of regret for previous violence, to the identical methods of his early years. I refer to his "Almanac of Independence" for the year 1860, in which amongst other things there is an attack on Sir Edmund Head, then Governor, that might have been taken from one of his old tirades against Sir John Colborne or Sir Peregrine Maitland.

Practically all that I have catalogued above is unknown to the Canadian people of to-day. Some of the points are vaguely treated in Mr. Charles Lindsey's book; others were wholly ignored by that writer.[5] Of No. 8 of course he knew nothing; that is a "find" of my own.

You say that "scant justice is done to Mackenzie's virtues and as much as possible made of his imperfections and weaknesses." I wonder at this statement considering the specific evidence given in some of my recent letters to yourself of my having intentionally omitted things which would have told against M. The things I mentioned to you were not all by any means. I am therefore able to meet with a direct denial the allegation that I made "as much as possible" of M's. failings.

Now as to doing "scant justice to M's virtues." I state deliberately that I have thrown into my book every scrap that fell in my way that told in his favour with the sole exception of some commendation in a letter of Joseph Hume's, of which a copy was kindly sent me by Mr. George Lindsey.[6] This I omitted because, considering the relations between the two men, and Hume's somewhat mischievous influence in U.C. affairs, I did not think that his commendation would do Mackenzie any good. But I will most gladly give it a place if anyone else thinks otherwise. But I repeat my statement—that wherever I found anything in M's favor I put it in—. Let me recall from memory a few favourable opinions.

—John Galt's as to his ability as a journalist.

—James Wilson's (of Prince Edward) as to his usefulness in the Assembly.

—Bidwell (I think) and Jesse Ketchum to the same effect.

—Donald McLeod as to his disinterestedness.

—Thos. S. Brown to the same effect.

—James Lesslie of the Examiner as to his public services in general and his personal integrity.

These men, it is true, were all, with the exception of Galt, his close political allies; but it is not my fault if a man who was so absolutely unsparing of his opponents, and who quite unnecessarily made opponents of so many men, did not receive any golden testimonials from them. In many places I have recorded my own opinion that in the man's nature there were elements of proof; that in money matters he had an underlying kindliness which his faults of temper sadly obscured but never wholly destroyed; that his general aims were benevolent. I have repelled the accusation brought against him of cowardice. I have spoken of the fidelity of the friends through whose protection and assistance he made his escape to to the United States; and to have faithful friends is always to a man's credit. I have contrasted his willingness to accept posts of responsibility and danger with the timidity of Rolph. I have said all I was warranted in saying about his affection for his family, and have mentioned his wife in terms of high respect. I do not see how I would have made more or better use than I have made of such data as I possessed telling in his favour. I gave the incident of his kindness to a woman who was a fellow-passenger with him on board the Steamer *Waterloo* and quoted his generous appreciation of the French Canadians. These are just the things I remember at the moment, but with the book before me I could point out others.

The fact is that while I omitted purposely many things which told against Mackenzie, I did not omit purposely one solitary item that came under my notice telling in his favour.

My own recollections go back to Mackenzie's latter days. No myth had gathered round him at that time, when events were still fresh in the recollections of the whole generation over 40 years of age. And is not this significant—that Mr. Lindsey, who published his life within a year after his death which occurred on the 21st August, 1861, has not published one scrap of newspaper comment called forth by that event? Turn to Robinson's book[7] and see what he has published about his father taken from journals of the period, to see what they did say on the occasion of his death; but as Mr. Lindsey had not given a line from any paper, save a poem that had been published in the "Globe," I did not think that anything very favorable to the deceased was to be found. The inference rather was that the comments were not favorable, but I did not go after them on that account.

You speak of me as defending the Family Compact. My chief defence of them has been drawn from Mackenzie's own writings [which] time and again mentioned particular members of the class with approval; [which] lauded their judges and appealed with confidence to their Courts; and [which] brought almost no specific charges against any of them, though he vituperated them in general in the grossest terms. Apart from this, any defence contained in my book consists of nothing more than asking or rather suggesting that the old system of government should be judged in reference to time and place. I could have gone much further than I did; for I could have quoted from the correspondence of Sir Charles Bagot (a governor with a high reputation for liberality) testimonials to the high personal worth of the members of the party so styled.

In more than one place I distinctly intimated that the system was one which the development of the country was more and more rendering obsolete and unsuitable; but what I have tried to hint is that the new system had and has its dangers, and that it does not do to assume that, because a system has a fine name it will work well without watching.

And what are the papers telling you every day about corruption and abuses, the waste of the public money and the public domain that have sprung up under responsible government? Do you think the people will not pardon me for saying—"Here is your problem—You thought you had solved it when you got a system called responsible government; but you haven't solved it yet, because you have only very partially succeeded in making governments responsible." There is nothing in that, let me tell you, to insult or even to offend a free people.

And now for the conclusion of the matter. I cannot make any substantial alteration in the book. I could not do it conscientiously, and therefore I will not do it at all. But far from objecting to emphasizing a little more whatever was good in M's character, I would do it with pleasure, if I could only see my way to it, and in reading the proofs I would keep that in view. I think every man is entitled to have his good points made as much of as they will reasonably bear. . . . If you want more than this, I cannot meet your view . . .

Do not suppose I have any grievance. I have none. You are as fully entitled to your point of view—needless to say—as I to mine. I simply know my own mind in this matter, and see a clear course ahead of me.

Faithfully yours,
W.D. LeSueur

20. The Task at Hand (1911)

W.D. LeSueur to John Lewis—December 26, 1911

I note what you say in your letter . . . about the "human element" and also your impression that Lindsey has not been fairly dealt with.

The human element appeals to me as it does to you: to whom does it not appeal who has any humanity in him? It depends however upon the sense a man has of the importance of the duty confided to him, how much he may yield to, and how much he must fight against, considerations of friendship, personal obligations, etc.

I felt that I had a very important task in hand. I was not over-confident of my ability to perform it in the best way. Several times I said to Morang that, *if I succeeded* in writing the book as I felt it ought to be written, it would constitute, I thought, a valuable and more or less permanent addition to Canadian history.

Mackenzie had never been adequately dealt with: the best had never been made of his good points *as a man*, nor had any one ever unveiled the full extent of his mischievous and unscrupulous demagoguism. Charles Lindsey had more or less disguised this under generalities; but Mackenzie, who had a character, was not a man whom you could describe in generalities. To say that he sometimes indulged in irrelevant arguments; that he was not very constant in his opinions; that he was not very accurate in his statements; that he was not always consistent in the positions he took—these are mere phrases: so long as you remember them you have received at second hand a conventional idea of the man. To make the image vivid, to make the man live, somebody must quote his own words: show how frequently the same indefensible, sometimes shockingly untrue, things were repeated, to what terrible

---

SOURCE: Lindsey Papers—Lindsey Section, Vol. v, File: "Lindsey vs. LeSueur—Evidence at Trial." Public Archives of Ontario. This letter in the Lindsey Papers does not identify LeSueur's correspondent, but the letter is quoted by Kenneth Windsor in the *Literary History of Canada* (Toronto: University of Toronto Press, 1973), p. 230, where the correspondent is identified as John Lewis, author of *George Brown* (1906) in the "Makers" series.

excesses of scurrility he did not hesitate to give way, how uniformly he ascribed the worst of motives to his opponents; how little he cared about misleading the ignorant as to the true condition of public affairs; how his hatred of opponents completely dominated his interest in practical measures of reform; and then show how, in spite of all this, there was a sound core of humanity in the man; that he had a soul above mere party politics; that, unscrupulous as he was as to means, he had, in the largest sense, good ends in view; finally that an indomitable soul went to wreck through the tempestuousness of its own passions.

Mackenzie emerges from my pages no ordinary man. Any one inheriting his blood has a chance of inheriting something verging on greatness. That deadly energy of his was almost genius in itself. .

Others emerge from my pages in a guise which will disappoint many. Colonial secretaries, lieutenant-governors, judges, office-holders under the old system have been ruthlessly robbed by me of those repulsive features under which an enlightened posterity has loved to contemplate them. They were all, or nearly all, decent old-fashioned folk doing their duty in the several stations to which they had been called in an honest old-fashioned way—not entirely unsuited to the comparatively undeveloped situation of the country. Morang no doubt rolled up his eyes to heaven and held up his hands in horror as he dictated to his type-writer the words (addressed to me): "You have defended the Family Compact!" To take away a favourite object of detestation is, I know, a worse offense against the public than to impair an object of worship. Still, if I was called to anything in this world I was called to the duty of speaking the truth. In this case it happens (I think it happens in most cases) that the truth is favorable at once to sanity and clarity of view, as it also is to charity in our appraisal of all the actors on the scene. A favourite word with Carlyle was "credible," as you will doubtless remember. Well I have not *aimed* at being "credible." A man must be content to be "incredible" some times, but my story has, in an eminent degree, if I am not mistaken, the virtue of credibility *because* founded on truth. . . .

21. The Teaching of History (1912)

To the Editor of *The Gazette:*

Sir,—Will you allow me to offer a few remarks in continuation of the discussion on the teaching of history, which took place at last Friday's meeting of the Protestant Teachers' Association, as reported in The Gazette of the following day. The principal speaker on that occasion appears to have been Prof. J.L. Morison, of Queen's, who, your report states, "could not find words strong enough to apply to the current text books which he referred to as one of the chief products of the devil," and who also declared that history "was singularly and almost universally badly taught," and that "the students who came to him were absolutely hindered by what they had learned in that branch." From this it may fairly be inferred that, if the students in question had learned nothing of history at school, they would be better prepared than they now are to pursue the study of history in a rational manner at college.

I am quite ready, myself, to believe that the professor's strong statement of the case does not seriously over-shoot the mark. The fundamental trouble I take to be the almost complete lack in the general mind of any true conception of what history is. Glancing far back into the past I recall an incident which perhaps may be used to illustrate my meaning. I was at the interesting age of ten or eleven when, in a reflective mood, I remarked to a school fellow of about my own years, who afterwards became a member of the Dominion House of Commons, that it must be a very difficult thing to write poetry, by which of course, I meant nothing more than making lines, measure and rhyme. "No, it isn't," was the reply, "all you've got to do is to buy a quite new book that no one ever saw before with poetry in it, and then learn the poetry off." The answer was given in all sincerity. To my companion's mind the book that nobody ever saw before—bookseller and printer seemed to have no place in his calculations—was a true First Cause of poetry, behind which nothing could be conceived. Being perhaps a little more given to abstract thought than he, I tried to show that there

---

SOURCE: *Montreal Gazette* (October 9, 1912), p. 11.

was something at fault in his theory of the genesis of poetry, but without much success.

Well, it is not going too far to say that there are many today who, to all intents and purposes look upon the book as the first cause and primal source of history; and consistently therewith the teaching of history is understood as the unloading on the child's mind of the information contained in prescribed texts. The truth of the matter is something very different, namely that we must make our history for ourselves almost as much as we must make our poetry, if our ambition chances to lie in that direction. The friend of my youth in those old Montreal High School days thought that taking poetry was the same thing as making it; and today children are taught to take history from books just as they might take apples from a barrel—the history just as authentic and finished and integral a product as the apple. But only in so far as we have a personal conviction well or ill-grounded, but sincere, as to how things happened in the past, and, as to the relation of one event to another, have we entered into the realm, or breathed the air, or caught the spirit of history?

How can school children, it may be asked, attain to such convictions? Can they investigate for themselves and boldly settle doubtful historical problems? Must they not receive some one version of history on authority? They should receive nothing on authority, I would reply. They should be distinctly told that in history there is no authority in the strict sense of the word; that there are simply authors, some better, some worse informed; some more, some less competent; some with clearer, some with obscurer vision; some more accurate in observation and statement, some less so; some with too little imagination, some with too much; some who theorize to excess, some whose facts have no theory to hold them together; some radical in their views and some conservative; some who have no fixed point of view; some swayed by national, some by theological prejudice; some whose judgments are warped by party passion or private interest; some flatterers of power, some of the populace; some mere rhetoricians, some special pleaders, some servile copyists, some simple prevaricators; finally that no one at his best is able to do more than approximate to the truth in his redaction or interpretation of facts.

Troja fuit: Troy was; it had its day, it ceased to be. The task of history is to enable us to re-live in thought that vanished life and other vanished lives. To the question, "Can these bones live?" we may well reply: "O Lord, Thou knowest." To my mind it adds vastly to the interest and fascination of history to regard it, not as a finished immutable record, something that may be taught with the same confidence as the use of the globes, or the chemistry of combustion, or the general sequence of geological phenomena, but as something in its nature imperfect because immense and inexhaustible,—a perpetual challenge to acuteness of mind, soundness of judgment, sureness of instinct and ripeness of knowledge to attempt at least some partial triumph of resurrection and reconstruction. The dry bones will certainly not come to life under the touch of Dryasdust.

One of the best of recent historical writers in the United States, Mr. Sydney George Fisher, has said:

> There is no person whose statement on any point can be absolutely accepted; and any one who supposes that he can write a final and authoritative account of any historical event is likely to find himself disappointed.

The conclusion of this sentence, in the general drift of which I wholly concur, seems to me a little weak; I should feel disposed to say: "has never grasped the true nature of history."

But I fear I am forgetting the value of your space, and must hasten my conclusion. For children of tender years, say, up to the age of fourteen, history considered as criticism and reconstruction is wholly unsuited; while history in the form of flat affirmation, or of appeal to local or national self-esteem, is absolutely injurious. Instead of history formally delivered as such, let them have ballad, epic, lyric or drama, with no more of a guarantee of the external facts narrated or assumed than you would give with a fairy tale. Let them simply know that this is Tennyson's, or Kipling's, or Kingsley's, or Macaulay's, or Shakespeare's, or Virgil's or Homer's conception of how things occurred. Let prose readings be given as well, and let them be credited not to history, but to the particular authors as interpreters, each in his own way and according to his own lights of the past. Do not make the Muse of History, who, after all, by her name, only claims to know things by report, responsible for all the deeds of her followers. Let the object be to instill noble conceptions, high views of life and duty into the minds of the young, and whatever can serve that purpose use freely. Do not guarantee the facts, but make sure that the ideals are such as shall help to upbuild a true manhood and womanhood. Even in college the teaching of facts as facts should be severely restricted as being at war with the essential nature of history, which is not affirmation but enquiry. The certificate that history gives is not that so and so is the case, but that, after such enquiry as the matter at present admits of, so and so appears to be the case. A registrar of lands does not certify that your title is good; he merely certifies as to the previous transactions which bear on the question of title. The student should be encouraged to read widely; but the main thing is to impress him with a true conception of history—its methods, resources, possibilities, limits, difficulties and inevitable uncertainties. In this region alone might almost be found the elements of a liberal education.

W.D. LeSueur
Ottawa, October 7, 1912.

22. History, Its Nature and Methods (1912)

. . . What I propose to consider is the nature of History, what history is, how we should regard it, and what we may expect from it. The law of development holds good here, as generally throughout human affairs. The modern notion of history could not have existed in any age when there was no specific demand for objective truth. There was a Muse of History in ancient times, but her name, Clio, meant little more than "report" and report is not a very solid basis for history. As that respectable writer G.F. Daunou once observed, the proper and safe equivalent of "on dit" is "personne n'affirme," or "rien ne prouve," and as regards most "on dits" it would be well to make a rule of taking the other side of the equation. "On" is not a responsible party. Etymologists tell us that it is a shortened form of "homme"; but until "homme" gives us his name and address, and signifies the source of his information, he is not highly entitled to credence.

The word "History," is of more promise, for it points to enquiry and knowledge founded on enquiry. It is in the sense of enquiry that Herodotus uses it in the opening sentence of his happily surviving narrative, in which, indeed, are many things difficult to believe, but which taken as a whole, makes delightful and not uninstructive reading.

The idea that history involved investigation was a fruitful one; and, as time went on, the need for objective truth in history was more deeply felt and more strongly affirmed. Not that the progress was unbroken. Allowance must be made for changing times and the varying tempers and capacities of different writers. The bow of a Thucydides could not be bent by a Xenophon, nor yet by a Livy. Each man exercises by preference his own special gifts; and Livy, with his *lactea uberias*,[8] aimed rather at literary effect and at flattering the national pride of his countrymen than at analysing political situations. Thucydides abstained from flattering the Athenians, though he shows a desire to

SOURCE: *Proceedings of the Royal Society of Canada* (1913), Appendix A, LVII-LXXXIII. This was LeSueur's Presidential Address to the R.S.C.

enable them to understand and duly value their best national qualities. With the break up of the Roman civilisation and the advent of a new order of things marked by the predominance of supra-mundane conceptions and interests, history sank to a far inferior level, from which it had gradually to rise, partly through the revival of letters in the Renaissance, and partly thorough the later development of the scientific spirit.

The idea we all have to-day is that history is a narrative—a true narrative—of past events. When a definition is given it is assumed that the terms of the definition are perfectly understood; but sometimes, upon looking into those terms, we find that they give us a good deal to think about. The word "narrative" gives us something to think about, and so does the word "events." If a man is to give us a narrative he must *connect* his events, as a string of disconnected events is not a narrative. Life flows like a stream; it is continuous, not discontinuous, and history must aim at showing us its continuity. When we say history we mean the historian, and it is upon the historian, the man, therefore, that we must depend to make history intelligible to us. Yet no one man can take a universal point of view. He can only see with his own eyes, measure by his own judgment, and understand with his own heart. Does the heart seem a strange thing to understand with? I seem to remember the phrase "an understanding heart," used in a book in which words are seldom misapplied. There must, therefore, always be a subjective element in anything that can be called history. Each man consciously or unconsciously has his own fundamental philosophy, his own insight into human nature, his own standards of the credible and the incredible. Would we strip him of all philosophy, of all cannons of judgment? In that case what could he do but stare like an infant at whatever phenomenon happened to be before his eyes? He certainly could not, in any true sense, understand it or make others understand it.

But if the narrator is influenced in the presence of events by his own subjectivity, there is more than a possibility that he will also be influenced in some degree by his social, political or national environment, or by all three at once. It is now very generally acknowledged that the histories written in the United States for nearly a hundred years after the conclusion of the struggle with the Mother Country, gave, with few exceptions, a most partial view both of the causes of the war and of the events that marked its course. To-day conditions have changed, and American historians are presenting a very different, and far juster, picture of the same series of events. Great Britain now appears rather as the patient and indulgent parent, erring in judgment at time, but never sinning past forgiveness, and usually willing to repair her faults as fast as they were pointed out. This more liberal and equitable spirit in which history has lately been written has doubtless acted upon public opinion, but a previous change in public opinion, a growing and deepening consciousness of the difficulties which the problems of government present, and of the defects in every form of government, has probably not been without influence on the historians themselves.

Allowance must be made for the difficulties attaching to the observation of facts. Pious Aeneas, when he was giving to Queen Dido the tragic particulars of the sack of Troy, was able to say "quorum magna pars fui,"[9] but it is impossible even for a man who is a great part of events to see everything. When you are engaged in street fighting, your attention is apt to be much occupied with the matter in hand; and if you happen to have your aged parent on your back, and to be making what speed you can from a scene of carnage, the opportunities for observation are not much improved. Still the pious hero made a thrilling narrative of it, too thrilling indeed for Dido's peace of mind. Like Desdemona, she loved him for the dangers he had passed, but unhappily he had business elsewhere. A fragment of Euripides that some one has preserved, says that Ares is favorable to falsehoods; and truly there has been a terrible amount of lying, or at least misrepresentation, about battles. After Borodino the Russian general reported that he had inflicted terrific loss on the French; putting on the soft pedal he added: "La nôtre a été sensible."

"In war," one of the leading English weeklies lately observed, "all the strongest passions of man unite to pervert or obliterate the truth." It assigns the palm for lying, however, to the painters of battle scenes; perhaps because they deliberately, and not under the influence of any excitement, paint into their pictures details that they know had no existence in reality. Examples of this indeed are not far to seek. But in much less exciting and more restricted affairs than battles observation is far from being so simple or so sure a thing as is commonly supposed. Eye witnesses differ in their testimony often in perfectly good faith:—everything depends on what catches one's attention. We go to see a conjurer, and lo! things without number are taken out of hats that never were in hats, and terrible acts of destruction are wrought on watches and other precious articles, which nevertheless emerge scathless from their trying adventures. All this is what our captured senses tell us; but it is not only when we visit such a performance that our senses are captured. The thing happens more or less every day. A transaction would have to be of a decidedly simple character, the situation of the observer a very favourable one, and his faculties very wide awake in order to preclude the possibility of error in reporting it. History must everywhere accept and make the best it can of human limitations.

History has been vitiated in the past by much of sheer misrepresentation; but in the use of so-called "authorities" many other points have to be guarded. The whole science of historical criticism comes in here. By what motives were the writers swayed? What pains, if any, did they take to be well informed? What were their sources of information? What degree of intelligence in the treatment of facts do they display? To what prejudices were they manifestly or probably subject? How far were they free to speak the truth? Truth has always been more praised than popular; and it is a very happy state of things where it can be told without reserve. Bishop Burnet got such a fright over the death on the scaffold of his friend Lord William Russell that he sought the favour of Charles II by offering to represent his actions in the most favorable light in the memoirs he was then writing. Yet, on the whole, the worthy and robust bishop has told a pretty fair story; though his anti-Catholic prejudices betrayed him sadly in the matter of the birth of a son to James II. As to biography the remark was lately made by one of the most prominent writers of the present day, Mr. H.G. Wells, that, speaking generally, it is false with "the worst of all falsehoods, the falsehood of omission," the reason, we must suppose, being that biographies are frequently written by those who have a direct interest in guarding the reputation of the subject, or by others upon whom they have imposed the obligation to do so. As materials for history, therefore, biographies, when proceeding from the environment of the subject are open to no small amount of legitimate suspicion. They may contain much truth; but how about the truth they do not contain? What says the learned Cujacius? "Quae non est plena veritas, est plane falsitas, non semi-veritas." In plain English: "Incomplete truth is not half truth but whole falsehood."

The claim is put forward in some quarters, that literary, as well as personal, reputations must be protected; and that, if a man has acquired glory for his nation by his works, that glory should be looked upon us as a national asset, not to be diminished by a belittling criticism. Thus, in the early part of the last century, Chateaubriand made a brilliant reputation for himself, and reflected glory on his nation, by such works as "Le Génie du Christianisme," "Les Martyrs," and "Les Révolutions." But, from the historical point of view, these works, notwithstanding their extraordinary eloquence and *éclat*, were of little value; and M. Jules leMaître, in a recent series of *Conférences*, ventured to say so, whereupon a French critic takes him to task as follows:

⸂ Supposing even the criticisms made to be well founded, it is just as unsuitable to touch, without due respect, the conception which, for the last century, we have been entertaining of the man, as it is to make too much of the tediousness of certain tragedies of Racine. It is not permitted to one of our own people to measure our heritage of glory by his own personal taste. Just as truly as superstitions *create* life, so prejudices *minister* to the moral life of nations. For our own part we are quite content to be blind, if, thanks to that weakness, we retain the power to act.

This is not the note of "magna est veritas," yet must it be confessed that a certain enfeeblement of popular ideals may in certain cases result from an unsparing literary or historical criticism. Truth has sometimes to be bought with a price. The fact is that history and criticism to-day are continually at war with the myth-making, legend-forming, tendencies of mankind. It is not what is true that takes the strongest hold on the popular mind; it is what is cast in a mould to fit popular needs; and when the people want to believe a thing it is very hard to prevent their doing so. The story of William Tell was long since proved by a number of historical investigators, including several Swiss ones, to be wholly without foundation; yet the popular belief in it is still strong, as is shown by the erection, as lately as the year 1895, of a fine statue of Tell, the work of the Swiss sculptor Kissling, in the market-place of Altdorf, and the opening in 1899, just outside that town, of a permanent theatre, in which Schiller's play of William Tell is to be represented every Sunday during the summer season.* Neither peoples nor individuals like to be disturbed in their pleasant illusions. Many a time has the hellebore of criticism extorted the cry: "Pol, me occidistis amici!"[10]

The greatest satirist of the age, Anatole France, touches in the preface of his not very edifying book, "L'Ile des Pingouins" on this question of the restraints put by popular prejudice on history. He represents himself as having applied to an historian of high repute for some hints as to how he should write a book of his own, which was to be of an historical character: "I come sir," he said on entering the learned gentleman's library, "to get the benefit of your experience. I am struggling with a work of history, and am not making much headway." Shrugging his shoulders the distinguished author replied:

My poor friend, why are you bothering yourself to compose a history, when all you have to do is to follow the general practice and copy the best known ones? If you have any new view or any original idea; if you present men and things in an unexpected light, you will take the reader by surprise, and readers do not like that. They only seek in a history the stupid things they know already. Try to instruct your reader, and you will only humiliate and vex him. Don't try to enlighten him; he will cry out that you are insulting his beliefs. Historians copy one another, and thus spare themselves toil and escape being thought conceited. Imitate them, and don't be original. An original historian is an object of universal distrust, scorn and disgust. Do you think, he added,

*Encyclopaedia Britannica, 11th edition, article "William Tell."

that I should have been considered and honoured as I am if I had put any novelties into my historical works? What are novelties? Impertinences.

The satirist here has indulged in a little humorous exaggeration, but he sets in a strong light the truth, that to revise history, where the prejudices, to say nothing of the interests, of men are concerned, is hardly less difficult than to revise a theological creed.

Not infrequently history is found to be corrupted in its very source. If an original narrative is false or exaggerated it may easily happen that the mistatements it contains will be repeated from age to age by a series of uncritical writers, and thus pass into unquestioned, not to say, unquestionable tradition. Count Frontenac, in a despatch to the French Government gave a greatly exaggerated official report of the Lachine massacre. Charlevoix took his word for numbers and details, and Charlevoix's account has become classic.[1ª] It is in all the popular histories. But how do we know that Frontenac exaggerated? Through the careful researches of the late Hon. Mr. Justice Girouard in parish registers. Not half the number reported by Frontenac as killed were missing after the disaster. In this case there were motives for misrepresentation. There was the ever-operative motive of trying to impress the French Government with the dangers to which the colony was exposed, so as to get more liberal supplies in men, money and material; and there was a special motive on the part of Frontenac who had just been sent back to Canada for his second term as Governor, of showing how terrible a calamity had overtaken the colony in his absence. Denonville, the retiring Governor, had just a few weeks before, ordered the abandonment and destruction of Frontenac's favourite fort of Cataraqui, and this did not help to put the two men, who already differed greatly in temperament and principles, on better terms.

Every student of Canadian history will remember Father Rochemonteix's criticism of the *Relations des Jésuites*, a series of annals which, on the whole, like the rest of the world, he highly esteemed.[12] He said in effect that they consisted of carefully selected incidents of a particular character and significance, and did not, therefore, correctly reflect the normal life of the country. What the good fathers had mainly in view was to interest their countrymen in the work of missions in Canada. From the despatches of Frontenac and the *Relations des Jésuites* to the Commentaries of Caesar is a far cry; but, perspicuous and doubtless, in the main, accurate as those famous writings are, it has been said of them, probably with truth, that they "were primarily intended to serve an immediate political purpose, and are indeed a defence, framed with the most consummate skill, of the author's whole Gallic policy and of his constitutional position." A parallel has been drawn between the position of Caesar in Gaul and that of Clive or Warren Hastings in India; and it is not difficult to imagine that the administration of the distant dependencies of a great empire, under conditions very far from static, might give rise to situations in which it would be practically impossible to keep within the prescribed bounds, or meet the demands of a public opinion formed at the seat of empire without any sufficient knowledge of local facts. Hence, no doubt, certain reticences and certain adroit turns in official correspondence, which later the historian or the historical critic must only do his best to discern and understand. Look where you will among the men of action and achievement, and the rule will be found to hold that, while they speak from a point of view of great command, and while what they have to tell us is of the highest interest and often of great moment, they do not tell us everything. They tell us what they consider it is good for us to know, and thus prepare the channels in which they think opinion should run. As a rule the absolute truth-tellers like Pepys and Rousseau have not been very edifying persons; nor has veracity always been illustrated in their daily lives. After all, what is truth? No more puzzling question was ever asked, and the mathematic that will solve it has yet to be invented.

In the year 1668 a French writer, La Mothe le Vayer, who had the honour of being associated with the education of Louis XIV, published a treatise entitled "Du peu de certitude qu'il y a dans l'histoire," which has been considered by some as marking that the beginning of wisdom in historical matters is to recognize with that sage writer the little certainty there is in history, as it has often, we may indeed say generally, been written, and its liability to error at all times. It is not impossible, in most cases of importance, to get dates right; and the same thing applies to names and places and all facts expressible in numbers or otherwise narrowed down to a point. The terms of original documents, treaties, charters, laws, edicts, etc., can be reproduced with exactness; inscriptions can be deciphered and more or less correctly interpreted; manuscripts can be collated, and texts purified; in all such matters a marked approach to accuracy and finality has been made within the last half century. There are flourishing schools of historical criticism in France, England, Germany, Italy and the United States; and writers are consequently held to a much stricter account for what they give to the world as history than formerly. It was a most inadequate and commonplace view of history that was put forward by the great Dr. Johnson when he said, *teste* Boswell:

Great abilities are not necessary for an historian; for in historical composition all the greatest powers of the mind are quiescent. He has the facts ready to his hand, so there is no exercise of imagination. Imagination is not required in any high degree; only about as much as is used in the lower kinds of poetry. Some penetration, accuracy, and colouring will fit a man for the task, if he can give the application which is necessary.

From the modern point of view to say that the historian has the facts ready to his hand seems hardly less than childish. It would be nearer the truth to say that he has no facts ready to his hand; for the careful sifting of facts is his particular duty. And then, what is a fact? At the outset it was remarked that, while it was easy to say that history was a narrative of past events, the terms of the definition might call for a good deal of consideration. So far we have been discussing what goes to the making of the narrative. Now we are confronted with the question, what is a fact? Is there such a thing as a simple fact? If there is I would venture to say it cannot have any meaning; certainly the nearer a fact approaches to absolute simplicity the less meaning it has. Caesar was assassinated——let us leave out place and date: is that a simple fact? By no means: it affirms the death of a man called Caesar, but it brings on the scene one or more assassins, on whose part are implied motives of hatred, envy, or patriotism according to the view that may be taken of the matter. They may all have been honourable men, or they may have been men who could not tolerate the sight of real greatness. To a man who had never heard of Caesar, and had no idea when or where he had lived, or how or why he had been put to death, the bare assertion of the fact would be wholly unmeaning. A good many years ago, news was telegraphed from the East that the Akhound of Swat had died. No doubt he was somebody; but so entirely ignorant were our western folk of where Swat was or what kind of person an Akhound would be when he was at home, that the announcement struck a clever New York journalist—a Canadian by the way—as surpassingly funny; and having a leisure moment, he wrote a kind of mock threnody on the sad event, which still survives as a jeu d'esprit of more than ordinary note. Just so might the announcement of the death of a European sovereign have struck the swarthy subjects of the Akhound, except that Easterns, not possessing the same exquisite sense of humour that we do, are not so much disposed to ridicule things simply because they know nothing about them. East or West, however, it remains true that a fact which calls up no other facts is meaningless. The root of the word "about" is "out." What lies *outside* of the thing must be apprehended before the inside of it can be understood. As Carlyle says: "Only in the whole is the partial to be truly discerned." Only through some knowledge of the state of parties at Rome, of the republican traditions of the state, of the civil struggles of the previous thirty or forty years, of Caesar's own career as statesmen and soldier, can we have any true conception of the meaning of his assassination by Brutus, Cassius and the rest. Failing such knowledge he is no more to us that the Akhound of Swat was to the man who set thousands laughing over the not essentially ridiculous fact of his demise.

The facts of life form a whole, consequently any analysis of them must be more or less artificial. When and where, for example, did the French Revolution begin? When and where did it end? Some doubt whether it has ended yet. We cannot pick an event or a fact off the tree of history as we pick an apple off an apple-tree. The apple will come off by itself, without necessarily disturbing other apples, and, when we get it, we get the whole of it. The fact does not come off by itself, and whole; it is vitally connected with other facts, and just where to sever it is often a troublesome question. This aspect of the matter must have been present to the mind of Carlyle when he exclaimed: "Consider history, with the beginnings of it stretching dimly into remote time, emerging darkly out of the mysterious enternity!" And again when he wrote:

By very nature it is a labyrinth and chaos, this that we call human history—an abbatis of trees and brushwood, a world-wide jungle at once growing and dying—you will find the fibrous roots of this day's occurrences among the dust of Cadmus and Trismegistus, of Tubal-cain and Triptolemus . . . At bottom there is no perfect history, there is none such conceivable. Histories are as perfect as the historian is wise, and is gifted with an eye and a soul.

If the Sage of Chelsea and the author of "The Rambler" have met in the Elysian Fields, they may perhaps have thrashed out this matter of the nature and bounds of history. Carlyle had the advantage of being born nearly a century later than Johnson and, it must be admitted, was much the profounder nature of the two. The great German historian Droysen speaks of the moral world as "an endless interlocking of actions, situations, interests and passions." It is clear that, from such an interlocking, facts cannot so easily be disengaged. To isolate a fact absolutely is almost as impossible as the task which was set Shylock of taking his pound of flesh without shedding a drop of blood.

Let two men work independently on the same period of history; give them access to the same documents and other sources of information, let them agree as to general methods, and let them be as free from prejudice as is possible for poor humanity, yet will they not tell you exactly the same tale. On some points they will agree, but not in all. "History," it has lately been said by an able writer, Prof. Henri Berr of the University of Toulouse, "is applied psychology." Each of us has his own psychology, that is to say his own conceptions as to how the mind of man works, as to the relative force of motives, the inward significance of outward actions. These conceptions we bring to bear on our understanding of the present, and these we also apply, with a certain allowance for historical parallax, to our interpretation of the past.

This is practically Emerson's view of the matter. The fact narrated, he says, must correspond to something in ourselves before it can be credible or intelligible to us. He holds that there is no age or state of society or mode of action to which there is not something correspondent in the life of each of us. As the psychologies of men differ, so will the versions they give us of past events differ. Is this a disadvantage? If it were there would still be no help for it; but fortunately we need not so regard it. On the contrary, if different interpretations are given to us, our minds gain in flexibility, in sympathy, in breadth, by entertaining, or at least considering, each in turn, nor are we by so doing, debarred from finally adopting the one that suits our own psychology best.

But is it not important, it may be asked, that we should know exactly how things happened? Is it not possible to get the truth without any admixture of personal elements? It is to be feared not. In the language of the apostle "Habemus thesaurum istum in vasis fictilibus"—"we have this treasure in earthen vessels." Give us some sublimated spirit, free from all earthly limitations and passions, to write history for us, and perhaps you might get what you want, and yet after all how could spirits of that kind, who knew nothing of human passion, deal with history that is full of human passions?

Very different views of the function and the value of history have been taken by different eminent persons. The great Bossuet, in the introduction to his "Discours sur l'Histoire Universelle," written, it will be remembered, for the instruction of the Dauphin, son of Louis XIV, says that, even if history were of little advantage to ordinary people, it should still be taught to princes, as the best means of enlightening them as to the passions and interests of men, as to times and seasons, and the respective effects of good and evil counsels. All that history contains seems to be for their special benefit and guidance. It was Lord Bolingborke, half a century later, who uttered the maxim that history was philosophy teaching by example. The Abbé Sieyes, on the other hand, had no faith in what he called "the alleged truths of history"—"les prétendues vérités historiques"; he thought the past could never be read aright, and that if it could there was nothing to be gained from it. This was also, practically, Jeremy Bentham's opinion. Not long ago a leading London weekly, referring to the troubles in Ireland, expressed the idea, in an article entitled "The Curse of History," that it would be a good thing if all history could be wiped out, so that the memory of old feuds might be obliterated. Napoleon described history as a "mensonge convenu." Prince Bismarck is stated to have been devoted to history. "In the full maturity of his experience," says a writer in the *Quarterly Review*,

> he delivered himself of the opinion that a properly conducted study of history must be the necessary foundation of knowledge for every statesman; that by this means alone can be learnt what is possible to attain in the various transactions with different states; and that the whole of the diplomatic art lies in the capacity for recognising the limits of the attainable.

Carlyle speaks of history as "the true fountain of knowledge, by whose light alone, whether consciously or unconsciously employed, can the present or the future be interpreted or guessed at." An able writer of our own time, John C. Crozier,[13] a Canadian by birth, but whose home has for years past been in London, England, agrees that "the present is ever a mystery to us until it is irradiated by some knowledge of the past"; he contends, at the same time, that while such knowledge may *account* for the conditions existing to-day it does not really explain those conditions, or point to the line of conduct which is best to pursue under them. To read history, says another—I forget at this moment who—is to travel through time, the knowledge thus acquired being analogous to that acquired by travelling through space. The observant traveller and the thoughtful reader will both be the better and the wiser for their excursions. The historian Froude, thinks that it is an abuse of history to try to make it teach any lessons whatever. "If," he says,

> Homer and Shakespeare are what they are from the absence of everything didactic about them, may we not thus learn something of what history should be, and in what sense it should aspire to teach.

It can teach, he holds, simply by bringing us into close and living touch with persons and events. It is a drama, and should be presented as such without hints as to how, in the opinion of the author, it ought to be interpreted.

The authors of a very comprehensive article of History in the *Grande Encyclopédie*, the MM. Mortet, recognize three stages in its development, the Rudimentary, the Literary, and the Scientific. In the Rudimentary we have songs, epics, sagas, legendary tales, narratives which more or less flatter the pride of princes or the ruling class, family annals, inscriptions, &c. In the literary stage which followed, and which was long predominant, history was regarded as a department of literature, and was often written as a kind of literary exercise, or to set forth party views or to support this or that system of thought. The accurate and impartial narration of events was a secondary matter. The third or Scientific stage, upon which History is supposed to have entered half a century ago or more, is the stage of careful and minute investigation, conducted on lines suggested by experience and designed to secure the maximum of accuracy and the best possible presentation of the subject in hand.

But if history has entered on its final and scientific stage, all minds in the community have not entered on that stage, and of course, the minds of the young have not entered on it. A vigorous onslaught was made by one of our university professors not long ago on the historical teaching given in the public schools, and especially on the text books. These, he went so far as to ascribe to a very sinister spiritual parentage. To the ears polite of this audience I shall not venture to name the party he made responsible for them. If the Professor was correctly reported, he said that "nothing so perplexed him as to know how to deal with the students who came to him, who were actually hindered by what they had learned in that branch." It follows that it would be better not to teach history at all in the schools than to teach it by present methods and with the present text-books. But if the methods of teaching in this particular subject are so bad, and the text-books of so shocking a character, what is the reason? Is anything wrong with the subject? Rousseau, many of whose views on education were sound enough, said that he had learnt history too soon, and that it had given him false ideas. He recommended that the teaching of it should be deferred till the pupil was fifteen years of age. But fifteen years of age in Rousseau's time would mean seventeen or eighteen in our day, so greatly has the period of childhood been extended. It may be that children are learning too young the kind of history that is presented to them. It may be that greatly abbreviated history is either falsified history or unintelligible history. I almost think one might venture to say that, the more history is abbreviated, the more knowledge of history it requires to make head or tail of it.

In which of its three stages, the Rudimentary, the Literary or the Scientific, may we say that history is most suited to youthful minds? In the first, it can hardly be doubted, though in the second it may also have some attractions and impart some benefit. Boys love to hear or read of battles and of victories won by their own side, if they have a side; and it is a bad sign if they have not. Some modern instructors would tell them,

> You shouldn't be so much interested in battles. Battles belong to a barbarous age; you should be interested in social progress, the development of political liberty, the advancement of the arts and sciences.

This good advice, however, simply means, "You shouldn't be boys, you should be men, and not ordinary men either, but men of a superior intellectual type." Such advice is vain: we must take boys as we find them and adapt our teaching to their condition of mental, and even moral, development.

It must be confessed, I think, that the conditions existing in a new country are not favourable to the teaching of history, at least to the young, and that may be part of the difficulty to which our professor referred. In an old country signs and monuments of the past abound. In a new country they are rare, and such as exist do not relate to a very distant past. A past in which our grandfathers lived is almost the present. But, in varying degrees, all historic monuments help to create the historic sense, that sense which makes the past real to us, while it widens and deepens our conception of the life of humanity. A German writer, Otto Jager, the author of an excellent handbook on the Teaching of History, is of opinion that decidedly the best means of arousing the historic sense is the teaching of Latin, inasmuch as it brings before the mind, as hardly anything else can do, the existence ages ago of a people, greatly different from ourselves, who spoke that language, a people who did memorable deeds, founded a powerful state, had their own political struggles, their own foreign wars, and who subdued nation after nation till, finally, the whole world as then known was subject to their sway. That our own language should be shot through with words and forms of speech which once came warm from the mouths of Cicero and Ceasar or flowed from the stiles of Vergil and Horace and Ovid, tends powerfully to give to the Latin language the double character of that which has been and yet is. Once make one past real, our author contends, and all pasts may become real. The tyranny of the present and actual has been broken.

All this may be true; for my part I am disposed to think it is true; but if so it simply means that the *best* mode of approach to history as a study is not open to the great majority of our young people; for it would be vain to think of introducing the study of Latin into the public schools. There is a further admission to be made which will be regarded, I fear, at least in many quarters—as a most damaging one—that history possesses a certain aristocratic character. Where family traditions and records exist the past is invested with a reality which it cannot have for those in whose personal lives it is practically a blank. Has not "ancient history" become a popular term of contempt? Again, history in its rudimentary stage, as has already been noted, introduces us to kings and heroes, to individuals who stand out from the crowd by the greatness of their deeds and their uncontested leadership. Homer and Shakespeare have both been denounced as incurable and shameless aristocrats; nor has Walter Scott, in times much nearer our own, wholly escaped the same condemnation. History tells of valiant opposition in times past to misgovernment and tyranny; but the opposers were in most cases aristocrats themselves—the barons who brought King John to terms, the Falklands and Sidneys and Hampdens who withstood the exactions of Charles I, not to speak of the Gracchi who championed the rights of the Roman plebs. It cannot be said, however, that its presentation of strong personalities renders history unsuitable to engage the attention of the young, for the contrary is the case; it is only as it deals with striking characters and stirring events that it can interest the young at all. At the same time, if its general tendency is unfavourable to democratic ideas, one can understand a certain instinctive, if not conscious, objection, or at least indifference, to it in communities like our own, in which the profession of such ideas is *de rigueur*.

As regards school text-books a difficulty presents itself in the fact that they are condemned beforehand to be written in a tone of dreary and passionless neutrality, whenever questions are touched upon in regard to which public opinion is divided, and with excessive glorification of men who have played a prominent part in the country. In works of this class it is not the good that such men have done that is interred with their bones, but on the contrary whatever in their several records might dim their lustre, or offend their partizans of a later day. This applies particularly to countries whose history does not run back very far. When a country reaches a certain age it can afford to have a few scoundrels in the background. But, even in older countries, the weakness referred to is exemplified. "Many text-books," says Herr Jager, speaking of the Prussian system of education,

have found it possible to assure our youths that Frederick the Great was really a sound Christian. I do not know (he adds) whether it is quite true that our nation is free from national pride, but I do know that a healthy nation or an intelligent man must be able to endure the truth.

But again, what is truth? Where public opinion is divided, or where, strictly speaking, there is no public opinion worth mentioning, but only conflicting party opinions, what is the man to do who must perforce avoid offending either side? Doleful complaints have been made by persons who have written school histories with the best intentions in the world, of the ruthless way in which higher authorities have insisted on rectifying the very slightest divergence from the strict median line. Has our Canadian Professor fully considered all these things?

It would be a mistake to suppose that the world had to wait till the nineteenth century for any recognition of the true principles of historical composition. Changes of intellectual habit do not come in like a

Noachian deluge. It would not be far wrong to say that almost every sound historical principle has at one time or other been exemplified, if not formulated, by writers of the so called Literary period. Thucydides had not very much to learn from the moderns. In abatement of the claims of Thucydides and Polybius to be considered scientific historians, it has been alleged that their object was to instruct the reader in public affairs. It is not obvious, however, that such a purpose is inconsistent with the scientific writing of history; on the contrary it seems to call for the most scrupulous accuracy in narration, for how can one instruct in public affairs unless he reports public affairs correctly? In the excellent "Histoire de la Littérature Grecque" by the brothers Croiset it is remarked that a wrong interpretation has commonly been placed upon the expression κτῆμα ἐς ἀει applied by Thucydides to his work. It has been taken in much the sense as Horace's "Exegi monumentum"; but it was not in that same spirit at all that the Greek historian used it.[14] What he meant was that he had written with the express object of producing something permanently useful, not merely temporarily entertaining, and had consequently striven to make his history accurate and trustworthy. It is claimed by the writers mentioned that Thucydides knew the value of documents almost as well as the moderns, and that, as an historian, he is neither an Athenian nor a Spartan but a scholar, a savant. He carefully estimates the material forces of the contestants; but, with characteristic wisdom, endeavours also to estimate their intellectual and moral resources on which the utilization of material elements so largely depends. He is disposed to think, indeed, that the most important factor in national life and development is intelligence, σύνισις, an interesting word, as it signifies *the throwing of things together, or the establishment of relations,* which really is the prime task of the intellect.

"He does not believe," to quote or rather translate M. Croiset,

that history is always a lesson of morality. He sees things as they are without any optimistic illusions; . . . He recognizes that interest and force, much more than absolute justice, take the lead in controlling events.

In this attitude of mind also Thucydides approaches the modern school. Thomas Hobbes, it is well known, made a translation of Thucydides, which, if not as exact as modern scholarship could have made it, has a terseness and vigour not unworthy of the author of "Leviathan." The great Englishman had a boundless admiration for the great Athenian. "If the truth of a history," he says in his Introduction, "did ever appear by the manner of relating, it doth so in this history, so coherent, perspicuous, and persuasive is the whole narration and every part thereof.'' Macaulay declared Thucydides to be the greatest Historian that ever lived. Nothing, we are told by Macaulay's biographer, put that great writer so much out of conceit with himself as the sense of his inferiority to Thucydides. In brilliancy of style and in range of knowledge Macaulay had the advantage; and in narrative and constructive power he was not inferior. Wherein then lay the superiority of the Greek historian? It must be found, I think, in his wider grasp and more complete command of his subject. While Macaulay seeks for telling antitheses, and entangles himself in arguments from which special pleading is not always absent, Thucydides sets forth his facts with unfailing insight and a calm and luminous impartiality. The first is the unrivalled advocate, the second is the consummate judge from whose decision it were rash to appeal. Much as we admire Macaulay, no one sits at his feet: Macaulay himself was willing to sit at the feet of Thucydides.

There are, indeed, many evidences that, in the ancient world, history was not wholly sacrificed to literature. Caesar had the narrative art in perfection and, as a record of facts, his work is of high value. It was probably a serious work that Asinius Pollio had in hand, when Horace addressed him thus in the first Ode of his second Book:

> You are treating of the civic troubles that broke out when Metellus was consul; of the causes of the war; the faults that were committed; the changing phases of the struggle; the play of fortune; the fatal coalitions of leaders; and bring before our view weapons still stained with unexpiated blood—a work full of hazard, for your path lies over fires slightly covered by treacherous ashes.

Here are surely the main elements of history. The character of Tacitus as an historian has, it must be acknowledged, been much debated. His style was one studiously designed to catch and hold attention; but clearly he had a sound conception of the historian's art. ''Before I enter on my task,'' he says,

> it is desirable that I should recall what the situation in the capital was at the time; what the disposition of the troops; what the state of feeling in the provinces; what was sound, and what unsound, throughout the world at large; so as to show, not only what particular things happened—a matter largely of chance—but how events stood related to one another and from what causes they sprang.

The Greek Lucian too, a little later than Tacitus, took a right view of the subject when he said:

> A writer of history ought, so far as that is concerned, to be a foreigner without country, living under his own law only, subject to no king,

nor caring what any man may like or dislike; but setting forth the matter as it is.

If it had not been for the break which came with the downfall of the Roman Empire, the science of history, so far as it is a science, might have been established on firm foundations much earlier than it was.

In spite of the concessions we must make, and should cheerfully make, to the Scientific school, I think it will have to be maintained that the great age of history is the Literary age. Omitting the works of the ancients, it was that age which gave us in England the histories of Clarendon and Burnet, of Hume and Robertson, of Gibbon and Macaulay, of Carlyle and Froude; and that produced in France those of Bossuet and Fleury, of Tillemont and Montesquieu, of Chateaubriand and Thierry, of Thiers and Michelet. In all these, with the exception perhaps of Chateaubriand, a measure, sometimes a large measure, of the scientific spirit is present; and to Chateaubriand much must be forgiven for the flashes of divination which light up so many of his pages, particularly in the "Memoires d'Outre Tombe." These writers have all had their respective points of view; but can history, it may be asked, be written to any good purpose, or at all, without a point of view? Some remarks made by Sir Francis Palgrave on this point may be quoted with advantage.[15] "No person" he says

can ever attempt this historical enquiry who does not bring some favorite dogma of his own to the task—some principle which he wishes to support, some position which he is anxious to illustrate and defend—and it is quite useless to lament these tendencies to partiality, since they are the very incitements to the labour. . . . I have exerted myself, (he continues) to see the objects before me clearly and distinctly. I have endeavoured to place them in a proper light; and I have approached them as nearly as I could in order to assure the utmost accuracy . . . and, whilst I am most ready to admit that my eyes may often have deceived me, I hope that those who see dif ferently will admit that they also may, with equal unconsciousness on their part, be labouring un under a similar delusion.

This was written eighty-two years ago, and the advances that have since been made in historical method have not deprived it of much of its force.

At the same time the fact cannot be overlooked that some writers are less judicial in their tone of mind than others, and that some important historical works are strongly marked, not to say marred, by bias. In some cases again critics who were themselves decidedly biassed have raised the cry of bias against works far less open than their own to that accusation. What to one man is bias is to another a fair and natural way of looking at things. Bias, after all, when it is honest, is little else than the psychology of which we have already spoken. Of two ways of understanding a character or interpreting events one may commend itself to one man and the other to another. This is a matter of constant occurrence in the affairs of life, nor do we always accuse of bias those who differ from us, nor do they necessarily so accuse us. There is, however, a kind of bias, if it may still be so called, which goes beyond mere psychology, and which causes a man to make rather than to adopt conclusions and to colour his narrative to suit the complexion of his own thought. Macaulay has accused Hume of this in very round terms. "Hume," he says,

> is an accomplished advocate: without positively asserting much more than he can prove, he gives prominence to all the circumstances which support his case; he glides lightly over those which are unfavourable to it; his own witnesses are applauded and encouraged; the contradictions into which they fall are explained away; a clear and connected abstract of their evidence is given. Everything that is offered on the other side is scrutinized with the utmost severity; what cannot be denied is extenuated or passed by without notice; concessions even are sometimes made, but this insidious candour only increases the effect of the vast mass of sophistry.

A formidable indictment!—one in which some may think a certain exuberance of verbosity is not lacking. Yet who is the accuser? A man who so wrote history as to draw upon himself censure of identical character. "Though he (Macaulay) practised little in the courts," says Mr. George Saintsbury in his *History of Nineteenth Century Literature*,

> he had the born advocate's gift, or drawback, of inclination to *suppressio veri* and *suggestio falsi*, and he has a heavy account to make up under these heads. . . . It has to be confessed that independent examination of separate points is not very favourable to Macaulay's trustworthiness. He never tells a falsehood; but he not seldom contrives to convey one, and he constantly conceals the truth.

Yet Saintsbury fully recognizes the magnificence of Macaulay's achievement considered as a whole. Of his view of the state of England at the death of Charles II he says that it

> may challenge comparison, as a clearly arranged and perfectly mastered collection of innumerable minute facts, sifted out of a

thousand different sources, with anything in history ancient or modern.

Nor have later writers than Macaulay, whose work was done over sixty years ago, always succeeded in maintaining an impeccable impartiality. Taine was trained in a very severe school, and was looked upon some years ago as a brilliant exponent of exact historical science: to-day critics are finding fault both with his methods and with his results. His whole presentment of the French Revolution is violently assailed by M. Aulard; while M. Paul Lacombe says that his generalizations are often mere arbitrary abstractions that twist facts all out of shape. The German Karl Fritzche is very much of the same opinion. I refer to these criticisms, not as either accepting or disputing them, but simply as showing that there is at least no immediate prospect of disputing them, but simply as showing that there is at least no immediate prospect of finality in the results of historical study.

At the same time it would be idle to deny that the rules and methods of correct historical procedure have been developed and formulated within the last generation with a completeness and self-evident authority never before attained. The old maxim holds that experience teaches. Men have been writing history now for a very long time. In doing so they have been betrayed into innumerable errors and weaknesses. But, just as these errors and weaknesses have been detected, they have called into existence precepts and cautions for their avoidance. History is full of pitfalls for the unlearned and the unwary; but to-day these pitfalls have all, practically speaking, been catalogued and charted, so that any one who wishes to avoid them, and is willing to take the necessary pains, may do so. Another point to be noticed is that the duty of impartiality is more fully recognized than ever before, and with results wholly beneficial to the interests of historical truth. It is felt that the writer, in order to be fair to the reader, must afford him, as much as possible, the opportunity to judge for himself in all disputed questions, and not merely guide him to an acceptance of the conclusions he has himself arrived at. A Macaulay leaves his reader no option save that of accepting his version of things or everlastingly perishing as an enemy of light. A Gibbon has a superbly ironical smile for all who do not believe that the eighteenth century has said the last word in philosophy. The Leckys and Gardiners and Greens, the Sorels, the Hanotaux and the Vandals, of our own day write more as if the final verdict lay with the reader, and it was no part of their business to force opinion either by an overwhelming eloquence, a crushing argumentative assault, or any assumption of superior wisdom and knowledge.

The mere avoidance of errors will not of course make a man an historian, any more than the avoidance of grammatical blunders will make him a distinguished writer; for, after he has got his facts right, he must let the world see how he understands and correlates them. A man of less learning will sometimes discover more meaning in facts and put a better construction on them than a man of greater learning. A word to the wise is more enlightening than many words to the foolish. Emile Reich says of specialists that they have a knack of dwelling on trivialities and neglecting the most important facts. The best way to acquire true historical insight, he thinks, is to knock about the world and come into direct contact with the hurly-burly of actual human life, and so to acquire varied and intense sensorial impressions. Ben Johnson said of Shakespeare that he was "naturally learned"; and his wisdom assuredly did not all come from books. . . .

. . . What should be the dominant note in history? I can imagine some adherent of the straitest sect of modern historical Pharisees exclaiming: "History wants no dominant note: all she has to do is to tell the truth and go her way." Well, I shall not revive the question already touched upon as to what is historical truth; but shall simply affirm that history, without being for one moment untrue to herself, may yet have a dominant note, and that that should be a note of *appeasement*. The past has been full of struggle, some effects of which are with us still. History may tell us of feuds and of battles, but history should not, itself, be a continuation of feud and battle. From an honestly and humanly written history we should rise with a better comprehension of the causes of past conflicts and of the motives of the participants; with compassion for error and all the effects of human fallibility. In a word history may be, and should be, a school of humanity, and that without the least suppression or distortion of facts. It has sometimes been made a school of hatred, and that with both suppression and distortion of facts. Let us hope that this is no longer possible. A great Quinquennial Historical Congress was held only last month in London. Men of the highest renown in historical science were there; and it is gratifying to know that, not only was this idea of the possibility of making history serve the purpose of healing breaches and cementing friendships, both between nations and within nations, earnestly dwelt upon by the venerable President, the Right Hon. Mr. Bryce, but that it was heartily responded to by other leading speakers. You will listen with pleasure, I am sure, to the following words taken from the President's address:

> Truth and truth only is our aim. We are bound as historians to examine and record facts without favour or affection to our own nation or any other. . . . Seeing that we are, by the work we follow, led to look further back and more widely around than most of our fellow-citizens can do, are we not called upon to do what we can to try to reduce every source of international ill-feeling? . . . As histo-

rians, we know that every great people has had its characteristic merits along with its characteristic faults. None is specially blameless; each has rendered its special service to humanity at large. We have the best reason for knowing how great is the debt each one owes to the other; how essential not only to the material development of each, but also to its intellectual and spiritual advance, is the greatness and welfare of the others and the common friendship of all.

I am glad to be able to borrow for the termination of my very imperfect discourse sentiments and expressions of this high and noble quality, and to know that they will be received by the members of this Society and the friends who are assembled here this evening with no less sympathy and approval than they were by the distinguished audience to which they were addressed.

Notes on the Text

1. John Henry, Cardinal Newman, *An Essay in Aid of a Grammar of Assent* (London: Longman's Green, 8th ed., 1889); Henry Longueville Mansel, *The Limits of Religious Thought* (Boston: Gould and Lincoln, 1870).

2. French littérateur and politician, exiled for his Republican opinions by Louis Napoleon from 1851-1870; friend of philosopher Victor Cousin and historian Jules Michelet.

3. "He who burns brightly weighs heavily upon the arts ranged beneath."

4. "I had a lot to do with these matters."

5. French statesman and historian (1787-1874). Author of numerous volumes of French, English and European history.

6. French moralist (1816-1880). Author of *Essay on Providence* (1883), *Mesmer and Animal Magnetism* (1855), *Eighteenth Century Studies* (1855), *Letters on Teaching* (1857) and other works.

1. Richard Proctor (1837-1888), British astronomer and regular contributor to the *Intellectual Observer, Chambers's Journal*, and other Victorian periodicals. His largest and most ambitious work was *Old and New Astronomy*, published posthumously in 1892.

2. English man of letters and statesman (1838-1923). Editor of the *Fortnightly Review* from 1867 to 1882, author of biographies of Cobden and Gladstone. For an excellent treatment of Morley, which describes his liberalism as "Christianity minus the Creeds," see Basil Willey, *More Nineteenth Century Studies; A Group of Honest Doubters* (New York: Harper and Row, 1966), pp. 248-301. Willey's book, as well as his *Nineteenth Century Studies* (Middlesex: Chatto & Windus, 1969), provides good contextual material for a reading of this volume.

3. *Scepticism in Geology and the Reasons for It* (London: John Murray, 1877, 2nd ed. 1878), was published under the pseudonym "Verifier." Its author was John Murray (the younger, 1808-1892), son of the prominent British publisher.

4. "Rome has spoken, the cause is finished." Spoken by St. Ambrose of the Bishop of Rome.

5. Henry Varnum Poor (1812-1905), lawyer, economist, and editor of

the *American Railroad Journal*, 1849-1863. The work referred to of Poor may be either *Money and its laws, embracing a History of monetary theories and a History of the currencies of the U.S.* (2nd ed., 1877), or *Resumption and the Silver Question* . . . (1878), both reprinted by Greenwood Press in 1919.

Sir Anthony Musgrave (1828-1888), colonial administrator who from 1850 to 1862 held posts connected with Leward Islands and Antigua. Governor of Newfoundland from 1864 to 1868; governor of British Columbia from 1869 to 1872. LeSueur's reference is probably to Musgrave's *Studies in Political Economy* (New York: A.M. Kelley, 1968 1875).

6. Oliver Wendell Holmes, *The Poet at the Breakfast Table* (Boston: Houghton, Mifflin, 1891). In his "Preface" to the volume, written in 1882, Holmes noted: "As I read these over for the first time for a number of years, I notice one character representing a class of beings who have greatly multiplied during the interval which separates the earlier and later Breakfast Table papers—I mean the scientific specialists. The entomologist, who confines himself rigidly to the study of the coleoptera, is intended to typify this class." (p. V)

7. "Morality and Religion" (unsigned editorial), Toronto *Mail*, January 10, 1880, p. 2.

8. "If you are looking for an example, look around you."

9. "Dagon" was deity of the Philistines in the form of a merman—its upper half human, lower half the tail of a fish. See 1 Samuel 5: 2-7.

10. For criticisms of *The Data of Ethics*, see "Herbert Spencer on the data of ethics" (Henry Calderwood), *Contemporary Review*, Vol. 37 (January, 1880), pp. 64-76; "Mr. Herbert Spencer's *Data of Ethics*" (Henry Wace), *ibid.*, Vol. 38 (August, 1880), pp. 254-269; "Mr. Herbert Spencer's Philosophy and the philosophy of religion" (A.M. Fairbairn), Part I, *ibid.*, Vol. 40 (July, 1881), pp. 74-92, Part II, Vol. 40 (August, 1881), pp. 209-228.

11. Spanish, meaning literally a "sentence of faith"—a sentence given by an inquisition; burning at the stake.

12. One who pretends to a knowledge of medicine; a quack. After Doctor Samgrad, physician (whose panacea was copius bloodletting and drinking of hot water) in the picaresque novel *Gil Blas* (1747) by René LeSage.

13. "Bentrovato," in modern Italian parlance, is a common form of greeting to someone met in the streets.

14. Sir Richard Owen (1804-1892), anatomist, paleontologist, and most prominent biologist in Britain on the eve of the Darwinian revolution; an opponent of natural selection but not the idea of evolution. Louis Agassiz (1807-1873), Swiss-born paleontologist and geologist. Professor of Natural History at Harvard after his arrival in America in 1846; a strong opponent of evolution. Charles Lyell (1797-1875), the premier geologist in Britain in the second quarter of the nineteenth century. A convert to Darwinian evolution, his *Principles of Geology*—which had exerted a profound influence on Darwin—had reached its eleventh edition by the time of the author's death. For biographical information and contextual material, see: C.C. Gillispie, *Genesis and Geology; the Impact of Scientific Discoveries upon Religious Beliefs in the Decades Before Darwin* (New York: Harper & Row, 1959); John C. Greene, *The Death of Adam; Evolution and Its Impact on Western Thought* (Ames, Iowa: Iowa State University Press, 1959); G. Basalla, William Coleman and

R.H. Kargon (eds.), *Victorian Science* (New York: Doubleday, 1970); Edward Lurie, *Louis Agassiz,.* abridged ed. (Chicago: University of Chicago Press, 1966).

15. See above, p. 91n23. Romanes' book, *Animal Intelligence*, was published in 1881.

PART THREE: *On Morality and Politics*

1. Edmund Burke, *The Writings and Speeches of Edmund Burke* (Boston: Little, Brown & Co., 1901). The passage quoted is from Vol. I, "Of the Present Discontents," p. 530. For other comments by Burke on "party" see Vol. I, "The Present State of the Nation," p. 271; Vol. VI, "On Protestant Ascendancy in Ireland," p. 390.

2. LeSueur here refers to the British Ballot Act of 1872, which introduced the secret ballot for all parliamentary and municipal elections. A similar bill was passed in Canada in May, 1874 (37 Victoria, Ch. 9, Sect. 27).

3. LeSueur refers here to the election of 1872, in which Macdonald's Conservative campaign preached the necessity of completing the federal union through the extension of a transcontinental railway to the Pacific. "If the union is to be complete, permanent and strong," he had said, "West and East must be bound together by an iron band." The Conservatives won only 40 of Ontario's 88 seats. See J.M. Beck, *Pendulum of Power* (Scarborough: Prentice-Hall, 1968), pp. 14-21.

4. Paley (1743-1805) was a natural theologian of the late eighteenth century whose writings served to show the evidences of God's plan in nature through illustrations of the harmonious relationship of its various parts: "There cannot be design without a designer; contrivance without a contriver; order without choice; arrangement, without anything capable of arranging. . . . Arrangement, disposition of parts, subserviency of means to an end, relation of instruments to an use, imply the presence of intelligence." Paley used the analogy of the "design" and arrangement of parts in a watch to illustrate this basic statement in his book *Natural Theology; or, Evidences of the Existence and Attributes of the Deity collected from the Appearances of Nature* (1802). Cited in Gillispie, *op. cit.*, pp. 36-37.

5. "Political Struggles," *Globe* (Toronto), Wednesday, September 4, 1872, p. 2. For defences of political partyism by the *Globe* which take issue with LeSueur's views, see "Political Corruption," Thursday, October 3, 1872, p. 2; "Political Corruption," Wednesday, October 16, 1872, p. 2; "Party Politics," Tuesday, November 5, 1872, p. 2.

6. Richard Lovelace (1618-1657) has variously been described as a poet, gentleman, and lover. During the Cromwellian Revolution—in 1642—he was imprisoned for seven weeks after presenting a royalist petition to the House of Commons. There, he wrote "To Althea, from Prison." In 1648, now a colonel, he was again imprisoned and wrote *Lucasta* (1649). Cf. *The Poems of Richard Lovelace*, intro. C.H. Wilkinson (1925).

7. This may possibly refer to "A Mush of Concession" by Philomachus, *The Nation*, Nov. 19, 1874, p. 331.

8. The "Canada First" movement. For background, see Carl Berger,

The Sense of Power (Toronto: University of Toronto Press, 1970), pp. 49-77, *passim*.

9. LeSueur refers here to Goldwin Smith.

10. Sir Thomas Erskine May (1815-1886), English constitutional jurist; from 1871 to 1886 Clerk of the British House of Commons. Author of *Rules, Orders and Forms of Procedure of the House of Commons* (1854); *Constitutional History of England since the Accession of George III, 1760-1860* (1861-1863); *Democracy in Europe* (1877).

11. Frederic Harrison (1831-1923) was England's leading positivist in the late nineteenth century. See his *Order and Progress* (London: Longmans, Green & Co., 1875).

12. "There are as many laws as there are men."

13. The American Pendleton Act (1883) provided for a bi-partisan, three-man Civil Service Commission for drawing up and administering competitive examinations to determine the fitness of applicants to the Federal Civil service on a merit basis. Five years earlier, Sir John A. Macdonald, responding to the pleas of a critic who wanted a non-partisan civil service, replied that creating one would be like trying to put Canada back to "the Age of Adam and Eve before the apple." Quoted in P.B. Waite, *Canada, 1874-1896; Arduous Destiny* (Toronto: McClelland and Stewart, 1971), pp. 19-20.

14. Henry Adams, *Democracy, an American Novel* (New York: H. Holt & Co., 16th impression, 1908). First published in 1880. This novel, by the grandson of President John Quincy Adams, was a severe moral indictment of American politics in the "Gilded Age." Had LeSueur ever turned his hand to the writing of fiction, he would doubtless have written a book not unlike *Democracy*.

15. "Sweet it is to see from the land the strenuous effort of another while the winds toss up the waves of the great sea."

16. Sir Henry Sumner Maine, *Popular Government: Four Essays* (London: J. Murray, 1885).

17. An English philosopher (1838-1900) known for his theories concerning ethics; lectured in moral philosophy at Cambridge, but resigned on religious grounds. Later, when the religious test was removed, he regained his Fellowship (1885). His major work is *Methods of Ethics* (1874), the three "methods" being egoism, utilitarianism, and intuitionism. See "Henry Sidgewick: The Pursuit of Complex Wisdom" in F.M. Turner, *Between Sceince and Religion, op. cit.*, pp. 38-67.

18. The Liberal Convention of June 1893. The Liberal platform that emerged from the convention was for lower tariffs, although its declared ideal was free trade. See H. Blair Neatby, *Laurier and a Liberal Quebec* (Toronto: McClelland and Stewart, 1973), p. 50. O.D. Skelton, *Life and Letters of Sir Wilfrid Laurier* Vol. I (Toronto: McClelland and Stewart, 1965), p. 152.

19. Literally, with "eyes not cast backward"—that is, "not looking back."

20. William Edward Hartpole Lecky's (1838-1903) major works were his *History of Rationalism* (1865), *History of European Morals*, 2 Vols. (1869), and *History of England in the Eighteenth Century*, 8 Vols. (1878-1890).

21. As well as being Editor and founder of the *Nation*, Godkin (1831-1902) became, after 1881, associate editor of the *Post* which, under his leader-

ship, broke with the Republican party in the 1884 presidential campaign. Godkin was a constant attacker of Tammany Hall, political "bossism" in general, and forcibly opposed "jingoism" and imperialism.

22. "Power without plan falls from its own weight."

23. James Russell Lowell, "Abraham Lincoln," in *My Study Windows* (Boston: J.R. Osgood and Co., 1875).

24. "The Descent is easy."

25. "Codlin and Short" are two characters in Charles Dickens' *Old Curiosity Shop*. Tom Codlin was the somber and cynical exhibitor of a Punch-and-Judy show; 'Short Trotters' Harris, his partner, was cheery and bright in contrast.

26. English statesman, poet and dramatist (1800-1886), connected with the Colonial Office for forty-eight years. His essays, drama, and lyric poetry appeared mainly in the *Quarterly Review*.

PART FOUR: *The Critic as Historian*

1. See A.J. Balfour, *The Foundations of Belief* (London: Longmans, Green & Co., 1895.

2. F. Bradshaw, *Self-Government in Canada, and how it was Achieved: the story of Lord Durham's Report* (London: P.S. King & Son, 1903). LeSueur was mistaken: the study was done for the London School of Economics, not Oxford. Reference is made to the book in LeSueur's original typescript of the Mackenzie biography (Ch. 20, p. 9n).

3. F.X. Garneau, *Histoire du Canada* 5 éd., rev., annotée et publ. avec une introduction et des appendices par son petit-fils, Hector Garneau (Paris: F. Alcan, 1913-1920), 2 Vols.

4. Le P. Camille de Rochemonteix, *Les Jésuites et la Nouvelles-France au XVIIIᵉ siècle, d'après des documents inédits* (Paris: Alphonse Picard et Fils, 1906), Vol. 2, pp. 126-128. Rochemonteix refers to letters of various French officers—Lévis, Montcalm, Bougainville—, historian Dussieux, and l'abbé Casgrain. Vaudreuil is there described as "incapable," "vain," "untalented," "corrupt," and "without intellectual honesty" or "independence of character."

5. Charles Lindsey (1820-1908), *The Life and Times of William Lyon Mackenzie* (Toronto: C.W., P.R. Randall, 1862), 2 Vols.

6. Lindsey to LeSueur, 6 November, 1906.

7. C.W. Robinson, *The Life of Sir J.B. Robinson* (Edinburgh, 1904).

8. Loosely, "flowing pen."

9. "I had a lot to do with these matters."

10. "Truly, you have killed me my friends."

11. Pierre François Xavier de Charlevoix (1682-1761), French Jesuit missionary who travelled widely in North America and wrote the "classic" description of New France to which LeSueur refers: *History and General Description of New France*, trans. with notes by John G. Shea (Illinois: Loyola University Press [1870], 1962). The original was published in 1744.

12. Camille de Rochemonteix, *Les Jésuites et la Nouvelle France au XVIIᵉ siècle d'après beaucoup de documents inédits* (Paris: Letouzey et ané,

1895-1896), 3 Vols.; *Les Jésuites et la Nouvelle France au XVIIIe siècle d'après des documents inédits* (Paris: Alphonse Picard et Fils, 1906), 2 Vols.

13. LeSueur meant John B. Crozier. See above, p. 22n.

14. Thucydides' Greek phrase translates as "possession for all time"; Horace's Latin equivalent is "I erected a permanent monument."

15. English critic and poet (1824-1897), editor of the *Golden Treasury* anthology, and friend of Gladstone, Tennyson, Browning, Matthew Arnold and many other prominent Victorians. LeSueur must be in error as to when his quotation from Palgrave was written, for it may safely be said that even Sir Francis was not sufficiently precocious as a child to be able to write the passage at age six!

A Bibliography of the Writings of W.D. LeSueur

Abbreviations: *CMNR - Canadian Monthly and National Review*
   RBCM - Rose-Belford's Canadian Monthly and National Review
   PSM - Popular Science Monthly
   Week - The Week
   UTM - University of Toronto Magazine

1871   "Ste.-Beuve," *Westminster Review* XCV (April, 1871), 208-227.

1872   "The Poetry of Matthew Arnold," *CMNR* I (March, 1872), 219-229.

——   "Party Politics," *CMNR* II (November, 1872), 447-455.

1874   "Bernardin de St. Pierre," *CMNR* V (April, 1874), 324-338.

1875   "Old and New in Canada," *CMNR* VII (January, 1875), 1-9.

——   "The Intellectual Life," *CMNR* VII (April, 1875), 320-330.

——   "Messrs. Moody and Sankey and Revivalism," pseud. "Laon," *CMNR* VII (June, 1875), 510-513.

——   "Prayer and Modern Thought," *CMNR* VIII (August, 1875), 145-155.

——   "Proofs and Disproofs," pseud. "Laon," *CMNR* VIII (October, 1875), 339-348.

——   "Modern Culture and Christianity," pseud. "Laon," *CMNR* VIII (December, 1875), 523-533.

1876   "Prayer and Natural Law," *CMNR* IX (March, 1876), 211-221.

——   "Liberty of Thought and Discussion," *CMNR* X (September, 1876), 202-212.

1877   "Science and Materialism," *CMNR* XI (January, 1877), 22-28.

1878   "Idealism in Life," *CMNR* XIII (April, 1878), 414-420.

1879   "The Bases of Education," *The Canadian Educational Monthly and School Chronicle* I (April, 1879), 193-201. Portion of a Presidential Address delivered before the Literary and Scientific Society of Ottawa.

—— "The Rev. Phillips Brooks on Popular Scepticism," *RBCM* III (July, 1879), 26-31.

—— "The Moral Nature and Intellectual Power," *RBCM* III (July, 1879), 104-105.

—— "A Few Words on Criticism," *RBCM* III (September, 1879), 323-328.

—— "The Scientific Spirit," *RBCM* III (October, 1879), 437-441.

1880 "The Future of Morality," *RBCM* IV (January, 1880), 74-82.

—— "Morality and Religion," *RBCM* IV (February, 1880), 166-171.

—— "Mr. Spencer and His Critics," *RBCM* IV (April, 1880), 413-422. Republished as "A Vindication of Scientific Ethics," *PSM* 17 (July, 1880), 324-337.

—— "Morality and Religion Again.—A Word With My Critics." *RBCM* IV (June, 1880), 642-655.

—— "Morality Without Theology," *RBCM* V (November, 1880), 522-528.

1881 "Is Civilization Declining?" *RBCM* VI (January, 1881), 95-97.

—— "Partisan Government," *North American Review* CXXXII (January, 1881), 52-63.

—— " 'Progress and Poverty' and the Doctrine of Evolution," *RBCM* VI (March, 1881), 287-296.

—— "Carlyle and Comte," *RBCM* VI (June, 1881), 639-642.

—— "The Influence of Superior Men," *RBCM* VI (June, 1881), 652-653.

1882 "The True Idea of Canadian Loyalty," *RBCM* VIII (January, 1882), 1-11.

—— "Materialism and Positivism," *PSM* 20 (March, 1882), 615-621.

—— "Physics and Metaphysics," *RBCM* VIII (April, 1882), 352-360. Republished as "Stallo's 'Concepts of Modern Physics'," *PSM* 21 (May, 1882), 96-100.

"Free Thought and Responsible Thought," *RBCM* VIII (June, 1882), 614-620.

—— "Mr. Goldwin Smith on 'The Data of Ethics'," *PSM* 22 (December, 1882), 145-156.

1883 "The Anarchy of Modern Politics," *PSM* XXIII (August, 1883), 444-453.

1884 "A Defence of Modern Thought. In Reply to a Recent Pamphlet, by the Bishop of Ontario, on 'Agnosticism,' " (Toronto: Hunter, Rose, & Co., 1884), pp. 40. Republished as "A Defence of Modern Thought" (abridged), *PSM* 24 (April, 1884), 780-793.

—— "Evolution and the Positive Aspects of Modern Thought. In Reply to the Bishop of Ontario's Second Lecture on 'Agnosticism.'" (Ottawa: A.S. Woodburn, 1884), pp. 43.

1885 "Evolution and the Destiny of Man," *PSM* 26 (February, 1885), 456-468.

—— "Mr. Arnold in America," *Week* II (September 17, 1885), 659-660.

1886 "Tecumseh—A Drama," *Week* III (March 4, 1886), 219-220.

—— "Reading and Intelligence," *Week* III (May 13, 1886), 381.

—— "Evolution Bounded by Theology," *PSM* 29 (June, 1886), 145-153.

—— "Ex-President Porter on Evolution," *PSM* 29 (September, 1886), 577-594.

1887 "The Service of Man," *Week* IV (March 31, 1887), 287.

—— "Creation or Evolution?" *PSM* 31 (May, 1887), 29-39.

1888 "Foot-prints of Creative Power," *North American Review* CXLVI (February, 1888), 219.

1889 "Science and Its Accusers," *PSM* 34 (January, 1889), 367-379.

—— "Mr. Mallock on Optimism" *PSM* 35 (August, 1889), 531-541.

1890 "Spiritual Influence," *Week* VII (May 23, 1890), 390.

—— "The Failure of Education," *Week* VII (June 6, 1890), 422.

—— " 'The Greatest Thing in the World,' " *Week* VII (July 18, 1890), 518.

—— "Moral and Religious Education," *Week* VII (July 25, 1890), 532-533.

—— "Grim Truth," *Week* VII (August 29, 1890), 614-615.

—— "The Coming Reform," *Week* VII (September 5, 1890), 630-631; VII (October 17, 1890), 725-726.

—— "Bigotry," *Week* VII (Oct. 3, 1890), 693.

1891 "The Late Bishop of Durham and the Author of 'Supernatural Religion,' " *Week* VIII (July 17, 1891), 530.

1892 "Review of 'Ballads from the Illiad' by Joseph Cross," *Week* IX (January 22, 1892), 122.

1893 "State Education and 'Isms,' " *Canadian Magazine* II (November, 1893), 3-7.

1895 "Problems of Government in Canada," *Queen's Quarterly* II (January, 1895), 198-209.

—— "Kidd on Social Evolution," *PSM* 47 (May, 1895), 38-48.

1896 "War and Civilization," *PSM* 48 (April, 1896), 758-771.

1900 "Notes on the Study of Language," *Transactions of the Ottawa Literary and Scientific Society* (1899-1900), 93-118. Read February 9, 1900.

1901   "The Problem of Popular Government," *UTM* I (April, 1901), 229-241; I (May, 1901), 257-263. A lecture delivered in the Chemical Building, University of Toronto, February 23, 1901. Also published in pamphlet form.

1906   *Count Frontenac* (Toronto: Morang and Co. Ltd., 1906), pp. 382. A volume in the "Makers of Canada" series.

1908   "In the Troublous Days of 1837—W.L. Mackenzie's Attacks," Toronto *Globe*, (Saturday, February 22, 1908), 8. Published anonymously, but there can be no doubt whatsoever that the article was by LeSueur.

1909   "Universities and the 'Idle Rich,' "UTM X (December, 1909), 81-83.

1911   "Education, Past and Present," *UTM* XII (May, 1911), 279-292.

1912   "Versions from Horace and Catullus," *UTM* XII (June, 1912), 391-392.

——   "Teaching of History," Montreal *Gazette* (October 9, 1912), 11.

1913   "History: Its Nature and Methods," *Proceedings of the Royal Society of Canada* (1913), Appendix A, LVII-LXXXIII. Presidential Address to the Royal Society of Canada.

1915   " 'Art Thou Weary, Art Thou Languid,' " *University Magazine* XIV (December, 1915), 563.

Note on the Editor

A.B. McKillop was born in Winnipeg and educated at the University of Manitoba and Queen's University. He has taught at Dalhousie University, Queen's University, and the University of Manitoba, where he is Assistant Professor of Canadian History. His publications include "Nationalism, Identity and Canadian Intellectual History" (*Queen's Quarterly*, 1974), and articles on various aspects of the political climate of Winnipeg during the depression. He is presently engaged in a study of the course of critical enquiry in Canada.

THE CARLETON LIBRARY